The Quest

The Quest

Christ Amidst the Quest

Lyman C. D. Kulathungam

WIPF & STOCK · Eugene, Oregon

THE QUEST
Christ Amidst the Quest

Wipf and Stock
An Imprint of Wipf and Stock Publishers
199 W. 8th Ave., Suite 3
Eugene, OR 97401

www.wipfandstock.com

ISBN 13: 978-1-61097-515-5

Manufactured in the U.S.A.

*For Sarojini
and Jaishan, Daniel, Mikayla, and Micah*

Contents

Images and Illustrations

Where there is no source indicated for an image, the material was located in the public domain.

Figure	With Permission of
Saddam Hussein	New York Times, December 31, 2006, AP Images
Superstructures of Christianity	Lyman C. D. Kulathungam
Superstructures of Other Religions	Lyman C. D. Kulathungam
Triquetra symbol, three entwined fish	The Holy Trinity Anglican Church, Sooke, Canada
The Holy Trinity Symbol 1	Koch, Rudolf with Fritz Kredel
The Holy Trinity Symbol 2	Conjubilant with Song blog. May 18, 2008
Greek Two	Lyman C. D. Kulathungam
Greek Three	Lyman C. D. Kulathungam
Greek Four	Lyman C. D. Kulathungam
Greek Tetrakyts of the Decad	Lyman C. D. Kulathungam
Trinity through Greek mathematical system	Lyman C. D. Kulathungam
Eye of God	
Rastafarian Johnson of Jamaica	Jonathan Kulathungam
Pluralistic Stance	Lyman C. D. Kulathungam
Exclusivist Stance	Lyman C. D. Kulathungam
Exclusive Universes	Lyman C. D. Kulathungam
Jesus amidst the Universes	Lyman C. D. Kulathungam
Chinese Tea Ceremony	Rex Ng
Statue of Confucius, Beijing	
Temple of Heaven, Beijing	Rex Ng
Yin-Yang	
Lu-Tung-Pin	
Tai Chi Devotee	Andy James
Sacred Gateway to Itsukushima Shinto Shrine, Japan	

Buddha, Dambulla, Sri Lanka	Reneta Thurairatnam
Reclining Buddha, Polannaruwa, Sri Lanka	K. Theivasagayam
Bodhisattva Avalokitesvara	Venerable Shanping, courtesy of Buddhist Cham Shan Temple, Toronto, Canada
Green Tara Buddha	Riwochi Tibetan Buddhist Temple, Toronto, Canada
Stages in Transcendental Meditation	Lyman C. D. Kulathungam
Ganesha	Paradise Print, Toronto, Canada
Hindu Kawadi Ritual	Anonymous, Sri Lanka
Statue of Shiva at CERN, Switzerland	*Giovanni Chierico*
Guru Granth being read	Guru Gobind Singh Children's Foundation, Toronto, Canada
Guru Granth Sahib at Sikh Gurwardara	Guru Gobind Singh Children's Foundation, Toronto, Canada
Sikh Khanda Emblem	
Dome of the Rock from Mount Scopus	
Shahadah	
Worship at Kabbah in Mecca	Muhammad Mahdi Karim
Sioux Prayer to the Mystery, 1908	Edward S. Curtis, Legends of America
Totem Pole, Vancouver, Canada	Angela Lum
Shaman from Amazonian Forest, Peru	
Christ of St. John of the Cross by Salvador Dali, 1951	© Culture and Sport Glasgow (Museums)

Foreword

IN THE WAKE OF technological developments in many fields, the globe continues to shrink, confronting the human family with increasingly complex and urgent problems. The tortured economic web is only one example. Some are sensing the challenge and are attempting to respond. Works by Thomas Homer-Dixon (*The Ingenuity Gap* and *The Upside of Down: Catastrophe, Creativity, and the Renewal of Civilization*) and Laurence C. Smith (*The World in 2050*) are illuminating, but not for the faint of heart. Some even dare to call those who assemble at the annual World Economic Forum in Davos, Switzerland the "New Champions," who are "transforming the future through change, innovation, and breaking old models, driving discussion and building a collaborative, optimistic future." They had better hurry.

Yet the futurists seem to have forgotten one important characteristic of the whole human race: religion. Philip Jenkins has honed in on that, particularly in his *The Next Christendom: The Coming of Global Christianity* and *God's Continent: Christianity, Islam, and Europe's Religious Crisis*. Pope Benedict XVI is also sensitive to the significance of global spiritual life, having assembled three hundred leaders from many religions in Assisi, Italy on October 27, 2011 to pray for world peace. His predecessor, Pope John Paul II, paved the way in 1986 and again in 2002 with similar gatherings.

It is in that super-heated context that Dr. Lyman Kulathungam's book must be seen. Dr. Kulathungam grew up in Sri Lanka and emigrated to Canada as an adult. He has lived in very different cultures, and he has experienced religious pluralism in extraordinarily diverse forms. He has taught "Hindu, Buddhist, and Islamic philosophy to Hindus, Buddhists, and Muslims at various universities" while being a deeply committed Christian himself. Life experience has given him a strong sense of the religious *mélange* of which we are all a part.

But this book is not a history of religions or a study in comparative religion, although Dr. Kulathungam could write either of those. It reaches much deeper than that. It is a response to the human *quest*. The quest is a longing to make sense of life, and, he says, "the quest encompasses all humanity, those religious in the traditional sense as well as the pre-religious, the post-religious and even the nonreligious; it is a human quest." Sounding a little bit like the famous St. Augustine ("our heart is restless until it finds its rest in you"), Kulathungam says, "Such a quest is very much an integral part of human DNA. Being made in God's image, we cannot but strive for God, whether we believe in him or not." A glance at the table of contents shows how widely he will range.

But he is fully aware of the difficulty of the task he is giving himself. He says, "When trying to capture the spirit of the quest of a religious community, one has to get a feel of the heartthrob of the community; one has to decipher the core of its deepest aspirations." To my knowledge, this is a unique and important undertaking. A historical or comparative study would be much easier. Dr. Kulathungam is venturing into human hearts, boldly reaching for understanding there in a way that no one else that I know of has done. But it is even more demanding than that.

Dr. Kulathungam is a Christian. Will Muslims, Aboriginals, and Sikhs recognize themselves authentically portrayed in this book? That question is particularly important because Kulathungam says, "This book endeavors to present Christ not as part of the human quest, but rather as the one who can satisfy that quest." This will certainly require, as he suggests, "a different conceptual framework," when he makes comments like, "Relating Christ to the quest of religious communities is very different from relating Christianity to other religions." This book will stretch most of its readers. It will challenge those Christians who usually do not see much or anything of value in other religions. It will challenge non-Christians, whether adherents of some other religion or of no religion to think about this person Jesus who occupies such a significant place in the human story.

And Dr. Kulathungam is equal to the task. Having taught with him for ten years, I know he brings a gentle, respectful, Christlike spirit to his work. Those who study under him admire him. He also brings a strong background in philosophy, particularly in formal logic. His unique character, education, and well-examined life experience constitute an excellent platform from which to explore what few have noticed or dared to pursue.

Rev. Dr. Ronald Kydd
Research Professor in Church History,
Tyndale University, Toronto
Canada

Preface

ONLY THOSE WHO HAVE been thirsty know what thirst really is. Perhaps they are the ones who can best talk about it. The venture to write a book entitled *The Quest* receives its impetus first of all from the fact that the author experienced a quest in his own spiritual journey and hence is hopeful that something sensible could be told about it. My encounters with people of different countries and cultures with both religious and nonreligious persuasions have enabled me to better understand the quest that people experience. Such a quest is not restricted to a particular sector of the human populace. It could express itself in religious as well as nonreligious communities. One may call such a quest a search for life's meaning, an attempt to get out of the predicament one feels that he or she is in, or a striving to enjoy a better quality of life. Even though such a quest is not restricted to the religious community, this book considers a mosaic of religious communities and their respective quests. Limiting the scope of the investigation to the quest of religious communities is due to my interactions with religious pundits, academics, and students of such communities. Participation in international and interreligious conferences both in Canada and abroad facilitated such interactions. I have had the opportunity of lecturing on Hindu, Buddhist, and Islamic philosophy to Hindus, Buddhists, and Muslims at various universities. One of the recurrent questions my students asked me through the years was "How would you relate Christ to the philosophical insights of Hinduism, Buddhism, or Islam that you have taught us?" This book is basically a response to such a query.

Let me invite you to journey through my response and listen to my plea. In order to relate Christ to people of various religious persuasions, we need an appropriate conceptual framework. The first two chapters provide such a framework for the examination of eight major living religions in the subsequent chapters. The first chapter attempts to look at religion by delving beneath its structural constructs, such as its creeds, belief systems, scriptures, organizational set ups, norms, rituals, and festivities, and deciphering the core aspirations of the people of a religion. There is often a temptation to be preoccupied with these superstructural constructs and lose sight of the aspirations that they express. Underlying these aspirations, one can sense among the adherents of religions a deep seated quest—a quest to get out of the predicament in which they feel entrapped, a salvific quest in which saviors prominently figure. This provides the rationale to describe religion as a quest. The second chapter attempts to find out whether one could in any way relate Christ to such a quest. In placing Christ amidst the quest of religious communities, one finds that he is not part of the quest, but on the other hand is well-equipped to satisfy such a quest.

Confucianism, Taoism, Shintoism, Buddhism, Hinduism, Sikhism, Islam, and Aboriginal religions figure in this investigation. They are not placed in the order of their origin. Buddhism precedes Hinduism, even though historically the former arose out of the latter; Buddha was born a Hindu. Grouping religions geographically into Eastern, Western, and Mid-Eastern traditions, though very helpful to get a full picture of the global multireligious world, does not adequately capture the strategy that this book adopts to view religions. Moreover, such a strategy is not based on an evolutionary scale; they are not in the order of how evolved they are as religions, how cogent their creeds, how theologically sophisticated their doctrinal stances, and how effective their organizational structures are. If so, Aboriginal religions, which are usually characterized as "primitive," should not be last in the line. The placement of these religions in this order is based on considering how relevant the quest of these faith communities is to Christ, ordered from least to greatest. Christ does not seem to be relevant at all to some of these religions when they first started, but the metamorphosis which took place in them with the passage of time makes Christ relevant to them now.

Relating Christ to the quest of religious communities is very different from relating Christianity to other religions. Christianity, like other religions, is a complex mixture of doctrines, practices, traditions, and organizational structures. When Christians adopt such strategies, they are like all others expressing their quest and articulating ways and means to satisfy it. Christianity cannot satisfy the human quest, but Christ can. In their quest, some Christians do meet Christ, while others live on substitutes like age-old traditions, cultural comfort zones, theological constructs, legalistic spiritualities, exhilarating experiences, and ecclesiastical efficacies: aspartame is sweet but it is not sugar!

Surveying religious communities does not imply that the quest is restricted only to religions. Such a quest existed before the rise of organized religions and will continue even if the world sees the demise of such religions as predicted by some prophets of doom. Such a quest seems to be built into the very makeup of human personhood. It may, of course, have a biological basis, but if one understands it merely in terms of biological or neurological dispositions, one tends to slip into a kind reductionism, as we shall see in the final chapter.

This book proposes that Christ could satisfy such a quest on account of the uniqueness of:

1. the strategy of his salvific mission;

2. his personhood; and

3. the means by which one could appropriate what he offers.

The strategy for liberating humanity originated in the hearts of leaders and founders in various religious communities, anguished by the pathos of the human predicament. These leaders were all humans, perhaps with superhuman insights.

The solution followed the problem. On the other hand, the plan to save humanity through Christ was conceived in the heart of God and that too before time began (Titus 1:2–3); here the solution preceded the problem. Such a strategy went beyond sound doctrines and good deeds; it involved the death of the Savior on the cross. Salvation of humanity was enacted by one who was both fully divine and fully human. This enabled him to be very much a part of humanity and yet able to free it from its predicament. The means to appropriate such a salvation is not through good deeds but through unmerited favor: grace.

This book attempts to understand and appreciate the relevance of Christ to the quest of religious communities without getting sidetracked with dichotomies that usually figure when comparing religions: dichotomies like true/false, better/best, elect/damned, spiritual/carnal, and even Christian/non-Christian. From the perspective of a God who so loved the world that he gave his only begotten son to save all humanity, all fall within the saving work of Christ and the ambit of his grace. It is within such a paradigm that one has to view Christ. If you plan to handle this book as a "how to" manual, let me assure you that you will be utterly disappointed and even frustrated. It does not present a set of strategies for evangelization, since I am more than convinced that in relating Christ to the quest of people, one should rather depend on God. He is smarter than our strategies!

Acknowledgments

*T*HE *QUEST* WOULD HAVE been just a dream if not for the enthusiastic support of a number of my mentors, colleagues, students, friends, and family members.

A venture such as this requires input from people who are knowledgeable in their own religious traditions. Imam Sayyid Muhammad Rizvi of the Islamic Shi'a Ithna-Asheri Jamaat of Toronto heading the Ja'ffari Community Centre Mosque has helped me in understanding the difficult concepts of Islam. Besides officiating as head imam in the mosque, he lectures on Islam at several interfaith conferences both in Canada and abroad and has often appeared on the television program, *Islam in Focus*. He is a prolific writer and scholar and has been a rich resource to me. Mr. Narain Ram Subramanian, who served as trustee and secretary of the Hindu Temple Society of Canada, president of Bharathi Kalamanram Canada, and director and co-chair of Panorama India, was my main resource person for the section on Hinduism. He has helped me appreciate its complexity and understand its multifarious stances. Rev. Shanping Sik, incumbent nun of Cham Shan Buddhist Temple in Toronto, is a Buddhist scholar and very involved in serving her community in the Greater Toronto area. She has been a great source of help in clarifying concepts, especially Mahayana Buddhism. Mr. Paramjit Dhillon, as coordinator of the Guru Gobind Singh Children's Foundation, is involved in mentoring Sikh youth, and fundraising for several charities, such as Plan Canada and The Hospital for Sick Children. He has greatly helped me to understand and appreciate Sikh beliefs and practices. All of these individuals have gone out of their way to provide valuable resources and constructive suggestions. They may not agree with some of my claims, but I sincerely respect their convictions.

Rev. Ashraf Beshara, senior pastor of the Gift of God Arabic Church in Mississauga, helped to clarify certain Arabic concepts and familiarise me with the Arabic culture and way of life. Rev. George R. Gunner, director of Aboriginal Pentecostal Ministries and senior pastor of House of All Nations, provided valuable information regarding aboriginal life and practices. Rev. David Loganathan's spiritual journey served as an ideal example of the Hindu quest for Christ. Rev. Peter McIntosh assisted by sourcing pictures, particularly from the Buddhist world.

Rev. David Wells, general superintendent of the Pentecostal Assemblies of Canada; Rev. David Shepherd, former district superintendent of the Western Ontario District of the Pentecostal Assemblies of Canada; Rev. Dr. Evon Horton, former president of Master's College and Seminary, and presently senior pastor, Brownsville Assembly,

Florida; and Rev. Dr. Irving Whitt, global education coordinator of the Pentecostal Assemblies of Canada, supported me throughout this venture and helped me through their insightful suggestions and encouraging endorsements. It is my distinct privilege to include their write ups for the cover leaf.

Rev. Dr. Ronald Kydd has taught in several universities, Bible colleges, and seminaries, authored books and articles of quality, and is deeply involved in ecumenical dialogue. Most recently he served as pastor of St. Andrews Anglican Church in Cobourg, and is now research professor in church history at Tyndale University. He has helped me immensely by reading parts of my manuscript and providing constructive suggestions. I am honored to have him write the foreword for this book.

Niran, my elder son, read through my manuscript with a particular focus on the theologically heavy or perhaps controversial sections. His responses led to lengthy but rewarding discussions which have helped to make my presentation more theologically palatable. He was also the *deus ex machina* during my times of technological calamities.

His wife Loria, my daughter-in-law, has journeyed with me since I started writing my first chapter. She spent countless long hours in not only typing most of my manuscript, but also copyediting and proofreading with meticulous attention to detail, patiently researching long-lost sources, and providing insightful editorial suggestions. She has helped to make this work more cohesive.

Jonathan, my younger son, edited a number of the images, and provided useful suggestions after reading sections of the manuscript, to add quality to my work. He researched the copyright regulations and offered me well-needed legal advice.

His wife Lilani, my daughter-in-law, typed parts of the manuscript, searched for some sources, and encouraged me at every stage of my project.

My niece, Christina Thurairatnam, helped me immensely by typing parts of the manuscript, and advising me regarding the publication process.

My niece, Lakshani Kulathungam, worked laboriously to search for pictures of various religions.

Shaun Jerome, my nephew, formatted the images in the book to meet the publisher's standards, organized my files, and carried out several internet searches for me.

To Sarojini, my wife, I owe the most. She not only encouraged me to venture on this project but also stood by me at every stage of this arduous journey. She read through the manuscript more than once and provided me with useful opinions to make it more reader friendly. If you still find some parts of the manuscript problematic, the fault is all mine.

I dedicate this book to her and to our grandchildren, Jaishan, Daniel, Mikayla, and Micah; to Sarojini, for her wholehearted commitment to make this book see the light of day and to our grandchildren, for they represent the future generation that will experience the challenges and opportunities of this rapidly growing intercultural, inter-religious global village.

COPYRIGHT NOTICES

1

Religion as a Quest

Now scorched, now froze, in forest dread, alone naked and fireless, set upon his quest, the hermit battles purity to win (Buddha on the ascetic quest, Majihima-Nikaya X11).

Just as there is fragrance in the flower, and reflection in a mirror, so similarly God lives within us. Search for him in your heart (Sikh scripture, Adi Granth).

As the deer pants for streams of water, so my soul pants for you, O God. My soul thirsts for God, for the living God. When can I go and meet with God? (Psalm 42:1–2).

Saddam Hussein's journey to the gallows on December 30, 2006.

ON DECEMBER 30, 2006 at 6:05 a.m. (EST) the world paused for the death of one man: Saddam Hussein. Amidst the medley of media reports, political pronouncements, and emotive outbursts there was a poignant expression of a core human aspiration—a quest for a better life, freed from the problems and pathos of human existence. The jubilant chants and prayers of relief of those who suffered under this dictator were glaringly evident. The judgmental statements of politico-religious pundits were loud and clear. Some shouted a loud amen to his being sent to the gallows. Others made scathing attacks on those responsible for his death, especially targeting what they called "the American devil." But such reactive expressions, though having a religious overtone, did not really exhibit the quest. Right at the very center of the enactment of this drama of death, there was a man, putting on a show of strength, but really in anguish, taking his last steps, grasping in his hands the Quran, and uttering some significant verses from it. His recurrent recitation was, "La ilaha Allah; Muhammad rasul Allah" (There is no God but Allah; Muhammad is the messenger of Allah).

The repetition of this creedal statement, called the Shahadah, is the most favorite religious ritual of the Muslims. But it is more than a confession of faith. When uttered with sincere conviction and repeated faithfully until death, it provides a Muslim the assurance to enter paradise—the very presence of God. Saddam Hussein died with these words in his mouth. Here was a man, a dictator who had controlled the destiny of his nation and impacted the politics of the world for decades, now desperately struggling to change his own destiny, yearning to be freed from his predicament. The actions and expressions of Saddam Hussein, in his journey to the gallows, exhibit an aspiration that we call the human religious quest. This book attempts to explore its nature and determine how Jesus Christ is relevant to such a quest. But once it is called a "religious quest," it may be placed in a category that we would like to avoid.

This book clarifies the quest in the context of some major religions, but it is not another book on world religions. There is adequate literature in the form of anthologies, introductions, surveys, and well-researched presentations on the history, organization, doctrines, and practices of the religions of the world. In a global village where people are exposed to various religions, one can naturally expect profuse publications on world religions in the future. Even though this book will be preoccupied with the aspirations of the people of some major religions, it does not want to be categorized as a typical book on the religions of the world.

It is also not another book on comparative religion. In recent times, there has been an influx of books on comparative religion. Such books attempt to compare religions, identifying common features, and pinpointing significant differences, especially in the areas of doctrine and practice. Such comparison enables one to determine which religion is better than the other and in what respects. There have been several taxonomies classifying religions based on different criteria. The evaluative criterion that the theory of evolution provides has proved to be conducive to the comparative analysis of religions. The strategy of categorizing life-forms into various species and placing them in the evolutionary ladder that biologists adopt has infiltrated into other disciplines. Religions came to be classified into types and assessed on how evolved they are. Scholars place Christianity alongside other religions and attempt to decipher the status of each religion in the evolution of human religiosity. Naturally, controversy arises as to which religion is most evolved. While some place Christianity as the highest expression of religiosity, proponents of other religions naturally resent what they consider a preposterous claim. If the difference between Christianity and other religions is one of degree, how can one claim that it is better than or even best among other religions? This book does not want to be preoccupied comparing Christianity with other religions and thereby become caught up in such a controversy.

If it is neither a world religions nor a comparative religion book, is it one on Christian apologetics—a defense of Christianity? If apologetics is merely theological polemics, working within the framework of true-false dichotomy, attempting to justify the truth of Christian claims and implying the falsity of other religious claims, then this book does not want to fall into such a category. But, if apologetics could present Christ as the fulfillment of the core aspirations of the people of religious communities, including those of the Christian community, then what is attempted in this book may be taken as an apologetic endeavor. It tries its best to identify the ways in which Christ is related to the quest of the various faith groups, rather than becoming entangled in the web of conflicting truth claims that religions make. It is an endeavor that wants to work within a parameter that encourages a mindset of "Christ and us" rather than "we and them." In the latter, "we" refers to Christians who exclude themselves from "them," non-Christians. In the former, "us" refers to all human beings in relation to Christ, whether Christian or not.

Most books on world religions, comparative religions, and apologetics seem to work on the assumption that religion is a distinct unit of the social fabric, having an organized structure, founded on belief systems, and executed through rituals and in-stitutions. On the grounds of such an assumption, one may characterize, compare, or defend religions. But the quest that we are concerned about is not to be confined to a conceptual framework that takes religion to be a distinct social entity. Viewing religion this way is a recent development and was not prevalent during biblical times.[1] In fact, Christ never spoke of religions in the modern sense of the term. When we describe "quest" with the term "religious," it indicates the aspirations that people of various religious persuasions exhibit, rather than a descriptive of religions per se, taken as distinct units of society. Moreover, the quest encompasses all humanity, those reli-gious in the traditional sense as well as the pre-religious, the post-religious, and even the nonreligious; it is a human quest. His Holiness the 14th Dalai Lama, a Buddhist statesman of our time, claims that the religious quest pervades all humanity. He points out that "all of us are the same, in wanting to find happiness and to avoid suffering."[2] Human beings, whether religious or not, are quest oriented. The quest encompasses all humans, and is not confined only to the religious. This book explores the expression of the quest of the people of some religions merely as typical examples of the human religious quest.

Such a quest is neither a theological dogma nor a mere biological instinct but something which arises from the core of human personhood—something that is intertwined with one's innermost aspirations. In fact, agnostic scholars belonging to disciplines other than religion have identified such a trait though not characterizing it specifically as a quest. Bertrand Russell, a reputed British philosopher statesman, who considered himself an agnostic, pointed out that the essence of religion lies in the very makeup of the human being, who he claimed to be a mixture of God and brute, a battleground between two natures: the finite self-centered and the other, the infinite, impartial, and universal. Human striving is a transition from the finite to the infinite

---

1. McDermott, *God's Rivals*, 12.
2. Dalai Lama, *Mind in Comfort*, 4.

mode of existence.[3] Charles Darwin compared human religious devotion to that of a dog's devotion to his master.[4] Ever since Darwin, biologists have attempted to explain human religiosity as an instinctive biological predisposition. What such scholars have accomplished is to provide a biological basis to the universality of religious behavior by making it part of the human genetic makeup. Dean Hamer, in his book *The God Gene*, attempts to show how faith in God is hardwired into our genes, how religiosity is biologically fostered.[5] In fact, such an attempt supports our contention that humans, whether religious or not in the traditional sense of the term, are quest oriented. It is our conviction that such a quest is very much an integral part of human DNA. Being made in God's image, we cannot but strive for God, whether we believe in him or not. Our main concern will be to find out how the quest works itself out through religions—how people of different religions articulate their quest.

Hence, we commence our study of religions at the grassroots level. People of different faiths no doubt share some beliefs, practice certain rituals, participate through some institutional structures, and prescribe themselves certain moral codes of behavior. But beneath such beliefs, rituals, institutions, and moral codes, there seems to be something that pertains to the core of the people of faith communities. Embedded in that core is a dynamic quest for something that would liberate them and provide them with a better quality of life.

Such a quest has been described in various ways: as a search for ultimate meaning or as a commitment to ultimate concerns. The series on World Spirituality that attempts to present an encyclopedic history of the religious quest came up with a working hypothesis to characterize human spirituality by identifying it with a dynamic quest for the transcendent. This is how the editors introduce the series: "The series focuses on that inner dimension of the person called by certain traditions 'the Spirit.' This spiritual core is the deepest centre of the person. It is here that the person is open to the transcendent dimension; it is here that the person experiences ultimate reality. The series explores the discovery of this core, the dynamics of its development, and its journey to the ultimate goal. It deals with prayer, spiritual direction, the various maps of the spiritual journey, and the methods of advancement in the spiritual journey."[6]

Radhakrishnan, former president of India and one of the most incisive thinkers of modern Hinduism, articulates human religiosity as a quest in his description of the essence of religion. He points out that religion is not to be confused with philosophy or an apologetic for an existing social order or even an instrument for social emancipation, but "a quest for emancipation . . . It is something inward and personal which unifies all values and organizes all experiences. It is the reaction of the whole man to the whole reality. We seek the religious object by the totality of our faculties and energies. Such functioning of the whole man may be called spiritual life, as distinct

3. Russell, "Essence of Religion," 565–76.

4. Darwin, *Origin of Species*, 470.

5. Hamer, *God Gene*, 6.

6. Sivaraman, ed., *Hindu Spirituality*, 1:xiv.

from a merely intellectual or moral or aesthetic activity or combination of them."[7] He observes that those involved in such a quest are incurably dissatisfied with and even exhibit revolt against anything less than what they are seeking for.[8]

Mahatma Gandhi's main goal was to achieve independence for India and rid her of some social evils such as the caste system. But, beneath such laudable pursuits, there lay a quest in the core of his being that perhaps motivated his pursuits. He is believed to have confessed: "What I want to achieve—what I have been striving and pining to achieve these thirty years—is self-realization, to see God face to face, to achieve *Moksha* . . . I live and have my being in pursuit of this goal."[9] Moksha in Hinduism refers to the liberated state that a devotee aims to achieve. Gandhi's confession is indicative of the salvific quest that motivated his life and mission.

Billy Graham describes "The Great Quest" as inherent in every human being. He identifies the quest in everyone when he commences his comment on it with the word "you." He states:

> You started on the Great Quest the moment you were born. It was many years perhaps before you realized it, before it became apparent that you were constantly searching—searching for something you never had—searching for something that was more important than anything in life. Sometimes you have tried to forget about it. Sometimes you have attempted to lose yourself in other things so there could be time and thought for nothing but the business at hand. Sometimes you may have even felt that you were freed from the need to go on seeking this nameless thing. At moments you have almost been able to dismiss this quest completely. But always you have been caught up in it again—always you have had to come back to your search.[10]

Karen Armstrong, in her book on Islam, identifies a quest that is distinguishable from the politico-economic facets of religious behavior. She points out that such a quest is an interior spiritual journey rather than a political drama; it is an exploration of the heart.[11]

When we examine the different religions in the subsequent chapters, we will find that religions characterize the quest in different ways. The goal of the quest and the ways of reaching the goal are not the same in all religions. But what has to be noted is that humanity seems to be involved in a quest that religions manifest despite their differences.

OUR PROPOSAL

Where does Christ stand in the midst of such a quest? This book endeavors to present Christ not as part of the human quest, but rather as the one who can satisfy that quest.

---

7. Radhakrishnan and Moore, *Source Book of Indian Philosophy*, 614–15.

8. Ibid.

9. Gandhi, *Autobiography*, vii.

10. Graham, *Peace with God*, 13.

11. Armstrong, *Islam*, ix.

The initial reaction to such a proposal could be that it exhibits a kind of spiritual audacity; that it claims the superiority of Christianity; that Christian beliefs are true while others are not; that Christ is authentic while awesome spiritual giants like the ancient Hindu gurus, Buddha, Lao-Tzu, Confucius, and Muhammad are all pseudo. Even though one can anticipate such a reaction, the proposal wants to avoid any exhibition of spiritual audacity. It is hoped that the reader will sense the spirit of the proposal, when exposed to the manner in which Christ is presented. The claim that Christ satisfies the quest of religious communities is somewhat comparable to the claim that water satisfies thirst. If water does not have the thirst-quenching quality, it cannot quench the thirst of people, however desperate they may be. On the other hand, if there are no thirsty people, water with all its thirst-quenching quality becomes useless. One finds it difficult to appreciate how water as thirst quencher relates to thirsty people in terms of a framework of analysis where water is taken to be superior and thirsty people to be inferior, where water is true while thirsty people are false. Likewise, in relating Christ to the quest of religious communities, it is not conducive to adopt a framework of analysis that takes Christ to be superior to those involved in the quest—that the claims of Christianity are true, while those of the other religious communities are all false. The successful articulation of the proposal necessitates a different conceptual framework. This will be our next task.

Articulating the Proposal

The first task will be to formulate certain methodological strategies that will facilitate the articulation of the proposal. The first one attempts to answer the question, "How to identify the quest of religious communities?" The second one responds the question, "How to understand Christ in the context of such a quest?" The rest of this chapter will deal with the first strategy, while the chapter following this one will handle the second strategy.

Identifying the Quest of a Religious Community

The quest originates amidst the adherents of a religion and not in its superstructural constructs, like dogmas, moral codes, organizations, or ritualistic practices. These may manifest, articulate, and nurture the quest, but do not conceive it. Hence, it is necessary to commence the analysis with the study of the religious communities at the grassroots level rather than with the superstructures of religions. Our main task is to decipher the quest of humanity that expresses itself through religious and sometimes even nonreligious avenues and then to determine whether Christ is in any way relevant to such a quest.

Religion, taken as a distinct facet of life, differentiated from the philosophical, political, and cultural facets of society is only a modern perspective. Separating the secular from the sacred and degrading the sacred is perhaps a post-enlightenment development. This was not so during the times when the apostles first presented Christ to the Gentile world. They did not view "other religions" as distinct from "their religion," since for them religion was not a distinct entity. No doubt, they recognized people worshipping other gods and being involved in ritualistic practices that they detested. But they did not consider "religion" in the modern sense—as a belief system or an institution that is separated from the rest of life. Even though religion today has become a recognizable, distinct entity of life, it is appropriate to relate Christ with the religious quest in terms of the biblical conceptual framework. In fact, Christ was more concerned about what the people needed and yearned for, rather than being preoccupied with their religious identity or social status. Nevertheless, since religion today functions as a distinct entity of society in such a pronounced manner we need to take into account its superstructural components. But we should not be sidetracked by the superstructures. It is best to commence by examining the cradle of the quest, the religious communities, and then relate these superstructures as expressions of the quest.

First of all, what is a religious community; what constitutes its identity? The Latin connotation of the term, derived from *idem*, or the Greek definition of identity in terms of "substance" are not helpful to characterize a religious community. Both these highlight that the identity of something lies in its sameness or permanence, but a religious community is so very dynamic. Any religious community, whether it be Hindu, Buddhist, Islam, or Christian is a dynamic plurality with significant differences among its adherents, both in areas of doctrine and practice. Moreover, religious communities undergo revolutionary shifts in their lifespan, giving rise to diverse versions. The Vedanta-Siddhanta Hinduism, Hinayana-Mahayana Buddhism, State-Domestic Shintoism, Sunni-Shi'ite Islam, and Catholic-Protestant Christianity are typical diversifications within religions, indicating that they are not static homogenous entities.

Hans Mol characterizes a religious community as a dynamic process of "sacralization"—a process that elevates certain things or persons to sacred status. According to him, sacralization occurs through four main "patterns." He describes them as patterns of a dynamic process rather than parts of a static entity.[12] They are "objectification"—creation of a set of beliefs;[13] "commitment"—an emotional attachment to a person, a group of people, or a set of beliefs that provides the members of the community a sense of belonging;[14] "ritual"—a set of formal behaviors; and "myths"—which reinforce in story form the worldview and actions of the community.[15]

The four patterns do change with the passage of time and are not exclusive of each other. They overlap in their functioning. Rituals help to activate commitment; beliefs express themselves in myths. Moreover, the patterns are not mere descriptions of what the community practices but what it wants to achieve; there is a sense of "oughtness," a normative thrust in the patterns. For instance, the set of beliefs are normative in that they indicate what the community aspires to achieve. Rituals, to be effective, have to be properly practiced, and myths, whether true or fictitious, are meant to drive home a point that would be transformative.

12. Mol, *Identity and the Sacred*, 5.

13. Ibid., 29.

14. Ibid., 13.

15. Ibid., 14.

What is significant is that when we take a religious community as a dynamic process that is striving for something, through certain "sacralized" patterns, we find that the community is essentially involved in a quest. The quest generates the process and gives direction to it. The founders of religions are motivated by a quest. The adherents follow or may even modify what the founder(s) propound. But the quest continues. It demands commitment on the part of the adherents—a wholehearted dedication to achieve what the quest is searching for. Rituals, in this context, do not apply only to certain religious ceremonies, like sacrifices and offerings, but have a wider reference. Rituals indicate the "sacralization of behavior," both individualistic and communal. There are certain communal structures, like the Christian church, the Buddhist sangha, and the Sikh Khalsa, that play a significant role in a religious community. They could be taken as arenas of communal ritualistic practice. They unify and integrate a religious community. Such ritualistic action becomes essential for the successful management of the quest. Finally, myths do not merely entertain a religious community. They may depict doctrinal truths through narratives involving conflicts and charismatic characters that evoke emotional responses. Myths like the Bhagavad Gita of the Hindus play a significant role in that they tend to find their way into the very fabric of the mindset of a community and thereby encourage its members to enthusiastically follow its quest.

The developments, divisions, and deviations that are common in the life span of religious communities indicate how people of a religious community modify, develop, enhance, or even supplant the strategies of articulating their quest. The history of a religious community, however variegated it may be, is basically a quest. The various patterns articulate the quest process. Our main concern will be to determine how articulation occurs though such patterns. But when exploring the patterns, one has to be careful to avoid abstracting them from the questing process. For instance, in the examination of the doctrines and belief systems of a particular religious community, the main concern should not be with the pros and cons of religious dogmas per se, but how the aspirations of the community find expression in the dogmas—how through them a community provides a theoretical basis for its quest.

An in-depth analysis of these patterns is neither possible nor necessary for an endeavor such as this. The strategy is to move beyond the question of what a religion is to a more germane inquiry as to how members of a religious community express, articulate, and manage their quest in and through the facets or patterns of religion; how do the Buddhists, Taoists, Hindus, and Muslims identify themselves through such patterns, in attempting to pursue their quest. Our next task will be to determine how these patterns relate to and express the quest of a religious community.

OUR GUIDELINES

In order to decipher the quest of religious communities, the following guidelines could be helpful: 1) Look without distorting the picture; and 2) judge not in haste.

Look Without Distorting the Picture

The quest of a religious community takes shape among the people who constitute it rather than in the superstructural components of religion, even though these do exhibit and administer the quest in various ways. Hence, when examining the superstructures one should be careful not to abstract them from the aspirations of the people who adopt them.

The strategy of assessing religions by comparing their superstructures is very popular in academic circles. The following diagram, depicting the comparison of Christianity with another religion, may clarify such a strategy:

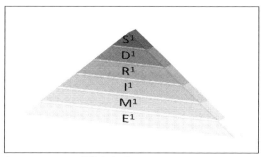

Superstructures of Christianity

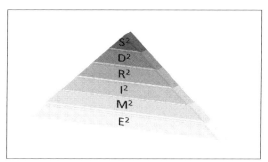

Superstructures of Another Religion

This legend will clarify the diagram:

S	Scripture
D	Doctrines
R	Rituals
I	Institutions
M	Moral Codes and Conduct
E	Experiences

The diagram represents the pyramid structure of a religion. Each facet is a layer in the pyramid. One may compare Christianity with another religion at various levels. The base of the pyramid, "E" signifies the foundational level of a religion. "E" stands for experiences of the people of a religion; it is here that the quest of a religious community originates. One may also select one or more superstructural facets of the religions and analyze in-depth and compare them. Such a strategy no doubt will provide some useful insights, but it also has the potentiality of bypassing the dynamics of the quest of religious communities.

A living religion is not a mere package of doctrine, rituals, organization, and moral codes. It is really the quest of a community. We may call it the faith of the community. Faith in this context is not a mere theoretical assent to a certain set of dogmas. Faith is a commitment, both personal and communal, that encompasses all the facets of life. The comparative method may encourage one to be preoccupied with a particular, perhaps significant, aspect of religion, but in the process lose sight of the big picture. Stephen Neil points out that things that are experienced as wholes are, in fact, not commensurable with one another, any more than one scent or piece of music is really comparable to any other.[16] The comparative method tends to view religions to be commensurable. But this often necessitates abstraction. For instance, one may pick out a specific doctrine, ritual, or an organizational structure and compare how each religion handles it and then attempt to assess which is better or the best. But, in such a selection, what is compared turns out to be an abstraction. Such a move tends to detach ideas from the dynamics of the communities that give rise to them and in doing so robs them of their life, comparable to the dissection of a specimen in a laboratory. A study of a dissected specimen no doubt gives us much information but does not capture the dynamics of the living creature. In the same way, comparison of the abstracted ideas of religions tells little about the underlying dynamics of the religious communities from which the ideas have been somewhat "violently disserved."[17]

Moreover, comparative assessment of religions often tends to concentrate too much on the doctrinal dimension of religions. Since scriptures are the most tangible expressions of doctrine, scholars naturally attempt to meticulously analyze the scriptures. There is, of course, merit in such a strategy. After all, scriptures of a religion express in the most definitive manner its doctrines. Hence, the study of scriptures will, to a great extent, help to determine doctrine and thereby make an objective comparative assessment of religions.

When attempting to find out the nature of the quest of religious communities through understanding their scriptures, there are certain precautionary measures to be taken. The doctrines of a religion, as presented through its scriptures, do not constitute a mere theoretical construct. They are intimately tied up with the dynamics of the religious community and may be taken as tangible expressions of its core aspirations. Hence, in exegeting the scriptures of a religion, one has to take into account the wider communal context that motivated and gave shape to those scriptures. William Graham's emphasis that scripture is a relational concept is well taken. He states that "the sacrality or holiness of a book is not an a priori attribute of a text but one that is realized historically in the life of communities who respond to it as something sacred

16. Neil, *Christian Faith*, 2.

17. Ibid., 2–5.

or holy. A text becomes 'scripture' in active subjective relationship to persons, and as part of a cumulative communal tradition. No text, written or oral or both, is sacred or authoritative in isolation."[18]

The founders and the followers, the priests and the prophets, the orthodox traditionalists, and even the heretics all constitute the dynamics of a religious community. Hence, in order to feel the real texture of the scriptures, we have to get into the fabric of the religious communities. For instance, to understand and appreciate the Quran, we have to journey into the spiritual struggles and aspirations of Muhammad. The Buddhist scriptures that contain Buddha's doctrines cannot be separated from Buddha. He insisted that his teachings were entirely based on his experiences. Concentrating on the text and abstracting it from the religious community will be a deterrent for finding out how the text expresses the quest of the community concerned.

Moreover, just because most religions have their own scriptures, we cannot apply the same hermeneutical methods to understand all scriptures. Since the nature and function of scriptures differ radically among religious communities, reducing their scriptures to a common denominator hinders interpreting them correctly. Winfried Corduan identifies a hermeneutical blunder that he calls "The Protestant Fallacy."[19] When one views the scriptures of other religions in the same way as Protestant Christians see the Bible, such a fallacy occurs. Classical Protestantism maintains that the Bible is the inspired word of God and that there is no other source of propositional revelation other than the Bible. The fallacy "consists in applying this understanding which is properly appropriate for the Bible, to the Scriptures of other religions. In other words, it means to hold that the essence of another can be distilled from its Scriptures, just as the essence of Christian belief and practice can be learned from the Bible."[20]

Scriptures function in very different ways in religions. The "orality of scripture" which William Graham highlights is characteristic of some of the scriptures of religions.[21] For instance, Avesta in Zoroastrianism is an accumulation of scriptures spanning several centuries (6 BC—637 AD). Even though one may profitably use Avesta to reconstruct Zoroastrian doctrines, it is not merely a doctrinal document. Most of Avesta is in the form of *gathas* (hymns) and rather difficult to understand. But in the Zoroastrian community, it was supposed to be not just a source of doctrinal information but rather a vehicle of worship, a ritualistic text recited at ceremonies of worship. The ritualistic practice of Avesta, rather than its doctrinal content, highlights the expression of the Zoroastrian quest.

Adi Granth, the sacred Sikh scripture, plays a very significant role in the Sikh community. The sacred text is recognized as the source of doctrine and binding authority for the Sikhs, but its role is not limited to that. As a collection of hymns and chants, it is very much a part of Sikh congregational worship. Gobind Singh (1666–1718 AD), the

18. Graham, *Beyond*, 5.

19. Corduan, *Tapestry of Faith*, 57.

20. Ibid., 58–59.

21. Graham, *Beyond*, 4–8.

tenth founder guru decreed that after him the one and only guru for the Sikhs will be Adi Granth. Sikhs venerate it like the other founder gurus—as the very embodiment of God's guidance to the community. We will do injustice to the community, if we take Adi Granth as merely a doctrinal revelation and apply the semantic and syntactic exegetical methods to understand it. As a congregational hymn book and an object of veneration its role is significant; it articulates the core aspirations of the Sikh quest to worship the one true God and thereby be freed from the shackles of human existence.

The Quran is the sacred text of Islam. For the Muslims, the Quran is a divine book, the original of it, Umm Al-Kitab, is found in heaven. For them, as Corduan observes, the Quran's "primary significance is not what it says, as important as that is, but its very existence."[22] It mediates God's presence in the lives of the believers. In fact, the most rewarding role of the Quran is to make Muslims feel the blessed presence of God through prayerful recitation. The poesy of the Quran makes its recitation both feasible and exhilarating. As the most perfect revelation of God, Quran is sometimes compared to the incarnation of God in Christ.[23]

Several scriptures contain quite a number of stories. Some of these stories appear to be unbelievable, especially in the contemporary scientific world. There is naturally a tendency to dismiss them as mere fables. But we have to view them in the wider context, in which they came into being and are believed. It was G. K. Chesterton who observed that "Fairy tales are more than true; not because they tell us that dragons exist, but because they tell us that dragons can be beaten."[24] Many the myths seem to convey that evil can be defeated. These myths should not be assessed on the criterion whether they are true or false, real or imaginary, but rather on the grounds of whether they express the hopes of the people who believe in them. Several among these myths express a core human aspiration: the hope to be freed from the entanglements of evil, in whatever form they may appear. In that sense, myths play a vital role in the salvific quest of religious communities.

When examining in the subsequent chapters the quest of the various religious communities, we will realize the variety of ways in which these communities view their scriptures. The citations of Zoroastrianism, Sikhism, and Islam are merely to point out that one should be cautious in understanding the scriptures of other religions in the way one handles the Bible. Care should be taken not to separate the doctrines expressed in scriptures or for that matter any other facet of religion, from their wider contexts where they are closely interwoven with the aspirations of the religious communities—aspirations that constitute their quest.

Moreover, while presenting the uniqueness of Christ and his salvation, one should not get entrapped with the parochial claim that there is truth only in Christianity and that all other religions are false—that the people of other religions have no knowledge about God or do not have any moral values. The Bible is unique not because truth is

---

22. Corduan, *Tapestry of Faith*, 62–63.

23. Denny, *Introduction to Islam*, 151.

24. Chesterton, as cited in Gaiman, *Coraline*, epigraph.

only found in it but because Christ, the Truth, is its central theme. When we examine the scriptures of some of the religions, we will realize that several claims pertaining, for instance, to the moral, psychological, metaphysical, theological, and social realms are true and even biblically acceptable. This leads us to the question as to whether God has revealed himself outside the Christian scriptures.

Revelation, in the Christian theological context, has been traditionally placed into two categories: special and general. Special revelation is taken to be God revealing to particular people at particular points in history. Today such revelation is associated mainly with written revelation, the Bible. Exposure to such revelation is claimed to have a redemptive impact, when one relates to Christ that the Bible presents. On the other hand, general revelation is viewed as a having a judgmental impact, in that there is no excuse for humans not to acknowledge God in their exposure to the marvelous constructs of the universe and through the sensitivity of their conscience. Psalms 19:1–4; Romans 1:16–17, 20; and 2:10–15 are the common texts cited to support general revelation. These verses highlight that revelation about God is available to all persons at all times and places. Walter Elwell points out that "General Revelation is that divine disclosure to all persons at all times and places by which one comes to know that God is, and what he is like."[25] The phrases "the work of his hands" (Ps 19:1) and "what he has made" (Rom 1:20), usually taken as referring to nature, could be taken in a wider sense to include not only the mountains, trees, and oceans, but also facets of human nature such as the human conscience and moral sensibility (Rom 2:14–15).[26] The avenues God provides are really open ended and the manner in which knowledge about him is obtained is also not at all restrictive, so much so humans do not have any excuse (Rom 1:20). Moreover, the Bible places God's revelation through the created order and human conscience in the context of the universality of the human predicament, that both Jews and Gentiles are all under sin and hence there is no one righteous before God, not even one (Rom 3:9–20). Such a placement indicates that general revelation is also salvific in intent. God gives a glimpse of his glory to those living in darkness with the hope that they would eventually see the light. Placing these two types of revelation in exclusive categories, special revelation as a means of redemption and general revelation as way of judging people seems artificial and really does mar the character of God, who is the facilitator of both special and general revelation. He is a God who wants all to be saved and none to perish.

Convinced by the unbounded grace and generosity of God revealed in Jesus Christ, Clark Pinnock accommodates world religions within general revelation.[27] It is inconceivable that the God who gave his only begotten son to save all humanity (John 3:16), would use general revelation to give just enough knowledge to humans to damn and not save themselves. The hesitancy in accommodating the endeavors of world religions within general revelation seems to be based on the assumption that

---

25. Henry, "Revelation," 944.

26. Corduan, *Tapestry of Faith*, 44.

27. Pinnock, *Wideness*, 18, 104.

any "religious idea" that comes from sources outside the orbit of special revelation is rebellious. Bruce Demarest's criticism of Clark Pinnock's position is based on such a view—a view that assumes that all religions that arise in response to general revelation is an act of rebellion.[28] But is such a dismissal warranted? Perhaps some endeavors of people of religious communities may well be taken as a sincere search for God rather than a demonic rebellion. Gordon Smith highlights this:

> All religion, it would seem more accurate to believe, reflects both an authentic search for God as well as human pride and rebellion. As such, then, we need to come to terms with the honest seeker after God whose only avenue of expression is the religious environment in which he lives. It seems rather preemptive to simply call this rebellion. It may be rebellion, but it could also be viewed positively as an authentic and sincere quest that is distorted by human fallenness.[29]

The distortion that human fallenness generates leading even up to rebellion could beset not only people of other faiths but also even those who claim to be authentic Christians. Moreover, just because many do not come to saving knowledge through general revelation does not mean that it is not part of God's salvific intent. Even those exposed firsthand to special revelation and have their being within the portals of the church do not have any idea of Christ as Savior.

Even before Pinnock, theologians like Hugh R. Mackintosh (1870–1936) and Wilhelm Schmidt (1868–1954) attempted to accommodate religions within the realm of general revelation. Seeing the worship of a Supreme Being, referred to as the High God, in some Aboriginal religions, Schmidt came to the conclusion that certain significant similarities among religions do indicate a "universal revelation."[30] Mackintosh claims that revelation has been occurring at all places and all times in and through nature, human history, and religions. But, according to him, that does not mean that the Christian message of salvation is superfluous. He points out that "a great missionary was once heard to say that he had never preached the gospel anywhere, without finding that God has been there before him. Yet that divine presence and action did not serve to make the Christian message superfluous, but to make it appreciated when it came."[31] The general revelation that is available to people of other faiths prepares them to receive or at least get an idea of Christ and the gospel message. We have to keep in mind that the facilitator of both general and special is God; he is a God who wants none to perish.

What is it that makes exposure to special revelation redemptive? It is not the "writteness" of the written word but Christ the Living Word, the incarnational revelation. The Bible without God's salvific actions climaxing in his incarnation in Christ would turn out to be another theological treatise on salvation. On the other hand, a non-biblical Christ turns out to be "humankind's begotten son"; a by-product of

---

28. Demarest, "General and Special Revelation," 202–5.

29. Smith, "Religion and the Bible," 18.

30. Schmidt, *Origin and Growth*, 262.

31. Mackintosh, "Does a Historical Study?," 514.

postmodern experientialism, as for instance, the New Age Cosmic Christ. David Fideler depicts Christ as "Sun of God" based on his extensive research on the way divine figures were represented as symbolic personifications of cosmic principles. But he himself admits that his depiction is not about the historical Jesus.[32] Such a Christ may be academically appetizing, but is not the Jesus of the Bible.

The efficacy of special revelation as a redemptive tool depends on two factors: first on the ontological reality of the incarnate Christ; second, on taking him into account when understanding the Bible. Viewing the Bible through the lens of Christ and his mission is a must to comprehend and appreciate the uniqueness of the Bible as "redemptive revelation." Perhaps since the invention of the printing press and as an aftermath of the Enlightenment, the written word has received glorified status at the expense of other modes of communication. The development of sophisticated modes of linguistic analysis have encouraged biblical scholars to be preoccupied with the mechanics of biblical exegesis, so much so that Christ becomes relegated to the background. It is here that one appreciates the vital role God the Holy Spirit plays in making the written word highlight the Living Word, Christ the Savior and not delimit him into a hermeneutical product.

Hence we could make the claim that all God's revelation is salvific in intent. But God does not orchestrate his intent through forceful means. Revelation is not divine imposition. There is always the option to accept as well as ignore, misunderstand, or even reject what is he is trying to reveal. We should also remember that both general and special revelation could be misinterpreted and modified in ways that what is intended to be conveyed through them is lost. In fact, God loses his copyright when he reveals himself, especially through the scriptures. When we accommodate other religions, we do not claim that all what they claim is acceptable. Anyhow, there is a rationale to accommodate certain articulations of the quest of religious communities within general revelation.

Such a quest usually originates with a sense of dissatisfaction with the existing state of affairs. Such dissatisfaction seems to be connected with, and perhaps provoked by, a moral sensibility, a prick in human conscience that something is not right. In the extremely popular yet profoundly philosophical movie, *The Matrix*, Morpheus's comment to Neo runs thus, "You're here because you know something. What you know you can't explain, but you feel it. You've felt it your entire life, that there's something wrong with the world. You don't know what it is, but it's there, like a splinter in your mind, driving you mad."[33]

Perhaps the splinter in the mind could be seen as human conscience. The Bible observes that Gentiles obey God's law, even though they are not aware of it. They are guided by a moral sensibility, their conscience, which gives them a sort of feedback on their actions and decisions (Rom 2:14, 15). Perhaps, it was this moral sensibility that disturbed the affluent, overprotected prince Gautama Buddha, when he was

32. Fideler, *Jesus Christ*, xv.
33. Wachowski and Wachowski, *Matrix*.

confronted with the sights of sickness, poverty, and death. The presence and even activation of such a moral sensibility does not mean that it eventually leads to awareness of God. The belief systems that such a sensibility generates in the hearts of religious leaders portray different images of God and paths to reach him. The knowledge that general revelation makes possible, namely the belief systems, the institutional structures, and moral codes differ drastically among religious traditions. It should be highlighted that general revelation embraces a moral-cum-spiritual dimension that plays a vital role in initiating and motivating the quest of religious communities. The doctrines and practices express and articulate the aspirations that constitute the quest of a religious community. These doctrines and ritualistic practices may not have salvific value. Nevertheless, the aspirations that are foundational to these doctrines and practices have salvific significance. For instance, when Paul addresses Gentile audiences (Acts 14:15–7; 17:22–31), he seems to assume that his audience does know something about the divine. When he was in the city of Athens, no doubt he was distressed with the idol worship of the Athenians. But, instead of running away, he addressed them as being "religious," when he commenced his sermon (Acts 17:22). He presented God in Christ as the fulfillment of something they had yearned for and believed in without knowing who or what it is: the Unknown God. He does not identify Christ with the idol of the Unknown God, but clearly states, "What you worship as something unknown I am going to proclaim to you" (Acts 17:23). Paul's use of the term "worship" to describe their religious behavior has to be noted. Paul was aware that the Athenians realized the necessity to give worth to and rely on a "God," even though they did not know who he was. Such a realization need not be satanic but could arise out of general revelation. The revelation that the Athenians already possessed provided the occasion for Paul to present Christ. Such a revelation had salvific significance. The distinction between salvific value and significance will become clearer when we examine each religion's superstructures in relation to its aspirations in the subsequent chapters. The very fact that the articulations of religious communities could be accommodated within general revelation prevents one from relating Christianity with other religions within a restrictive paradigm dictated by the true-false dichotomy.

Hence, when attempting to examine the religions, so as to decipher the quest of the religious communities, these guidelines will be helpful. First, when examining the superstructural facets of religions, one should not abstract them from the aspirations of the religious communities. Second, stay clear of the temptation to view other religions in the way one views Christianity, especially in the area of understanding scriptures. Finally, be willing to accommodate some of the articulations of religious communities as part of what God has orchestrated through general revelation in the world at large. These guidelines would enable one could look without distorting the picture.

Judge Not in Haste

Contemporary developments have tended to transform the world into a multicultural, multi-religious global village. Factors such as demographic shifts, urbanization, technologies of travel and communication, availability of religious literature, and media exposure providing graphic illustrations of what transpires when religious people clash in various parts of the world, have intensified the awareness of religious diversity. This has almost forced those committed to a specific religion to determine how one should view other religions—as to how to be faithful to one's commitment in the face of challenges that religious diversity presents. In such a global village of religious plurality, the question naturally arises as to whether there is any justification to claim that one religion has the best way to satisfy what we call the human religious quest.

Any analysis of the quest of the religious communities has to be placed within a wider framework of reference rather than within the polemical paradigm that encourages making hasty judgments. In fact, as we will see in subsequent chapters, some of the dogmas, rituals, and moral injunctions that articulate the quest of religious communities serve to highlight how Christ is relevant to such a quest. Examining religious communities in such a wider framework of reference does demand patience and a willingness to suspend judgment on the doctrines and practices of other religions. But, that does not mean that one is indifferent to truth claims or has abandoned all objective criteria to distinguish between valid and invalid claims, legitimate and pseudo spiritualities. When trying to capture the spirit of the quest of a religious community, one has to get a feel of the heart throb of the community; one has to decipher the core of its deepest aspirations. Providing meticulous hermeneutical analysis of religious texts, comparing and clarifying the concepts of religious dogma, extracting the philosophical insights from the preachings and teachings of the gurus of religion, assessing the organizational structures of religious movements, analyzing the sociology of religions through statistical strategies, and laboriously tracing the dissensions and conflicts in the religious world are all legitimate academic pursuits. But preoccupation with such pursuits in a piecemeal manner, isolated from the dynamics of the life of religious communities, will not serve our purpose. Unless such pursuits are interwoven with the life of the religious communities, the attempt to decipher and characterize their aspirations will not be facilitated. This is vital to the endeavor to capture the relationship between Christ and the quest of religious communities. Hence, it is in such a wider framework of reference that we will attempt to identify the quest of religious communities and locate their deeper aspirations. Hasty judgments, condescending comments, and derogatory condemnations of the articulations of other religious communities will not help.

CONCLUSION

As stated earlier, this book is not and cannot claim to be an exhaustive volume on world religions covering the various facets of religions. Nevertheless, when relating Christ to each religion, the book will make some observations of the religion's origin and development, its doctrinal formulations and dissensions, its organizational structures and ritualistic practices, its moral codes and even political involvements. Nevertheless such observations will not be the focus of attention. They will be of interest to the endeavor, as multifarious expressions of the quest of the religious community concerned. This book does not want to be preoccupied with the superstructures of a religion and thereby miss the dynamic flow of a religious community. For in that flow we detect the religious quest of the community, its core aspirations, and this is where we find Christ relevant to the religious community. As scholars who realize the changing face of missions point out, "Religion, although molded by culture, is more than a cultural phenomenon. The search for God and the need for relationship with him—the inner essence of religion, its spiritual core—are embedded within the human psyche."[34] It is in this sense that a religion could be characterized as a quest. Christ will be presented as the fulfillment of the religious quest of humanity within such a paradigm. In order to provide a rationale for such a claim, the second methodological strategy becomes necessary. This strategy will attempt to find out who Jesus Christ really is and why he is not part of the quest but, on the other hand, the one who could satisfy the human religious quest. This will be our next task.

34. Pocock, *Changing Face,* 83.

2

Christ among Saviors

Everyone who drinks this water shall be thirsty again, but whoever drinks the water I give him will never thirst (John 4:13).

WHEN RELATING CHRIST TO the quest of religious communities and suggesting that he is the one who can adequately satisfy such a quest, we have two preliminary tasks. First we need to establish that he is not part of the questing humanity. Second, we have to show that his very personhood enables him to be the one who could satisfy such a quest. This chapter deals mainly with these two tasks, which really pertain to the identity of Christ, as to who he really is.

Once this is accomplished, there will be an appropriate conceptual framework to articulate our claim. In the subsequent chapters, we will examine the faith communities that we have chosen. We will find out first whether the people of a religious community are involved in a quest; second, how the founders and subsequent leaders articulate the quest; and third, how the superstructures of religion express the quest. Then, we will attempt to identify certain indicators that make Christ relevant to the quest of the community concerned. We will examine each religion within such parameters.

The proposal that Christ can satisfy the religious quest of humanity cannot be justified unless we can show that he is not part of the quest. In order to articulate such a claim, we have to place him outside of the realm of humans involved in the quest. This is precisely where the problem lies. After all, Jesus Christ lived on this earth as a human being at a specific period of history. If he was just a carpenter's son, however profound his teachings, sensational his miracles, compassionate his ministries, and sacrificial his death may have been, he was still human and hence one among the questing humans. Perhaps he was another person attempting to lead thirsty people to the well where he quenched his thirst, but is not the one who quenches the thirst.

John Hick, the reputed pluralist, takes religions essentially as "paths of salvation." He proposes that even though "salvation" is primarily a Christian term, it could be taken in a wider functional sense, applicable to other religious traditions. When so taken, "salvation" appears as "the transformation of human existence from self-centeredness to reality centeredness."[1] Whether Hick's generic characterization of "salvation" is acceptable or not, his grassroots level approach highlights the salvific quest of religious communities. His observation that these communities are all aspiring for a "transformation" is well-taken. Nevertheless, his attempt to present all religions as providing "paths of salvation" leads him to consider Christianity as one of them and Christ as one of the many saviors. In order to place Christ in this category, he makes it a point to stress the humanity of Jesus at the expense of his divinity. He acknowledges that there is a logical connection between the claim that Jesus is the only Savior and that he is God. He puts it this way:

> There is a direct line of logical entailment from the premise that Jesus was God, in the sense that he was God the Son, the Second Person of the Divine Trinity, living in human life, to the conclusion that Christianity and Christianity alone was founded by God in person; and from this to the further conclusion that God must want all his human children to be related to him through his religion, which he has himself founded for us; and then to the final conclusion, [that] 'outside Christianity, [there is] no salvation.'[2]

Hick has to downplay the deity of Christ in order to justify his pluralistic stance that there are several saviors offering different ways of salvation. He identifies a common trend among religious communities to exalt their founders to divine status. He claims that the history of Christianity also exhibits such a development, when Christ "the Son of God" was exalted to "God the Son." Hence for him, the incarnation of Christ turns out to be a myth. Hick's downplaying of the deity of Christ allows him to place Christ in the same category as religious leaders like Buddha, Lao-Tzu, Confucius, and Muhammad, whose identity resided in their humanity, or rather in their super-humanity. Identifying Christ in this way makes him very much a part of the human religious quest. If Christ is merely a human being who provides a way of salvation, then it would mean that there is no qualitative distinction between his way and the other paths of salvation. But can Christ, though fully human, be taken as merely human?

Our proposal is founded on the conviction, that Jesus Christ is God; he is God the Son. That does not mean that we do not take the humanity of Jesus lightly. A Christology from "above" rather than from "below" seems to be the approach the writers of the gospel adopt. When the gospels were written, Christ had already ascended. The arrangement and content of the gospels seem to be determined by the fact that Jesus came from above and has gone up above.[3] Such an approach is helpful to substantiate the proposal that Christ is able to satisfy the human quest on the grounds of his unique divine-human personhood.

Nevertheless, the claim that Jesus Christ is "God the Son" faces a formidable theological challenge. If God is one, how can Christ also be God? The monotheistic stance challenges the legitimacy and logic of the claim that God is one, and Christ is also God.

---

1. Hick, "Religious Pluralism," 54.
2. Hick, *God Has Many Names*, 58.
3. Macleod, *Person of Christ*, 16.

Considering God as a triune being is helpful to substantiate such a claim. There has been significant work done in recent years highlighting the necessity of a trinitarian framework of reference to capture the nature of God especially as a relational being.[4] But, conceiving God as a triune being carries with it controversies: first, whether there is biblical justification for the doctrine of the Trinity; second, whether the claim that "God is one but three" is logically consistent. Can one be a monotheist and still conceive God as Trinity?

The Councils of Nicaea (325 CE) and Constantinople (381 CE) presented a full-blown doctrine of the Trinity. The doctrine, which received expression subsequent to the composition of the Bible, turned out to be controversial since its key terms are not found in the Bible. The doctrine was articulated mainly through Greek and Latin concepts. But, if a key term of a doctrine is not explicitly mentioned in the Bible, does that mean there is no justification to articulate a doctrine using nonbiblical vocabulary? Even though the term "Trinity" is not explicitly used in the Bible to describe God, there are several ways in which the Scriptures indicate the workings of the trinitarian God. Since adequate study has been done on the biblical grounds for the doctrine,[5] we would highlight certain hermeneutical and epistemological considerations that have to be taken into account when claiming its legitimacy.

First of all, why did God not reveal himself as triune being during Old Testament times? Second, even though the workings of God as Father, Son, and Spirit are evident in the New Testament, why does it not explicate the doctrine? Third, why did the articulation of the doctrine take almost four centuries to be fully developed in the councils of Nicaea and Constantinople? To respond to these questions, it is helpful to look into what Rodney Stark identifies as one of the most neglected Judeo-Christian premises of God's revelatory strategy. He calls it "Divine Accommodation." According to such a premise, God's revelations are always limited to the current capacity of humans to comprehend them. That, "in order to communicate with humans, God is forced to accommodate their incomprehension by resorting to the equivalent of 'baby-talk.'"[6]

There are some anticipations of the concept of God as triune being in the Old Testament. But, during the Old Testament era, God's intent seems to be to make the children of Israel, who had come out of a polytheistic religious world, believe in him and only him. He had to reveal himself in a manner comprehensible to a people who despite his repeated warnings, tended to slip into the worship of other gods, such as Baal. In such a context, to present God as "One in Three" would have confused the Israelites, and perhaps even encouraged them to go back to polytheism. God's postponement to reveal his trinitarian personhood is quite in keeping with the premise of divine accommodation.

The New Testament era commenced with two major historical events: Christ's incarnation and the outpouring of the Holy Spirit on the day of Pentecost. These

---

4. Kruger, *Great Dance*; Olson and Hall, *Trinity*; Witherington and Ice, *Shadow*; Hill, *Three-Personed God*; Lee, *Trinity*; Panikkar, *Trinity*; Welch, *In This Name*.

5. Bickersteth, *Trinity*, is a comprehensive study of the biblical basis for the doctrine of Trinity.

6. Stark, *Discovering God*, 6.

made an indelible mark on the understanding of God. The monotheistic Jews needed something much more than a dogma or an innovative ritual to view God as triune being. When Jesus was born, the angelic proclamation that he is Immanuel, meaning "God with us," and the miracles associated with his birth were no doubt spectacular (Matt 1:23; Matt 2:16; Luke 2:8–14), Moreover such an event was not merely extraordinary but really a fulfillment of Old Testament prophecy and hence turned out to be a reality show enacted in the Jewish arena traumatizing the monotheistic mindset. The carpenter's son from Nazareth claiming to have a unique filial relationship with God, though it seemed blatantly blasphemous, had to be reckoned with. Moreover, Jehovah, who had categorically declared that there was no god beside him, proclaiming Jesus as his beloved son (Matt 3:13–17), shockingly provided the divine stamp of approval on Jesus' identity. The very fact that God raised him up from death, and the human encounters of the risen Christ poignantly pointed out that he was more than a mere human. Moreover, Pentecost publicly enacted God the Father's promise being fulfilled through Christ his Son baptizing people with God the Holy Spirit (Acts 1:4–8). It was a significant historical moment of the triune God in action. These historical happenings served as object lessons to drive home the point that God is Father, Son, and the Holy Spirit. They provided the experiential fabric for the weaving of the tapestry of God as triune being.

The early church fathers responded to what happened in history that, though controversial, was undeniable. The presentation of God as triune being originated not as a theological dogma but as a pastoral response to congregational practice. Dyadic (Father and Son) and triadic (Father, Son, and Spirit) patterns of addressing God became evident in church liturgies and catechetical practice. Church fathers like Clement of Rome and Ignatius exhorted their mostly Jewish flocks by highlighting God as Father, Son, and Spirit. They were called upon to provide a biblical rationale for the congregational behavior in their churches. Believers, both Jew and Gentile, exhibited modes of worship that were novel even to them. For instance, Irenaeus's catechetical instruction gives a fair picture of church practice of the time. He points out that "This, then, is the order of the rule of our faith . . . God the Father . . . the creator of all things: this is the first point of our faith. The second point is this: the Word of God, Son of God, Christ Jesus our Lord . . . And the third point is this: the Holy Spirit, through Whom the prophets prophesied . . ."[7] Prayer and worship were directed to God, Jehovah (*Yahweh*), but addressed as Father of Jesus Christ. Moreover, Jesus came to be worshiped based on the recognition of his divine exalted status (e.g., 2 Peter 3:18; Rev 1:5–6). Even though the Holy Spirit was not openly worshiped, there was a spontaneous experiential realization that the Spirit was the divine presence that enabled people to proclaim Jesus as Lord. Greetings, baptisms, and doxologies came to be in the name of the Father, Son, and Spirit. Jesus' command to baptize "in the name of the Father, of the Son, and of the Holy Spirit" (Matt 28:19) naturally turned out to be the rule of faith. About the year 150 CE, Justin

7. Kelly, *Early Christian Doctrines*, 89.

Martyr mentions that the candidates for baptism "receive the washing with water in the name of God the Father and Lord of the universe, and of our Savior Jesus Christ, and of the Holy Spirit."[8] The doxologies also exhibited a similar pattern. Such modes of worship and church practice exhibited a threefold pattern in the Christian experience of God, and thereby testified to the divinity of not only Jehovah but also of Christ and the Holy Spirit. A popular evening hymn of the second century is still preserved in the liturgy of the Greek Orthodox Church:

> Serene Light of the Holy Glory
> Jesus Christ
> Having come to the setting of the sun,
> And seeing the evening light
> We praise the Father and the Son
> And the Holy Spirit of God.
> It behoveth to praise Thee
> At all times with holy songs,
> Son of God, who has given life;
> Therefore the world glorifieth Thee.[9]

The hymn indicates that, as early as the second century CE, God was worshiped as Father, Son, and Spirit. Christ is glorified as one who rendered life to people. Such modes of worship did not arise out of theological speculation but rather as a result of two very significant historical events: incarnation and Pentecost. Incarnation refers to the birth of Jesus Christ in Bethlehem. The angelic messages concerning Jesus, given to his mother Mary, the wise men from the East, the shepherds and the prophetic announcements made by those who met the baby Jesus all point out that he was not just an ordinary baby, but God incarnate. Pentecost refers to the outpouring of the Holy Spirit on the day of Pentecost (Acts 2). These events facilitated the understanding of God as a triune being. Kelly points out that the early catechetical and liturgical formulae represent a pre-reflective, pre-theological phase of Christian belief. They came out of the worship and preaching of the church and provided the raw material for theologians to construct the Christian doctrine of the Godhead.[10]

The trinitarian doctrine served as a way of rendering legitimacy to such a Christian experience by providing a conceptual framework for the practice of the new modes of worship and liturgy. The early church fathers could not just ignore the Christ event. Some of them were converts from a Greco-Roman background. Hence it is understandable that they employed the conceptual tools available to them, especially in Greek philosophy, to articulate Christian doctrines; the doctrine of Trinity is one of them. For instance, Clement of Alexandria (150–215 CE) pointed out that Greek philosophical concepts could help Christians to articulate some of the scriptural dogmas and thereby present a better understanding of their faith.[11] The participants of the Nicene and Constantinople

8. Quasten, *Patrology*, 25.

9. Quoted in Quasten, *Patrology*, 159.

10. Kelly, *Early Christian Doctrines*, 90.

11. Chadwick, *Alexandrian Christianity*, 18–19.

councils, as well as the theologians like Irenaeus and Tertullian who preceded them, also came from such a world. It is not surprising that they used Latin and Greek concepts to make the doctrine more comprehensible. The term "Trinity" does not occur in the Bible. Its Greek form "trias" seems to have been first used by Theophilus of Antioch (181 CE) and its Latin form "trinitas" by Tertullian (200 CE), who is believed to have developed the formula that God is "one in substance but three in persons." Such an articulation of the doctrine employing Greek and Latin concepts exemplifies the working of God's revelatory strategy of divine accommodation. For God in his wisdom sometimes allows his revelation to be explicated, not modified or added upon, through extra-biblical concepts and modes, so as to make it comprehensible. The explication per se is not God's revelation but enables comprehension to an extent. The trinitarian formulation of God's personhood may be taken as an example.

The articulation of God as triune being took shape in a Jewish world that claimed only Jehovah is God. Ascribing divinity to Christ amounted to blasphemy. The early Christians, constituting many Jewish converts, were influenced by Jewish ideas about God and were naturally hesitant to accommodate any God besides Jehovah. The controversies that arose out of new forms of worship and practices pertained to acknowledging Jehovah as the Father of Jesus Christ and the deity of the Holy Spirit. This made it necessary to defend God as a triune being. The challenges both within and outside the church called for expressing the mystery of the Trinity in some acceptable way. What the early Christians believed came to be expressed in graphic form. One of the earliest symbols used to represent Trinity was the equilateral triangle. During biblical times Priscilla and her husband Aquila accompanied Paul on some of his journeys (Acts 18). St. Priscilla's catacombs discovered in Italy have several symbols used by the early church during the second and third centuries CE. One of the tombs in the catacombs contains a palm branch symbolizing martyrdom and victory and an equilateral triangle depicting the Holy Trinity.[12]

The following diagram shows a representation of the Trinity that has been in vogue since postbiblical times.

Emblem of the Holy Trinity Anglican Church, Sooke, British Columbia, Canada

This symbol, called the *Triquetra* (in Latin *try-ket-ra* means three-cornered), is one of the oldest to depict Trinity. The fish is believed to be the oldest symbol for Christ. The equal arches of the circle that the three fishes depict could be taken as representing the equality of Father, Son, and Spirit, while the interwoven blending of the arches could indicate the indivisibility of the persons of the Trinity and the unity in the Godhead. Note the equilateral triangle that is at the center. The *Triquetra* seems to represent the God as triune being by depicting it as a triangle. Such a depiction has been found in church altars and archi-

12. Webber and Cram, *Church Symbolism*, 40.

tecture, especially in the Roman Catholic and Orthodox churches. The following diagrams exemplify such a representation:[13]

The Holy Trinity (Symbol 1)

The Holy Trinity (Symbol 2)

There seems to be a rationale for the early church to pick out the triangle to depict the Trinity. Let us look at the historical context of such a symbolism.

The logical inconsistency in asserting that God is one yet three is obvious. In simple arithmetic vocabulary, how can 1=3 or 1+1+1=1? When we adopt the Arabic number system, we are bound to identify a mathematical fallacy. But nowhere in the Bible is it stated that we should adopt such a number system to articulate a biblical doctrine. In fact, this system was not available during New Testament times. Apostle Paul, the erudite scholar and legal pundit, would have been embarrassed had he been confronted with a mathematical problem using Arabic numerals.

It was in a Greco-Roman world that the early church started to establish itself. Greek and Roman mathematics were very popular until approximately the middle of the second century of the Christian era. Greek mathematics was based mainly on the Pythagorean number system, attributed to Pythagoras (580–500 BCE). This was the predominant mathematical system of the New Testament and early church period. Hence, the early church fathers, who were responsible for the formulation of the doctrine of the Trinity, would most likely have worked with Greek mathematical concepts and methods. If so, we need to examine the doctrine of Trinity through the concepts and norms of Greek rather than Arabic mathematics. How did the Greeks understand the nature and purpose of mathematics?

GREEK MATHEMATICS IN NEW TESTAMENT TIMES

For the Greeks, religion, philosophy, science, and mathematics were inseparable. Pythagoras was not only a mathematician but also a philosopher and the founder of a religious cult. Plato considered mathematics indispensable to philosophy. Over the porch of his school, the Academy, he is said to have placed the warning: "Let no one unversed

13. Symbol 1: Koch, *Christian Symbols*, New Testament, line 5. Symbol 2: Conjubilant with Song, "Trinity Sunday."

in geometry enter my doors."[14] Xenocrates, one of the principals of the Academy, is reported to have turned away an applicant who did not know geometry with the words, "Go thy way, for thou hast not the means of getting a grip of philosophy."[15]

Pythagoras did not write any books and not much is known about his life. Those who claimed to be his followers and those who developed on his theories, like Plato and Aristotle, may be taken as part of the Pythagorean tradition. In this tradition, the four main branches of mathematics were arithmetic, geometry, astronomy, and music. Two key concepts, number and magnitude, determined such a classification. Arithmetic was concerned with number, while geometry's focus was magnitude; music dealt with number in ratio-relationships, while astronomy observed magnitude in motion—the motion of planets. Arithmetic, as a theory of numbers, was geared to understand things rather than to count them. Calculation may have been its secondary function, but its primary function was to understand reality, which for Pythagoras exhibited a kind of harmonious order.

Pythagoreans shared the Greek conviction that philosophy could transform lives. The Socratic dictum, "Knowledge is virtue," claimed that knowledge made people virtuous. Philosophy was taken as the means to make this possible. Plato expressed this idea in one of his dialogues, *Phaedo*, that is believed to have been inspired by Pythagorean doctrines. Plato's allegory of the cave drives home the point that philosophers were not mere otherworldly-minded speculators, but liberators of prisoners in the cave under the captivity of ignorance. Arithmetic functioning as a significant component of the philosophical endeavor turned out to be a means of liberation. Pythagoras believed in the transmigration of souls and claimed that human beings were trapped in the cycle of rebirth. His religious order shared with the Orphic religious communities certain rituals, music, and rules of abstinence as modes of "purification" meant to release one from the cycle of births.

Pythagoras, being a philosopher mathematician, elevated arithmetic beyond the needs of commerce and used it as a mode to understand the nature of reality. Through such knowledge, he proclaimed with religious gusto that one could be released from the cycle of rebirths. It is neither possible in this chapter nor necessary to explore all the areas of Pythagorean arithmetic, but, it will be of help to get a glimpse of the key concepts of his theory of numbers—those which are particularly relevant to gain a better understanding and thereby a fairer assessment of the doctrine of Trinity. It was in such a mathematical context that the doctrine took shape.

PYTHAGOREAN THEORY OF NUMBERS

We understand arithmetic as a tool for calculation, but for Pythagoreans it is a science that considers numbers in themselves: a theory of numbers. Plato, who belonged to the Pythagorean tradition, points out that arithmetic as an art of calculation is only

14. Heath, *History*, 24.
15. Ibid.

preparatory to the true science where numbers are used to understand reality rather than count things.[16]

Number, for Pythagoreans, is not just a numeral but could represent a celestial power, a blueprint of creation that is divine in itself. Pythagoreans took numbers as principles of things. Aristotle notes this in his *Metaphysics* when he states that, "In the time of these philosophers [Leucippus and Democritus] and before him the so-called Pythagoreans applied themselves to the study of mathematics, and were first to advance that science; insomuch that having been brought up in it, they thought that its principles must be principles of things . . . these thinkers seem to consider that number is the principle both as matter for things and as constituting their attributes and permanent states."[17] In other words, numbers provide identity to things; things are numbers. How can that be?

For Pythagoras, numbers have magnitude and hence have to be shapes. Pythagoreans identified numbers with geometric figures like straight lines, triangles, and squares.

In describing numbers as shapes, Pythagoreans introduced two concepts: "dot" and "field." Perhaps due to the use of pebbles, dots were called "boundary stones." The area they mark out is the "field."[18] The dot or, in familiar terms, the point, has position and is taken as a *unit* of number. A point becomes a number when it receives shape, and for that there must be a field (area) covered. A point needs another point at least to possess area; then the points become "boundary stones" for the area covered between them. The following diagram could help to get an idea of number as shape. Let "A" and "B" be points and "F" the field (area) bounded by them.

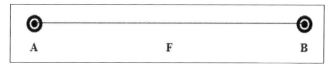

"A" and "B" act as "boundary stones" for the area "F." Pythagoreans called this shape number two.

But, what about number one? We should note that "0" has not yet been accommodated in the number series. The Pythagoreans considered "one" in Greek, the monad, not as a number but the "principle of unity" out of which the continuum of numbers emerge. In fact they called "one" god Apollo, which means "not of many." "One" functioned not as a number but as providing the basis for all numbers. As Aristotle points out, the "one" is regarded as not being itself a number, because a measure is not the things measured, but the measure, or the "one" is the beginning or principle of number."[19] Moreover, "one" as a point has location but no shape, and hence does not qualify to be a number, even though without it, there can be no number. In the Arabic

16. Plato, *Republic* in Heath, *History*, 13.

17. Aristotle, *Metaphysics*, in Heath, *History*, 67.

18. In Burnett, *Early Greek Philosophy*, 104.

19. Quoted in Heath, *History*, 69.

system, "one" is very much part of the number series, while in the Greek system it is that which makes the series possible, but is not part of the series.

On the basis of "one," other numbers generate. Number two is depicted as a straight line, while number three takes the shape of a triangle. Let us examine the features of number three as a triangle.

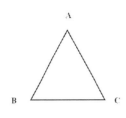

Greek number three

The popular definition of triangle as a plane figure bounded by three straight lines is euclidean, and hence has to be understood in terms of Greek mathematics. What the definition tries to convey is that a triangle is a single unit of space that is bound by points: "A," "B," and "C." The points function as boundaries for the area "F." Number three, when depicted as a triangle, is singular; just as number two is one elongated from "A" to "B," number three is one enclosed by points "A," "B," and "C." Plural numbers start with number four, which is square or rectangular in shape that contains two triangles, as the following diagram shows:

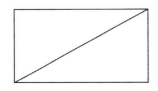

Greek number four

Three, as triangle, is not plural, but singular. Pythagoreans attributed not only mathematical but also religious significance to triangular numbers.

Pythagoreans picked out the triangular number, "tetrakyts of the decad," namely number ten and called it the perfect number. They found in it some significant mathematical features.

Each side that binds the triangle has four boundary points (stones); hence the field of the triangle was bound equally, expressing symmetry. Moreover, it is the first number that has in it an equal number of prime and composite numbers. It shows at a glance that $1 + 2 + 3 + 4 = 10$. On account of these significant features, the decad as triangle

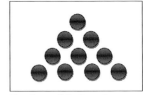

Tetrakyts of the Decad

became an effective tool to understand the cosmos; the decad expressed the symmetry of the universe.

Hence, the Pythagoreans swore by this number and even took it as an object of worship in their ritualistic exercises.[20] In other words, the triangular decad received salvific value. The Pythagoreans believed that through devotionally contemplating on this mathematically perfect number, they could be freed from the "wheel of birth."

Pythagoreans also related the theory of numbers to musicology. For them, the Tetraktys expressed not only arithmetic and geometric relations, but also harmonic relations. Sextus Empiricus claimed that Pythagoreans came to the conclusion that the universe was organized on harmonic principles through an examination of the Tetraktys. He stated, "This number (i.e., ten) is the first tetraktys and it is called 'the fount of ever flowing nature' because it is their view that the whole universe is organized on harmonic principles, and harmony is a system of three concords (the fourth,

20. Burnett, *Early Greek Philosophy*, 102.

the fifth and octave), and the ratios of these three concords in the four numbers I have already mentioned—that is in 1, 2, 3, and 4. The fourth constituted by 4:3, the fifth by 3:1, and the octave by 2:1."[21]

Hence, the theory of numbers served as an ideal gateway to obtain knowledge of the symmetrical and harmonious nature of reality. Such knowledge served as the means to be freed from the "wheel of birth." It was within such a conceptual framework that the doctrine of Trinity took shape. Hence, the best way to understand and evaluate it is to place it in its proper context.

GOD AS TRIUNE BEING THROUGH THE GREEK LENS

The primary purpose of Greek mathematics was to understand the nature of things. Hence, when we view God as Trinity through the Greek theory of numbers, we have to use it to understand God rather than trying to count him. But, can we really understand God? Perhaps that is why the Nicene and Constantinople creeds were both confessional expressions of belief rather than explanations of God, they started with the confession, "We believe." Such a belief provided an understanding of God that was never claimed to be perfect. The trinitarian formulation is really a case of faith seeking understanding. It is very much in line with the medieval philosopher St. Anselm's stance. His plea to God was, "I do not seek to understand so that I may believe; but I believe so that I may understand."[22]

In the claim that God is a triune being, he is one yet three; "one in substance" and "three in persons." We need to understand the concepts "one" and "three" in the way the mathematical system of the day viewed them. We should not confuse "one" with the Arabic numeral "1," which was the first number and very much part of the numerical series 1, 2, 3 . . . "One" in Greek, called the *monad*, was not a number per se, but made the number series possible. The Pythagorean philosopher Theon of Smryna (115–140 CE) viewed "*Monad* as the principle of numbers."[23] In presenting God as "one" the term "one" means that he is the one who makes all things possible, but not one of those things, in the way "one," as the unit of number, makes the number series possible, but is not a number as such.

The other key term is "three." In the Greek system "three" is a triangular number: singular and not plural. Let us attempt to try to capture the description of God as "three" in Greek mathematical terms. Let us go back to the diagram that depicts number three and apply it to comprehend God as triune being.

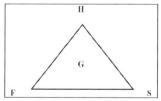
Trinity through Greek mathematical system
Trinity through Greek theory of numbers

"F" stands for God the Father, "S" for God the Son, and "H" for God the Holy Spirit. The field bounded by "F," "S," and "H" is "G," which stands for God. "F," "S,"

21. Sextus Empiricus, *Against the Professors*, quoted in Waterfield, *First Philosophers*, 102.

22. Anselm of Canterbury, *Proslogion*, 87.

23. Theon of Smyrna, "Mathematics," 13.

and "H" act as boundary points for "G." In other words, the Godhead is bound by Father, Son, and Holy Spirit; there is no God beyond the boundary points. Moreover, the triangular area "G" is a single unit of space. The number "three," represented as a triangle, is a singular number. The triangle is really "one" elongated and enclosed; three is really one, strange as it may seem! In such a conceptual framework, the trinitarian claim, "God is one and yet three," is not contradictory, even though paradoxical. The world had to wait till the Christ event to really appreciate the truth inherent in the paradox. Hence, criticizing the doctrine of Trinity as being logically inconsistent is mainly a result of a hermeneutical fallacy of employing an inappropriate tool to understand a doctrine.

Moreover, Greek served as the doctrine's language of expression. As Johannes Quasten notes, Christianity was a Greek movement until almost the end of the second century; Greek was the original language of patristic literature. Both the New Testament writers and the church fathers wrote in Koine, which was a compromise between classical Attic and popular Greek.[24] It offered some key concepts that enabled the church fathers to crystallize doctrine. Some of them were converts from Hellenistic religions and conversant with the trendy philosophical concepts of the day. They were able to elucidate the concept of God as Trinity using terms which were meaningful to the wider Hellenistic society.

The trinitarian formulation contained two key philosophical terms, "substance" (or "essence") and "person." The confessions and later the creeds of the early church claimed that God is one in essence (substance) but three in persons. Athanasius's creed states that while each of the persons is increate, infinite, omnipotent, eternal, and so on, there are not three increates, infinities, omnipotents, eternals and so on, but one.[25]

The trinitarian dogmas, as articulated by the Nicene (325 CE) and Constantinople (381 CE) councils and confirmed by the subsequent synods provide us with the Greek and Latin formulations of the doctrine. These formulations characterize God as triune being; that God is one power and substance (*ousia, substantia*) in three distinct persons (*hypostaseis, personae*) and both Son and Spirit are of one identical substance (*homousion, unius substantiae*) with the Father. Such formulations pinpoint that God is one in substance but three in persons.

In the Greek vocabulary, particularly in Platonic terms, "substance" is that which gives reality (existence) and identity to a thing. Hence, the dogma that God is one and that Father, Son, and Spirit are identical in substance amounts to the claim that all three of them are substantially one and the same.

"Person" however is a relational term indicating that even though Father, Son, and Spirit are substantially one, they are distinct and are related to one another.

The semantics of the trinitarian doctrine articulated through Greek philosophical concepts "substance" and "person" cannot be fully understood without the syntactic provided by Greek mathematics. The syntactic representation of the doctrine through

---

24. Quasten, *Patrology*, 20–21.

25. Kelly, *Early Christian Doctrines*, 273.

the "triangle" enables us to capture the sense in which the concepts "substance" and "person" were used to make the claim: God is one in substance but three in persons. Hence, when we view the doctrine of Trinity through the Greek lens, we should put on the bifocals of its syntactic and semantics.

Let us refer back to the previous diagram, which will help us to see how we so view the doctrine.

In this diagram God (G) is the whole triangle; Father (F), Son (S), and Spirit (H) are integral to the triangle and cannot be separated from it; they are one in substance. But "F," "S," and "H" can be distinguished as boundary points—distinguishable as "persons." As Athanasius's creed points out, one cannot divide the substance; the triangle is a single unit and when divided it loses its identity. But the points can be distinguished in the triangle, all of them equally necessary to make up the triangle. As the diagram indicates, Father, Son, and Spirit are related to one another but they are not related to God, since they are substantially the same.

Rudolf Koch presents an early symbol for the "Eye of God" in this manner.[26] The eye is placed in the area of the triangle and not in one of the three points of the triangle that represent Father, Son, and Spirit.

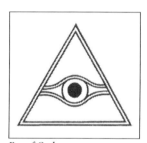
Eye of God

Hence, when we view the trinitarian doctrine through the bifocals of Greek mathematical and philosophical concepts we can appreciate the creedal claim that God is one in substance and yet three in persons. Such a perception of God as triune being enables us to understand better the biblical references to Jesus Christ as God the Son, and the relationship between God the Father and Jesus Christ. For instance, if *Logos* refers to Jesus, how could Jesus be *with* God and yet *be* God (John 1:1)? Likewise, Jesus' claims "I and my Father are one," or "If you have seen me you have seen the Father." The trinitarian doctrine viewed through the Greek lens helps us to understand such seemingly contradictory claims as paradoxical insights. Conceiving God as triune being implies that Christ is God just like God the Father. In this sense he is not one among the questing humans.

This takes us to the second issue concerning Christ. Is he the only one who could satisfy the human religious quest? When there are other ways of salvation available, why should one claim Christ as the only Savior? In subsequent chapters we will determine the specific ways in which Christ is related to the salvific quest of each of the major religious communities. But, before that, we need to choose a framework of reference that would best represent the relationship between Christ and other saviors; a framework that will neither misrepresent the personhood of Christ nor demean the salvific endeavors of other religious. This will be our next task.

26. Koch, *Christian Symbols*, Old Testament, line 1.

FRAMEWORK OF REFERENCE TO RELATE CHRIST TO SAVIORS

We may characterize the world of today not only as scientific, technological, industrial, information laden, media-managed, shrinking global village, but also as spiritual.[27] Such spirituality shows itself in both conventional and nonconventional ways and aims to be transformational. People yearn to be transformed. There has been a significant growth and multiplication of cults and new religious movements, identified as alternative religions. These are not mere doctrinaire edifices, but rather expressions of the aspirations of people who want to be freed from the predicament in which they perceive themselves to be. In turbulent times of rapid social change and global economic collapse people tend to resort to anything that would free them from their predicament and give them a sense of security. Usually they find it in something beyond the mundane material realm, something to be realized through the spiritual.[28] The Jamaican Rastafarian movement is not a major world religion and has of course racial-political overtones but may be cited as a nonconventional expression of a millenarian expectation.

Rastafarian Johnson of Jamaica

When asked to describe his ultimate goal in life, Johnson replied that, as a Rastafarian, he strives to follow the "High God" with the hope that he would liberate the world, especially the black nation.

While there has been a global expansion of Christianity, all the major religions are experiencing a revival. Such a revival is not just an academic preoccupation with certain theological doctrines, but rather a concerted effort that strives to transform human lives and even change human destiny. Religions like Hinduism that have been, through the ages, content to keep within their demographic boundaries are becoming enthusiastically evangelical. The motivating factor of such a religious resurgence seems to be salvific in the sense that people want to be freed from the predicament in which they are. The adherents of the religions are very proud and protective of their respective ways of salvation. In such a context, Christ, as the only Savior, becomes naturally controversial.

There have been three popular responses to this question. Exclusivism claims that Jesus Christ is the only Savior and that confession of him is necessary for one to

27. Bruxy Cavey, author of *The End of Religion*, contends that religion as a distinct organizational structure of society is fast dying. But that does not mean that people are not religious, especially in the sense of being spiritual.

28. The popular television series *Heroes* (NBC, 2006–2010) seemed to be based on the theme that in order to conquer evil, people need to be endowed with supernatural powers.

be saved. On the other hand, pluralism contends that there could be many saviors and paths of salvation. Inclusivism, in the middle, maintains that Christ is the only Savior, even though explicit confession of him is not a must for salvation.[29] According to this view, some people of other faiths could be included within the saved, even though they do not know Christ personally. While we will associate ourselves with some of the views of these approaches, it seems not conducive to articulate our proposal within the parameters of such taxonomy. Working within it seems to force us to be preoccupied with peripheral issues rather than being concerned with our central concern of trying to decipher why and how Christ satisfies the human religious quest. Nevertheless, we will make reference to some of these views when we articulate our proposal.

The term "savior" in religions encompasses a multiplicity of types. A savior may be a historical or a mythical figure, a prophet, a teacher, a person with extraordinary spiritual powers, a deified human, a moral or theological doctrine, or even a ritualistic practice. In a context of such multiple "saviors" how can we relate Christ to them? We need a framework that best reflects the relationship between Christ and this group of "saviors." In order to capture this relationship, a framework that attempts merely to compare and contrast Jesus Christ with them, by taking him as one of them, seems inadequate.

Venn's diagrams used in set theory are helpful to construct an appropriate analytical framework of reference.

When relating Christ to other saviors, two main stances stand out: Jesus is one among many saviors and Jesus is the only Savior. The claim that Jesus is a savior among other saviors, a member in the group of "saviors" can be represented thus:

$$U^1$$

(Diagram 1) Pluralistic Stance: S^1 = set of Saviors, $\underline{S}^1$ = complementary set of S_1

Here, the universe of discourse, symbolized as U_1 refers to the group of humans who acknowledge that there is something drastically wrong with existence, especially human existence. S_1 represents the group of persons claiming to rectify the problem: "saviors." $\underline{S}_1$, as the complement of S_1 refers to those persons excluded from the membership of S_1: "not saviors"; they could be those who are followers of saviors or even agnostics and atheists who deny the legitimacy of saviors. The universe of discourse (U_1) contains both S_1 and $\underline{S}_1$; $U_1 = S_1 + \underline{S}_1$. When we view the pluralist stance through

29. Leading advocates of these views include Ronald Nash for exclusivism, Clark Pinnock for inclusivism, and John Hick for pluralism.

such a framework, Jesus finds a place as a member of S1, like other saviors; the notation "x" in S1 indicates that the set is not empty; it could have more than one member, that is, more than one savior. S1 could have J (Jesus) and other saviors too. Moreover, since Jesus belongs to S1 and since S1 is part of U1, he is also a part of the universe of discourse made up of humans who realize that there is something drastically wrong with existence; some among them claim to be saviors attempting to find a way out, while others either follow these saviors or are skeptical of them. Placing Christ in such a universe helps to justify the pluralist stance that there are several ways of salvation and Christianity provides one way, Jesus, as one among other saviors, all belonging to the realm of questing humans.

The claim that Jesus is the only Savior would be that Jesus is the one and only member of the set of saviors S2. The following diagram shows this:

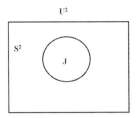

(Diagram 2) Exclusivist Stance: J ε S², S²=U²

In this diagram J stands for Jesus and S2 stands for the set of saviors. The diagram indicates that the set of saviors (S2) is the same as universe of discourse (U2). We should note that Jesus (J) is not a set even though placed in a circle. J is not a set but a member of the set S2. A member of a set, in this Jesus (J), and the set of saviors (S2) are not of the same logical order; the Greek letter *epsilon* (ε) is used to indicate the relationship between member and set. The above diagram shows that Jesus is the one identified as the member of the set of saviors S; this could be represented thus J ε S2.

But can we justify that Jesus is the one and only Savior, as shown in Diagram 2? Let us have a look at diagrams 1 and 2.

Firstly, in diagram 2, the universe of discourse (U2) is the same as the set of saviors (S2). U2= S2. But in diagram 1, the set of saviors (S1) is a set within the universe of discourse (U1), which is a wider set. It is the group of people who acknowledge that there is something drastically wrong with existence, and includes both saviors and non-saviors. Hence, the universes of discourse (U1 and U2) are different.

Secondly, the set of saviors (S1) in diagram 1 could accommodate more than one member. But in diagram 2, the set of saviors (S2) has only one member, Jesus. The question is, when there are other "saviors," how Jesus could be the only Savior? How can we justify that Jesus is the only member of the set of saviors? We are forced to contrast them with Jesus by placing all of them in the same category. But this does justice to neither Jesus nor the other saviors. Presenting Jesus as being different from, and perhaps superior in some ways to other "saviors" may allow us to claim that Jesus is better than or even the best among "saviors," but will not warrant the claim that he is the only Savior. Moreover, such contrasting demeans the other saviors. They appear to be inferior to Jesus. Such a claim seems to be too particularistic if not pedantic!

Viewing God as a triune being allows us to accommodate Jesus as God the Son. He is unique by virtue of his personhood. Jesus, though born at Bethlehem, pre-existed and in fact did not have a beginning. He was involved in creation of the universe (Gen 1:1) and the plan of salvation through him was conceived in the heart of God the Father, before time began (Titus 1:2). Though Christ was put to death, he rose from the dead and his life knows no end. Hence, we cannot place Christ in the universe of discourse (U1) which accommodates saviors who belong to the human realm; the set of saviors where Jesus is the only member (S2) cannot be the same as the set of saviors in diagram 1 (S1).

We need an entirely different type of "universe of discourse." Let us look once again at diagram 1 that depicts the pluralist claim: Jesus is one among other saviors. The universe of discourse U1, as given in diagram 1, is made up of two sets: set of saviors S1 and its complement S1. These sets represent two types of responses of people to the problem, that there is something drastically wrong with existence. The first type of response is from the group of people who claim to solve the problem, the "saviors" (S1). The second type of response is from the group of people who follow these saviors or are even skeptical of them (S1). Such responses, as represented in S1 and S1, are human oriented. Even though some saviors belonging to S1 may claim to be God aided or even have been deified, they all fall within the human category. Pluralists like John Hick make it a point to consider Jesus as one of them. But, if we take Jesus as God incarnate, he cannot be cannot be placed in such a set of "saviors" (S1) or even in the universe of discourse (U1), which however universal it may be, is still very human based. He has to fall within an entirely different universe of discourse; one that views the human predicament and attempts to liberate humanity from a divine perspective; one that is exclusive of the universe of discourse found in diagram 1. The following diagram shows the type of universe of discourse in which we could place Christ:

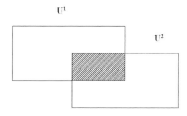

(Diagram 3) Exclusive Universes

U1 stands for the universe of discourse found in diagram 1; as noted earlier, a universe that is basically human based, in that the members of this universe are all part of the questing humans. Christ, though human, is God incarnate and cannot be placed in U1; we need another universe of discourse, U2, that is exclusive of U1. The above diagram shows that U_1 and U_2 are exclusive of each other; the intersection of U_1 and U_2, marked with diagonal lines, is empty. Christ should be placed in U_2.

Combining diagrams 1, 2, and 3, we get the following diagram:

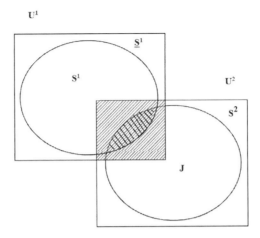

(Diagram 4)Jesus Amidst the Universes

This diagram shows that the universes of discourse U_1 and U_2 are exclusive of each other; the intersecting square of U_1 and U_2, marked with diagonal lines, indicates that it is empty. Set S_1 which is the set of saviors as represented in diagram 1 falls within the universe of discourse, identified as U_1. S_2, the set where Jesus is the only member, as shown in diagram 2, is found in U_2. Sets S_1 and S_2 are exclusive of each other because they fall within two exclusive universes of discourse (U_1 and U_2). The intersection of S_1 and S_2 as shown in the above diagram, marked with diagonal lines, is empty. Hence, J (Jesus) the only member of the set S_2 is totally exclusive of set S_1. Moreover, since $S_2=U_2$, there is no possibility for anyone else other than Jesus to be savior in the universe of discourse U_2.

There are of course legitimate "saviors" as members of the set S_1 found in the universe of discourse U_1. They are all part of the quest that besets in humanity. They attempt to provide a way out of the predicament in which they and their fellow beings are caught up. They may be successful at providing an effective salvific strategy, arising from and articulated by human beings; they are saviors yet very much part of the human quest. But, Jesus, though fully human, yet God incarnate is not part of the human quest. The salvation wrought by him arises from and articulated by one who is fully human yet fully divine. Hence he is not a member of the set S_1, and also falls outside the universe of discourse U_1, where S_1 occurs. Since J and S_1 fall within two exclusive universes of discourse, we cannot and should not claim that Jesus is superior while other saviors are inferior. One cannot compare apples with oranges.

Hence, presenting Christ as the only Savior through a framework of reference, adopting Venn's set theoretical tools, helps us in more than one way. We are able to a great extent avoid the polemics of elevating Jesus as superior to other "saviors";

he belongs to an entirely different universe of discourse. Comparative assessment is legitimate of things that belong to the same category. Jesus' ontological identity as God incarnate justifies his placement in a universe of discourse that is exclusive of the human-based universe U1. Moreover, such a placement helps us to provide a rationale for claiming that he can satisfy the religious quest of humanity on the grounds of his personhood.

The superstructures of religions do not really need Christ, but the communities of faith, whose aspirations such superstructures express, need Christ. It is precisely at this pivotal point that Christ becomes pertinent to the religious communities. In the framework of reference that we will adopt to relate Christ to these communities, we will try to capture the areas in and modes by which they express their need for "salvation." We will place Christ in the midst of such expressions and determine whether he is any way relevant to such a need. The description of the need for "salvation" will be different between Christianity and other religions. The modes articulated to meet the need are also not the same. But the need is very much there and Christ seems very relevant to that need.

In the subsequent chapters we will attempt to relate Christ to the quest of each of the major religions, adopting the framework of reference which diagram 2 shows. In such a conceptual framework, we acknowledge the legitimacy of saviors presented by various religions. We do not deny all that they proclaim as false or invalid. When we relate Christ to these saviors we recognize that they belong to a universe of discourse that is different from that where Christ belongs. Judaism, being so much intertwined with Christianity, needs a different conceptual framework to relate Christ to the Jews and hence we do not include it. Confucianism, Taoism, Shintoism, Buddhism, Hinduism, Sikhism, Islam, and Aboriginal religions figure in this investigation. They are not placed in the order of their origin, but rather how relevant the quest of these faith communities is to Christ, ordered from least to greatest. Christ does not seem to be relevant at all to some of these religions when they first started, but the metamorphosis which took place in them with the passage of time makes Christ relevant to them now. But what is significant is that all these religious communities exhibit a quest which makes Christ relevant to them.

3

The Confucian Quest

Do not do to others what you do not want them to do to you. —Confucius

Do to others as you would have them do to you. —Jesus

CONFUCIANISM, TAOISM, AND BUDDHISM are the most prominent expressions of Chinese religiosity. But they do not fit into the conventional model of theistic religions. For instance, the concept of a personal transcendent God and the collective practice of faith through an institutional structure do not seem to figure much in Confucianism. It has no priesthood or clergy. Its scriptures, though revered, are not taken as divine revelation. It has a faint doctrine of an afterlife. Confucius, the founder, never claimed even to be a prophet of God.

If we merely pick out the popular proposals of Confucianism, we could characterize it as a sociopolitical reformist movement led by Confucius, who was convinced that training civil servants would generate good government. No doubt his teachings provided the basis of the curriculum for civil service training that have lasted until recently. While he aimed to establish a politically stable society, he went much further than providing a program for political reform. He attempted to orchestrate a strategy of transformation, both personal and communal, that encompassed the intellectual, political, economic, moral, and spiritual facets of life. It was transformational in a holistic sense. Such an endeavor exhibits an underlying salvific quest, and this is where Christ becomes relevant to the Confucian quest.

The founders of Taoism and Confucianism, Lao-Tzu and Confucius, lived during the sixth century BCE, a turbulent period identified as the "Period of Warring States" in Chinese history. They were caught up in the anguish of the times and realized that there was something rotten in the state of China. Each attempted to provide a way out. Even though their ways were not the same, they were essentially salvific in intent; they were "ways of salvation" to enable the Chinese to get out of their predicament. Hence there is some justification for calling both Confucianism and Taoism "salvation religions."

Nevertheless, in using such nomenclature to characterize these religions, one has to be careful not to understand them through inappropriate theological concepts. Terms like "salvation" and "savior" are theologically loaded. One may wonder why Confucius' program for political reform may be described as a way of salvation. The preponderance of ethical and political content in the teachings of Confucius might prompt one to view Confucianism as a Chinese version of secular humanism rather than a religion, but this view reflects a compartmentalization of the secular and the sacred that is foreign to the context in which Confucianism arose. Religion as a sacred entity distinct from secular society was absent from the China of Confucius; in fact, there were no distinct terms in Chinese for "religion" and "philosophy" until the late nineteenth century. The Japanese introduced the term for "religion" through translations of European works, while the term for "philosophy" was an adaptation from Western vocabulary.[1] During the time when Confucianism was taking shape, there was no marked distinction between religion and philosophy. To describe Confucianism as a philosophy of political reform, devoid of all religiosity, would therefore be an attempt to characterize it through conceptual categories that are foreign to it.

Confucianism was a response to the desperate need of the Chinese people to be freed from the despicable conditions in which they found themselves. It was a way of liberation. But in a context where religion, culture, philosophy, and ethics were so intertwined, such a way turned out to be a quest not merely to provide a better political system, but to transform the Chinese people both individually and collectively in the process. Hence, taking into consideration the then-prevalent Chinese conceptual framework, we may with justification describe the Confucian political strategy as a "way of salvation," and the Confucians as being involved in a salvific quest.

The World Spirituality series accommodates Confucianism in two volumes entitled *Confucian Spirituality*. One of its editors, Mary Evelyn Tucker, presents Confucianism not as a religion in the conventional sense of the term, but rather as a religious worldview with a distinctive spiritual dimension. According to Tucker, a religious worldview gives the community that holds it a comprehensive defining orientation to certain "ultimate concerns." Spirituality is that which enables a faith community's deep yearnings to relate to those ultimate concerns.[2] Even though the ultimate concerns of Confucianism may not be those of traditional theistic religions, the fact that they are all geared to freeing the Chinese from their predicament justifies the categorization of Confucianism as a salvific endeavor. In order to capture the character of the Confucian quest, we have to examine how founders of Confucianism and the leaders who came after them articulated this quest. That will be our next task.

THE ARTICULATORS OF THE CONFUCIAN QUEST

Confucius, Mencius, and Hsun-Tzu are the most prominent articulators of the Confucian quest. Confucianism gets its name from Confucius, whose family name

---

1. Weiming and Tucker, eds., *Confucian Spirituality,* 15.
2. Ibid., 2–3.

was K'ung. His followers addressed him as K'ung-Fu'Tzu/Kongzi (Master K'ung/Sage-Teacher). "Confucius" is a Latinized form of "Kung Fu Tzu."

The historicity of Confucius is not in doubt; biographical material about him is extensive. Sima Qian (145–85 BCE), the court historian of the Han dynasty, in his work, *Records of the Ground Historian (Shiji)*, cites many legends surrounding Confucius. The problem is to separate fact from fiction. Confucius (551–479 BCE) was born in the Chinese state of Lu, modern Shantung, and lived in Chu-fou, about one hundred miles northwest of the believed birthplace of Lao-Tzu, the founder of Taoism.[3] Confucius came from an aristocratic family that had lost its wealth and status due to the collapse of the feudal states. His father, Shu-liang Ho, was a reputed military commander in the state of Lu; he died shortly before the birth of the child. Despite the challenges she faced as a poor single parent, the widowed mother provided her son the best education then available. He followed the traditional school curriculum, which included poetry, Chinese history, music, hunting, fishing, and archery. This education had a lasting effect on his life and mission. A master teacher should first go to school!

Even though Confucius was keen to continue his studies, the family's financial straits forced him to resort to menial jobs. In his late teens he managed to get a minor position in government, and this opened his eyes to the corrupt administration of his time. He was married at nineteen and had two sons, but his marriage ended in divorce. In his mid-twenties he lost his mother. Being the devoted son of a loving mother, he became utterly depressed and went into mourning for about three years. During this disturbing time of his life, he resorted to the study of ancient Chinese ceremonial rites and governmental institutions.

Eventually he emerged from his isolation and began a career as a teacher. He turned out to be a master teacher, an advocate of principles of good government, a mentor, and an exemplar of ideal moral conduct. His reputation as teacher earned him an invitation to serve in a high ministerial position in the government of the duke of Lu. In this new position he tried to put into practice his teachings on good government based on the principles of propriety, or *li*. *Li* in Chinese means "propriety," "courtesy," "decorum," and "good form"; it is that which characterizes heaven, regulates the universe, and provides the norm for people's conduct. It is believed that due to Confucius' relentless efforts, crime rate dropped during this period and China experienced peace.

This did not last long, however. Due to jealousy and rivalry among state officials, he was forced to resign in utter frustration. But this did not dampen his spirit, for he was committed to a mission in life that went far beyond achieving political gains. He lived in a period of political chaos and social disintegration. The Golden Age of the Chou dynasty had disintegrated into feudal anarchy. Feudal lords held more power than kings, ministers assassinated their rulers, and sons killed their fathers. It was in such morally degraded, politically disintegrated China that Confucius' mission in life took shape. Even though he had failed in his attempt to make the rulers adopt his

---

3. Main sources for biographical details: Nigosian, *World Faiths*, 196–99; Hopfe, *Religions of the World*, 222–24; Carmody and Carmody, *Ways to the Center*, 172–73; Hutchison, *Paths of Faith*, 217–18; Riegel, "Confucius."

ideas, he did not fatalistically accept things as they were, for he was convinced that there was a way out.

He began educating prospective public servants in the hope that they would reform the government and thereby restore order in China. Characterizing his strategy as religious in the conventional sense of the term does not do justice to what he was hoping to accomplish. He was neither trying to establish a religious institutional structure nor presenting a strategy for mere political reform. He was fully committed to his mission of establishing political and social order, but his way out was not merely to reform the state's administrative structure; he was convinced that to reform the state one had to start with the individual. In his view, rectification of the individual was fundamental and took precedence over reforming the state. For him, such a rectification was not merely making the individual more politically astute, but rather orchestrating a transformation that encompassed the intellectual, moral, spiritual, and social facets of a person. The ideal individual, *Chun-tzu* (true gentleman), was not a self-centered person, however accomplished he might be, but one who personified the virtue *jen*. *Jen* characterizes the ideal relationship that ought to prevail among people, and may be understood as goodness, benevolence, altruistic love, or human-heartedness. Confucius considered *jen* to be the virtue of virtues. His strategy aimed to find ways and means to inculcate this virtue in the individual, especially the prospective public servant, and thereby transform the sociopolitical fabric of decadent China. In this sense, Confucius articulated a holistic strategy that was salvific in intent.

Moreover, he identified himself as one caught up in the predicament of China at the time, and hence was very much part and parcel of the quest. This is evident in his confession, which runs thus:

> At fifteen my mind was set on learning. At thirty my character had been formed. At forty I had no more perplexities. At fifty I knew the Mandate of Heaven (*T'ien-ming*). At sixty I was at ease with whatever I heard. At seventy I could follow my heart's desire without transgressing moral principles (Analects 2:4).[4]

This confession shows clearly the quest of Confucius to align himself with Heaven's Mandate (heaven's will). He was himself involved in a spiritual journey, the perceived success of which encouraged him to emphasize personal rectification as the starting point for any type of transformation.

Confucius died in 479 BCE. Even though his disciples deeply mourned his demise, his teachings were not taken seriously during his lifetime. However, after his death conditions in China deteriorated badly. Interstate warfare increased, family loyalties gave way to army rule, and despotic manipulations by feudal lords replaced moral values. Such despicable conditions forced the desperate Chinese to take Confucius more seriously and resort to his salvific strategy.

China's political, social, and moral disintegration forced into focus the question: "What is the root cause of the cancer that has stricken the Chinese society?" Two

---

4. Chan, *Source Book*, 22. Unless otherwise mentioned, quotes and citations from the works of Confucius, Mencius, and Hsun-Tzu are translations by Chan.

leading disciples of Confucius, Meng-Tzu, known as Mencius in Latin (375–312 BCE), and Hsun-Tzu (310–219 BCE), responded to this question in almost diametrically opposite ways, in terms both of their diagnosis of the disease and their cures for it. Nevertheless, their proposals were significant developments in the articulation of the Confucian salvific strategy. Moreover, these post-Confucian developments enable us to appreciate how Christ becomes very relevant to the Confucian salvific quest. Let us first get a glimpse of the lives and aspirations of these leaders who were responsible for such developments.

The book that bears Mencius' name, Book of Mencius, and other legendary sources attempt to draw parallels between him and Confucius. Like Confucius, Mencius was the only child of a poor widow who struggled to provide him with an education. Like Confucius, he became a teacher and sought the position of a political adviser. Like Confucius, he had a sense of mission to free the Chinese from their predicament by attempting to persuade rulers to accept his strategy for solving the problem of endless wars among feudal states. Like Confucius, he served as a government official but was unsuccessful in changing the quality of administration. Like Confucius' Analects, the Book of Mencius records the aspirations of one who was struggling to free himself and his decadent community. As in the case of his master, Mencius' death was mourned, but his teachings were not acclaimed.[5]

Even though Mencius followed in the footsteps of his master, there were some significant deviations. While Confucius no more than implied that human nature is good, Mencius declared explicitly that it is inherently good. Such a view of the human being may be traced to Mencius' view of heaven. According to him, heaven is present within the human heart, and this is what makes human nature inherently good.[6] His emphasis on the innate goodness of human nature had a ripple effect on the character of the Confucian way of salvation. According to Mencius, since human nature is basically good, moral power is inherent in human nature; everyone can become a sage. Nevertheless, he acknowledged that all do not act virtuously. He traced this to the environment generated by the sociopolitical structure of a community, and believed that through self-cultivation one could uncover one's innate good nature. This confidence in human potency resonates with the typical humanist claim that one need not resort to any superhuman source, that humans can liberate themselves. Perhaps this is why Confucianism is typically regarded as a humanistic sociopolitical philosophy rather than a religion.

Nevertheless, the Book of Mencius exhibits an interplay of confidence and doubt. In the opening sections he claims that despite the grim realities of wars, starvation, and death of his day, those in political leadership can change the tide because they possess the capacity for humanness and rightness. In his discussion with kings Hui of Liang and Xuan of Qi, he appears very confident in human potency.[7] But in the closing

5. For details about the life and aspirations of Mencius, the following works are helpful: Chan, *Source Book*, 49–51; Nigosian, *World Faiths*, 203–4; Hopfe, *Religions of the World*, 227–31.

6. Oxtoby, *World Religions: Eastern Traditions*, 398.

7. Bloom, "Practicality," 234–35.

sections of his book, perhaps due to the challenges of aging and the stark realization that his teachings were not being accepted, Mencius exhibits a level of doubt amounting almost to despondency.[8] He seems to have doubted whether one could attain sagehood through self-cultivation. Such pessimism naturally threw a wet blanket on Mencius' proposal that humans could liberate themselves on the grounds of the innate goodness of human nature.

Such doubt arising from the leading advocate of the goodness of human nature was obviously contagious. Moreover, the increasing atrocities of the period intensified this doubt. Hsun-Tzu (298–238 BCE), a native of Chao (now known as Shansi in North China), articulated a doctrine that human nature is innately evil. Acclaimed as an eminent scholar, he had served as a magistrate for some years. He was contemporaneous with Mencius, even though it is not known for certain whether they ever met.[9] After Hsun-Tzu lost his government position, he spent the rest of his life propagating a strategy to liberate ailing China. His works are in the form of essays such as "On Nature," "The Rectification of Names," and "the Nature of Man as Evil." Nevertheless, like the writings of Confucius and Mencius, Hsun-Tzu's works were also articulations of one who felt very much the anguish of the turbulent times and strove to find a way out. Since he started with the premise that human nature is essentially evil, he had to provide aggressive ways not only to rectify the evil nature of human beings but also to enable them to attain a wholesome quality of life, both personal and communal.

Desires arising from human nature, which is essentially evil, tend to be selfish. Conflicts among people are bound to occur, necessitating some type of determined imposition of order. For Hsun-Tzu, such an imposition was not mere political programming but a comprehensive strategy that touched every facet of human life. Persistent study, adhering to the laws of nature, enforcement of the laws of propriety (*li*), the proper practice of rites and rituals, and good works that would align one with the Way of Heaven (Heaven's Mandate) all played a significant role in this strategy. They were all vital to Hsun-Tzu's way of liberating humanity by reforming an intrinsically evil human nature.

Confucius and his successors Mencius and Hsun-Tzu were the leading articulators of the Confucian salvific strategy during the axial period of Chinese religious history. Even though they could be called "saviors," all of them shared the anguish of the turbulent times and were very much engaged in the quest themselves. For instance, Confucius was conscious of his limitations. He confessed his love for virtue and wisdom, describing himself as one "who, in the eager pursuit of knowledge, forgot his food, and in the joy of attaining to it forgot his sorrow."[10] Such a confession amply justifies placing Confucius within the Confucian quest rather than making him part of its object. The people living in the time of these founders did not wholeheartedly acclaim their teachings, but what they had articulated did not die with them.

---

8. Ibid., 235.

9. For biographical details about Hsun-Tzu see Chan, *Source Book*, 115–16; Nigosian, *World Faiths*, 203–4; Hutchison, *Paths of Faith*, 234–35; Hopfe, *Religions of the World*, 229–31.

10. Qouted in Chan, *Source Book*, 32.

The Confucianism that took shape during this axial period of Chinese history was not a static given. It faced several challenges. During the Chin dynasty (221–206 BCE), Confucians were under severe persecution, almost to the point of being extinguished. A deliberate attempt was made to kill Confucian leaders and burn their scriptures. During the Han dynasty (206 BCE—220 CE), despite imperial patronage, Confucianism fell into utter disrepute. Taoism, Buddhism, and then Christianity turned out to be formidable challenges. Maoists and later Communists dismissed Confucianism as archaic. But the Chinese did not give it up. They found in it not merely a curriculum for effective civil service performance, a program for political reform, and an avenue for Chinese patriotic expression, but notably a salvific strategy that would generate a wholesome quality of life. When times became turbulent, the motivation to find a way out naturally intensified. This was one of the underlying motivating factors for subsequent developments and modifications to the strategy, leading up to the Neo-Confucianism that extended into Korea and Japan.

The arrival of Buddhism in China and the impact of indigenous Taoism naturally posed a challenge to Confucianism. But the Confucian response to this challenge shows how the Chinese accommodate different religious ideas. A story is told that around the sixth century CE the emperor asked a reputed Chinese scholar whether he was a Buddhist. The scholar pointed to his Taoist cap. Asked whether he was a Taoist, he raised his robe to reveal his Confucian shoes. Naturally, the emperor was puzzled and posed the question, "Are you then a Confucian?" Whereupon the scholar tugged at the Buddhist scarf he was wearing. The Chinese took Buddhism, Taoism, and Confucianism as mutually inclusive and complementary. The main reason for such an accommodative attitude is not that these religions were fully compatible in doctrine and practice. Rather, the followers of each religion considered themselves to be involved in a salvific quest and viewed those of another religion as fellow travelers taking a different path. They borrowed from one another whatever would better their own way of salvation. For instance, Tung-Chung-Shu (179–104 BCE), who was responsible for making Confucianism the state religion, and Yang-Hsiung (53 BCE–18 CE) combined the Taoist world view with Confucian ethics to articulate a salvific strategy. They took the universe to be a great mystery (*Tai-hsuan*) that manifests itself through the Taoist principle of *yin-yang*. *Yin* and *yang* are two pervasive forces of the universe, opposing yet complementing each other. The human being, as a part of the universe, also manifests *yin-yang* in his own being: human nature is a mixture of both good and evil. Humans could liberate themselves by developing the good in them through the practice of ethics.[11]

Confrontation with Buddhism and Taoism did not kill Confucianism, but rather helped to revive it. Neo-Confucianism best represents the blending of Confucian ideas with Buddhism and Taoism. However, this does not mean that Confucians never criticized these religions. Han Yu (768–824 CE) and Li-Ao, the forerunners of Neo-Confucianism, attacked both Taoism and Buddhism, while Chu His (1130–1200

---

11. Chan, *Source Book*, 271.

CE), reputed leader of the Neo-Confucian rationalist school, criticized Buddhism. Their criticisms were meant to make their followers appreciate the Confucian salvific strategy and follow it. Wang-Yang-Ming (1472–1529 CE), the founding leader of the intuitionist school of Neo-Confucianism, highlighted the importance of introspective intuition, which resembles Buddhist psychotherapeutic meditative methods.[12]

The articulators of the Confucian quest, both the founding leaders such as Confucius and Mencius and those who followed them, were very much participants in the quest. Confucianism has been and still is a dynamic quest founded on the conviction that there is a way out not only for the Chinese but for all humanity. Our next task will be to find out how the Confucian scriptures express this quest.

SCRIPTURAL EXPRESSIONS OF THE QUEST

The Confucian scriptures comprise a variety of writings spread over a long period of time. Most but not all of them came out of China. The Chinese classics, the writings of Confucius, Mencius, and Hsun-Tzu, the writings that predated them, and those of the subsequent Neo-Confucians all belong to the compendium of Confucian scriptures.

Out of these, the most well-known scripture is Confucius' Analects (Lun-Yu). It has twenty short chapters containing quotes and anecdotes that express some of Confucius' aspirations and thoughts on moral, political, and social topics. After his death, his disciples compiled the contents and included materials belonging to different time periods. Some sections may not have actually been authored by Confucius. The Analects, as well as Mencius's Book of Mencius and the essays of Hsun-Tzu, may be taken as major expressions of Confucian aspirations and strategies to attain them.

In order to fully capture the scriptural expressions of the Confucian quest, we must go beyond merely analyzing the texts in question; we must view them within a larger framework. These scriptures arose out of the aspirations of the Chinese to free themselves from the predicament in which they found themselves. They differentiated these scriptures from other writings and gave them sacred status. The reason for such a "sacralization" was the conviction that these texts contained key ideas and strategies to transform the disease-stricken Chinese society. The articulators who first gave shape to these scriptures did not consider themselves to be communicating divine revelation, but rather as fellow Chinese striving to provide a way out. But if the works of these founders are the Confucian scriptures, how can writings that predate them and those that came centuries after them also be taken as sacred scriptures?

The pre-Confucian classics, called the Five Classics, were formulated long before Confucius arrived on the scene. They are divergent in genre and cover a wide range of topics. The reverence given to them reflects the importance of tradition for the Chinese. The Classic of Changes (I-Ching) deals mainly with divination attributed to the sages of old. The Classic of Documents, known also as The Book of History (Shu-Ching), contains speeches of kings and chief ministers on various political matters including principles of good government. The Classic of Songs, or The Book of Poetry

---

12. Weiming and Tucker, eds., *Confucian Spirituality*, 91–92.

(Shih-Ching), is a collection of poems and songs. The Classic of Rites or The Book of Rites (Li-Chi) is a comprehensive compendium of regulations for the proper administration of rites and rituals, stipulating proper etiquette for special social occasions and sacrifices. The Institutes of Chou (Chou-li) describes ideal government offices during the time of the Chou dynasty. The fifth classic, Spring and Autumn Annals (Chun-ch'iu), provides information about the state of Lu and traces the collapse of its political and moral order. The common belief is that these classics were edited by Confucius and that the last one may have been even authored by him. But even so, why should they be included in the Confucian scriptures? Here we need to take into account Confucius' strategy. He was convinced that in order to liberate Chinese society, he had to appeal to the high quality of life that prevailed during the Chou dynasty, the Golden Age of Chinese history. He identified in the classics some of the key concepts of this Golden Age, and believed that revitalizing and transmitting them could cure China's disease. Hence he accommodated the ancient texts as providing certain key concepts forming part of his salvific strategy. He considered himself the transmitter rather than the creator of the strategy. He puts it thus: "I have transmitted what was taught to me without making up anything of my own. I have been faithful to and loved the Ancients" (Analects 7:1). The Book of Changes and The Book of History contain views about the universe that the Confucian world view accommodates. The Book of Rites highlights Confucius' obsession with rituals.

But even though he resorted to the classics to inform parts of his strategy, he did not merely import all they contained. He believed that the most effective way to free China from its decadent state was to resort to Chinese tradition at its best and adapt it to conditions of his time—a strategy of "deliberating tradition."[13] Confucianism embraces not only the views of Confucius, but also some key concepts, customs and rites that have been in vogue in China from of old. Hence we cannot fully appreciate the nature and dynamics of the Confucian quest by concentrating only on the Analects.

The Five Classics, along with The Analects, The Book of Mencius (Meng-Tze), The Doctrine of the Mean (Chung-Yung), and The Book of Great Learning (Ta-hsio), provide the main scriptural sources of orthodox Confucianism. They were not canonized like the Bible, or even taken as final. Those who subsequently articulated the Confucian quest did not limit themselves to what these scriptures said, but took them as foundational rather than final. For instance, Hsun-Tzu, in the book named after him, developed his version of Confucianism on the assumption that human nature is essentially evil, a view that the works of Confucius and Mencius did not uphold. Neo-Confucians accommodate certain Taoist and Buddhist metaphysical and mystical elements that the original scriptures did not highlight. Some of the above scriptures were further modified and regrouped and new scriptures came to be added as the challenge of Buddhism and Taoism led the Neo-Confucians to look into their religion and update it. They made selective use of the original scriptures, The Analects, The Book of Mencius, The Great Learning, and The Doctrine of the Mean to face the new

13. Smith, "The Way," 198.

challenges. Neo-Confucians in Korea were interested in the relationship between human nature and emotions, so they had recourse to The Book on Learning of Human Nature and Principle (Songni hak) as a significant scriptural source.

The Confucian salvific quest, then, neither commenced nor concluded with the writings of Confucius. The classic texts to which Confucius had recourse anticipate some components of his way of liberation, and post-Confucian scriptures significantly developed what he had articulated. But what must be noted is that those who articulated the Confucian salvific strategy, whether they be associated with the ancient classics, the Confucian, or post-Confucian scriptures, were very much part of a salvific quest. The authors of these sacred texts claimed to be endowed with wisdom that was providential rather than supernatural; the scriptures record their insights and enlightened admonitions in their quest to find a way of salvation. The scriptures should not be abstracted from the aspirations of those who articulated and revered them; they were not revelations from on high, but aspirations from below. Our next task will be to identify the main characteristics of the Confucian way that arose out of these aspirations.

THE WAY OF THE QUEST

A Humanist Way

Confucianism is undoubtedly humanistic, but it cannot be equated with secular humanism as we know it. Humanism in China was not an outgrowth of philosophical speculation but of desperate social and political conditions. Such conditions necessitated a way out. Humanism served this purpose as a salvific strategy founded on the assumption that humans have the potential to liberate themselves. We could identify expressions of humanist trends before Confucius' time, but it became fully grown in Confucius, who articulated it into a definitive salvific strategy. Moreover, post-Confucian developments added some new features to this humanism. In order to explore fully the humanistic character of the Confucian salvific quest, we need to accommodate both pre-Confucian and post-Confucian views.

Confucian humanism proposes that to liberate a community, one must commence with the individual. One of the pre-Confucian scriptures, The Book of Great Learning, which is a chapter in The Book of Rites, puts it this way:

> The ancients who wished to manifest their clear character to the world would first bring order to their states. Those who wished to bring order to their states would first regulate their families. Those who wished to regulate their families would first regulate their personal lives. Those who wished to cultivate their personal lives would rectify their minds. Those who wished to rectify their minds would first make their wills sincere. Those who wished to make their wills sincere would first extend their knowledge. The extension of knowledge consists in the investigation of things. When things are investigated, knowledge is extended, the will becomes sincere; when the will is sincere, the mind is rectified; when the mind is rectified, the personal life is cultivated; when the personal life is cultivated, the family will be regulated; when the family is regulated, the state will be in order; and when the state is in order, there will be peace throughout

the world. From the Son of Heaven down to the common people, all must regard the cultivation of the personal life as the root or foundation. There is never a case when the root is in disorder and yet the branches are in order.[14]

This passage highlights the significant role of the individual in the enhancement of society. In a society fraught by internal wars, corrupt administration, extortion, and disregard for moral values, the individual functioned as a pawn in the hands of the powers that were. To elevate the individual to a place of dignity in such a society demanded a determined effort on the part of Confucius. Such a determination arose out of his conviction that to reform society he had to start with the individual, and in his emphasis on the significance of the individual, he could be called a humanist. In general, humanism is a view that gives significance to the human being and makes a concerted effort to identify and eliminate any dehumanizing factors. Phrases like "self-realization," "self-cultivation," "self-integrity," or "self-flowering" that figure prominently in Confucian writings may incline us to label him as a typical humanist. But as the above passage highlights, the "cultivation of personal life" was not meant to idolize the individual, but rather to drive home the point that rectification of the individual is vital to enhance the quality of life of the community, whether it be the family, the state, or the world at large. Such a communal enhancement is the ultimate end.

Moreover, some of the dehumanizers identified by contemporary versions of humanism become catalysts for humanization in Confucianism. The "individual" and "society" figure as polar terms in contemporary humanism, which places the human being on a pedestal and jealously protects it from dehumanizing agencies such as society. But the Confucian conceptual framework took "individual" and "society" not as polar terms but rather as integrally interconnected and complementary. In Confucius' view of life *jen* figures as the virtue of all virtues. Etymologically the character for *jen* is a combination of the character for "man" and for "two"; it depicts the ideal relationship that should prevail among people. Confucius' view of the human being may be depicted thus:

Human Being = I & Y

What this depiction tries to convey is that Confucius viewed the human being not as an individual but as a social being. The human being is not an isolated individual "I" but one in relation with "Y" ("You"), that is, in relation with some other such as a relative, friend, or associate. For Confucius, anything that limits the social facet of a human being and highlights his individualism is dehumanizing. Confucian morality seeks to develop the social aspect of the human being by enhancing the virtue of altruistic goodness (*jen*), a virtue that manifests itself only when a human being is in harmonious social relationships. When that occurs, the human being is truly human, and can provide the starting point for the society to be transformed. Hence Confucian humanism claims that human beings have the potential to reform themselves and society only when they are in harmonious relationship with one another.

14. Rosemont, "Universal Path," 184.

Contemporary humanism views with suspicion any attempt to degrade the human being to a mere physical organism of the natural order. The Confucian worldview, on the other hand, recognizes humans as being embedded in and dependent on the dynamics of nature, a view that was "anthropocosmic."[15] Tu Weiming articulates this vision thus:

> Human beings are . . . an integral part of "the chain of being," encompassing Heaven, Earth, and the myriad of things. However, the uniqueness of being human is the intrinsic capacity of the mind to "embody" (*ti*) the cosmos in its conscience and consciousness. Through this embodying, the mind realizes its own sensitivity, manifests true humanity, and assists in the cosmic transformation of Heaven and Earth.[16]

This "anthropocosmic" vision implies that human beings are very much a part of the cosmos, integrally connected with the dynamics of nature, as Thomas Berry observes, "What developed in China was a remarkable sense not of individualism but of humanity having both a microphase and a macrophase. The microphase is the limited particularity of the individual in oneself; the macrophase is the same individual as present to the entire order of reality."[17]

The "sage" in China was not one who renounces the world as illusion, but one who is integrated with nature. The classics, especially The Book of History, The Book of Ritual, and The Book of Changes, tried to integrate the "microphase" and "macrophase" of the individual. But it was Confucius who really provided the way for such integration by pointing out that personal discipline is needed for an individual human being to be in harmony with the world of nature.[18] Those who came after him built on this strategy. The "process of cultivation of personal life" that Confucian humanism advocates is first of all a means to make the individual aware of his real nature as a cosmological being. Such knowledge would then serve as a catalyst to transform the society of which the individual is a part.

Secular humanism considers religion to be a dehumanizing factor. Confucius and those who followed him, by contrast, were not atheists or agnostics; reverence for a "High God" was prevalent even before Confucius, and he did not demean or deny such reverence. In fact, the struggle he underwent in his personal spiritual journey to be aligned with "Heaven's will" (Analects 2:4) indicates his religiosity: "Heaven" really takes the place of the "High God" during this time. In this context, religiosity taken as reverence for and alignment with a supernatural being enhances rather than dehumanizes the human being.

The Confucian strategy is essentially humanist, since it is founded on the dictum that the human being has the potentiality to liberate himself and humanity. But this kind of humanism takes society, the world, and even the divine as integral to the

15. Weiming and Tucker, eds., *Confucian Spirituality*, 20.

16. Ibid., 132.

17. Berry, "Individualism and Holism," 44.

18. Ibid., 46.

THE QUEST

individual's humanity rather than as dehumanizing. Having harmonious relationships with these are absolutely essential for the human being to be genuinely human and so function as a catalyst for the transformation of society, the true objective. This takes us to certain significant features of this humanist strategy: its moral, ritualistic, and religious facets.

A Moral Way

The Confucian humanistic strategy has a pronounced moral overtone. Confucius claimed, "It is man that can make the Way great, and not the Way that can make man great" (Analects 5:28).

The Way (*Tao* in Chinese vocabulary) has been a key concept of the Chinese worldview; Taoism, the other major Chinese religion, takes its name from this term. Taoists take *Tao* to be the ultimate dynamic principle embedded in the very texture of the universe, as well as intimately connected with the destiny of human beings. The manner in which one responds to the flow of the Tao determines one's destiny. According to Taoism, when one passively flows with the Tao, one can be liberated.

Confucius challenged the Taoist way as being too fatalistic. He claimed that the human being determines destiny, that man makes the Way great and not vice versa. What determines destiny is one's moral caliber, which enables good deeds; human beings can and should act morally in order to generate good deeds. The classical Confucian dictum on human nature states that "by nature men are alike. Through practice they have become far apart" (Analects 17:2). Although this claim seems to be neutral with regard to human nature, yet Confucius' teachings in general imply the goodness of human nature. There has been a lingering feud among Confucians as to whether human nature is inherently good or evil. Mencius claimed that human beings are good by nature, while Hsun-Tzu considered human nature to be evil. According to Mencius, "Man's nature is naturally good just as water naturally flows downward. There is not man without this good nature; neither is there water that does not flow downward" (Book of Mencius 6a:2). He acknowledged the possibility of water running uphill against its nature, through artificial means; likewise, one could be led to do evil against one's very nature. But he pointed out that moral action provides the means of enhancing the goodness inherent in human beings; any program of moral action would therefore be in keeping with human nature. On the other hand, Hsun-Tzu, who took human nature to be evil, had to propose a more aggressive program of moral action. According to him, "The nature of man is evil; his goodness is the result of activity . . . Crooked wood must be heated and bent before it becomes straight. Blunt metal must be ground and whetted before it becomes sharp. Now the nature of man is evil. It must depend on teachers and laws to become correct and achieve propriety and righteousness and it becomes disciplined."[19]

For Hsun-Tzu, an aggressive program of moral education and legal imposition is necessary to change inherently evil human nature. Both views, even though opposed

19. *The Hsun-Tzu* in Chan, *Source Book*, 128.

50

concerning the original nature of a human being, are in agreement with the basic Confucian dictum that moral action is necessary to change human destiny.

In the Chinese context, we can with justification characterize moral action as virtuous action. "Virtue" (*te*) played a significant role not only in Confucianism but in the times that preceded it, but it was not understood in the same way at all times. From ancient times, the Chinese have acknowledged a Supreme Power called *Ti* (the Lord), who blessed and punished people. He protected in battle those whom he favored, and approved the appointment or dismissal of state officials.[20] Hence people tried their best to please him in order to gain his favor, and "virtue" meant the quality of pleasing this Power. Beginning with the period of the Chou dynasty, however, the concept of heaven (*T'ien*) gradually replaced this Supreme Power as the ultimate spiritual reality, a development that led in turn to a change in the character of this supreme reality. It is believed that the founders of the Chou dynasty, having overthrown the Shang dynasty, had to justify their right to rule. Hence they developed the doctrine of the Mandate of Heaven, a moral law based on virtue.[21] Confucius often spoke of heaven (T'ien). But for him, heaven was no longer an anthropomorphic deity but rather a supreme reality that is morally purposive and generates moral codes of conduct to be followed by people. In this view, human destiny ultimately depended on adhering to heaven's moral law. Hence, Heaven's Mandate or Will (*T'ien Ming*) was a moral will, one that expected people to behave according to certain moral injunctions. This came to be called the Way of Heaven (*T'ien Tao*), or the Principle of Heaven (*T'ien Li*). Heaven does not bless people according to its pleasure but on the grounds of a lifestyle that is in harmony with its moral criteria. In this context, a virtuous person was one who was aligned with heaven's moral will; "virtue" meant the quality that reflects heaven's morality. This is why Confucius lauded virtuous action, since it had a significant impact on human destiny. When he claimed that the human being determines human destiny and that man makes the Way great and not vice versa, he made it a point to state that it is the moral caliber of the human that is vital to this capacity. Confucius' own spiritual struggle to follow Heaven's Will, as confessed in Analects 2:4, testifies to this conviction. He consciously cultivated a lifestyle, through apprehending the truth and trying to grasp Heaven's Mandate, that would harmonize his desires with heaven's moral principles. Such a confession confirms the Confucian tenet that a human being can liberate himself through cultivating a lifestyle that is in accord with heaven's morality.

Moreover, this option is available to any human being, since Confucius believed in the perfectibility of all humans. He radically modified one of the key Chinese concepts, *Chung-Tzu* (the superior man). Originally this term meant "son of the ruler." Gradually it came to mean "superior man" on the grounds that nobility was a quality determined by status, specifically by heredity.[22] But out of 107 times this term is used in the Analects, Confucius uses it most often to refer to a morally superior person of

20. Chan, *Source Book*, 3.

21. Ibid., 3–4.

22. Ibid., 15.

any status; nobility for Confucius was no longer a matter of heredity or social stratum but of character.[23] He selected as models certain emperors from the Golden Age of Chinese history, the period of the Chou dynasty, such as Yao of the third millennium BCE and his successor Shun. But they were picked out as morally ideal persons with political achievements rather than on the grounds of heredity or social status. It was the "sage," including the sage emperors, that typified the morally superior man.[24]

The question arises how one could cultivate such a destiny-changing moral life-style. First of all, Confucius took the individual as one in relation with others. Hence the strategy of moral development was always relational. Self-transformation or self-cultivation was a communal act. The morally transformed person, *Chung-Tzu*, was one who exhibited *jen* in thought, word, and deed. The term *jen* in pre-Confucian writings usually referred to the virtue of kindness or benevolence, but Confucius broadened its scope; he regarded it as a general virtue.[25] For him, *Chun-Tzu*, the Superior Man, is a man of jen. He is "a man of humanity," who, "in wishing to establish his own char-acter, also establishes the character of others, and in wishing to be prominent himself . . . also helps others to be prominent" (Analects 6:28). Jen is the quality of altruistic humanness that, when cultivated, acts as a catalyst for the transformation both of self and society. Hence the moral strategy that Confucianism adopted was relational in character and communal in scope.

Secondly, this strategy was oriented more towards duty than rights. The individu-al is always viewed in relation to others. Placing an individual in a web of relationships entails mutual obligations and responsibilities rather than individual rights.

Obligatory relationships are essential for transforming not only the individual but also the community. Mencius makes explicit five relationships:

> According to the way of man, if they are well fed, warmly clothed, and comfort-ably lodged but without education, they will become almost like animals. The Sage [emperor Shun] worried about it and he appointed Hsieh to be minister of education and teach people human relations, that between father and son there should be affection; between ruler and minister there should be righteousness; between husband and wife there should be attention to their separate functions; between old and young there should be proper order; and between friends there should be faithfulness. Emperor Yao said: "Encourage them, lead them on, rec-tify them, straighten them . . . so they discover for themselves their moral nature" (Book of Mencius 3a:4).

Mencius did not invent these relations. They were already in vogue in Chinese so-ciety. This passage indicates that he approved the sage's attempt to educate the people to practice these relations. All involve reciprocal obligations. Mencius's emphasis on these obligations is founded on the conviction that human transformation, whether personal or communal, could only be effected through proper moral relationships. The potentiality to exhibit proper moral relations is what distinguishes humans from

23. Ibid.
24. Ibid.
25. Ibid., 16.

animals. Moreover, the morality that could transform humans has to be oriented towards duty rather than rights, communal rather than individualistic.

In order to cultivate such a duty-oriented communitarian morality, The Book of Great Learning provided a program of moral education. The first chapter of this book is supposed to contain the views of Confucius, while the ten subsequent chapters are taken to be views of one of his followers, Tsen-Tzu. This book suggests eight practical steps: investigate the nature of things, extend knowledge, cultivate sincerity of will, rectify the mind, cultivate personal life, regulate the family, harmonize with the natural order, and, finally, be a catalyst for world peace.

The steps indicate that both acquiring knowledge and cultivating sincerity of will are integral to becoming moral. The question is which is prior: knowledge or will? Neo-Confucians were divided on this issue. Chu-His (1130–1200 CE) was convinced that to lead a moral life one should sincerely will to become good, and for that to occur, one should first of all know "the nature of things." According to him, such knowledge produces the "virtuous sage." This resembles the Socratic dictum "Knowledge is virtue." On the other hand, Wing-Shou-Jen (1472–1529 CE) insisted that no true knowledge is possible without cultivating "sincerity of will," that one should sincerely will to become good in order even to know what is good.[26] Even though there is a difference of opinion between the two Neo-Confucian schools, both agree that humans have the capacity to become moral through learning, that one can learn to become a sage. This highlights the humanistic character of the Confucian moral strategy. Nevertheless, the same controversy also highlights the limitations of human nature, especially the weakness of the human will. Confucius seemed to be aware of this. In order to enable people to live morally, he believed it was necessary to resort to ritualistic and religious practices.

A Ritualistic Way

Rites and rituals have been very much a part of the Chinese way of life. The Classic of Rites provides a compendium of Chinese rites and rituals pertaining to almost every facet of life.

Confucianism, born and bred in China, naturally gave an important place to the practice of rites and rituals, but with a character and function that was typically Confucian. Ritual facilitated the efficacy of the Confucian salvific strategy. In this garb, it provided prescriptions for proper conduct in highly specific situations that would enable the participants to be liberated.

In order to appreciate the salvific import of the practice of rites and rituals, we have to examine the Chinese notion of *li* that is foundational to its performance. As a generic notion, *li* may be taken as "propriety" or "proper conduct." Implicit in this notion is the idea of rule-governed conduct. Since orderly performance of rites and rituals is eminently rule-governed, *li* came also to signify "ritual propriety."

26. Ibid., 84–85.

Originally li gave the rules for pleasing the spirits and obtaining their blessing. Later on it acquired a moral overtone and became connected with the notion of rightness (*yi*). Firstly, *yi* provided the moral criterion for the practice of li in that it determined whether specific rules were the right ones to regulate given types of ritualistic practice. Secondly, yi also provided the rationale for the application of *li* in ritualistic practice.[27] Hence li came to be understood as ritual propriety having an ethical rationale. Confucianism based the practice of rites and rituals on such "ritual propriety."

Confucians all claimed that ritual practice was effective to liberate people, even though there was difference of opinion among them regarding human nature. For those following Mencius, the practice of rites and rituals served as a catalyst to enhance the goodness inherent in humans and thereby transform their quality of life. On the other hand, those following Hsun-Tzu, who claimed that human nature is inherently evil, accorded a more aggressive role to ritualistic practice, regarding it as both corrective and transformative. It had to first change human nature in order to make it wholesome. A. S. Cua identifies three functions of *li*: delimiting, supportive, and ennobling.[28] In the first instance, li acts as a preventive by limiting the pursuit of self-interest. It has a supportive function in giving a sense of satisfaction to one who acts within the limits of proper conduct. But what highlights the salvific character of Confucian ritualistic practice is the ennobling function of li. It not only limits self-interest and supports wholesome desires, but also transforms the one who adheres to it.

For Confucians, ritualistic practice is a properly ordered, morally justified mode of behavior: li directed by yi. In a communal context it enables the participants to develop altruistic humanness (jen), which also has a transformative impact. Confucians, especially those following Hsun-Tzu, claimed that without constructive human effort human nature cannot be transformed, and that such effort has to be orchestrated through ritualistic practice.[29]

Confucius highlighted the intimate connection between the ritual and the participant in his conversation with a disciple, Tzu-Kung. It runs thus:

> Tzu-Kung asked: "What would you say about me as a person?"
> The Master said: "You are a utensil."
> "What sort of utensil?"
> "A sacrificial vase of jade." (Analects 5:3)

During Confucius' time, ornamented vases of bronze and jade filled with grain were used in sacrificial harvest offerings. These vases were taken to be sacred. Yet their sacredness did not reside in the preciousness of the bronze, the beauty of the jade, or the edibility of the grain that was in them. The vase was sacred because it was an integral part of the ceremony; its identity lay in its participation as a constitutive element of the ritual. Unlike utensils in general, the sacrificial vase had no significance apart from the ritual. What distinguished it from other vases was its ritual function.

---

27. Cua, "Ethical," 255.

28. Ibid., 255–63.

29. Ibid., 258.

In using the metaphor of a sacrificial jade vase, Confucius poignantly points out that he wants human beings to become not mere utensils, useful though they may be, but utensils involved in the ritual of life. For him, a participant is not a mere utensil but very much a part of the ritual, like a sacrificial vase. Unlike utensils in general, this particular utensil has no other use than to be part of the ritualistic ceremony. In fact, some ceremonial utensils had holes in them, emphasizing that their value lay in being part of the ritual and not in their aesthetics or utility.

The Confucian way aimed to transform people not through mere acquisition of knowledge or performance of duties, but through whole-hearted ritualistic participation. When asked about filial piety, Confucius responded, "Filial piety nowadays means to be able to support one's parents. But even dogs and horses are fed (can support their parents). If there are no feelings of reverence, wherein lies the difference?" (Analects 2:7). The act of nourishment becomes a ceremonial ritual of dining wherein the participants exhibit a sense of reverence, and such a ritual is transformative. On account of this, the ritual takes precedence over the individual participants. Confucius pinpointed this when he responded to his disciple's concern over killing a sheep as a part of a sacrificial rite. He said, "You love the sheep, but I love the ceremony" (Analects 3:17).

The practice of rituals has a communal impact. Confucius emphasized that "Virtue never dwells in isolation; it will always bring neighbors" (Analects 4:25). Rituals orchestrate the enactment of *jen* (altruistic humanness), and hence they are communal in their impact. As Herbert Fingarette points out:

> Man is transformed by participation with others in ceremony which is communal. Until he is so transformed he is not truly man but only potentially so—the newborn infant, the wolf-boy of the forests, or the "barbarian." Ceremony is justified when we see how it transforms the "barbarian" into what we know as man at his best. When we see man as a participant in communal rite, rather than as individualistic ego, he takes on to our eyes a new and holy beauty just as the sacrificial vessel.[30]

In the Confucian context, ritualistic practice can be transformative to individuals as well as communities, provided the participants do not treat it as mere formality; they need to make an honest effort to participate in the ritual. Confucius pointed out, "If a man is not humane, what has he to do with ceremonies? If he is not humane, what has he to do with music?" (Analects 3:3). For him, ritual performance without sincere commitment becomes hypocrisy. Commenting on the ritual of sacrifice, he points out, "If I do not participate in the sacrifice it is as if I do not sacrifice at all" (Analects 3:12).

In our commercialized, rat-race culture, where we gulp coffee in fast-food nooks, a popular Chinese ritual like the tea ceremony may appear a time-wasting ordeal. But in the Chinese context it is a meaningful ritual with wholesome benefits to the participants. It exhibits the vital role rituals play in the life of the Chinese people. The Chinese

---

30. Fingarette, "Confucian Metaphor," 238.

wedding tea ceremony ideally exemplifies this, enabling the principal participants, the groom and the bride and their families, to commence a binding relationship.

Contemporary version of the Chinese tea ceremony

The participants, meticulously following proper procedure, become very much part of the ritual. In the process of their performance, they exhibit propriety (li) that generates the virtue of altruistic humanness (jen). After all, these two virtues are necessary for marital harmony!

Ritualistic practice aims to rectify the individual and thereby transform the community. Some rituals aim to bring about transformation on a universal scale encompassing both earth and heaven, the physical and spiritual realms. Such rituals, honoring heaven, earth, sun, moon, ancestors, and so on, aim at enabling the participants to be in harmonious relationship with the universe extending beyond the realm of human earthly existence. This takes us to the religious facet of the Confucian way.

A Religious Way

We may characterize the Confucian way as religious, provided we do not view it through traditional western conceptual categories. The humanist, moral, ritualistic way of Confucianism was essentially salvific in intent, in the sense that it attempted to provide a way of liberation that was transformative. That in itself would qualify it to be a "salvation religion." Confucius was concerned with finding a way out of his community's perceived predicament. Of course, his proposal contains some political strategies, but it was basically pragmatic in a salvific sense. Moreover, it had a moral overtone. He was concerned about how people of his time behaved. His aim was not merely to effect political reform, but also to bring about moral enhancement in society, a wholesome quality of life. Any religion worth its name has a moral component, and Confucianism qualifies as a religion on this count. Although it is possible to characterize it as merely a program for political reform with a moral overtone, there is certainly room to view it as religious when we look into the manner in which Confucians articulated their quest.

What characterizes people involved in a religious quest is their resort to something beyond themselves. For Confucius, that something was not a transcendent personal God but heaven (T'ien), a trans-human reality that was very much part of Chinese religiosity through the ages, a reality that lies beyond the human and in some sense encompasses the human. As noted above, it was once acknowledged as a Supreme Power called Ti, but Confucius and Mencius preferred to regard it as heaven (T'ien). They claimed that human destiny depended on cultivating a harmonious relationship with heaven through abiding by its will. Confucians aspire to cultivate this relationship, a relationship that generates a transformation and is thus salvific in its impact.

Sacrifices and the rites of passage associated with certain important stages in one's life such as birth, puberty, marriage, and death were very much in vogue in the China of Confucius. He did not give up on these rites. For instance, he continued the practice of funeral rituals, even though he did not have a full-fledged doctrine of life after death. Perhaps there was a longing for life after death, but first death itself had to be reckoned with. Funeral rituals were meticulously practiced in the hope that the dead would survive death. Confucius proposed that immortality (*shi er buxiu*) depended on cultivating virtues (*lide*), using proper speech (*liyan*) and doing good deeds (*ligong*).[31] The belief that living a good life and cultivating these virtues would generate life after death motivated Confucians to meticulously practice funeral rituals. In earlier times, the Chinese had performed such rites resorting to spirits, including ancestral spirits. Confucius seems to have had an "as if" attitude toward the existence of spirits when he offered sacrifices to them (Analects 3:12), but this attitude was not a skeptical denial; it was rather a faith in what seems not to be obvious. In fact, he revolted against the hypocritical performance of sacrifices, saying, in the same passage, "If I do not participate in the sacrifice, it is as if I did not sacrifice at all." For him, sincere participation in the ritualistic was vital to the cultivation of a lifestyle founded on propriety (*li*). Such a practice indicates the religiosity of the Confucian quest.

Confucius and Mencius never claimed to be God or even superhuman. They considered themselves to be very much part of the people and like them caught up in the predicament in which they found themselves. But after their death, and perhaps much to their dismay, these leaders were deified by their followers, who built temples for them and made sacrifices and offerings to them. Such deification also indicates the religiosity of Confucianism. Confucians need a God.

Developing one's moral character, cultivating a lifestyle of propriety through the practice of rituals, trying to be in a harmonious relationship with heaven, and deifying their founders are all interrelated in the Confucian salvific quest. These are what lend to Confucianism its religious character. The strategies of self-cultivation, moral development, and ritualistic practice were all meant to liberate humanity, qualifying Confucianism not only as a humanistic moral strategy but also as a "salvation religion." This is where Christ becomes relevant to the Confucian salvific quest.

THE RELEVANCE OF CHRIST TO THE CONFUCIAN QUEST

If the Confucian quest is merely a humanist program for political and social reform, then Christ, as Savior, is not relevant to Confucians. But the Confucian quest is at its core salvific. The humanist, moral, political, ritualistic, and religious facets of the quest are all geared to providing a way of salvation. Hence it is in order to ask how Christ becomes relevant to the Confucian salvific quest.

---

31. Chan, *Source Book*, 13.

Christ's incarnation to redeem humanity becomes pointless if humans do not need to be redeemed. Christianity characterizes the human being as destined to be in harmonious relationship with God. But due to the sinfulness that besets all humanity, this relationship is severed, necessitating Christ's salvific incarnation and sacrifice.

Confucianism similarly understands that humans are destined to be in harmony with heaven (*tianreheyi*). Confucians believe that humans have the potential to be aligned with heaven, since they are endowed with a heavenly nature that enables them to be morally sensitive and respond to the Mandate of Heaven. In fact, this capacity is taken to be the defining characteristic of humanity. Such a description highlights the potential of humans to respond to the superhuman. Christians believe that humans, being created in God's image, have the potential to respond to God. There is something in the very make up of human beings that drives them to search for something beyond themselves, whether we call it "God" or "heaven."

Nevertheless, Confucians acknowledge that humans do not meet such expectations. The morally decadent China of Confucius glaringly exhibited how far humans were from the ideal. The popular Chinese myth, "Separation of Heaven and Earth," describes the discrepancy between the ideal and the actual in human existence. The myth runs thus: Once upon a time humans and deities did not intermingle. Humans, for their part, held gods in reverence, while deities descended among them from time to time through intermediaries (shamans). Hence the spheres of the divine and the earthly remained distinct. There were no calamities. But there came a time when humans and deities started to intermingle without the aid of shamans. As a result, people lost their reverence for the deities, the gods violated the rules of conduct, and calamities arose. It was at this point that an ancient sage-ruler Zhuanxu, believed to have lived in the twenty-fifth century BCE, intervened, presumably with the approval of the God-on-High. He arranged the cosmic order by separating heaven and earth, thereby blocking communication between humans and heaven.[32]

The myth depicts the disruption in the cosmic order caused by the rift between heaven and humanity. In a similar way, the biblical narrative about the fall of the first humans, Adam and Eve, highlights how sin separated humanity from God. Nevertheless, according to both Confucianism and Christianity, this separation goes against the very nature of human personhood. Humans are crafted to be in harmonious relationship with the superhuman reality: "heaven" for the Confucians and God for the Christians. For Christians, since humans are made in God's image and destined to have fellowship with God, the aspiration to regain that relationship is undeniably present. The Christian claim is that, since humanity is incapacitated by sin, such an aspiration can only be fulfilled by Christ, who is not himself part of the quest. For Confucians, the belief that humans are endowed with a heavenly nature drives them to strive to be aligned with heaven (tianrenheyi). The aspiration to bridge the gap is that which motivates the Confucians in their salvific quest.

32. Bodde, "Myths," 65–70.

Both Christians and Confucians claim that there is a way out of the human predicament. Christians resort to Christ, while Confucians resort to a humanistic, moral, ritualistic program with religious overtones. But in the articulation of their strategy Confucians seem to suggest that what they are really longing for is Christ. This articulation is not confined to the views of the founding fathers, but extends to cover the views of those who followed them. All of these articulators were very much engaged in the quest. In confessing the challenges he faced in trying to lead a moral life and how he strove to overcome these challenges through proper learning, Confucius acknowledged his humanity. He compared himself to "Old Peng" (Analects 7:1), supposed to be an official of the Shang dynasty (1751–1112 BCE), who loved to recite old stories. A teacher's reputation depends to a great extent on the acceptability of his teachings, but Confucius was not popular during his lifetime. After his death, China experienced turbulent times. Civil wars replaced family loyalties, and after the brutal reunification of China by the Chin and Han dynasties, despotic state control prevailed. However, to stabilize China, cultured administrators rather than ruthless army officers were required. This is where Confucius became indispensable to the Confucians. The Confucian classics became the basis for civil service examinations for government officers. Confucius' teachings came to be accepted as indispensable to equip the bureaucrats with the moral virtues. His teachings were sought for their salvific value and he came to be venerated as a savior-sage. Within a few hundred years of his death, Confucius came to be venerated by his family members, political leaders, and even by the emperor, to the point of deification. Temples were devoted to the worship of Confucius, not only as a model of unselfish public service but also as one who embodied the virtues that would liberate decadent China. Statues of Confucius became objects of worship; offerings and sacrifices were made to them. The Confucian temples in Beijing and Taiwan are standing monuments of the Confucian quest for a savior-god.

According to certain ancient Chinese texts, when a person dies, the body decays while the spirit survives. The spirit is invoked through the use of spirit tablets during sacrificial offerings. The spirit tablet found in the Confucian temple in Zhanghua, Taiwan reads thus: "Supreme Sage and Premier Teacher Confucius."[33] This indicates that the spirit of Confucius may have been invoked during sacrificial offerings. The humble teacher and political reformist who died in frustration eventually turns out to be worshiped in temples, offered sacrifices, and invoked for help. Not only Confucius, but also some of his disciples, such as Mencius, came to be venerated. Several temples contain their statues.[34] These leaders were venerated as gods because of their salvific potency. They modeled the teachings that would save the Chinese. Such veneration expresses a deep aspiration: what the people needed was not just a profound teacher with a viable salvific doctrine, but one who transcends the human and is thereby able

33. Weiming and Tucker, eds., *Confucian Spirituality*, footnote to photo 3, 162–64.

34. Weiming and Tucker, eds., *Confucian Spirituality*, footnote to photo 15, 162–64, states that major figures of the Confucian tradition are venerated in temples and shrines. For example, the statue of Mencius is enshrined in a small temple that marks his birthplace south of Qufu in Shandong province.

to help humanity. The deification of Confucius and his disciples indicates that people needed more than a sage. The "Lord on High," replaced by "heaven," of course received divine status, but was distant from humans and not directly involved in saving desperate people. This is where the deified Confucius becomes significant. What such people craved was not a "God on High" or a "heaven beyond," but one who could relate to them and enable them to be freed from their predicament. What they were desperately longing for was a "Savior God"; one, in fact, who is very much like God in Christ. This is one of the ways Christ becomes relevant to the Confucian quest.

The belief that humans are endowed with a heavenly nature may imply that they do not need any help. But Confucians did not believe this to be the case. Dong Zhongshu, a Confucian scholar and statesman of the Han

Statue of Confucius at Confucius Temple in Beijing, China

dynasty (206 BCE—220 CE), stressed the necessity of the sage-king in the transformation of his subjects.[35] While Dong accepted that people are endowed with heavenly nature, he realized that they needed further help. He claimed that only a sage-king could render such help. Such a king would have the authoritative power over his subjects to provide transformational instruction. As a sage, he would also have the wisdom and moral caliber to act as the model and motivator to effect the transformation. Just as only a potter can shape clay on a potter's wheel and only a smith can cast metal in a mold, Doug Zhongshu claims that only a sage-king can transform his subjects.[36] So, although Confucianism commenced by emphasizing the adequacy of self-effort, it eventually resorted to the help of the sage-king because people are unable to make it on their own. The justification for such help is that the sage-king has authority, mandated by heaven, on the grounds of his moral maturity. He is both ordinary and exceptional. Sarah Queen points out that the sage-king is imitable, since that which enables him to become a sage, his human nature, is possessed by all human beings equally. Yet he is inimitable to the extent that he transcends his fellow human beings in fulfilling the moral propensities of this nature. This is precisely why he can lead others onto the path of ultimate transformation.[37]

The resort to the sage-king shows that people desperately need help from one who is very much one of them and thus able to relate to them, yet not caught up in their

---

35. Queen, "Way of the Unadorned King," 312.

36. Ibid., 313.

37. Ibid.

predicament or bound by their limitations. He must have the authority mandated by heaven, and the ability enabled by the strength of his own personhood, to liberate them. Confucians did not invent sage-kings; legendary figures like the Three Sovereigns (San-hunag) and the Five Emperors (Wu-ti) have populated Chinese mythology from ancient times.[38] But Dong Zhongshu highlighted the salvific role of the sage-king: for him, a sage-king is not merely an inspiring legendary figure but rather a historical figure that actually changes the destiny of a nation by transforming the people.

In stipulating the role of the sage-king, Dong Zhongshu articulates a core aspiration of the Confucians. They are seeking one who would be part of humanity and yet able to liberate humans; one who is both immanent and transcendent, able and willing to liberate humanity. Could it be Christ they are seeking? For Christ is both human and divine. He is immanent in his incarnation, yet transcendent as God the Son.

Sacrifices have been an integral part of Chinese religious life. There are significant features in the Confucian adoption of the Chinese sacrificial system that poignantly suggest a longing for the Christ depicted in the Bible as the sacrificial lamb and high priest. Confucians attempted to structure a sacrificial system that would liberate as well as reconcile them with heaven (t'ien), the "unity of heaven and humans" (T'ianrenheyi) being the goal of their salvific quest.

Belief in a spirit world is a given for the Chinese. Maintaining proper relationship with spirits is normative. Ancestral spirits, nature deities, deified humans such as sage-kings, and a host of spirits and gods leading up to the Lord on High (Shangti) are all part of the spirit world. Rites, rituals, and sacrifices are employed to relate people to the spirit world and gain the favor of spiritual beings. Many of these spirits and deities are indifferent to human welfare. They even interfere with human lives at their own pleasure. Hence humans had to strive to be on good terms with these beings through sacrifice.

The Confucians introduced certain modifications to the Chinese sacrificial system so as to make it more effective and the sacrificial act more meaningful. It is here that Christ and his sacrifice become relevant to the Confucian salvific quest. During the time of Confucius, sacrifices had turned out to be mere formalities orchestrated by unscrupulous shamans and power-hungry rulers. Shamans claimed to have special ability to commune with spirits through divination using oracle bones. These were cattle bones and tortoise shells in which people's problems, confessions, and appeals were inscribed. By observing the patterning of the cracks that showed in these objects on being heated, the shamans interpreted the message the spirits had for people. The penitents depended on the shamans to be assured that their confessions had been heard by the spirits. While the shamans became rich, extorting money for their services, the procedure degenerated into an empty formality so that there was little evidence of any sense of piety or devotion on the part of the penitents.

Confucius reacted against this. For Confucians, sacrifices were supposed to transform one estranged from heaven into one reconciled with it. The belief was that

---

38. Oxtoby, *World Religions: Eastern Traditions*, 355.

heaven would respond favorably to people who followed its moral dictates. "Sin," in this context, was not merely an act that displeased spirits and deities but that which corroded the character of people, distancing them from the character of heaven. Sin, taken as moral failure, carried with it moral guilt. Sacrifice came to be understood as a means of reconciling with heaven through moral rectification. For that to happen, the penitent had to be more than a mere onlooker depending on the shamans' skills; he had to be an active participant in the sacrificial act. Since moral rectification pertains to the innermost part of one's being, the sacrificial act had to be internalized; the penitent had to be seriously involved in it. This is why Confucius stated, as quoted above, "If I do not participate in the sacrifice, it is as if I did not sacrifice at all." He emphasized that the efficacy of rites does not reside in mere ceremonial acts *per se*, but in performing such acts with a humane heart (Analects 3:3). For Confucians, sacrifice is a transformative ritual that demands the sincere participation of the penitent. When transformation occurs through the sacrificial act, the participant is reconciled with heaven. Sacrifice has a salvific impact, provided the participant is sincerely involved in the sacrificial act. In the context of this emphasis we can appreciate Confucius' comment to Tzu-Kung, that he is a "sacrificial vase of jade." What the Confucians really want is a sacrificial procedure that has a transformative impact on the persons participating in it. When such participation occurs, the penitent can appropriate the sacrifice. This resembles the Christian teaching that the salvific impact of Christ's sacrifice on the cross can only be appropriated when the participant sincerely repents.

Moreover, the sacrificial victim in the Confucian sacrifice had to be acceptable to heaven. Confucians developed the practice of offering one's best, whether it was the most expensive precious stone, such as jade, or an animal without blemish. They took the perfect animal or the jade as analogous to moral perfection and hence acceptable to heaven. What they needed was a "sacrificial victim" that, by its perfection, would be acceptable to heaven and thereby enable them to be reconciled with heaven. Christ on the cross, the sacrificial lamb without blemish, meets the requirements that the Confucian sacrificial system stipulates for the sacrificial victim.

The practice of human sacrifice, though not common, was still extant in China; the Confucian classics confirm the practice, but do not approve it. Confucius condemned even the symbolic representation of human sacrifice: he detested sacrificing or dismembering human effigies or even wooden figures in the shape of humans.[39] We can appreciate his condemnation of the sacrifice of human beings, for that would have been unacceptable to heaven on moral grounds. However, if Confucians condemned human sacrifice on moral grounds, would the sacrifice of Christ be disqualified as not meeting Confucian requirements?

Nevertheless, in certain exceptional circumstances, Confucians accommodated human sacrifice. Heaven for them being an abode of spiritual beings who are sincerely concerned about humans, the only sacrificial victim acceptable to heaven was one who was totally altruistic and sincerely concerned about the sins of penitents.

39. Ibid., 369, 394.

A story is told in the Confucian classics about King T'ang, the founder of the Shang dynasty (1751–1123 BCE). After successful conquests, his kingdom experienced years of drought. Diviners told him that heaven (t'ien) could only be placated by human sacrifice, whereupon King T'ang, after purification, placed himself on the firewood and prepared to offer himself vicariously to the Lord on High (*Shangti*) on behalf of the people. But rain fell and quenched the fire. The king survived and the drought ended.[40] There is controversy about whether this event is historical or legendary. Either way, however, it is notable that this event is remembered with admiration by Confucians. Even though they oppose human sacrifice, they seem to accommodate it under very exceptional circumstances: when the one who is sacrificed is motivated only by altruistic motives, when there is no other way to please heaven, and when there is no one else who could be the sacrifice. In this context, the human sacrifice is neither murder nor suicide, but carried out because there is absolutely no one else who could do it. It becomes a vicarious act. What Confucians seem to require of such a sacrifice is ideally fulfilled by Christ's vicarious death on the cross, motivated by agape love.

Moreover, the person who performs the sacrifice, the officiator, plays a vital role in the Confucian sacrificial act. The efficacy of the act depends to a great extent on the caliber of the person offering the sacrifice. Confucians insist that this person must be of high moral caliber. Hence they opposed the participation of morally questionable shamans in sacrifices. They identified the emperor to be the best person to perform the sacrifice, believing that the officiator had to be of the same status as the one to whom the sacrifice is offered. Regional officers could address spirits of similar rank; higher officers could sacrifice to higher gods, while only the emperor could sacrifice to heaven, the "Lord on High." Confucians believed that there is a hierarchal order both in the world of spiritual beings and in the world of humans. The highest in the spiritual ladder was heaven, often identified with the Lord on High (Shangti). The highest in the human order was the emperor. For the votive gift to be acceptable, the officiator was required to be of the same hierarchal status as the one to whom the sacrifice was offered.[41] This is the rationale for appointing the emperor to perform the sacrifice.

Moreover, the officiator had to be acceptable also on moral grounds. Hence not all emperors were automatically qualified to be effective officiators. In order for the sacrifice to be acceptable to heaven, the officiating emperor needed to be a sage-king. Confucians idealized such an emperor, calling him the Son of Heaven since heaven would accept him as its own.

The present impressive complex of the Temple of Heaven in Beijing, China, dates back to the Ming dynasty (1368–1661). It accommodates the Hall of Prayer and the three concentric open-air terraces. The middle terrace is where the emperor made sacrifices to heaven (the Lord on High) on behalf of the people.

---

40. Ibid., 361.

41. Sommer, "Ritual and Sacrifice," 206.

Temple of Heaven in Beijing, China

Confucians made certain specific demands concerning the nature and role of the emperor as officiator. They wanted him to be the Son of Heaven as well as the High Priest of the World. In their view, for the sacrifice to be effective, the officiator had to be acceptable to heaven; in fact, taken by heaven as its own "son." Moreover, he needed to be able to intercede for all the people and execute the sacrificial rites in the most effective way on their behalf, as a high priest capable of representing all. What Confucians longed for was an officiator accepted by heaven as its very own, and who would be able to act and intercede on behalf of all the people, even willing to giving up his life for them.

Christ, as God's only begotten Son, is heaven's very own; he is the great high priest who not only intercedes with God the Father on behalf of humans, but also gave his life for them. Hence Christ meets the Confucian requirements of an ideal officiator.

Confucianism is a humanist, moral, ritualistic way that is both philosophical and religious. But all these facets of Confucianism display an underlying motivating factor: Confucians want their way to be most of all salvific and not merely speculative theory or ritualistic formality. They want to be freed from their predicament and transformed into a wholesome state, both collectively and individually. The Confucian teachings, moral codes, and ritualistic practices are all meant to serve that purpose.

When we look at the complex Confucian spectrum as a whole, we find that it is not a mere political program or moral code of conduct, or even a meticulous practice of ritualistic rules, but rather a dynamic salvific quest, aspiring for a Savior-God. The founders of Confucianism believed in the power of human potential, and highlighted self-help as an effective means of salvation. But Confucians eventually realized the need for a savior figure, and found it in the sage-king.

Confucianism no doubt stresses the indispensability of proper moral living. In fact, Confucian moral theory is in no way inferior to that of Christianity. When Tsu-Kung asked Confucius, "Is there one word which can serve as the guiding principle for conduct throughout life?" he replied, "It is the word altruism (*shu*). Do not do to others what you do not want them to do to you" (Analects 15:3). This is really the negative version of Christ's golden rule, "Do to others as you would have them do to you" (Luke 6:31). But to put into practice what the moral norm demands, whether it be in positive or negative form, human capacity in itself is not enough. Perhaps that is the reason why Confucians eventually resorted to something superhuman, deified

Confucius, and religiously practiced sacrifice. This was a desperate plea for mercy. On the grounds that good works, meticulous ritualistic practice, and cordial social relationships founded on sound morality are necessary but not sufficient to liberate humanity, Confucians resorted to mercy, which could be taken as a type of favor based on merit. From a Confucian perspective, the above-mentioned strategies have meritorious value for salvation, but this merit in itself is not adequate; there is a need for some added favor, which resulted in the resort to the superhuman. But what the Confucians really need is unmerited favor—that is, grace.

God's grace enacted through Christ as God the Son, Savior, and perfect sacrifice fulfills these core aspirations of the Confucians. Understood in this way, Christ seems very relevant to Confucians, even though Confucianism and Christianity as religious structures seem to be so far apart.

4

The Taoist Quest

TAOISM, THE OTHER MAJOR religion of China, shows itself as a multiplicity of dynamic activities of diverse sects stretching over several centuries. But amidst such diversity, we can identify an underlying quest among the various Taoist communities—a struggle to liberate themselves from the predicament in which they feel they are caught. Such a salvific quest seems to be at the core of the mosaic of Taoist communities. The etymological root for the term "Taoism" is *Tao/Dao* which means "Way." In this sense, Taoism by its very name indicates that it is a way of liberation that resorts to the "Way."

The acclaimed founder of Taoism is Lao-Tzu. Both he and Confucius provided the basis not only for Taoism and Confucianism, but also for subsequent Chinese religiosity. But the Taoist salvific quest neither commenced nor concluded with Lao-Tzu. The ancient Chinese classics like the *Book of Odes* (*Shi-Jing*) contain ideas and strategies similar to those found in the writings of Lao-Tzu and his disciple Chung-Tzu. What is significant is that these ancient writings express definitive anticipations of the Taoist quest. Concepts and practices which figure in Taoism, such as filial piety, ancestor veneration, worship of multiple deities, resort to spirits, locating the underlying principle of nature in *Yin-Yang*, and divination, may be taken as expressions of age-old longings of the Chinese people to find ways and means of release from the predicament of human existence. Lao-Tzu, and later Chung-Tzu, developed these concepts and practices, reforming them to function more effectively as channels of their salvific endeavor.

There is a popular misconception that the insights of Lao-Tzu and Chung-Tzu were philosophical rather than religious, so much so their legacy gets the label "Philosophical Taoism." But their philosophical insights were not merely speculative. These dogmas arose out of the anguish that the founder leaders experienced due to the decadent sociopolitical system of the day. They intended their dogmas not merely to be philosophically appetizing but to serve as directives to transform the individual and thereby enhance the quality of communal life. During a period of social upheaval, preoccupation with metaphysical speculation becomes a waste of time. Chung-Tzu is believed to have described the logicians of his time as those who were able to subdue other people's mouths, but could not win their hearts.

With the passage of time, Taoism exhibited certain developments which one traditionally associates with religion, such as ritualistic and liturgical modes of worship, hierarchy of gods, resort to messiah figures, prescriptions for wholesome living, and strategies for attaining immortality. These developments functioned as catalysts for the transforming life that the founders aimed for. Even though some of these latter developments appear to be very different and even opposed to the views of the founders, there was an underlying motivating factor that related the religious with the philosophical facets of Taoism: the quest to liberate the Chinese people from the predicament in which they perceived themselves to be. It is in this sense that we could call the Taoist endeavor, both of the earlier and latter periods, as a salvific quest. Rodney Stark distinguishes elite and popular forms of Taoism, but is careful to point out that both are "salvational." In order to highlight the salvific character of Taoism, he cites Henri Maspero, the French Sinologist who was murdered by the Nazis in 1945. Maspero pointed out that Taoism was the Chinese attempt to create a salvation religion that aimed to lead faithful devotees to life eternal.[1] Julia Ching supports such a characterization when she points out that "Taoism can be called a 'salvation' religion [on the grounds that it assumes] a fallen state from which one is to become whole again or healed."[2]

One may justifiably characterize Taoism as a quest that aimed to free its participants from the predicament of human existence so glaringly exhibited in the turbulent years in which its founders lived—a quest that aimed at flowing with *Tao* (Way).

THE ARTICULATORS OF THE QUEST

The founders of Taoism, Lao-Tzu and his disciple Chung-Tzu, provided the philosophical and theological basis for the quest that was until then articulated predominantly through ritualistic practices. The founders did not initiate the quest but rather provided it a conceptual basis. Moreover the articulation of the Taoist quest did not end with what the founders had accomplished. After, them there were several Taoist leaders, leading up to the Neo-Taoists. Neo-Taoism transformed Taoism in certain significant ways during the third to sixth centuries CE. An examination of the lives and teachings of both the founders and their followers will help us to appreciate their respective roles in the articulation of the Taoist quest.

Lao-Tzu

Lao-Tzu is controversial in more than one way. Whether he is merely a legendary figure or a historical individual is uncertain.[3] The first mention of Lao-Tzu is in the book, *Chung-Tzu*, believed to have been authored by and named after his disciple

---

1. Stark, *Discovering God*, 260.

2. Oxtoby, *World Faiths: Eastern Traditions*, 429.

3. Kaltenmark, "Lao-Tzu," 315–18.

Chung-Tzu. Here the writer mentions that Confucius was his master-teacher who worked as a curator in the archives of the Chou dynasty. He also mentions that Lao-Tzu had met with Confucius. Ssuma Chien's *Shih-Chi* (*Historical Memoirs*), the first book on the history of ancient China, written around the second century BCE, contains a sketchy biography of Lao-Tzu. This book locates Lao-Tzu's birthplace in the village of Chu-Jen, which corresponds to the modern town of Luyi in the province of Honan, in central China. A temple called *Taich'ing Kung* (the Palace of Great Purity) along with a twelve feet high statue of Lao-Tzu now stands on the spot traditionally held to be his birthplace.

There is also controversy concerning Lao-Tzu's names. According to *Shih-Chi*, Lao-Tzu's real name was Li-Erh (surname and given name) or Li-Tan (surname and public name). But, interestingly he is called Lao-Tzu and rarely by these names. In a world where age was venerated and taken as the repository of wisdom, the name Lao-Tzu, meaning Old Master, was an honorific title.

The Chinese historian Ssuma Chien's account has some helpful observations to provide insight into Lao-Tzu's life, provided they could be taken as authentic. According to Ssuma Chein, Lao-Tzu was a court archivist of the Chou dynasty kings. Confucius is said to have visited him. Finally he went on a journey toward the west, dictated his book Tao-Te-Ching, and never returned.[4] Lao-Tzu's quest started in the court of the Chou dynasty, when he served as the curator of the archives. Such exposure allowed him to be reminded of the past glories of the Chou dynasty and also made him despondent when he realised that the China of his day was far from what it had been during the Chou dynasty. The feudal political structure that provided peace and prosperity to China was quickly crumbling. The old norms of social conduct lost their authority. While some feudal lords were unable to protect their subjects from invading armies, other lords became ruthless in the pursuit of their own selfish ambitions. While serfs became landowners and a new merchant class came into being, the old aristocratic families that were the backbone of the feudal agricultural economy became poor and powerless. Contact with the so-called barbarian neighbors forced the peripheral Chinese states to adopt new principles of governmental organization, agricultural management, and warfare strategy. Historians identify these tumultuous centuries as the "Period of Warring States."[5] It was the turbulence of such disturbing times that perpetuated an anguish among the intellectuals, an anguish that motivated them to propose diverse solutions to the problems facing the country. Confucius and Lao-Tzu best represent these intellectuals in anguish. Lao-Tzu could not bask in the glories of the Chou dynasty preserved only in the archives and at the same time experience the pathos of a society that was cracking at its core. It was such an anguish that forced Lao-Tzu to leave the comfort of his curator job and start on a journey to the west—one that is so symbolic of his quest.

4. Ibid., 318.
5. Ibid., 311–14.

The issues that Confucius and Lao-Tzu identified may appear to be political in nature, and some of their solutions have political overtones. But, we should avoid the temptation to understand the Chinese world through Western categories, by imposing the typical taxonomy of separating the political from the religious. Lao-Tzu's frustration of the sociopolitical fabric of his day had a spiritual impetus. What he offered was not a mere strategy for social reform. He presented a way for the Chinese to be liberated and thereby experience an enhanced quality of life. His book, Tao-Te-Ching, expresses glimpses of his aspirations and strategies to fulfill them. In such an endeavor, he identified himself as very much part of the quest. He never claimed to be God or even one endowed with superhuman powers.

Chuang-Tzu

Chuang-Tzu (399–295 BCE) developed on Lao-Tzu's ideas. Both agreed that the foundational strategy for liberating the Chinese is resorting to and flowing with the *Tao* (Way).

Chuang-Tzu is believed to be a contemporary of Mencius, the disciple of Confucius, and was a native of Meng. Some locate it in the province of Honan, south of the Yellow River. There is a common belief that Lao-Tzu and Chuang-Tzu came from southern China, while Confucius and Mencius were from northern China. Chuang-Tzu also authored a book that was named after him, Chuang-Tzu. Like Lao-Tzu's Tao-Te-Ching, this book also took shape during the turbulent "Period of Warring States." The author of Chuang-Tzu despised politics and advocated asceticism. It is reported that Prince Wei had once offered him the position of prime minister but he had bluntly refused it.

Chuang-Tzu's despise for the pomp and glory of politics had a rationale. In his view, there was an alternative way of flowing with the Tao; that of ascetic mysticism. His work contains descriptions of spiritual journeys, ecstatic practices, techniques of meditation such as sitting and forgetting, and mind-testing, all for the sake of experiencing a mystical union with the Tao.[6] In this respect, he seems to have gone further than his master, Lao-Tzu, in stressing the necessity of flowing with the dynamic *Tao* through mystical experiential ways.

After the Founders

After Lao-Tzu and Chuang-Tzu, there were several articulators of the Taoist quest. One group developed on the philosophical and theological ideas of the founders and the other group searched for ways and means to extend life through dietary and alchemic devices. Taoism had to confront the impact of other religions, mainly Confucianism and Buddhism. For instance, Yang Hsiung (53 BCE—18 CE) attempted to highlight the Taoist views about the world by introducing certain Confucian views. He claimed that the world originated from what he called an ineffable transcendent one who could be described only as "non-being." Neo-Taoism transformed Taoism during the third to

---

6. Oxtoby, *World Religions: Eastern Traditions*, 423.

sixth centuries CE. It was a multifaceted movement that accommodated both philo-sophical and aesthetic expressions. The most prominent articulators of Neo-Taoism were Wang-Pi/Wang Bi (226–249 CE), Hsiang Hsu, and His Kang/Xi Kang who be-longed to the group called the "Seven Worthies of the Bamboo Grove." This group was known to be a movement that protested against rules and doctrines through noncon-formist actions. One of them, Liu Ling, is supposed to have walked naked in his home. Some were lavish drinkers. Some reinterpreted Confucius as a sage united with the Tao, thus placing him higher than Lao-Tzu. The Heavenly Masters sect was greatly responsible for highlighting the religious facet of Taoism. A member of this group, Chang Ling (also called Chang Tao-ling) claimed that Lao-Tzu appeared to him on a mountain. Such an event rendered superhuman status to Lao-Tzu. This group stressed the importance of confession of sins and praying for the sick.

Our survey of the founder articulators and those who followed them has been brief and sketchy. One has to be careful in making claims concerning their lives and accomplishments, since there is considerable controversy as to whether some of them even existed. Even if they were real historical individuals, the question arises to wheth-er one could accept as authentic all that is ascribed to them. On the other hand, if their historicity is denied, one has to accommodate them as legendary figures. Nevertheless, as historical or legendary figures, they continue to have a significant impact on Taoists. Legendary though they may be, they typify the innermost aspirations of people caught up in tumultuous times such as the "Period of Warring States." These articulators played a significant role in giving shape to the Taoist quest over the centuries. The motivation for such articulation came from the fact that they were very much part of the quest and the anguish of the times. They were not divine beings revealing a way out to the people in predicament. They lived amidst the anguish of the turbulent times of Chinese history. They were determined to free themselves and their fellow beings from such a state, on the conviction that resorting to and flowing with the Tao would liberate them. Such a conviction impelled them to articulate their thoughts and strate-gies in and through their inspirational literary works and exemplary, sometimes even erotic, lifestyles. This takes us to find out how Taoist scriptures function in expressing their articulations.

SCRIPTURAL EXPRESSIONS OF THE QUEST

The most well-known scripture of Taoism is Tao-Te-Ching. The title literally means "The Classic of the Way (*Tao/Dao*) and its Virtue (*Te*)." Compared to the scriptures of other religions, Tao-Te-Ching is tiny, made up of little more than five thousand words organized into eighty-one chapters. Poetry, riddles, and paradoxes characterize its lit-erary style. There is controversy concerning its authorship. Tradition claims that Lao-Tzu dictated Tao-Te-Ching on his exit from China to the west, at the request of the guardian of a frontier city gate. But many scholars are of the view that Tao-Te-Ching is the work of several authors belonging to different regions and time periods ranging from the sixth to the third century BCE.[7]

Whether the author of Tao-Te-Ching is one or many does not really belittle the claim that the book expresses the quest of the Chinese to be liberated by resorting to the Tao. The book takes shape during times that historians call "The Period of Warring States." If the source of some of the ideas contained in the book could be located in centuries before it was written, there is reason to believe that the author(s) did not initiate the quest but rather developed on it by supplying the philosophical concepts that provided a theoretical basis for the Taoist quest. The turbulent times of the period prompted the author(s) to express their aspirations to be freed from the predicament they felt they were in through such a work. The fact that such a philosophical endeavor arose out of spiritual anguish of the authors shows how intimate the connection was between the philosophical and the religious. Whether Lao-Tzu was a real historical individual or a legendary figure who typified the aspirations of the anguished intellectuals of the turbulent times is uncertain. But one may safely conclude that Tao-Te-Ching expresses with poetic finesse the Taoist quest that the Period of Warring States generated.

The next best known Taoist scripture is that of Chuang-Tzu, the disciple of Lao Tzu. The book is called Chuang-Tzu, in keeping with the prevalent tradition of titling the book after the name of the author. Both Tao-Te-Ching and Chuang-Tzu arose out of the turbulence that the decadent sociopolitical system of the day generated. The authors of both the books wanted to get out of such a predicament. But there are some significant differences between them. Tao-Te-Ching, though applicable to the Chinese populace, seems to be specifically addressed to those in political leadership. On the other hand, Chuang-Tzu coming from the heart of a mystic seems to stress the personal and emotional facets of the strategy of getting aligned with the Tao. Such a book would naturally have a wider appeal. But neither books claim to be divinely inspired or infallible or even binding in an authoritative way. The alleged authors of the books never claimed to be recipients of divine revelation. They identified themselves with the people struggling to be free and used practices like divination and trances to obtain insights that would enable them and their fellow citizens to be free. Moreover, one cannot expect poetical and subjective mystical expressions of the insights that these works contain to be upheld as authoritative divine revelations. People took them and still continue to take them as inspirational guidelines in their quest for liberation.

The host of Taoists scriptures that came after the two classics arose from articulators belonging to a variety of sects. The present Taoist canon, containing over one thousand texts, is believed to have been compiled in 1445 CE. It includes accounts by mystical practitioners, poems, encounters with deities, advanced meditation practices, methods of achieving immortality, and so on. One naturally cannot expect these scriptures to be consistent with one another. In fact, some seem to contradict one another or even seemed to go against the views expressed in the Taoist classics.

---

7. Kaltenmark, "Lao Tzu," 326.

But such scriptural discrepancies do not deter the Taoists in considering these books as sacred scriptures. Adopting a typical Chinese syncretic mindset, Taoists tend to pick and choose whatever is conducive to enhance their life. The scriptures in Taoism function as catalysts for transformation rather than presentations of coherent doctrinal systems.

Our next task will be to examine the way of the quest that such scriptures expressed. Such an examination would also enable us to determine how Christ becomes relevant to the people involved in the Taoist Way.

THE WAY OF THE QUEST

The leading articulators of the quest, Lao-Tzu and Chuang-Tzu, received their impetus from the turbulence of their times. Considering the historical context, it is reasonable to surmise that they would have identified the corrupt political system as the cause for such a chaotic China. But, when we take into account their proposals, it is evident that they did not want to merely treat the symptom and ignore the cause of the disease. They attempted to provide a way that would generate not merely a reformed political structure but, more fundamentally, a wholesome quality of life, both individual and communal. Lao-Tzu's proposal had some political teachings addressed to rulers, but he went much further than providing a plan for political reform. Chuang-Tzu went so far as to advocate a mystical ascetic way, resulting in withdrawal from politics and even society. Nevertheless both their proposals were salvific in intent.

The Taoist way of salvation is woven around the concepts of Tao, Yin-Yang, and Wu-Wei. They were very much part of the Chinese conceptual world from age old times. The articulators used these Chinese concepts to provide a philosophical and theological basis for their salvific strategy. Speaking in the language of their culture, they naturally could relate with the people. The concept of the Tao figures foremost in their strategy.

A Way founded on Tao

Tao/Dao literally means "way," "path," or "road," and is sometimes extended to mean the principle underlying the nature and operation of the universe. Taoists had no monopoly on either the term or its meaning. But what is significant is that the Taoist thinkers, Lao-Tzu and Chuang-Tzu, gave the Tao a vital role in their way of liberation. They claimed that resort to the Tao and aligning with its dynamic flow is a must for one to be liberated. Developing on some of the meanings given to Tao in Chinese thought, these thinkers characterized it as the Transcendental, Immanent, and Normative Way. In whatever way they understood the Tao, they found it to be indispensable to the way of liberation they presented. Let us see how the Tao, taken in the above senses, functioned in the Taoist salvific strategy.

Tao as the Transcendent Way

Taoism posits the Tao as a Transcendent Way. Tao-Te-Ching characterizes it as un-nameable, indefinable, imperceptible, indiscernible, formless, and a cosmic mystery. In fact the opening lines of Tao-Te-Ching highlight how the Tao is beyond human description; that it is conceptually transcendent: "The Tao (Way) that can be told of is not the eternal Tao; The name that can be named is not the eternal name. The Nameless is the origin of Heaven and Earth; The Named is the mother of all things."[8]

To claim that the Tao is nameless was radical in Chinese literary tradition that insisted on a direct correspondence between names and what they refer to. Such a tradition considered that if something cannot be named it is not real. Lao-Tzu went against such a view. He proposed that the Tao is nameless, that it eludes literary depiction and does not fall under the typical linguistic categories (Tao-Te-Ching, chapters 32, 37, 41). But, that does not mean that the Tao could be dismissed as a mere figment of imagination. The Taoists could not afford to dismiss it thus. If their way of liberation was dependent on flowing with the Tao, it cannot be unreal. If so, any attempt to liberate oneself would be pointless. For, if what one seeks for is illusionary, then the journey would be mere dream walking and dream walks do not exhibit strategic direction. Hence the Tao, even though nameless, had to be real. Lao-Tzu's struggle to assure himself of the reality of the Transcendent Tao, despite its mysterious elusiveness, is explicit when he voices his conviction thus: "There was something undifferentiated and yet complete, which existed before heaven and earth. Soundless and formless, it depends on nothing and does not change. It operates everywhere, and is free from danger. It may be considered the mother of the universe. I do not know its name; I call it Tao. If forced to give it a name, I shall call it Great."[9]

The Tao as the Transcendent Way, even though beyond human existence and comprehension, is taken to be real. Lao-Tzu ascribes certain characteristics to the Transcendent Tao, while maintaining its mysterious elusiveness (Tao-Te-Ching, chapters 25, 32, 34, 35, 37, 39, 41, 67). It is significant that these characteristics are indispensable for the Tao to function as the ontological basis for the salvation of humanity; they are in fact salient, salvific features. Tao, as the Transcendent Way, is undifferentiated yet complete; beyond human conception (soundless, formless . . .); everything depends on it but is not dependent on anything; eternal and omnipresent; free from the limitations of human bondage, it is tranquil and not perturbed by the calamities of life; it is unique and does not resemble anything else; it provides for all to become perfect. All these features are necessary for any being to serve as the ultimate resort for those seeking to be liberated. They also feature in the God of Christianity, but there is one significant difference. The Tao is impersonal while the God of Christianity is personal. The attributes associated with personhood do not feature in the Transcendent Tao.

---

8. Quoted in Chan, *Source Book*, 139. All quotations/citations are from Chan's translation of Tao-Te-Ching unless otherwise noted.

9. Chan, *Source Book*, 152.

Tao as the Immanent Way

Presenting the Tao as a transcendent reality is necessary but not sufficient to provide an efficacious salvific strategy. After all, human beings are those who need liberation. They are the ones who are suffering in a decadent world. Hence the Tao has to be somehow or other related to humans and their world of existence. This is where Tao, as the Immanent Way, becomes indispensable to the salvific aspirations of those who resort to it.

The mysteriously elusive Tao should also be related in some tangible manner to the world of humanity. Tao, as the Immanent Way, is not only the cosmic principle of the universe but also acts as the vital principle of life. "The Great Tao flows everywhere. It may go left or right. All things depend on it for life, and it does not turn away from them. It accomplishes its task, but does not in turn claim credit for it. It clothes and feeds all things but does not claim to be master over them."[10]

In this sense, the Tao is not merely the transcendent "Ground of all Being," but also very much part of human life.

Nevertheless the Tao, as the Immanent Way, is an impersonal, amoral force that permeates all life and nature. Lao-Tzu employs metaphors like water, uncarved wood, valley, and void to describe the dynamic immanence of Tao. Lao-Tzu points out that: "Analogically, Tao in the world (where everything is embraced by it), may be compared to rivers and streams running in to the sea."[11]

Flowing water captures the inherent character of the immanent Tao. Water bypasses and gently wears away obstacles, it seeks its own level, reaches without effort the lowest levels, and nourishes living things without aggressive effort. As Andy James puts it: "Water is soft and yielding, accommodating itself to all circumstances and environments and flowing down to even the lowest of places. Yet life cannot exist without water. Even in its gentle state, it can dissolve the hard—a trickle of water in time will dissolve a mighty mountain. Water not only accommodates change but also can lend itself change. It can be a raging river, a towering tidal wave, a massive iceberg, or a scorching jet of steam."[12]

The Tao as the Immanent Way, metaphorically characterized as water, enables the Taoists to take the world of nature and life as a dynamic process.

Tao as the Normative Way

As an inherent dynamic principle of nature, the Tao also determines human behavior, in that it prescribes to humans how they should live in order to liberate themselves. In this respect, the Tao appears as a normative way. Lao-Tzu used water as a metaphor to describe the dynamics of the Immanent Tao. The symbolism is also ethical. He attempted to derive moral lessons from the properties of water. When Lao-Tzu describes

---

10. Ibid., 157.
11. Ibid., 156.
12. James, *Spiritual Legacy*, 51–52.

water as good, beneficial to all, non-competitive, non-aggressive, dwells in lowly places which all disdain, the moral overtones of the properties of water are evident.[13]

When Lao-Tzu insists that one ought to act like water, in order to flow with the Tao, morality gets involved in the Taoist way of salvation. Moral attitudes and modes of behavior play a significant role in the Taoist way of salvation. Hence, the Tao does not merely describe life as it is but how life ought to be. The main thrust of the moral codes is to enable the Taoist, who is struggling to be liberated, to flow with the Tao.

Flowing with the Tao

The problem arises when one attempts to swim against the current. The central thesis of Taoist founders was that the way out for the people of decadent China was to stop resisting the flow of the Tao and start flowing with it. Their metaphorical poetry and parables were meant to aid people change directions and flow with Tao. They traced the cancerous cause of decadent China to resistance to the Tao's flow, orchestrated especially by those who controlled the politics of the nation. But, what the Taoist thinkers proposed went far beyond political reform. They presented a way of salvation through resort to a mysteriously elusive but immanent dynamic principle of all life and nature, the Tao. The "fallen" state occurs when people resist the flow of the Tao. On the other hand, when they swim with the current and are aligned with the Tao, they are on their way to liberation. Now the question is how to flow with the Tao.

How to Flow with the Tao

Lao-Tzu and Chuang-Tzu characterized their strategy of flowing with the Tao in a certain way and their presentation may be described as the orthodox Taoist way of salvation. But, their strategy received some significant modifications and amplifications during the centuries which followed them. An examination of the original proposal along with the subsequent developments will enable us to identify the key features of the Taoist way of salvation. Such an exposure also makes us realize how Christ is relevant to the Taoist quest for "salvation." Let us first identify the main characteristics of the proposals that the founders leaders Lao-Tzu and Chuang-Tzu offered.

A Way Based on Human Experience

Lao-Tzu and Chuang-Tzu had lived through the turbulence of their times and resorted to the Tao as their source of refuge. In their struggle to find harmony with it they adopted some strategies that they found to be successful. On the grounds of such perceived success, they encouraged their fellow beings to adopt their way. The justification of their way was founded on the insights that the experience of their personal spiritual journey offered. Hence their way of liberation originated from and was shaped by the challenges they faced in life rather than from any sort of divine revelation.

13. Chan, *Source Book*, 143.

A Way Directed by the Dynamics of Yin-Yang

From ancient times, the Chinese viewed the universe as being orchestrated by two contrary yet complementary elements or forces called *Yin* and *Yang*. Such a dichotomy not only characterizes material things but also persons, events, concepts, moral values, and even the spirit world. Yang, described as masculine, represents the active, bright, positive, dry, and warm facets of the universe. On the other hand, Yin, described as feminine, stands for the passive, dark, negative, moist, and cool aspects of the universe. The Yin-Yang is more than a simplistic taxonomy; it is rather a way to comprehend the core character and inner workings of the world of nature, spirits, and humans.

Yin and Yang are taken to be not only opposite but also complementary to each other. The popular diagrammatic representation of Yin-Yang exhibits how each is related to the other.

Yin-Yang

The dark section in the circle represents the Yin, while the white section shows the Yang.

As the diagram shows, Yin and Yang bulge into each other. Moreover, there is a dark Yin spot in the white Yang area and a white Yang spot in the dark Yin area. This means there cannot be anything that is totally Yin or Yang; in any realm, even in the realm of moral values, there is nothing that is totally good or fully bad. There is something that is good in bad and vice versa. The Taoist thinkers saw the whole of reality, the heavenly and the earthly, and every facet of life through the lens of Yin-Yang. Lao-Tzu points out that when people look at their world, they recognize the dynamics of Yin-Yang. He puts it this way: "When people of the world all know beauty as beauty, there arises the recognition of ugliness. When they all know good as good, there arises the recognition of evil. Therefore: Being and non-being produce each other; difficult and easy compel each other; long and short contract each other; high and low distinguish each other; sound and voice harmonize with each other; front and back follow each other."[14]

Lao-Tzu captures the dynamics of Yin-Yang in heaven thus, "The Way of Heaven does not compete, and yet it skilfully achieves victory. It does not speak, and yet it responds skilfully to things. It is not anxious about things, and yet it plans well . . . "[15]

Chuang-Tzu went a step further and claimed that opposites are really identical. According to him, dualities such as like and dislike, large and small, life and death, knowledge and ignorance, finite and infinite are identical aspects of one and the same reality. Tradition has it that once Chuang-Tzu had dreamt that he was a butterfly. After waking up he is supposed to have stated, that he did not know whether he had dreamt that he was a butterfly or whether he was butterfly dreaming that he was Chuang-Tzu.

The Taoist articulators not only saw the whole of reality, the earthly and the heavenly, through the Yin-Yang dynamics, but went a step further and used it as a

14. Ibid., 140.

15 Ibid., 173.

directive in the way of healing of the body and more fundamentally in the liberation of humans. Yin-Yang is the basis for Chinese medicine. Since Yin and Yang, though opposites yet are complementary, health (Yang) is not totally devoid of sickness (Yin). There is bound to be some sickness in health and vice versa. Chinese medicine is geared to make a person healthy by creating a state of balance where Yang is not over shadowed by Yin.[16]

The Taoist is directed to cultivate the Yin-Yang dynamics in his or her quest for liberation. Lao-Tzu's directive runs thus: "Act without action, do without ado, taste without tasting. Whether it be big or small, many or few, repay hatred with virtue. Prepare for the difficult while it is still easy, deal with the big while it is still small."[17]

One could identify the play of Yin-Yang dynamics in these directives which are asking one to do opposite things, such as "taste without tasting."

When a person is liberated, he or she exhibits the Yin-Yang interplay at its best. This liberated state receives the name Wu-Wei. It refers to the climax point of the Taoist way of salvation. The popular English translation of the term as non-action gives a wrong idea that Wu-Wei is merely negative passivity. Wu-Wei is not mere absence of action, but rather being active while being passive. This is taken to be the perfect harmony that Yin-Yang dynamics generate. Lao-Tzu identifies a person who has reached this state of Wu-Wei as a sage; as one who exhibits virtue (*te*). He characterizes a sage as one who manages affairs without action, spreads doctrines without words, produces things but does not take possession of them, and accomplishes his task without taking credit for it. Such a sage does not strive to be great and yet has achieved greatness.[18] Hence the founders gave a vital role to Yin-Yang dynamics in their way of salvation. Yin-Yang provides the directive to be followed to flow with Tao, and the perfect balance between Yin and Yang exhibits the core character of the person who had been liberated—Wu Wei.

A Way that is Salvific Rather than Reformative

What Lao-Tzu and Chuang-Tzu proposed was much more than a strategy for political and social reform. Their way was holistically transformative rather than merely reformative; they were spiritual articulators rather than mere social reformists. Their strategy aimed to provide what they described as "tranquility." This quality of "tranquility" characterizes Tao, which is free from all desires.[19] For Lao-Tzu, when one returns to the flow of the Tao, "tranquility" results. He puts it this way: "All things come into being, and I see thereby their return. All things flourish, but each one returns to its root. This return to its root means tranquility. It is called returning to its destiny. To return

16. Maciocia, *Foundations*, 1; James, *Spiritual Legacy*, 87–89.

17. Chan, *Source Book*, 169; also 157.

18. Ibid., 140, 157.

19. Ibid., 158.

to destiny is called the eternal (*Tao*). To know the eternal is called enlightenment. Not to know the eternal is to act blindly, to result in disaster."[20]

Return to the Tao results in the seeker being enlightened. "Tranquility" is not acquired through mere reformatory methods, whether political, ethical, or even psychological. It is made possible through a definitive change of directions in the spiritual journey of a seeker. There are two ways a seeker could take: the way of flowing with the Tao or the way of flowing against it. Problems arise when one attempts to swim against the current. But, when a seeker changes directions and flows with the Tao, he or she is on the road to liberation; to Wu-Wei, which entails "tranquility."

But, to flow with the Tao, one has to first know about it. Lao-Tzu claims that knowing the eternal Tao leads to enlightenment, while not knowing it ends in disaster.[21] But, what type of knowledge does one need to accomplish such a task? Since the Tao is beyond human comprehension, one needs to resort to a kind of intuitive wisdom rather than traditional modes of knowledge. Knowledge, validated through the laws of non-contradiction and excluded middle will not help a seeker to flow with and be identified with the Tao. Its mysterious elusiveness and the interplay of Yin-Yang in its dynamics challenge the very foundations of the logic of traditional knowledge. The law of non-ontradiction stipulates that contradictory claims cannot coexist, while the law of excluded middle states that, if one makes a claim about something, then asserting its contradictory is excluded. Then how could one accommodate these laws of logic foundational to traditional knowledge, and at the same time claim that contradictions are complementary and even identical? That is why Lao-Tzu claimed that a seeker should possess a superior intelligence or *ming* (light), to be equipped with the type of knowledge that would enable one to know the Tao and thereby flow with it. For him, such knowledge is not intellectual or even spiritual in the sense of being in fellowship with a personal god. It is a matter of identifying oneself with the Tao through an inward realization of its unity, simplicity, and emptiness.[22] Chuang-Tzu, who claimed that opposites are identical, had to go further than Lao-Tzu's superior intelligence (*ming*). Chuang-Tzu insisted that the spiritual journey had to be founded on mystical experiences, demanding ascetic withdrawal from activities of the mundane world.

Moreover, the "tranquility" that Taoist enlightenment generates is still conditioned by Yin-Yang dynamics. Even though the state of Wu-Wei exhibits a harmonization of Yin and Yang, yet it cannot be an absolute permanent state of existence. Wherever Yin-Yang is at work, there is bound to be change; there is always the possibility for Yin to overshadow the Yang and thereby put the state of Wu-Wei out of balance. Hence Chuang-Tzu claimed that the spiritual journey is not a final return to Origin (*Fe*) and staying there permanently. For him life is an eternal transformation (*hua*) from one state to another. He takes the spiritual journey as an infinite process of

---

20. Ibid., 147.

21. Ibid.

22. Kaltenmark, "Lao-Tzu," 327.

change or transformation that involves ceaseless mutations with no final end. Chuang-Tzu no doubt acknowledges that when a seeker attains Wu-Wei there is a "tranquility" that transcends description. Even though Wu-Wei is the ideal state in the process of transformation, it is not an absolute end. Every stage in the process, including Wu-Wei, is conditioned by the dynamics of Yin-Yang. Wu-Wei does exhibit the harmonic interplay of Yin-Yang, but such a state, ideal though it may be, would not last forever. Hence the enlightenment that Wu-Wei depicts carries with it a sense of insecurity. It is not surprising that the Taoist leaders who followed Lao-Tzu and Chuang-Tzu made desperate attempts to provide ways and means to overcome this sense of insecurity. We will have occasion to discuss their attempts later on in this chapter.

A Way Based on Human Effort

The passivity that features in flowing with the Tao could prompt us to conclude that the Taoist way of salvation involves no human effort but is rather a fatalist acceptance of things. This is only partially true. No doubt when one flows with the Tao there is a progressive surrender to it. But, such a progressive passive surrender to Tao does not imply that the Taoist way does not involve human effort.

The Tao is an impersonal dynamic force. It flows in its own way and no one can change its course. It is not a person and hence it cannot be sensitive to the needs of those who want to be aligned with its flow. It cannot help and one cannot expect any sympathy from it. Those who seek liberation have to passively allow themselves to get in line with the flow of this impersonal force. This means that the passive resignation to the Tao's flow is really a kind of effort; the seeker has to flow with the Tao rather than get its help. Lao-Tzu's advocacy of acquiring "superior intelligence" and Chuang-Tzu's preference for mystical encounters are meant to enable one to flow with the Tao; they are salvific strategies based on human effort.

The Taoist strategy of the founders was essentially salvific, even though it did not exhibit the traditional features of a religion. Nevertheless, it was more than philosophical speculation or strategy for social reform. These founders were mystic poets articulating a spiritual quest that arose out of the turbulence of their times—a quest that was determined to provide a way to be in harmony with the Tao, in order to be liberated. Even though the founders had completed their task, the quest of their followers did not come to an end. The amplifications and modifications that the followers brought about are significant in more than one way. First of all, these developments added to Taoism attributes that are so characteristic of a religion. Moreover, these changes indicate that the followers found the way of liberation their leaders had formulated lacking in some respects. The revisions wrought by several Taoist sects were meant to make the Taoist way of salvation more productive.

Most significantly the subsequent developments in Taoism exhibit some fundamental facets of the quest of the diverse Taoist sects: the search for God, resort to messiah figures, striving for eternal life, plea for "grace," and attempts to be assured of one's salvation. We could place these subsequent developments under the heading, "The

Quest of Latter Taoism." This is where Christ becomes more relevant to the aspirations of the Taoists.

THE QUEST OF LATTER TAOISM

The Search for God

Deities and demons have been very much part of the Chinese life. Lao-Tzu and Chuang-Tzu no doubt downplayed deities but they could not deter their followers searching for God, and that too for a Savior God.

One thing the Tao lacked was personhood. Dynamic though it may be, it could not, by its very nature, respond to the anguish and innermost aspirations of human beings; it could not in any way express its feelings, whether love or hatred, to the people who resorted to it.

What Taoists needed was Tao as a person—someone with whom they could relate. Hence, they resorted to a diverse pantheon of gods: celestial beings, immortals, divinized human heroes, and personifications of nature. But amidst such varied resorts we could identify a significant trend—a search for a God having the character and capabilities to save humanity. Some gods displaying such characteristics were already there in China. During the period of the Shang dynasty (1751–1123 BCE) the Chinese worshiped a deity called *Shan-Ti* or *Ti*, one who ruled from high. During the period of the Chou dynasty (1122–256 BCE), *Tian* (heaven) replaced *Shang-Ti*. He was worshipped as a supreme power of the heavenly regions, governing the world through rewarding the righteous and punishing the wicked. After the time of the Han dynasty (206 BCE—220 CE) a triad of gods came to be worshiped, under different names: *T'ien* (the Heavenly One), *Ti-Yi* (the Earthly One) and *Tai-Yi* (the Great One). The first two came to be personified as the transcendent and immanent emanations of the Tao. The third one was Lao-Tzu deified. In fact, what was called the Three Pure Ones, *Yi-Ch'ing* (Jade Pure), *Shang-Ch'ing* (Upper Pure), and *Tai-Ch'ing* (Great Pure) were taken as different manifestations of Lao-Tzu. Their role was to save mankind through teaching his doctrines and expressing his compassion. Lao-Tzu never claimed to be God, but after his death, Lao-Tzu came to be deified. It is believed that such deification commenced around 165 CE, when Emperor Hunan ordered a statue of Lao Tzu to be erected and rituals to be performed at his birthplace.[23] When Taoists deified Lao-Tzu, they had in their quest for salvation a source of superhuman help. The depiction of Lao-Tzu as a savior god took many forms. Some Taoists believed that he emerged originally from a state of chaos and eventually achieved an incarnate form and came as savior to humans.[24] Some attempted to accentuate his super humanity by claiming that his mother carried him in her womb for seventy-two years.[25] After the arrival of Buddhism in China, some even claimed that he was a Chinese manifestation of Buddha. This clearly indicates that the Taoists needed much more than Lao-Tzu's

23. Baldrian, "Taoism," 293.

24. Boltz, "Lao Tzu," 455.

25. Baldrian, "Taoism," 293–94.

teachings, profound though they may be. They wanted him to be savior god. Yu-huang, the son of an emperor, was another human deified. He was venerated as one ruling heaven, controlling the destiny of people, ruling them with justice and compassion. Another popular divine triad was *San-kuan* (three officials). They ruled over the regions of the universe and helped mankind in many ways. *Tien-kuan*, Ruler of Heaven, granted happiness, *Ti-kuan*, Ruler of Earth, granted remission of sins, while *Shu-kuan*, Ruler of the Watery World (hell) protected people from evil. Their compassion for people was unbounded. But such compassion could only generate from the heart of a person and not from an impersonal Tao. Such a resort to gods and deifications of humans indicate that the Taoists need a personal god, who could share their feelings, understand their anxieties, and help them in ways they as humans could handle—a god who they could worship, praise him for blessings, blame him for their problems, ask him forgiveness for their sins, and take refuge in him.

The "tranquility" that results, when one attains Wu-Wei, whether through supersensory knowledge or mystical experiences, lacks that personal relationship with the source of help. The "tranquility" that one claims to experience is similar to the confidence one gets when swimming with the current rather than against it. The Taoists could resort to the Tao but could not take refuge in it. They needed a source of help that was personal, and hence they resorted to a god, who has personhood.

Moreover, such a god should not only be compassionate but also be capable to save. What is the point of having a kind god who does not have the capability to help humanity? Amidst the pantheon of gods, the Taoists developed a hierarchy of gods; the most powerful god ranked highest on the ladder. During the second century BCE, this was *Tai-Yi* (The Great One). A triad of gods arose to popularity, because of the power attributed to them. "The Primal Celestial One" controlled the past, "The Precious Celestial One" controlled the present, while The "Way-and-its Power Celestial One" had power over the future. Some claim that the similarity between the Taoist and Christian formulation of Trinity is due to the influence of Nestorian Christianity, which was present in China during this time.[26] Whether or not we accept such a claim, we could justifiably conclude that the veneration of powerful gods suggests that the Taoists were searching for not only a kind and compassionate god, but also one who had the power to save them: an almighty god.

A god could be extremely compassionate and powerful, but unless such a god takes some concrete salvific action there is no benefit to the suffering humanity. Such a god should show his power and compassion in and through definitive salvific action.

Theophanic episodes may be taken as salvific acts. According to a popular Taoist sect, the Heavenly Masters, Lao-Tzu featured as Lord Lao, had appeared to the founder of the sect, Chang-Ling, through a theophany, and had instructed him about the correct way of liberation. Tradition has it that Chang-Ling ascended to heaven, received his mandate from Lord Lao and established the Heavenly Masters sect, whose doctrines and practices are founded on Lord Lao's instructions. Hence, Lao-Tzu came to

---

26. Oxtoby, *World Religions: Eastern Traditions*, 430.

be taken as more than a teacher; he was given the status of a divine being enabling Taoists to be saved in and through theophanies.

Incarnations constitute another kind of salvific action. Lu-Tung-Pin, one of the Eight Immortals, became very popular among the Taoists. He is believed to have been a doctor and scholar during his lifetime (755–805 CE). After his death he came to be venerated as the King of Medicine and many temples were built in his honor. The reason for his popularity was not merely his knowledge of medicine, but rather his incarnations, which proved to be salvific in nature. According to popular belief, he incarnates from time to time to guide people into a healthy and righteous way of life and thereby enables them to attain immortal life.

Lu-Tung-Pin, most popular of the Eight Immortals

No doubt the Tao as the Immanent Way has an incarnational feature, in that it is very much part of the dynamics of world, including humanity. But, the incarnations of Taoist deities, like immortal Lu-Tung-Pin, are very different from those of the Tao as the Immanent Way. Lu-Tung-Pin, being a divine person rather than an impersonal force, incarnates as a result of an act of will compelled by compassion to save humanity. Even though the Taoists acknowledge the Tao as the Immanent Way, and flowing with it is necessary for salvation, they love, venerate, and worship Lu-Tung-Pin as a god who incarnates to help them in their time of need.

The search for god that latter Taoism exhibits is one that longs for an almighty, compassionate god who saves humanity in and through definitive salvific acts such as incarnations. The efforts of latter Taoists to personify the Tao, deify leaders like Lao-Tzu and emperors, construct a hierarchy of gods based on their respective powers, adore gods who show their power and compassion by becoming part of humanity in times of crisis are all facets of the Taoist search for a savior god. Such efforts help us to appreciate the relevance of Christ to the Taoist quest.

Resort to Messiahs

The resort to messiahs is closely tied up with the Taoist search for a savior god. Both these trends have the same impetus: the realization that self-effort is inadequate and hence resort to other sources of help—human or superhuman—becomes an absolute necessity.

The Taoism that Lao-Tzu and Chuang-Tzu articulated was a way of salvation essentially through self-effort. Seekers had to rely on their own ability to become aware of the way in which Tao operates and to align themselves with it. Even the mystical path that Chuang-Tzu advocated was individualistic, depending on one's own spiritual strength.

During the first and second centuries, Taoist messianic movements led by charismatic leaders multiplied. An ancient sacred text, Tai-ping Ching/Taiping jing (Classic of the Great Peace) stated that one could hope for an age of great peace. Building on this idea, several messiah figures cropped up claiming to usher in that age of peace. They were either gifted or divinely empowered. Some even claimed to be reincarnations of Lao-Tzu. These messiahs appeared during times of political crisis. Even though they attempted to free the Chinese from political anarchy, they were more than political reformists; they used Taoist ideological strategies to generate a state of harmony, Wu-Wei, on an individualistic as well as on a communal basis. Some of them claimed to have divine empowerment. Hence, their impact was more than political. It was salvific in nature, aiming to transform not only the individual but also the community, and in fact all humanity.

The resort to messiahs forcibly suggests that Taoists need help from sources other than their own. They need a messiah that is equipped with an effective salvific strategy which would not merely solve the immediate political problems but generate a wholesome society. For such a task to be accomplished the messiah has to be divinely empowered. Christ seems to meet the requirements of the messiah that the Taoists long for. He is not only divinely empowered but is divine. He does not need to adopt any salvific strategy; he is himself the way of salvation.

Striving for Eternal Life

Taoism does not dismiss human life as an illusion but places a high value on life. This naturally leads to finding ways to lengthen it. Latter Taoism developed some significant strategies to lengthen life that are significant in more than one way. They helped Taoism to become popular, especially among the masses. People want to live long. The longevity practices aimed to meet this longing. Chinese believe that a human being contains three life principles: the generative force/semen (*Ching*), the vital life force/breath (*Ch'i*), and spirit (*shen*);[27] when these three are activated, the human being could have a longer and, in fact, an immortal life. Based on such a belief Taoists developed several methods to extend life. They fall into three main categories: practices which aim to make the body healthy, those which attempt to equip the mind, and those that try to strengthen the human spirit. Since the Taoists do not separate the body, mind, and spirit, these practices intermingle in their functioning to lengthen life.

Practices like dietary regulations, fasting, sexual restraint, respiratory techniques, and alchemy aimed to enable the body to function efficiently. Some adopted strict dietary rules, restricting the eating of solid foods and even living on saliva and air. Some employed breath-control techniques similar to those used by Hindu yogic hermits. Alchemy was another popular means of extending life. Some used minerals like gold to prevent the body from decaying. Some second and third-century Taoist texts

27. Ibid., 433.

mention alchemic experiments.[28] Practices like vocalizations, absorption of solar energy, breathing techniques, visualizations, and meditations, though meant to equip the mind, also help the body. Combined in various ways these methods today are known as *Chi'kung* or energy training.

Both the alchemist experiments and *Chi'kung* exercises took Taoists into the realm of the divine. They realized that gods could be involved in the magic of their alchemy. As stoves were used in their experiments, they began to offer sacrifices to the god of the stove, *Taso Chun*. Eventually several other gods came to be included in the alchemic ritual of extending life. Through their help, Taoists claimed that they were cured of sicknesses. Priests used certain formulas to restore vital energy *(ch'i)* and some performed exorcisms to ward off evil spirits. Prophets, divine healers, and occult practitioners enabled Taoism to become a popular common man's religion.

Such strategies attempted not merely to lengthen life but also enhance the quality of life; they had a transformative thrust. They turned out to be a means to free oneself from the bondage of present life end enter into an ideal mode of existence. Such a move carried with it a noticeable replacement of the goal of the quest. The search for immortal life turned out to be a striving for "eternal life"; the latter understood as qualitatively different from the former. This is where Christ, as the provider of eternal life, becomes relevant to the Taoist striving.

Lao-Tzu claimed that the way to lengthen life is to be aligned with the Tao. Latter Taoists resorted to personal gods, which gave them a life-model to aim for. Even though the lives of some gods could not qualify as "models" to be emulated, deities like the Eight Immortals, and the deified Lao-Tzu, were reputed for their character and compassion; their lives served as ideal models to be followed. Hence, the longevity practices became means to become like gods and thereby achieve a quality of life that is not only immortal but also wholesome. Julia Ching points out: "True, the quest for physical immortality may seem rather earthly, yet the wish for immortality contains within itself a quest for transcendence. To become godlike—powerful like the gods or immortal like the gods—has always been the deepest of human longings."[29]

When Taoists compared their lives with those of some gods, the difference was obvious. They realized their decadent state and craved for a "godly" life. In their quest for wholeness, they began to associate human decadence and sickness with "sin," understood as an offence against the gods. In and through longevity practices, they attempted to free themselves from such "sin" and attain a godlike life.

In 1972, in Mawangdui, near Chang Sha, Hunan, archaeologists discovered a body from second century BCE. It was well preserved and immersed in a liquid containing mercuric sulphide. There were talismans designed to conduct the diseased to her eternal residence into the presence of the Lord-on-high.[30] What is significant about this find is that the longevity practice included not only alchemic use but also some

---

28. Ibid., 434.

29. Ching, "East Asian Religions," 429.

30. Ibid., 434.

ritualistic techniques to usher the deceased into a life that is not mere continuation of the present life but one that is in god's presence. The transformative thrust of Taoist longevity practices is evident in such a find.

Inner alchemy or embryonic respiration is a longevity practice involving complex meditation and physical techniques. The complex esoteric technique aims to transform the person to a transcendent level of existence, where the human spirit could function without the encumbrances of the flesh. This enables one to have out-of-body experiences and a foretaste of the life in the spirit that is believed to occur after death.[31] Such practices were geared to deliver a quality of life that was different from the mundane life on earth; they attempted to transform rather than lengthen life.

Another type of meditation involving the channeling of vital energy is *Taijiquan*, popularly known as *Tai-Chi*. Though very much a martial art, it became a technique to provide a mode of existence that is different from the aggressive rat-race life. Tai-chi looks like swimming in the air, involving continuous non-aggressive circular movements. Taoism claims that "salvation" is possible only when one flows with the Tao, and not against it. Tai-chi is a mode of exercise aimed at becoming aligned with the flow of the Tao, and thereby generating a tranquil state. Hence, Tai-chi is much more than physical exercise for healthy living. Utterly disappointed with attempts to market Tai-Chi in the West as an exercise routine to be mastered in a weekend or even in minutes, Andy James points out that "this is a pity because the secret of *taijiquan's* mysterious benefits lies as much in the intention (*yi*) behind the physical movements as in the shape (*xing*) of these movements. The adage in *qigong* that the *yi*, or intention guides the *qi*, which in turn guides the physical body, applies no less to *taijiquan* and to other internal martial arts—not to mention meditation and the rest of our lives. In our scramble for the "quick fix", we may be casting aside one of humanity's true pearls."[32]

No doubt Tai-chi involves physical exercise, but such exercise is impelled by one's intention to free oneself from the entanglements of aggressive life and attaining a harmonious life attuned to Tao. Andy James describes the holistic character of the exercise thus: "*Taijiquan* is unique and remarkable because it is an extremely effective martial art, a moving meditation, a mind-body exercise, and a physical expression of Daoist yin-yang philosophy, all wrapped in a beautiful package of dancelike movement."[33]

The transformative overtone of Tai-chi is evident in the way Taoists practice it.

Devotee performing Tai Chi

31. Ibid., 11. See also Fisher, *Living Religions*, 197–98.

32. James, *Spiritual Legacy*, 122.

33. Ibid., 124.

The transformative thrust of these longevity practices changes the search for immortality to a striving for "eternal life." When Taoists attempt to attain a godlike life, free from the sins of the flesh and able to transcend the body, the quest is for an entirely different type of life. The mortuary rituals of the Taoist sect, Celestial Masters, also exhibit such a thrust. Funeral rites generally included exorcisms to prevent evil spirits from harassing the dead. The Celestial Masters, led by Zhang Daoling, went further in the practice of mortuary rites over the deceased. They promised "liberation from death and promotion to celestial transcendence."[34] The funeral procession was taken as symbolizing "the soul's journey from the tomb to transcendence."[35] The Celestial Masters hoped that through such mortuary rites and funeral rituals the dead could attain a life that transcends life on earth; a life in the presence of gods who were taken as emanations of Tao itself. What these Taoists were really striving for was not immortal life but a type of life that is qualitatively different from lengthened human life: eternal life.

Plea for Mercy

Wu-Wei is the arrival point of the spiritual journey of a Taoist. The "tranquility" that it offers gives Taoists a peace of mind, a sense of confidence that they are swimming with the current and not against it. Even though enthralled with the "tranquility" that Wu-Wei generates, the devotees are still unable to forget the "sins" of their past. There still lingers a conscience-pricking sense of guilt for "sins." Flowing with the Tao and attaining Wu-Wei does not include any repentance or confession of sins. One cannot repent or confess to an impersonal Tao. Hence, they needed a way to be freed from the haunting sense of guilt that sin entails.

A sect called The Way of Great Peace (*Taiping-Tao*) of the Han dynasty period (206 BCE—220 CE) developed such a strategy. Its scriptures, *Taiping-Jing*, tells how one could handle the "guilt of sin" through certain rituals. The penitent was put into a private chamber to purify oneself through fasting, meditation, reflection on past deeds, and appealing to various gods for help. This was followed by repentance of sins; expressions such as "remember one's sins," "meditate on one's trespasses," and "face one's sins" were commonly used. Confessions for this sect were not merely to relieve stress. The practice of confession arose out of a worldview that *Taiping-Jing* presents.[36] It explains the interaction between sins and diseases by positing a primordial spiritual energy (*yuangi*) permeating the three main components of existence: heaven, earth, and humanity. This energy divides itself into three factors: spirit (*shen*) associated with heaven, essence (*jing*) with earth, and vital energy of harmony (*yi*) associated with humanity. Human beings contain in microscopic manner these three powers.

When a human being commits "sin," the flow of energy of heaven and earth is cut off. In fact, the spirit deserts the body, leaving the sinner morally decadent, spiritually dead, and leading a life akin to beasts. Heaven hates this state of affairs and inflicts

34. Nickerson, "Opening," 60.
35. Ibid., 73.
36. Masaaki, "Confession," 39–57.

sickness on the sinner. As Tsuchiya Masaaki points out: "According to the *Taiping-jing*, sickness is therefore the expression of displeasure at human misdeeds on the side of the spirit(s) of Heaven (*tianshen*) and not the automatic effect of an imbalance or disharmony of energy."[37]

For sickness to be heaven's expression of displeasure of human "sin," heaven has to be a person with moral sensitivity and not a mere impersonal force. Latter Taoists personified heaven and call it the Lord of Heaven (*tianjun),* who judges and evaluates human behavior with the aid of numerous deities and spirits. What we have to note here is that the Taoists of this religious sect developed the concept of "sin" in relation to the personhood of heaven. It cannot be displeased with "sin" unless it is a person. The infliction of sickness on the sinner is because heaven hates sin as evil.

Such a worldview that posits a connection between sin and sickness provides the rationale for confession. To enable the spirit to return to the body of the sinner, and thereby cure the sickness, the body first has to be purified. Sitting in an "incense chamber," fasting, meditating, practicing bodily refinements, and abstaining from sexual activities and passions were all taken as effective means of purification, but in themselves inadequate to free the sinner from sin and its bondage. This is where the act of confession becomes indispensable in the purification process. It aids in the expulsion of the defilement of sin.[38] In and through confession, the sinner accepts one's sin and also realizes the inability to free oneself from sin. This is where confession turns into an appeal to heaven. Heaven being personified has the capacity to hear human pleas, recognize human sincerity, react with pity and compassion, and grant forgiveness. But forgiveness from heaven cannot be mechanically orchestrated; the sinner had to depend on heaven's mercy. This is where the quest of the latter Taoists, as articulated especially by the members of The Way of Great Peace, turned out to be a plea for mercy.

Taoists wanted to be freed from sin, its guilt and bondage and formulated a strategy that exhibited a desperate plea for mercy. This is another place where Christ becomes relevant to the Taoist quest. Repentance of sin is indispensable to be freed from it through Christ.

Strategies to be Assured of Salvation

The search for gods, resort to messiah figures, striving for eternal life, and plea for mercy all have an underlying salvific motive. Taoists resort to such strategies so that they can be freed from the predicament in which they feel they are in and attain a mode of existence that would be rewarding. But they need one thing more. If and when they achieve what they strive for, they need an assurance that they have arrived, that what they hope for has been realized. What they so desperately need is "an assurance of liberation."

37. Ibid., 44–45.
38. Ibid., 45.

Latter Taoists did not, of course, forsake their foundational dictum—that flowing with the Tao is indispensable for their salvation. Nevertheless they could not expect the impersonal Tao to provide the assurance they needed. Hence, they had to resort to something personal. This they found in gods. Being personal in nature, they were capable of being sensitive to the penitent, compassionate to their confessions, forgiving of their sins, and merciful to their pleas. But, the question still lingers. What is the assurance that their confessions have been heard, their sins have been forgiven, and mercy has been granted? Taoists orchestrated several strategies to be assured of their salvation. These could be placed under two main categories: ritualistic and revelatory.

Amidst several Taoist rites and rituals, two are noteworthy. They help to understand how Taoists use rituals to assure their salvation. These modes pertain to certain kinds of offerings and written documents.

Taoist offerings include incense, flowers, tea, wine, vegetarian and non-vegetarian foods, money, jewelry, and even utensils. Through such offerings the devotees want not only to convey a message to the deities but also be assured that they respond to it with favor. Though the message contained a multiplicity of appeals for various kinds of blessings, it was essentially a salvific plea. The response anticipated was that the plea has been granted, that salvation has been assured.

Offerings were both a way of expressing the penitence of the devotees and a way of assuring them that the deities have responded with favor. No wonder the practice of offerings to deities was so meticulously structured. Priests officiate in the offering ceremonies since the penitent devotees need a holy mediator. Even today in Taiwan the priests belonging to the lineage of Celestial Masters perform this ritual following meticulously the directions given in a sacred text, *Yaoyang wupin dan* (*List of Essential Goods*).[39] Foods offered to deities were carefully selected, delicacies that they would relish. Offering fruits is popular in many religions. But in Taoism it receives an added salvific significance. Fruits for such offerings should be fresh, washed, and clean. Pomegranates and other fruits supposed to contain unclean and muddy substances were excluded. The fruits have not only be palatable to the gods but also very much like them. Numerous ritual texts in the Taoist cannon list fruit as a key offering.[40] Other Taoist texts exclude vegetables fertilized by manure or human waste, as they are taken to be impure.[41] What we find in such a meticulous selection is the emphasis that the offering has to match the high gods in their purity to be efficacious as a means to obtain their favor. The offerings were taken to be a means to please the gods and thereby feel assured of the salvation of the penitent devotees

Eating meat is generally understood to defile the soul. Usually both the officiating priests and the participating devotees are forbidden to eat meat prior to and during the ritual. But Taoists accommodate meat offerings. Goats are offered to gods like the Jade Emperor, who the Taoists treated as a supreme deity, comparable to a traditional

39. Haruji, "Offerings," 274–75.
40. Ibid., 286.
41. Ibid.

Chinese emperor. The offering to him had to be in the form of a royal banquet with high class goat meat.[42] The purpose of meat offerings was to please the gods by giving them the meal that would satisfy their taste and thereby gain their favor.

The second strategy to be assured of one's liberation may be described as revelatory. A key component of Taoist rituals was the use of various forms of written documents—memorials, petitions, pronouncements, letters, and inscribed utensils. Such documents enabled the Taoists to have a well-defined systematic interaction with the other world. The penitent devotees used the documents to articulate their pleas. Moreover, the writs, orders, and pronouncements taken to be responses from the deities gave the assurance the devotees craved for—the assurance that their pleas have been granted. There is a salvific overtone characterizing these documents. Usually a ritual commenced with an announcement. One such announcement runs thus: "Respectfully and sincerely, your servant prays for mercy and grace from the Great Dao. I humbly beg that you grant my wish. From now on, day and night, let us receive your radiance of grace and accept our testimony of deliverance and salvation. To this end, I humbly present the various talismans and writs I have, properly sealed and executed by me."[43]

The Taoists used such announcements to articulate their confessions in a liturgically structured manner. The response to such confessions came in the form of writs of pardon, pronouncements of deliverance, and orders to the spirits of the underworld not to harass the penitent devotees. These fall under the revelatory strategy. The officiating priest took upon himself the role of a heavenly bureaucrat. He opened the sealed talismans and read the contents on behalf of heaven, pronouncing pardon and deliverance.[44] It is here we see how Taoists combined ritualistic and revelatory methods in order to be assured of their liberation. The penitent devotees felt assured that they have been pardoned on the grounds that the announcement came from heaven enacted through the officiating priest. Taoists rigorously practiced such rituals so as to be assured of their salvation.

The search for a savior god, resort to messiahs, striving for eternal life, pleas for mercy, and strategies to be assured of "salvation" that characterize latter Taoism makes Christ very relevant to the Taoist quest.

THE RELEVANCE OF CHRIST TO THE TAOIST QUEST

Whether we characterize Taoism as philosophical or religious, ritualistic or mystical, we could justifiably claim that the Taoists are seriously involved in a salvific quest. The foundational dictum of the Taoist quest is that one could attain liberation, Wu-Wei, only by becoming fully aligned with the Tao, the Way.

Lao-Tzu and Chuang-Tzu had stipulated certain requirements the Tao should meet to function as the ontological basis of the Taoist way of salvation. Later on, Taoists made some additional stipulations for the Tao to function more effectively.

42. Ibid., 281.

43. Hiroshi, "Documents," 256.

44. Ibid., 272.

When one takes into consideration both the original and subsequent characterizations of the Tao, one is able to discern what Taoists are really aspiring for, what type of Way (Tao) they are attempting to construct as an ontological basis for their way of salvation. It is precisely here that Christ becomes relevant to the Taoist quest. Christ seems to fulfill what the Taoists aspire Tao to be, both in character and function.

Taoism commences with the stipulation that the Tao should be both transcendent and immanent. It should not be in any way dependent on the humanity that is striving to be liberated. Nevertheless it should also be somehow or other intimately connected with humanity. Taoists stipulate that what they resort to for their salvation should be involved with humanity and yet not caught up in their predicament. God in Christ meets both these requirements. Christ, as God, is transcendent and hence not caught up in the predicament of sinful humanity. Yet through his incarnation he becomes very much part of humanity. He is God in human flesh and yet totally free from sin that besets humanity.

Taoists also realized that what they resort to should be personal in nature. Hence, they searched for a personal savior god. This they found in a hierarchy of gods, leading up to the Three Pure Ones. What the Taoists need is a divine personal being, who would be able to liberate them in a personal manner—one who would be sensitive to their needs compassionate to their cries, forgive their sins, and free them from their bondage, someone who would intentionally help them and with whom they could relate in a meaningful manner. An impersonal Tao, however dynamic it may be, just could not meet such deep typically human yearnings. Only a being, that could relate to humans as a person and yet be much more than human, ideally a god, could satisfy the Taoist aspiration. What the Taoists aspire for, Christ fulfills. For, he is not an impersonal cosmic force but God himself with a personhood, fully human yet not entangled with the sin of humanity. God in Christ is both willing and able to relate with humanity at its point of deepest need and help individuals in a very personal manner. For salvation through Christ is not following a formula nor attempting to align oneself with an impersonal force, but having a personal relationship with Christ, the Savior God.

The God of Christianity is a person. In fact, the creation of the world was an act of a personal God and not an emanation from an impersonal energy (Gen 1:1). God's personhood is best revealed in his only begotten Son, Jesus Christ. Christ reveals God's character and personhood not through theophany or prophetic utterances but in flesh and blood. The disciples of Christ did not deify Christ. There was no need for it, since he was Immanuel, "God with us," at the time of his entrance into earth (Matt 1:23). What Taoists are aspiring to achieve through their strategies to personify the Tao and deify Lao-Tzu, Christ already is.

Taoists need a God who is all-powerful and compassionate so as to save humanity. The Bible makes it clear that the God of Christianity is almighty and compassionate beyond limits (2 Cor 1:3). It was God's love that sent his only begotten son to save humanity (John 3:16).

Moreover, Taoists long for a God who will become part of humanity to save it. The various theophanic and incarnational episodes of Taoist deities indicate such a longing.

But Christ's incarnation differs from Taoist incarnations in significant ways. First of all Christ is not a deified human who had achieved immortality like Immortal Lu-Pung-Pin. Christ is eternal. There are several deities who have incarnated in the Taoist religious history, but Christ is the one and only incarnation. Lu-Pung-Pin had to incarnate from time to time, since the impact of an incarnation ended as years went by. But the impact of Christ's incarnation, as effected through the cross does not diminish with the passage of time. What Taoists are aspiring for is a personal almighty, all-loving God who incarnates to save all humanity, once and for all. Christ meets these aspirations.

We have noted that the search for immortality eventually turns out to be a striving for eternal life—a life that is god-like and free from the bondages of human life. Christ, through the cross, provides humanity not just a better quality of human life, but eternal life.

In their striving for eternal life Taoists came to a point when they realized that human effort, however efficacious it may be, is inadequate. This is when the quest of latter Taoists, as articulated for instance by the members of the Way of Great Peace, turned out to be a plea for mercy. What Taoists eventually realized was that works alone cannot liberate humanity, that helpless humanity needed divine mercy. Moreover, such mercy has to come from a being that is both compassionate and powerful. Such a being has to be compassionate in order to be sensitive to the sins of the suffering. Such a being should also have the ability to liberate those in bondage. What the Taoists aspire in their desperate plea for mercy, salvation through Christ fulfills. For, such a salvation is orchestrated through grace that emanates from God in Christ, who is both compassionate and almighty to save humanity, including the Taoists.

In order to be assured of their salvation, Taoists resort to rituals and pronouncements. The meticulous and sometimes repetitive performance of rituals gives the penitent devotees the confidence that their confessions have been heard and their sins have been forgiven. The devotees take the announcements such as the writs of pardon, when read by the officiating priests on behalf of gods, as revelatory confirmations from heaven. What Taoists desperately hope for is an assurance of their salvation. But one cannot be assured of one's liberation on the grounds of obtaining divine mercy dependent on human effort. For there will always be a lingering doubt whether human effort is good enough to obtain mercy. On the other hand, the assurance of salvation that a repentant sinner receives when accepting Jesus Christ as savior is something that is definitive and totally independent of human effort; it is an assurance founded on God's grace. We will have occasion to differentiate between mercy and grace in the last chapter.

Our examination of the dynamics of Taoist salvific quest has given us some insights into the aspirations of Taoists. The resort to the Tao is core to the Taoist way of salvation. According to Taoists, what they resort to, the Tao, should be transcendently immanent and also be divinely personal. Moreover, resort to the Tao should be able to provide eternal life, facilitate the granting of mercy through compassionate deities and render the "assurance of salvation" to the penitent devotees. Christ seems to fulfill these core aspirations of the Taoists in their salvific quest.

5

The Shinto Quest

SHINTO IS THE INDIGENOUS religion of Japan. But the Japanese did not use the term Shinto to refer to their religion until about the sixth century CE. The entry of Buddhism, Taoism, and Confucianism from China spurred the crystallization of indigenous religious practices and beliefs. Shinto collectively denotes such practices and beliefs. *Shinto* or *Shen-Tao* means "the way (*tao*) of the divinities/spirits (*shen*)." The preferred Japanese term that describes this religion is *kami-nomichi*, which also means "the way (*no-michi*) of the gods/spirits (*kami*)."[1] The concept of *kami* figures in every version of Shinto and at every stage of its dynamic history. Though *kami* is usually translated as "divinities" or "spirits," it does not refer to an absolute transcendental being, but rather to a quality or an occult force that emanates from elements in nature, animals, and humans, evoking a sense of awe, attraction, or even repulsion. Ceremonies, rites, and rituals center on the awareness of kami, founded on the belief that one has to be in tune with kami to be freed from the problems of life. Shrines in various parts of Japan serve as locations for the perpetuation of these practices. Such practices existed among the Japanese long before Shinto religion received an identity of its own. The quest of the Japanese to be sensitive to and aligned with kami predates the recognition of Shinto as a distinct religion.

For centuries Shinto literally meant the "the way of the *kami*." These terms were virtually synonymous. But in the thirteenth century Shinto came to be used to identify the indigenous religion of Japan, differentiating it from especially Buddhism, Confucianism, and Taoism. The earliest recorded instance of such a usage is in a collection of replies by thirteenth-century Judo sect priest Shinzui (1279 CE) and Shingnon priest Tsukai (1234–1305 CE), when they pointed out that even though Buddhism is very similar to their religion, it has an identity of its own.[2] Shinto, no doubt, was made in Japan but with Chinese parts! The Japanese, in using the term Shinto, wanted to give an identity to their religiosity, but they also accommodated several Buddhist, Tao, and Confucian elements. Such an accommodation was mainly with the intention

---

1. Nigosian, *World Faiths*, 218.
2. Kasahara, ed. *History*, 299–300.

of making their quest to liberate themselves more effective. The emergence of Shinto schools during the thirteenth century CE points out that Shinto is not a static given but a dynamic process. The multiplications and diversifications that continue to happen among these schools and sects indicate that Shino is still evolving.

Here is a typical example of a faith community that does not exhibit the traditional components of religion such as a reputed founder, a canonized set of sacred scriptures, a codified doctrinal statement, an ecclesiastical structure like the Vatican of the Catholic Church, or a well-defined set of moral codes. Shinto is, rather, a collective term referring to a multitude of practices, some indigenous and some borrowed from other religions and cultures. Nevertheless, beneath the multifarious conglomeration of ceremonies, rituals, shrines, mountain asceticism, ancestor veneration, and emperor worship there are expressions of the same core aspirations of a significant sector of the Japanese populace. Such aspirations are indicative of an underlying salvific quest, a quest that exhibits itself in divergent ways, such as state, shrine, sectarian, and domestic Shinto.

State Shinto was founded on the principle of *saisei-itchi*, according to which the political and religious dimensions of a community are inseparable. This is best seen in the emperor-headed Shintoism that prevailed in Japan for several years. During this era the emperor was not only the ruler but also the nation's priest, serving as the guardian of the country's kami, on which the nation's destiny depended. Hence, commitment to the country and loyalty to the emperor turned out to be religious duties with a salvific purpose. The Japanese worshiped the emperor with the conviction that he would engineer the nation's kami and thereby protect and transform Japan. In 1868 Emperor Meiji established a theocratic state based on Shinto. This state lasted until December 15, 1945, when Japan was finally defeated in World War II. In response to the order issued by the commander of the Allied forces, on January 1, 1946, the emperor publicly denounced the notion that he was divine and the belief that the Japanese were superior to other races and destined to rule the world. Even though such a declaration was catastrophic to state Shinto, the Japanese continued to express their religiosity in other ways.

The emperor is dead but kami is very much alive in the hearts and lives of the Japanese. From ancient times shrines have occupied a central place in the Japanese religious life. They are taken to be locations where kami resides. The earliest places of Shinto worship are believed to be trees or groves demarcated as sacred. Eventually as shrine complexes developed, tall gate-frames known as *torii* (sacred gateway) became the traditional entrance, separating the sacred space of the shrine grounds from the profane space outside. *Torii* is an open gateway indicating that all are welcome. A typical major shrine has two buildings: the outer and inner shrine. Anyone can enter the outer shrine, but beyond that is the *honden*, the sacred sanctuary of the kami. Only priests can enter this area. The kami that is believed to frequent this area is invoked to dwell in a natural object or even a mirror. Complex ceremonial rites are performed to encourage the kami to dwell in the sanctuary. The myth *Nihongi* tells about the establishment of the shrine in Izumo, which is taken to be the most ancient of all

Japan's worship centers. It is a popular place to get blessings from kami for happy marriages and family relationships. Shrines like the Ise Grand Shrine, consisting of the Inner Shrine (*Naiki*) and the Outer Shrine (*Geku*) became very popular pilgrimage centers and locations for corporate worship. Kami Amaterasu, the sun goddess, is believed to be located in this shrine. The Itsukushima Shrine is located in the island of Itsukushima (popularly known as Miyajima) in the city of Hatsukaichi in Hiroshima. The whole island is taken to be the shrine. It is another popular shrine both for devotees and tourists. Devotees flock to this shrine since it is associated with kamis, which are very much needed. It is dedicated to the goddess Itsukusima-Hima, daughter of the storm goddess Susanovo-o-no Mikoto, the god of seas and storms and brother of Amaterasu, the sun goddess. The Japanese want to be protected from earthquakes and storms and need the sun for their agriculture. Tourists are attracted to this shrine especially because of its picturesque entrance (*torii*) located off the shores of the island. Such an entrance demarcates the sacred area from the profane. The placement of the *torii* in the watery region has symbolic significance. Washing one's feet and hands is a common practice in many shrines and temples. When devotees go through the watery entrance, they are believed to enter the sacred.

The *Torii* (sacred gateway) to the Itsukushima Shrine, Japan.

Shrines also became the centers of activity for sects. Every religion has sects, and Shinto is no exception. Shintoists at first practiced their rites and rituals individually in shrines. Eventually during the period of state Shinto sects began to develop. In 1882, Emperor Meiji's government recognized thirteen sects. They had to function under government control and fulfill certain obligations. New sects had to become affiliated with state-recognized sects to gain acceptance. Nevertheless, state control did not deter the growth of sects. At first they were financed and administered by the state. But with the demise of state Shinto, sects became independent and had to finance themselves. These thirteen sects fall into five main groups: pure Shinto (3), Confucian Shinto (2), mountain Shinto (3), purification Shinto (2), and redemptive Shinto (3).

Sects are vital to the articulation of the Shinto quest in more than one way. The grouping of believers in sects led to organized ecclesiastical structures that facilitated corporate ritualistic practices, codified doctrine, prescribed norms for moral living, and provided strategies for spreading Shinto. Moreover, members of each group, headed by clergy located in shrines, highlighted certain doctrines and strategies that they thought were conducive to liberation. For instance, the pure Shinto sects claimed that they represented "pure" Shinto, free from foreign influences. Their teachings are based on the classical myths and emphasize gratitude to ancestors and loyalty to emperors. The Confucian sects accommodated Confucian ethics and exalted patriotism. Believing that mountains harbor kamis, the mountain sects elevated mountain worship as the ideal way of liberation. Mount Fuji and Mount Ontake became sacred locations. The purification sects made ritualistic performance the means for purification. The redemptive sects, also called "faith healing" sects, attempted to make Shinto a religion that redeems people through revelatory messages. The Shinto quest became channeled through organized corporate structures highlighting different facets of Shinto doctrine and practice.

One would have expected the demise of Shinto with the collapse of state Shinto, the termination of government support to sects, and Japan's rapid industrialization and scientific advancement after World War II. But Shinto is still alive and well. The first impression one gets when visiting the industry-laden, commerce-stricken, technocratic country of Japan is that the rat-race-orchestrated Japanese are far from religion. But, when one visits their homes and detects their *kami-dana* (god-shelf), one realizes how the Japanese are still Shinto at heart. *Kami-dana* does not always contain the statue of a god; it may have the name of a benefactor or ancestor, an object bought from a reputed shrine, or even a family heirloom. This becomes venerated specifically because it is believed to have the spiritual force, kami, that would protect and transform the family. Domestic Shinto is homegrown.

The ceremonial practice of rituals in shrines, the culmination of state Shinto in emperor worship, the specialization of sectarian Shinto in articulating versions of Shinto doctrine, and the rise of domestic Shinto providing the Japanese ways to express their religiosity at home are all truly Shinto. In whatever way the Shinto believers exhibit their religiosity, they are all seen to be involved in finding out ways and means of liberating themselves. Of course, as in any religion, there are bound to be nominal Shintoists pompously participating in ceremonies and in the mechanics of ritualistic practices. Nevertheless, underlying all the divergent ways the faithful express their religiosity, there seems to be a resort to a spiritual force, kami, to enable them to transform life. This justifies calling Shinto a quest and furthermore a salvific quest. In order to get at the character of such a quest and capture the spirit of those involved in it, one needs to examine its expressions. Such an examination helps us to see the relevance of Christ to the Shinto quest: "the way of the gods" seems to call for "Christ the Way."

EXPRESSIONS OF THE SHINTO QUEST

When dealing with other religions, scriptures as an expression of the quest of the people following those religions, find a special place. But when it comes to Shinto, it is difficult to give such a place to scriptures. There is no set of canonized scriptures. Shinto seems to be closely intertwined with the social and behavioral facets of the Japanese way of life. Hence, in order to identify the quest of the Shintoists it is more helpful to examine their patterns of social and personal behavior than to be preoccupied with their scriptures. Myths and magic, rites and rituals, shrines and structures of the state, sectarian feuds and domestic practices would help us get at the nature of the Shinto quest.

There are some chronicles compiled between the eighth and tenth centuries that provide information about ancient Japanese life. Two of these works are taken to be the oldest and most important to get at the roots of Shinto worldview and practices. They are the *Kojiki* (*Records of Ancient Matters*) completed in 712 CE, and the *Nihon-shoki* (*Chronicles of Japan*) completed around 720 CE. The main works of the eighth century are the *Kogoshui* (a historical account of early Japan) and the *Manyoshu* (a collection of ancient poems). The latter helps us to get a feel for the yearnings of the people. Two other documents, *Shinsen Shojiroku* (a compilation of the register of families) and *Engishiki* or *Yangi-shiki* (records of codes of the Engi era), of the ninth and tenth centuries, are helpful to get an idea of early Japanese lifestyle.

These chronicles are not taken to be divinely inspired or even as authoritative documents. They contain several historical narratives and some of them are myths. In fact, one cannot really distinguish between myth and historic factuality in these chronicles. For instance, *Kojiki* and *Nihon-shoki/Nihongi* provide the main sources for the Shinto view of the divine origin of Japan tied up with the creation of the world. A section in the chronicle, "The Age of the Gods," describes how the creation of the world occurred, especially Japan. Such an account may seem a mere myth to a contemporary historian, but where no distinction was drawn between the historical and the mythical, such accounts are foundational to Shinto beliefs and practices. Some chronicles contain poems and prayers for ceremonies such as the agricultural festival and rituals to placate kami. Ballads and poems, prayers and praises, rites and rituals to kami and the pantheon of gods/spirits that came to be eventually added were part and parcel of Shinto practice, whether it be state, sectarian, shrine, or domestic. Here we see how narrative myths play a significant role in expressing the articulation of the Shinto quest. For instance, Ise Shrine's popularity could be traced to a myth that locates the sun goddess kami Amaterasu in this shrine. Affinity with nature and veneration of mountains may be taken as another age-old expression of Shinto. Such an expression has its roots in myths recorded in these chronicles, which pointed out Japan, including its natural beauties, to be a divine creation.

Nevertheless, the quest of the Shinto followers finds expression in prominent ways through extra-scriptural avenues such as worship in shrines, mountain pilgrimages, emperor worship, ceremonies and festivals, and domestic activities. Merely examining the chronicles is not helpful to get at the core aspirations of the Shintoists.

THE WAY OF THE QUEST

The Shinto quest to find a way of "salvation" is not based on a static set of codified doctrine and moral prescriptions given once and for all in canonized scriptures. The Shinto way evolved in and through several stages of Japan's history. It is still evolving. First, let us identify the foundational features of the way—those that have prevailed amidst the changes. Then we will examine the latter developments and attempt to determine their significance.

Foundational Features

The feature that poignantly characterizes the Shinto way is veneration of and resort to kami. Kami does not refer to God, understood as a transcendent personal being. But there are certain interesting features attributed to kami which make it relevant especially to the Christian characterization of God. *Nihongi/Nihon-shoki* (*Chronicles of Japan*) describes the origin of kami as a self-created deity thus: "In primeval ages, before the earth was formed, amorphous matter floated freely about like oil upon water. In time there arose in its midst a thing like a sprouting, and from this a deity came forth of its own."[3]

The chronicle *Kojiki* (*Record of Ancient Matters*) goes on to state that the world was created through three deities. "Now when chaos had begun to condense, but force and form were not manifest, and there was nought named, nought done, and who could know its shape? Nevertheless Heaven and Earth first parted, and the Three Deities performed the commencement of creation."[4]

Even though these chronicles are not divine revelations, those who made such proposals and those who believed in them seem to have an insight into the possibility of a self-created creator god who, as three deities, was involved in the act of creation. Such a self-created triune deity is believed to have manifested itself in male and female kami forms, called Izangi (male) and Izanami (female). The union of this primal couple and their descent from heaven led to the creation of the islands of Japan and several forms of kami-like deified powers, elements of nature, ancestral spirits, and spirits of well-known historical figures.[5] The myth called *Nihongi/Nihon-shoki* has it that Izangi and Izanami consulted each other and concluded that they needed to produce someone to be lord over the natural world they had created. Thus came into existence kami Amaterasu, the sun goddess.[6] Those who formulated the myth thought that the world needed not only a creator but also a sustainer. Perhaps, impressed by the awesome natural beauty of blossoming mountainous Japan, its inhabitants thought and still think that there should be a creator as well as a sustainer of such a world. Despite the natural and man-made calamities Japan has experienced through the years, it is still a country of resplendent natural beauty. People are still awed by it and set store by the message of the myth that there should be a god responsible for creating and sustaining such a beautiful country. Such an insight could well be taken as an instance of general revelation.

Kami is both singular and plural, for it refers to a single essence manifesting in many ways. It can manifest itself in good as well as in bad ways. It refers to a quality

---

3. Adapted from *Nilon-shoki* 1:3, in Picken, *Shinto*, 10.

4. In Smart and Hecht, eds., *Sacred Texts*, 320.

5. Oxtoby, *World Religions: Eastern Traditions*, 377.

6. Smart and Hecht, eds., *Sacred Texts*, 321.

that can evoke both wonder and dread in us. It includes anything that deserves to be revered or even dreaded for its extraordinary powers. Its actions need not be only good or noble but can be even malignant.[7] The strange, the unknown, and the inexplicable were taken to be the workings of kami. This rather peculiar awareness of kami as being present in things of different character provides a worldview that does not separate the spiritual from the material, the revered from the dreaded, humans from animals and the elements of nature. Wherever kami is found it evokes awe, wonder, or even dread.

The recognition that kami could help as well as harm people naturally led people to find ways and means to please it. The Shinto way is essentially an attempt to reconcile with kami in order to be freed from life's calamities. Shinto did not commence with a doctrinaire strategy to ward off the evil effects of kami, but rather resorted to taboos and rituals in a haphazard manner. Certain Shintoists were picked out as having special spiritual powers. Through meticulous performance of rites and rituals, they attempted to ward off the evil effects of kami. They turned out to be the Shinto shamans.

Shinto had its roots in an agricultural community. Farmers, naturally wanting their harvests to be plentiful, had to be on good terms with the kami that enables good crops. Sunlight is necessary for good vegetation. Hence, rituals to praise and placate kami Amaterasu, the sun goddess, became necessary. Celebrations and festivals provided occasions to honor as well as gain favor from the sun goddess. The spring and autumn harvest festivals were such occasions. Shrines came to be locations for such occasions. The Grand Shrine of Ise, dedicated to sun goddess Amaterasu, was and is still a favorite farmer shrine. The account found in the scripture *Nihon-shoki/Nihongi* indicates how the Ise shrine came to be taken as the abode of Amaterasu:

> Now the Great Goddess Amaterasu instructed Yamato-hime saying: "The province of Ise, of the divine wind, is the land whither repair the waves from the eternal world, the successive waves. It is secluded and pleasant land. In this land I wish to dwell." In compliance, therefore, with the instruction of the Great Goddess, a shrine was erected to her in the province of Ise. Accordingly an Abstinence Palace was built at Kawakami in Isuzu. This was called the Palace if Ise. It was there the Great Goddess Amaterasu first descended from Heaven.[8]

Earthquakes and storms are common in Japan. They are disastrous to agriculture as well as life. Hence the kami associated with storms had to be placated. The Miyajima shrine, dedicated to kami Itsukushima, the daughter of the storm god kami Susanowo, became another popular location for ritualistic practice. Festivals provided the ceremonial occasions while shrines served as locations for the practice of rituals.

Japan taken as a divine creation, and elements of nature like the mountains and rivers, became places of veneration. Mountain worship has been an ancient Japanese tradition, based on the belief that there is an indwelling kami on certain mountains. Shrines were erected on such mountaintops to invoke through rites, rituals, ceremonies,

7. Moore, ed., *Japanese Mind*, 25.
8. de Bary et al., eds., *Sources of Japanese Tradition*, 34–35.

and arduous pilgrimages the favor of the indwelling mountain kami. Mountains Fuji and Ontake are favorites as centers of Shinto mountain worship. Eventually Jikko-kyo, Fuso-kyo, and Mitake-kyo became popular Shinto mountain sects.

Early Shinto way was not based on an explicit, well-defined set of doctrines put into practice through structured programs. It was rather a compendium of rites, rituals, and ceremonial purifications performed at festivals, shrines, and mountains. Rituals rather than doctrine characterized such a way. It had neither a legalistic code of ethics nor a creed based on sacred scriptures. But however haphazard the ritualistic performances were, they had a salvific purpose. In early Shinto, there was no concept of sin understood as something that is immoral and repelling to a holy God. Hence, repentance as a penitent reconciliation with God entailing a change of character was not required. However, Shinto acknowledged the presence of a quality of impurity or misfortune, called *tsumi*, that may offend the kami and bring about calamities such as famine, drought, and war. Tsumi arises through defilement by corpses, menstruation, and improper relationships between humans or between humans and nature. The evil impact of tsumi is got rid of through purification rites rather than through repentance.[9] Those participating in such rites wanted to be in line with kami in order to enrich their lives or be freed from their calamities. They believed that through purification rituals one could be freed from the evil impact of tsumi and be reconciled with kami. Such purification could be enacted personally or communally. Bathing in a waterfall or participating in a ceremonial ritual, *oharai*, where a priest waves a piece of wood with streamers attached over the person(s) who need purification were popular rituals. Today this ritual is performed even on cars and buildings.

The resort to kami (sometimes manifested as gods and goddesses) and the meticulous practice of multifarious rites and rituals in order to please the deities and/or purify oneself provide some rationale to consider the early Shinto as a salvific way. But some significant developments took place in the articulation of the Shinto way that have to be taken into account to get a more comprehensive view. This will be our next task.

LATER DEVELOPMENTS

Plea for Superhuman Help

State Shinto, which prevailed from 1865 to 1945, is a significant episode in Shinto history. The rationale for the claim that one could effectively practice the Shinto way of salvation through political channels is the principle of *saisei-itchi*, according to which the political and religious dimensions of life are basically one. Moreover, the roots of state Shinto could be traced to certain myths in the chronicles. They indicate that Japan had a divine origin and the lineage of emperors had a divine commencement. According to one myth, the sun goddess Amaterasu, who was created to be lord over Japan and its people, was dissatisfied with their disorderly conduct. She commissioned her grandson Ningi to descend and rule them. Later his great-grandson, Jimmu, became the first human emperor to rule Japan in 660 BCE. Every emperor

---

9. Fisher, *Living Religions*, 210.

after him was considered a descendant in an unbroken line from the sun goddess, Amaterasu. Through the centuries, farmers performed rituals at the Ise shrine that was dedicated to the sun goddess Amaterasu because she was the kami that enabled good harvests. During the state Shinto era the shrine received status and significance for another reason: it was the emperor's temple, since the lineage of emperors was traced to Amaterasu. Under the patronage of emperors, the Ise shrine became popular as a location for ritualistic practice connected with the nation's destiny.

The emperor's divine roots gave him a status that no human political head could claim. He became the guardian of the nation's kami, which made him the most effective channel to protect the people, liberate them from external threats, and guide their destiny as a nation. By the fourteenth century, the emperor's relationship with kami was well-defined; the way of the emperor turned out to be the way of the kami. As a living incarnation of the sun goddess he was considered God in human form, and his commands were taken to be inviolable. In fact, some believed that he was the ruler of all humanity, not just of the Japanese. To a Western mindset that separates religion from politics, such a claim seems audacious, but it highlights the deep need people have for superhuman help. They need someone more than a priest or a shaman, someone with divine roots to change their destiny both individually and communally.

Plea for Life After Death

State Shinto was partly a reaction to the challenge of Chinese religions, especially Mahayana Buddhism, which entered Japan during the sixth century CE. While Shinto became more self-conscious as a result of the impact of such religions, it also began to assimilate some of their beliefs and practices. Early Shinto's rites and rituals were geared to enable the participants to be free from the problems of this life. But is there life after death? If so, how can one be assured of a peaceful afterlife? This is a lingering concern of all humans. The Japanese were no exception. Mahayana Buddhism, especially the Pure Land sect that came to Japan, addressed this concern. Pure Land Buddhism proclaimed that after death one could enter a heaven, Pure Land, with the help of a legendary/historical figure called Amiddha Buddha. A movement called Ryobu (Two Aspect Shinto/Dual Shinto), attempting to find common ground between Shinto and Buddhism, came into prominence in Japan between the sixth and ninth centuries. Shinto texts influenced by esoteric Buddhism were composed. The most popular of these is the *Tenchi Rekil Ki* (*The Esoteric Teachings of the Cosmos*).[10] The Ryobu Shinto adherents took the Buddhas and Bodhisattvas as manifestations of kami. Hence Amiddha Buddha became a kami manifestation that would enable one to be assured of a peaceful afterlife. Here is a good example of how Shinto adherents resorted to a Buddhist strategy to be assured of their afterlife.

---

10. Kasahara, ed., *History*, 307.

Plea for Moral Transformation

The spread of Buddhism in China gave rise to a fear that Shinto would eventually be obliterated in Japan. Buddhism emphasized the role of quality moral conduct in one's spiritual journey, while Shinto was preoccupied with rites and rituals. Hence to meet the challenge of Buddhism Shinto had to come up with a morality that would be rewarding to its followers and prevent the Shintoists from converting to Buddhism. Shinto reformists tried their best to revitalize Shinto through emphasizing the necessity of moral transformation. But a people caught up in a ritualistic mindset found it difficult to envisage the possibility of transforming life and changing destiny through moral reformation.

It was only during the military leadership of the Tokugawa regime (1600–1867) that Shinto got the boost it needed in this respect. Militant leaders supported Shinto and aggressively pushed away outsiders, including the Buddhists. But even though Confucianism was foreign, these leaders accommodated it because Confucian ethics helped to enhance the quality of the military leadership. The *samurai*, functioning as a guard or mercenary soldier serving a lord, was part of Japanese society from ancient times. But during this era, Samurai was idealized and a warrior code, called *Bushido*, was established based on Confucian ethics. A samurai was expected to be loyal to his master, courageous, polite and gentlemanly, and willing to die to for his cause. All these are Confucian values. The suicide ritual *hara-kiri* (belly-cutting) best exemplifies the emphasis on proper conduct. When a samurai thought that he had failed in his conduct and wished to redeem whatever honor had been lost, he performed this torturous ritual. The main purpose of the Confucian sects Shusei-ha and Taisei-kyo was to highlight the indispensability of proper moral conduct in the Shinto way. They relied on prayer and meditation to gain inner tranquility. Confucianism acted as a catalyst to move the Shinto way in the direction of a moral way attempting to transform the seekers internally and thereby liberate them.

Plea for Internal Purification

Closely connected with the emphasis on moral transformation is the claim that purification ought to be enacted with sincerity and not merely a ritualistic formality.

The practice of purification rites and rituals has been in vogue in Shinto from age-old times. But two sects, Shinshu-kyo and Misogi-kyo, gave a special place to these rituals to purify the participants and ward them from evil. The Shinshu-kyo purification rites, such as the fire-subduing ceremony and hot water ritual, were all performed with prayers.

The Misogi-kyo sect emphasized proper breathing ritual, not merely for physical and mental health but especially because proper breathing could direct one to be aligned with the divine will. What is significant to note is that the purification sects did not want ritualistic practice to be a mere external formality. They emphasized that the practice of rites and rituals when done with sincerity could have a transformative impact on the participants.

Plea for Redemption

The redemptive sects developed from the emphasis that purification sects placed on internal transformation. The Shinto way has always been, in a sense, salvific in its purpose. The performance of rites and rituals was meant to keep people out of trouble. But the redemptive sects went a step further and insisted that redemption should change not only the character but also the destiny of people. Kurozumi-kyo, Konko-kyo, and Tenri-kyo belong to this group of sects. The founders of these sects, after having spiritual experiences, proclaimed a message of redemption. Moreover, these sects pointed out that faith in a divine power is a must for redemption.

After three spiritual crises, Kurozumi Munetada (1780–1850), the founder of the Kurozumi sect, proclaimed that Amaterasu, the sun goddess, is the source of all happiness and well-being. He established seven rules for a person to be redeemed: faith in the sun goddess, humility, self-possession, compassion, sincerity, gratitude, and industry.[11] Even though he never claimed to be God, after his death he was deified and worshiped along with the sun goddess. Faith healing was one of the chief attractions of this sect. The sect used several methods of healing, but the most important one was faith in the sun goddess.

The peasant Kawade (1814–1883) was the founder of the Konko-kyo sect. As a result of a vision Kawade had in 1859, he claimed that he was commissioned to mediate between Tenche-kane-no kami (Great Father of the Universe) and human beings. This god, taken to be the source of infinite love and mercy, is a later addition to the Shinto pantheon. According to the followers of Kawade, humans suffer because of two basic failures: ignorance of Tenche-kane-no kami's infinite love, and the violation of his laws. To be redeemed, one should have faith in the Great Father of the Universe, love others, fulfill one's duties, and pray for peace.[12] Kawade became the mediator for such redemption.

Another peasant, a woman named Nakayama Miki (1798–1887), was the founder of the Tenri-kyo sect. Emerging from a trance in 1859, she claimed that she was possessed by a god, Tenri-o-no-mikito (God of Divine Reason). Following his command, she gave up everything and devoted herself to presenting a message of redemption through teaching, faith healing, and mental cures. According to Nakayama Miki, human beings follow their own selfish ends and not the will of divine reason and thereby end up in misfortune and suffering. She claimed that one could achieve original purity by getting rid of the vices and having faith in the god Tenri, thereby earning his favor.[13]

What is significant is the shift that took place in the Shinto way of liberation over the course of these developments. It started by claiming that one should get in line with an impersonal force, kami, manifesting itself in humans, animals, elements of nature, and sometimes through deities. It ended up emphasizing the reality of a divine being who is the source of all existence and controls the destiny of human beings.

11. Nigosian, *World Faiths*, 236.

12. Ibid.

13. Ibid., 237.

Through the centuries Shinto was essentially a way of works, emphasizing the necessity of the performance of rites and rituals. More lately the redemptive sects, on the other hand, placed the emphasis on faith and trust in the favor of one or more gods. Such developments naturally make Christ relevant to the Shinto. Our next task is to find out how he is relevant.

THE RELEVANCE OF CHRIST TO THE SHINTO QUEST

How can Christ be related to a quest that is so preoccupied with occult practices, magic, divination, and rites and rituals performed to appease kami believed to reside in animals, humans, heads of state, trees, mountains, rivers, sun, moon, and family heirlooms? As we have already noted, beneath these multifarious activities there is a salvific quest, one that motivates Shinto followers to participate enthusiastically in such activities. It is here that Christ becomes relevant to the Shinto quest.

The Shinto way is founded on a worldview that acknowledges the world, particularly Japan, to be a divine creation. Moreover, the divinity that created the world and its people is also concerned about them. The sun goddess Amaterasu's regret over the disorderly conduct of the Japanese, and her decision to send her grandson Ningi to make matters right, may be dismissed as mere myth. But in a context where the demarcation between myth and historical fact is so faint, such a story has considerable impact in making the Japanese believe that a divinity is concerned with their destiny. This conviction provided the rationale to worship the emperors, whose lineage was traced to the sun goddess; it indicates that the object of Japanese aspiration was ultimately a divinity that would become incarnate and provide the supernatural help to give them a better quality of life and change their destiny. Does this not make Christ relevant?

The Shinto way started out as essentially a way of works. The rites and rituals performed at domestic, communal, and national levels are all meant to make people fall in line with kami. This way is meant to be salvific in the sense that the practice of it should bring about a change in the quality of life of those participating. But there are some noteworthy latter developments in Shinto. They exhibit some core aspirations, and it is here that Christ becomes relevant to the Shinto quest.

Early Shinto practice of rites and rituals was aimed mainly at warding off the calamities of this life. But, as a result of Buddhist influence, those involved in such practices also wanted to be assured of a peaceful life after death. The Pure Land Buddhism that came into Japan assured a peaceful and happy life after death in a heaven called Pure Land in the Western hemisphere. To reach that heaven one had resort to Amiddha Buddha's mercy. He would respond when his name was chanted. Later Shinto adopted Amiddha Buddha as a manifestation of kami. Hence the appeal to his mercy became a popular strategy in order to be assured of a peaceful life after death. What the Japanese aspire to, in other words, is not merely a good life now but also a life after death that would be even better. Christ's provision of eternal life satisfies such an aspiration, for the eternal life that Christ provides is not merely immortal life but a life that is qualitatively distinct from the present life. Moreover, such life is assured on the grounds of grace rather than on good works. The sincere, prayerful chants of Shinto seekers in shrines, festivals, and in the secrecy of their homes are a cry for the grace that only Christ can provide. But the grace that Christ provides does not depend on the meticulous practice of rites and rituals; it is given unconditionally.

Rites and rituals are prone to become mere formalities devoid of any real change of heart—a mere external performance without internal transformation. Early Shinto was characterized by keeping out of trouble by fulfilling obligations through certain rituals, but there were some significant latter developments in Shinto that highlight the importance of character transformation. Responding to the impact of Confucian ethics and the challenge of Buddhism, Shinto began to place an emphasis on morality, attempting to transform the seeker internally. The samurai code depicted not only a courageous warrior but also a man of character, a gentleman who considered the welfare of others. The purification sects interiorized Shinto ritualistic practice by emphasizing that it should bring about a change in the character of those involved in it. According to these sects, merely meticulous performance of the rituals is not enough; it should also generate a wholesome change in the Shinto believers. What the Japanese really wanted was a way that would bring about a character change in them.

The redemption that Christ offers entails a change of character, but it does not occur through the efficacy of human deeds. From the Christian perspective, deeds by themselves, however good they may be, cannot bring about the sought-after holistic character change in the believer. Human beings are sinful by nature; they need superhuman help. Resort to God becomes a necessity. Faith in God in Christ and dependence on his grace become indispensable for one to be redeemed.

The redemptive Shinto sects of the eighteenth and nineteenth centuries made certain proposals that radically changed the Shinto way. According to early Shinto, falling in line with kami was an absolute necessity in order for a person to be liberated. Kami was taken to be an impersonal force, found in the elements in the universe and evoking a sense of awe or even dread. But the redemptive sects attributed qualities to this kami that made it more like the God professed by theistic religions. It turned out to be an absolute, transcendent, and personal being. The Kurozumi-kyo sect came to see the sun goddess as the source of all things and the one who sustains and guides those who trust in her. Konko-kyo's Great Father of the Universe and Terri-kyo's God of Divine Reason had similar attributes: each is the all-powerful source and sustainer of things and is more of a person than an impersonal force or quality, a transcendent being who is nevertheless sincerely concerned with human beings and even incarnated. It was the sun goddess who, out of compassion, sent her grandson to the Japanese. The redemptive sects of later Shinto resorted to a personal, all-powerful divine being rather than to an impersonal quality or force in order to find liberation.

Moreover, these sects emphasized that faith in such a being is a must for redemption. Mere performance of rites and rituals was not enough. The founders of these sects did not claim to be gods themselves; their spiritual struggles led to certain experiences that motivated them to proclaim a redemption possible only through faith in an almighty personal god. They were all part of the quest. Their message of redemp-tion reveals what they and their followers were really craving in their struggle to be redeemed: a divine being who had the power to save and in whom they could place their faith. The "unknown God" who can redeem them is God in Christ. He meets their requirements and fulfills their aspirations.

Dick Wilson, in commenting on contemporary Japanese religiosity, observes that Japan seems to have attained the freethinking attitude of healthy secularism that characterizes much of modern western society.[14] But he also concedes that amidst the current Japanese secularism, a type of religiosity is growing. Trying to identify the root cause for such a growth, he quotes the novelist-turned-politician Shintaro Ishihara:

> There is spiritual void at the core of the Japanese nation, a moral degeneration that characterizes everything that happens in this society . . . Japan offers a glar-ing example of a highly developed level of cultural development . . . supported by a pitiful mediocre . . . moral philosophy . . . Post-War Japanese have been so alienated that they have been unable to realize their responsibility and sense of duty as individuals and unable to conceive a moral code.[15]

Our examination of Shinto suggests that such a void cannot be filled by rites and rituals, modes of meditation, a moral code, an orthodox creed, an organized religious structure, or even pious participation in religious ceremonies. Later developments in Shinto, such as the plea for superhuman help, for life after death, and for wholesome transformation and redemption, may be taken as definitive pointers to Christ as the one who can fill that void. Francis Xavier brought Christianity to Japan in the sixth century, but despite the ardent efforts of missionaries and leading Japanese Christians such as Dr. Toyohika Kagawa, Christianity has not flourished in Japan. The Japanese have successfully adopted some of the Christian ceremonies; many Shinto believers re-ligiously follow Christian wedding traditions and even liturgy, and during Christmas festivities one finds it difficult to distinguish between a Christian and a Shinto believer. But Santa Claus seems to be more victorious than Christ in commercialized Japan. The void is still very much there! The followers of Shinto do not need Christianity, but they do need Christ.

14. Wilson, *Sun at Noon*, 90.
15. Ibid., 95.

6

The Buddhist Quest

Here was a man who, in the prime of his life, left the luxury of his father's mansion where he had been secluded from casualties and calamities and started on a journey that epitomizes the Buddhist quest. Seeing a crippled old man, a suffering sick person, a corpse carried to be cremated, and a decrepit hermit were traumatic revelations to the overprotected prince. These experiences led him on a tortuous journey to find the cause and cure for the misery of human existence. Such a quest ultimately ended up in finding a way out, which he advocated to those around him.

"Buddhism" is a Western title given to what is commonly called *Buddha Dharma* in Asian countries, best translated as "the way of the Buddha." The term *Buddha* means "the awakened or enlightened one." It refers primarily to Siddharta Gautama, or Sakyamuni (sage of the Sakya clan), who lived in India during sixth century BCE. Born into a rich, royal, noble-class family, nurtured in luxury, and secluded from the mishaps of life, he lived in comfort and opulence. Legend has it that his father was warned by astrologers that his son would either be a world ruler if he stayed at home or an ascetic if he left home. Naturally his overprotective father gave him all the comforts of life and arranged for his marriage to a beautiful woman, Yasodhara. He lived in luxury, but by the time his first son was born, he showed signs of restlessness, for there is no other reason for him to name his son Rahula, meaning "fetter." The four traumatic experiences he had outside his haven of comfort precipitated the crisis and started his quest. Leaving his wife, son, parents, and the comfort of his home, he set off to find an answer to his soul's yearning. The life of wealth and pleasure, that he had so far enjoyed, could not satisfy him. He followed the Hindu gurus of his time and underwent their ascetic austerities, including self-torture. But nothing could satisfy his innermost yearnings. One day, seated under a tree (since then known as the Bodhi or bo tree, "the Tree of Wisdom") on the banks of river Neranjarain in Buddha-Gaya, he attained enlightenment, *nirvana*, after which he came to be known as Buddha "The Enlightened One." In his first sermon after enlightenment, he presented Four Noble Truths, including the Eightfold Path, which he was convinced was the way that would liberate humanity—that which would satisfy the human spiritual quest.

Though born a Hindu, he claimed he had a spiritual awakening that motivated him to teach a way of liberation, *dharma*, which was significantly different from Hindu doctrine and practice. *Dharma*, understood in its original sense, denotes a fundamental truth or law for gods, humans, and animals alike. Buddha in his enlightenment had been "woken up" to such a truth and thereby became liberated. He presented his dharma with the conviction that it would lead to enlightenment, which he had himself experienced. Amidst some speculative insights that Buddhism presents, it seems to make orthodoxy subservient to orthopraxis; that one's lessons from experience could generate doctrine. Hence, to understand and appreciate Buddhism, we should not separate theory from practice. Buddhism is essentially a path to liberation, founded on experience. The core concepts of Buddhism, such as *dukka, nirvana, boddhisattva,* and *dhyana* have to be interpreted as concepts which are associated with one's spiritual quest for liberation—one's salvific endeavor.

Edwin Arnold introduced Buddhism to the Western world in 1879 through his book entitled *Light of Asia*, one of the classics of English Buddhist literature. He presented Buddhism through the lips of a Buddhist with the belief that the spirit of Asiatic ideas could best be articulated from an Oriental rather than a Western perspective. The opening stanza of his ode runs thus:

> The scripture of the Savior of the World
> Lord Buddha-Prince Siddhartha styled on earth
> In Earth and heavens and Hells Incomparable,
> All honored, Wisest, Best, most Pitiful;
> The Teacher of Nirvana and the Law.[1]

These words indicate how a Buddhist views Buddha— that he is a historical figure, in fact the best of all humans, who is treasured for his teachings which enable one to attain nirvana, the ideal state of freedom and liberation. This legitimizes him to be acclaimed as the savior of the world. He is savior in the sense that he taught the path to liberation which he had himself discovered.

Buddhism may not fall under the category of what we usually label as theistic religions. But that does not prevent us from describing it as a salvific quest. The Buddhist delegates at the 1993 Chicago Parliament of World Religions presented Buddhism thus:

> Sakyamuni Buddha, the founder of Buddhism, was not God or a god. He was a human being who attained full Enlightenment through meditation and showed us the path of spiritual awakening and freedom. Therefore, Buddhism is not a religion of God. Buddhism is a religion of wisdom, enlightenment and compassion. Like the worshippers of God who believe that salvation is available to all through confession of sin and a life of prayer, we Buddhists believe that salvation and enlightenment are available to all through the removal of defilements and delusion and a life of meditation. However, unlike those who believe in God who

---

1. Arnold, *Light of Asia*, 11.

is separate from us, Buddhists believe that Buddha which means "one who is awake and enlightened" is inherent in us all as Buddha-nature or Buddha-mind.[2]

Buddhism presented thus is obviously a path of "liberation," though not theistic. Such a path enabled Buddha to be "liberated," and those who follow this path are involved in a quest to be "liberated," just as he was. In this sense, Buddhism is essentially a salvific quest. It is in the light of such a depiction of Buddhism that we will attempt to find out whether Christ is relevant to the Buddhist quest and, if so, in what ways?

The Buddhist quest arose out of a world where Hinduism had deteriorated to a slavish subservience to the authority of corrupt Hindu priests. They were exploiting the masses by demanding money for performing multifarious rituals. Although meticulously followed, the age-old socioreligious customs turned out to be mere formalities. Such a world was not conducive to help people fulfill their aspirations, and hence they reacted. Such a reaction expressed itself in what historians identify as the "Sramana Movement." It reacted against such empty religiosity and tried to explore more satisfying paths of liberation. The fatalists (Ajivikas), the naturalists (Lokayatas), the agnostics (Jains), and the Buddhists may be taken as expressions of this reaction.

Buddhism commences with Gautama Buddha, but after his death Buddhists grouped themselves into many sects which all claimed to be faithful to the original teachings of Buddha, even though their versions of Buddhism reveal significant differences. Over a period of time, these sects gradually merged into two main schools: *Hinayana* (Lesser Vehicle) or *Theravada* (Teachings of the Elders) and *Mahayana* (Greater Vehicle). The former school represents the way early Buddhists interpreted and followed the Buddha Dharma. Mahayana characterizes how with the passage of time Buddhists continued to follow the Buddha Dharma, adopting it to their needs. It should be kept in mind that both Hinayana and Mahayana Buddhism are not homogenous in character. Hinayana is supposed to be the orthodox teachings of the elders, yet there are significant differences between doctrine and practice among Hinayanists. Mahayana Buddhism is a conglomeration of diverse sects like the Tibetan Vajrayana, Zen, Pure Land, and Nichiren. It is significant that underlying both the Hinayana and Mahayana expressions of Buddhism there lays a salvific quest, initiated by Buddha; the Mahayana sects claim to enhance and not negate the path for liberation that Hinayana proposes.

We will attempt to first examine the quest as formulated in the Hinayana tradition and then trace how the quest developed in latter Buddhist Mahayana and Tantric traditions.

BUDDHA THE INITIATOR OF THE QUEST

The quest of Buddhism originated with Buddha (563–483 BCE). The manner of his birth, his spiritual struggle, enlightenment, teachings, denials, silences, and finally

2. "A Message from Buddhists," 53.

his death provide us with sufficient material to find out how Buddha initiated the Buddhist quest, being very much part of it.[3]

The Birth of Buddha

Siddharta Gautama, later called Buddha, the enlightened one, was born about 563 BCE in Lumbini near Kapilavasthu in present day Nepal. Legend has it that Buddha had a miraculous birth. One night Queen Mahamaya, Gautama's mother, dreamt that a white elephant with six tusks had entered the right side of her womb and that a multitude of heavenly beings bowed down to her. When she woke up she was with child. The Venerable Ananda, a cousin and a close disciple of Buddha, provides us with some details about the birth and life of Buddha. Ananda claims that Buddha had confessed to him that he was a bodhisattva, who hailed from Tushita, "Heaven of the Contended," and descended into his mother's womb.[4] Bodhisattva in Buddhism refers to one who is seriously striving to attain enlightenment. According to Ananda, divine beings in the "Heaven of the Contended" implored Siddharta Gautama to be born on earth to become a Buddha and thereby show the path of enlightenment to all human beings.[5] The "Heaven of the Contended" was the abode of those who could eventually be enlightened. Such a description of what preceded his birth indicates that Buddha was born as a bodhisattva to become a Buddha; he was born to be enlightened.

Buddha's Quest

Buddha's quest commenced with a spiritual crisis amidst a luxurious and overpro-tected life. He is supposed to have said that night and day a white parasol was held over him so that he would not be touched by cold or heat, by dust, or weeds, or dew. Traumatic exposures to an old man, a sick man, and a corpse made him question the point of the luxuries of life if everything ended with death. His encounter with a her-mit helped him to decide what to do to get out of the crisis. He renounced everything and commenced his spiritual journey.

But the journey was not easy. First he turned to the types of meditations that were available to him. His mentors advised him to practice Hindu modes of medita-tion. These enabled him to reach exalted levels of concentration, but he found them inadequate as they did not lead him to what he was really seeking.

Then he resorted to asceticism, self-mortification involving tortuous bodily prac-tices and solitude in life-threatening places, but even these proved to be futile. As a last resort, he went and sat cross-legged under a bo tree, naked and weak. Ananda quotes Buddha regarding his struggle for liberation from the bondage of the cycle of rebirths (*samsara*): "Before my enlightenment, while I was still only an unenlightened

---

3. Sources for Buddha's biographical details: Nanamoli, *Life of the Buddha*; Dhammananda, *What Buddhists Believe*; Bercholz and Kohn, eds., *Buddha and His Teachings*; Kohn, *Life of the Buddha*, 3–44; Pande, "Message of Gotama Buddha," 3–33.

4. Nanamoli, *Life of the Buddha*, 3.

5. Bercholz and Kohn, eds., *Buddha and His Teachings*, 4.

Bodhisatta being myself subject to birth, ageing, ailment, death, sorrow, and defilement, I sought after what was also subject to these things. Then I thought: Why being myself subject to birth, ageing, ailment, death, sorrow and defilement, do I seek what is also subject to these things? . . . seeing danger in them, I sought after the unborn, unageing, unailing, deathless, sorrowless, undefiled supreme surcease of bondage, Nibbana."[6] Realizing that the predicament besetting all humanity included himself as well, Buddha started on a quest to be free from such bondage.

Hermann Hesse's short novel, *Siddharta*, is a creative attempt to pinpoint the quest of Buddha, here called by his family name Siddharta: "It is the story of a soul's long quest in search of ultimate answer to the enigma of man's role on this earth. As a youth, the young Indian Siddharta meets the Buddha but cannot be content with a disciple's role; he must work out his own destiny and solve his own doubt—a tortuous road that carries him through the sensuality of a love affair with the beautiful courtesan Kamala, the temptation of success and riches, the heartache of a struggle with his own son, to final renunciation and self-knowledge."[7]

Buddha, like several founders of religion, finds that there is something rotten in human existence, that all humanity, including himself, is caught up in such a predicament and that he has to get out of it. This motivates in him a quest to be freed from such a predicament.

Buddha the Enlightened

Statue of Buddha at the Golden Temple, Dambulla, Sri Lanka. Buddha explains the Noble Truths in his first sermon after enlightenment.

Dhammapada, a Sutta Pitaka discourse, records the words of Buddha just after his enlightenment:

6. Nanamoli, *Life of the Buddha*, 10.
7. Hesse, *Siddhharta*, back cover.

Seeking but not finding the House Builder,
I traveled through the round of countless births:
O painful is birth again and again.
House Builder, you have now been seen;
You shall not build the house again.
Your rafters have been broken down;
Your ridge pole is diminished too.
My mind has now attained the unformed nibbana
And reached the end of every kind of craving.[8]

Buddha's exuberance at his enlightenment also indicates the struggle he had experienced to attain it, the joy of being freed from the crippling bondage of cyclic rebirths. Such a victorious exuberance could have tempted him to glorify himself as god or at least superhuman, but he wanted the world to remember him as the enlightened one and nothing more.[9]

Even though enlightened, he was hesitant to become involved in philosophical issues, such as whether the universe is infinite, whether the soul is different from the body, and whether there is life after death. He was careful to present his views based only on what he had experienced in his spiritual journey. He presented his teachings with the sole purpose that those who follow them would also be enlightened like him. The first sermon delivered to his first disciples in Deer Park in Benares contains the gist of his teaching: the Four Noble Truths including the Eightfold Path. For the next forty-five years, he wandered from place to place in central India, explaining the truth (dharma) he had discovered.

Buddha's Death

His death, believed to have occurred in 483 BCE, is described as entering the state of *parinirvana*, which means "nirvana without remainder,"[10] implying that there are no rebirths after it. Buddha knew that he would soon die, and on the strength of his enlightenment, he indicated that he was prepared for death. Death for him was the consummation of nirvana; the total release from the cycle of rebirths. He did not consider himself to be eternal and remained silent when asked whether he would exist after death. When Ananda and his other disciples wept as he was about to die, Buddha comforted them, saying that it is in the very nature of things that anything that is component in nature will dissolve, that all will die. When Ananda asked him who would be their teacher when he died, Buddha replied: "I am not the first Buddha to come upon earth; nor shall I be the last. In due time, another Buddha will arise this world, a Holy One, a Supremely Enlightened One, endowed with wisdom, in conduct auspicious, knowing the universe, an incomparable leader of men, a master of devas and men. He

---

8. Nanamoli, *The Life of the Buddha*, 29.

9. Ibid., 188.

10. Oxtoby, *World Religions: Eastern Traditions*, 230.

will reveal to you the same Eternal Truths which I have taught you. He will proclaim a religious life, wholly perfect and pure, such as I now proclaim."[11]

To Ananda's query, "How shall we know him?" Buddha replied, "He will be known as Maitreya, which means kindness or friendliness."[12] The portrayal of the coming Buddha, especially as the one who will be known for his love, interestingly resembles Jesus.

The last words of the Buddha to Ananda and the other monks present were, "Behold now, I exhort you: Impermanent are all compounded things! Work out your salvation with earnestness."[13]

Statue of the recumbent (reclining) Buddha in Polannaruwa, Sri Lanka, built during the reign of Parakramabahu the Great (1153–1186 CE)

Buddha's life and mission is a story of a man who articulated a quest to free humanity on the grounds of his own personal journey. But the articulation of the Buddhist quest did not terminate with him. Significant developments occurred in Buddhism as it evolved into a religion that accommodated lay people and spread into countries like Burma, Sri Lanka, Thailand, Korea, China, and Japan. Such an expansion necessitated certain modifications in the doctrine and practice of Buddhism. In fact, such a trend still continues. Buddhadasa of Thailand and the present Dalai Lama of Tibet are well known contemporary articulators. But all the schools and sects of Buddhism accept the core concepts of Buddha's way of liberation. Our next task will be to find out how Buddhist scriptures express the way of the quest.

11. Dhammananda, *What Buddhists Believe*, 45–46.

12. Ibid.

13. Rahula, *Way to Peace*, 158.

THE SCRIPTURAL EXPRESSIONS OF THE QUEST

The oldest Buddhist scriptures are Tipitaka (Sanskrit Tripitaka) which means "Three Baskets." They were written in Pali, the language in which Buddha spoke and taught and were collected after Buddha's death by a council of five hundred elders. Many of them are believed to have had personal contact with him and his teachings. The Venerable Ananda, a close disciple of Buddha, contributed greatly to the collection of these scriptures which were eventually written down on palm leaves and stored in baskets. Perhaps, the label Tipitaka arises from the ancient practice of storing palm-leaf manuscripts in wicker baskets. Early Buddhism got the name Theravada (teachings of elders), since it was based on these scriptures codified by the elders. In addition to this Pali canon, several non-canonical commentaries on the scriptures and Jataka tales came to be accommodated as Buddhist sacred literature. The Jatakas refer to a voluminous body of literature, constituting poems and stories mainly about the previous lives of the Buddha. In Theravada countries like Cambodia, Laos, and Thailand the Jatakas are to this day performed in dance, drama, and recitation. Narratives play a vital role in conveying some Buddhist doctrines in forms palatable to the people. For instance, the Jataka stories present how rebirths function on the road to enlightenment by narrating Buddha's past births and lives in an interesting manner; that on the way to become a Buddha, he passed from life to life by being at various times a bird, a hare, a monkey, a prince, a merchant, and an ascetic. In each case the challenges he faced enabled him to cultivate virtue, patience, and compassion which eventually led him to enlightenment.[14]

Each of the three-part scriptures (Tipitaka) played a vital role in the practice of early Buddhism. Sutta Pitaka is in short verse or prose form. It contains particulars about Buddha's life and teachings. His teachings, which came out of his experiences, presented the path to liberation. It was difficult for him to articulate such supramundane experiences. Moreover, only a person who has been enlightened like Buddha would be able to comprehend such concepts. Hence, Buddha had to put his concepts in a verbal format that his disciples could memorize, with the hope that in recollecting them they would eventually internalize the concepts that the cryptic verses contain. Vinaya Pitaka provides the rules for the *sangha*, the community of monks and nuns. These rules are not presented in a rigid legalistic format but expressed in story form to drive home the purpose for which the rules have been laid down. The monks and nuns were expected to capture the spirit of the rules rather than legalistically follow them. At a time when Hindu Brahmin priests were legalistically imposing rules of conduct on the community, Buddha's approach to religious norms was revolutionary as well as refreshing. Abidhamma Pitaka (100 BCE—100 CE), literally means discourses about dharma (doctrine). It is an interpretative exposition of the teachings of Buddha as found in the crisp formulations of Sutta Pitaka.

These scriptures are not to be viewed in the same way we take the Bible. One needs to be particularly careful in not committing the "Protestant fallacy," when handling

---

14. Kawasaki and Kawasaki, *Jataka Tales*, vol. 1, 12.

Buddhist scriptures. They are not revelations to be taken as providing authoritative divine directions for religious practice but rather as insights and practical guidelines arising from the experience of enlightened Buddha. These scriptures express the aspirations of Buddha's quest and the insights that his enlightenment generated. Such scriptures were codified and presented by his disciples with the conviction that what had worked for the master would also work for them.

Early Buddhism proposes that one could be liberated through self-effort. The scriptures serve as an aid in this effort. The Venerable Punnaji claims that the scriptures are not to be accepted on faith or treated as an authority but handled as a flashlight to guide those in darkness to find the path themselves.[15] Citing an early Buddhist scripture called Kalama Sutta he describes the role of the scriptures in the Buddhist quest for liberation thus, "Buddhist scripture is the word of the Buddha that instructs and inspires the human being on his way to goodness. The purpose of Buddhist scripture is to help followers find their way through life in the pursuit of goodness."[16]

Punnaji tries to highlight that the Buddhist scriptures are essentially Buddha's words, rather than God's words, and they are inspirational in that they aid the seeker to attain that higher quality of life, "goodness," which Buddhism identifies as nirvana. The memorizations of the crisp formulations, the discerning of the spirit of the monastic rules, and the insightful expositions of the doctrine are all meant to aid the seeker to attain what Buddha had achieved.

Buddha's enlightenment was a transcendental experience that could not be fully expressed through words. He hesitantly attempted to communicate the insights of his experience by reinterpreting the role of words. The Vedic semantics of the time claimed that seers who authored the scriptures beheld truth in words. Others need to grasp the truth in and through words. But the whole point of Buddha's message was that one should directly and personally attain enlightenment—that he could only point the way. Hence he tried to confine himself to practical directions, avoiding verbal and conceptual pictures of transcendental truths, which he thought were beyond words. His silence to the questions about transcended human experience, such as "Is there life after death?" and "Is there a god?" was meant to drive home this point. Hence, in interpreting what Buddha communicated through language, one needs to take his linguistic expressions as practical guidelines and exhortations for enlightenment rather than divine revelations of transcendental truths.

With the passage of time, as developments and divisions occurred within Buddhism, its scriptures increased in number and changed in content and function. The subsequent compendium of Buddhist sacred texts falls under the category of Mahayana scriptures. Dating from the first century BCE, there came into being a new and wide range of scriptures which went beyond what was expressed in the Pali canon. Buddhism started as a religion of the monks and nuns but later lay people became Buddhists. The later scriptures reflect the aspirations of Buddhists who were frustrated

15. Punnaji, "Place of Scripture," 6.
16. Ibid., 12.

with the way monastic Buddhism articulated the scriptures. Monks and nuns lived in isolated monasteries, under the patronage of kings and rich merchants. Having neither financial worries nor family responsibilities, these secluded monks and nuns were able to devote themselves to sophisticated doctrinal studies and meditative methods that were far beyond the comprehension and capabilities of lay people. These were turbulent times that gave rise to spiritual anguish among the population at large. What was needed was a way of liberation that could be understood and practiced by the ordinary lay people. The latter Buddhist scriptures were expressions of such aspirations.

The Avatamsaka-Sutra (The Flower Adornment Sutra), the large corpus of writings collectively called Prajnaparamita (Perfection of Wisdom Sutras), the Vimalkirti-Nirdesa Sutra, the Diamond Sutra, the Lotus Sutra, the Heart Sutra, and the Tibetan Tantric sutras may all be taken as expressions of the spiritual aspirations of latter Buddhists belonging to the Mahayana tradition.

The Diamond Sutra contains the core teachings of Buddha's teachings, stressing that everything is impermanent. In its emphasis on the role of the bodhisattva, this sutra may be taken as a bridge from Hinayana to Mahayana views.[17]

Most of the Mahayana scriptures, diverse though they may be, resorted to Buddha to establish their legitimacy. These sutras claimed that they too were records of Buddha's ideas, even though not made public until the right time came. For instance, the Avatamasaka Sutra records the teachings of Buddha immediately after his enlightenment, but known only to some. According to a popular Mahayanist story, once when Buddha was teaching, he took a handful of leaves from the forest and pointed out to his disciples that the leaves in his hand were very much less than the leaves of the forest. He compared the teachings given openly to the handful of leaves and the teachings that were to be given in secret to the leaves of the forest. The Mahayanists believe that Buddha communicated his insights based on the need and spiritual maturity of his listeners.

Vimalkirti-Nirdesa Sutra, originally in Sanskrit, was later translated into Chinese and Tibetan languages. This contains more of the insights of Vimalkirti than those of Buddha. The popularity of this sutra is not based on the historicity of the expounder Vimalakirti, as no one knows whether such a person really lived; the name Vimalakirti means "one who has a spotless fame." He denotes a historical prototype that represents the spiritual aspirations of the times. He was referred to as a bodhisattva in that he was trying to help others rather than meditate in a monastery. In the context of early Buddhism where only monks could aspire to be enlightened, a layman being designated as bodhisattva indicates how Buddhism was becoming a layman's religion. Moreover, this sutra employs a dramatic technique that ordinary people could relate to.

Mahayana sutras express the salvific aspirations of latter Buddhists in very definitive ways. At its beginning, Buddhism advocated self-effort as a means of liberation. Scriptures belonging to this tradition provided guidelines to help individuals attain liberation by themselves. But resort to "other-help" gained prominence in latter

---

17. Sahn, *Compass of Zen*, 125.

Buddhism. The shift from "self-help" to "other-help" had a significant impact on the function of latter Buddhist scriptures. This is most evident in Pure Land scriptures. Its main scriptures, The Longer and Shorter Sukhavatiuyuha, Amitayurdhyana, and Pratyupanna Samadhi Sutras describe ways and means to get the help of Amitabha (Amida), one who had attained enlightenment centuries ago and is now helping those who resort to him to gain entrance to heaven, the pure land.[18] There seems to be a significant shift from self-effort through good works to resort to other help, in these sutras. The longer sutra gives a prominent place to good works, while the Shorter Sutra emphasizes resort to Amitabha through repeating his name as the ticket to Pure Land.

The Lotus Sutra best represents Mahayana quest for liberation through resort to "other-help." Buddha in this sutra is deified and becomes an object of worship and the poetic stanzas of the sutra become a means of appealing to his help. Buddhism at first was essentially a religion for the monks and nuns. But when lay people became Buddhists, they needed an assurance that they also could attain nirvana. A single line of the Chinese text of the sutra "Not one fails to become a Buddha" is expanded in the Japanese version thus, "All will attain Buddhahood: the sutra says. And we the unenlightened mortals, hearing it, are glad."[19]

The sutra's declaration that all could attain Buddhahood provided that assurance and hence the Lotus Sutra became a popular object of veneration. Devotees used the title of the sutra as a mantra. Some volunteered to write copies of the sutra with the hope to gain merit.[20]

The growing trend to venerate Buddha and his teachings is evident in the manner these sutras came to be placed on the altars of Buddhist temples. But just like the early Buddhist, latter Buddhist scriptures express the aspirations of the Buddhists, and should not be taken as God revealed just because they contain theistic ideas and are even venerated. They are expressions of the spiritual insights and aspirations of those involved in the Buddhist quest. They may be taken as generating from divination, but are not to be confused with divine revelations. When we understand the Buddhist scriptures in this manner, the teachings that commenced with Buddha and later developed by several sects turn out to be spiritual insights and aspirations of the Buddhist religious community. The biblical presentation of the life and mission of Jesus, on the other hand, is based on the assumption that the Bible is God's revelation. The Christ of the Bible and Buddha of the Buddhist scriptures belong to different categories, necessitating different hermeneutical methods to understand them. To understand Buddha of the Buddhist scriptures, we have to find out what Buddha taught and how the religious community that followed him viewed Buddha. On the other hand, to understand Christ of the Bible, we have to find out what God in his revelation through scripture has revealed about Christ. Through the scriptures, Buddha provided a way of liberation that he had personally experienced in his

18. Prebish, *Buddhism*, 119–22.

19. Kasahara, ed., *History of Japanese Religion*, 95.

20. Ibid., 92–98.

spiritual journey, while the Bible presents Christ as the way of salvation. Our next step will be to examine the Buddhist way of salvation.

THE WAY OF THE QUEST

The Buddhist quest commences with the traumatic experiences Buddha had when he encountered poverty, sickness, and death. The Four Noble Truths, including the Eightfold Path, revolve around the realization that suffering (dukka) characterizes human existence. Buddha clarifies this in the first Noble Truth: "What now is the noble truth of suffering? Birth is suffering; decay is suffering; death is suffering; sorrow is suffering; lamentation, pain, grief, and despair are suffering; not to get what one wants is suffering; In short, the five aggregates (*khandhas*) of clinging are suffering."[21]

Buddha's description of suffering (dukka) in terms of the fivefold cravings (*khandhas*) that beset all existent beings implies that it is not be understood as mere physical or emotional pain that some experience. Buddhism highlights that such suffering is not to be taken as pain of disagreeable sensations nor as pain caused by the absence of happiness, but pain caused by the inherent restlessness and transitoriness of all phenomena (*samkhara-dukkata*). Such suffering arises out of the very nature of existence, impermanence (*anicca*), the fundamental property that characterizes all things. This truth points out that there is inherent inadequacy in everything, due to the fact that everything is causally conditioned (*pattica-samuppada*), and whatever is conditioned is impermanent and ultimately bound to perish. It is a suffering that is grounded on the temporality of human existence. The disease of suffering that besets humanity is not restricted to a single lifetime but covers the whole cycle of rebirths (samsara). This is the suffering that Buddha agonized over and that initiated his quest; he was determined to find the cause of suffering.

According to Buddha's diagnosis, the core cause of suffering is craving (*tanha*). He presents his diagnosis in his second Noble Truth: "What now is the noble truth of the origin of suffering? It is craving which gives rise to repeated existence, is bound up with pleasure and lust, and always seeks fresh enjoyment here and there; that is sensual craving for existence and craving for non-existence."[22]

In Buddha's view such a craving arises out of a deception caused by a warped view of who the craver is and what is being craved for. The craver takes for granted that he or she is a soul, a permanent identity, and the things craved for are lasting. But Buddha challenges both these assumptions. He claimed that there is no-soul (*anatta*) and the world is inherently impermanent (*anicca*) The Buddhist doctrine of *anatta*, as presented in the scripture, Samyutta-nikaya, states that no self exists in the sense of a permanent eternal entity, that the soul is no more than a transitory and changing aggregate of mental and emotive states. Hence, the tragedy is that human beings crave, unaware that both the craver and the things craved for are transitory. This is the

21. Bodhi, "The Buddha's Teachings," 62.
22. Ibid., 62–63.

Buddhist depiction of *maya*. Such deceptive craving places the human being in the bondage of the cycle of rebirths.

Chandra Wickramasinghe's poetic description of maya runs thus:

> Maya . . . that creates its own reality,
> Through a thousand self-reflecting mirrors of the mind,
> Tricks you into a suave duality
> Of the real unreal and the unreal real,
> Leaving you in a perfect bind.
> Your steady feet will cleave,
> With Heraclitean re-assurance,
> The waters of many rivers
> In a fleeting moment,
> As the mind travels in light years
> And jumps back into the crumbling moment
> Of life's division of space into time.
>
> Ah! How the illusion holds,
> Even in an unromantic heaven,
> With an eclipsed moon and remote stars,
> Where the dreamer
> Would still fantasize with consummate ease,
> The unseen glory
> And its hidden romance!
>
> Flux, unchanging flux!
> Stands on its head,
> Zeno's theory of static dots,
> And the Mind—the Great Deceiver!
> With quicksilver logic,
> Assures linear progression
> To seekers of mastery over it—
> Through self-effacement and self-denial,
> Till one slips into the formless continuum,
> Of zero infinity!
>
> "Moderation"—the distilled gospel of the ages,
> Lacks the glitzy mystique
> And the heady élan
> Of flaunted religion.
> The Greeks,
> With their humanistic idealism,
> Expressed it with succinct elegance,
> In "Meden Agan"![23]

Heraclitus and Zeno are Greek philosophers who had diametrically opposite worldviews. Heraclitus thought that everything in the world was in a state of flux, that one could not step into the same river twice. Zeno claimed that nothing moves,

23. Wickramasinghe, "Maya."

that change is an illusion. *Meden Agan* is a Greek phrase meaning "middle way." Wickramasinghe makes an insightful connection between the human predicament of being caught up in deceptive maya and the way out of it. In the context of "flux, unchanging flux" it is wise to resort to a "middle path": a moderate way.

This takes us to the next two Noble Truths which render the prognosis for the disease that besets humankind and the medicine of moderation that would cure it.

Buddha's third Noble Truth provides assurance that problem could be solved. He states, "What now is the noble truth of the cessation of suffering? It is the complete fading away and cessation of craving, its forsaking and abandonment, liberation and detachment from it . . . "[24]

This truth provides the strategy to get out of this bondage: one has to get rid of the cause of suffering (dukkha), which is craving (tanha).He claims that since suffering is caused by craving, if one removes the cause, the effect will cease; when one annihilates craving, suffering will be no more. This gives a strategic direction to the quest.

In order for the strategy to succeed, Buddha provides his fourth Noble Truth, which runs thus, "Now this, O monks, is the noble truth of the way that leads to the cessation of pain: this is the noble Eightfold Path, namely, right views, right intention, right speech, right action, right livelihood, right effort, right mindfulness, right concentration."[25]

This truth provides the means to execute the strategy. Buddha recommends the Eightfold Path as a way to escape the bondage of rebirths and attain liberation (nirvana). In order to eradicate suffering, its cause has to be destroyed and to achieve this goal Buddha presented a practical way, a way leading to the cessation of suffering.

The Eightfold Path may be presented thus:

1. Right Understanding—Wisdom/Knowledge (*prajna*)
2. Right Thought/Intention
3. Right Speech—Moral Discipline (*shila*)
4. Right Action/Conduct
5. Right Livelihood
6. Right Effort/Endeavor
7. Right Mindfulness/Contemplation (*Samadhi*)
8. Right Meditation/Concentration

Buddha presents the Noble Truths and the Eightfold Path as practical strategy to be liberated from what he perceives as the human predicament. The Eightfold Path provides the treatment for the disease that besets humanity. As Bihikku Bodhi puts it, "To each of the four truths the Buddha assigns a specific function, a task to be mastered by the disciple in training. The truth of suffering to be fully understood, the craving and defilement which originate it are to be abandoned, nirvana as deliverance

24. Bodhi, "The Buddha's Teachings," 63.
25. Radhakrishnan and Moore, eds., *Source Book*, 275.

from suffering to be realized, and the Noble Eightfold path that leads to deliverance to be developed."[26]

Such a path has some significant features.

A Nontheistic Path

The grouping of the eight steps into three interrelated activities—wisdom, moral discipline, and mediation—helps us understand the stages by which a seeker attains enlightenment (nirvana). One starts with a minimal degree of right understanding of the nature of the self that seeks and the world that is sought. Such knowledge (*prajna*) enables proper moral conduct (*shila*) which eventually leads to meditation (*samadhi*) that ends in nirvana. All three stages are taken to have salvific value in that they help the seeker to be liberated.

The third Noble Truth pinpoints that one could be released from the bondage of suffering that the cycle of rebirths (samsara) generates. That state of release is what Buddhism calls nirvana. The Eightfold Path provides the way to attain it. The Eightfold Path is essentially a "way of salvation." When Buddha presented this way, he did not claim that it would lead one to God or one could become divine. God does not play any part in the path to liberation. It should be noted that his path is nontheistic and not atheistic. Buddha does not deny God but is silent on the question of whether there is a God.

Punnaji points out that one does not become a Buddhist by birth or even by ritualistic practices but by a character transformation—a change of personality[27]—a transformation that is articulated through one's own effort rather than resort to divine help.

A Path Generated by Human Experience

Based on the path he took in his quest for liberation, Buddha prescribes the Eightfold Path. What he had achieved through his quest, he recommended to his disciples, so that they too might be liberated. Hence, the Four Noble Truths should not be taken as a theoretical construct of a speculative thinker but rather as a documented journal of Buddha's quest; it is an expression of the Buddha's personal quest, which after his enlightenment is presented as an earnest recommendation to his disciples. In the Dhammapada (The Path of Virtue), which is part of the Sutta Pitaka, Buddha states, "Going on this path, you will end your suffering. This path was preached by me when I became aware of the removal of the thorns [in the flesh]."[28]

Buddha's promise that following the path will end bondage and suffering is founded on his own experience. He himself followed the path and attained enlightenment and recommends it in his first sermon thus:

26. Bodhi, "The Buddha's Teachings," 64–65. See also Bodhi, *Noble Eightfold Path*, which highlights the therapeutic role of Buddha's Noble Truths.

27. Punnaji, *Becoming a Buddhist*, 2–3.

28. Radhakrishan and Moore, eds., *Source Book*, 313.

As long as in these noble truths my threefold knowledge and insight duly with its twelve divisions was not well purified, even so long, O monks, in the world with its gods, Mara, Brahma, with ascetics, brahmins, gods, and men, I had not attained the highest complete enlightenment. Thus I knew.

But when in these noble truths my threefold knowledge and insight duly with its twelve divisions was well purified, then, O monks, in the world . . . I had attained the highest complete enlightenment. Thus I knew. Knowledge arose in me; insight arose; that the release of my mind is unshakable; this is my last existence; now there is no rebirth.[29]

Hence, the Buddhist path came out of Buddha's spiritual struggles and episodes and not as divine revelations or as philosophical constructs.

A Middle Path

Buddha claimed that his way of liberation is a "middle path," a path of moderation that avoids the life of pleasure that the Indian Materialistic schools (*Carvaka*) advocated as well as the tortuous austerity of Hindu asceticism. He had tried both of these extreme paths and had not found them helpful.

He introduces his way of liberation in his first sermon thus: "These two extremes, O monks, are not to be practiced by one who has gone forth from the world. What are the two? That conjoined with the passions, low, vulgar, common, ignoble, and useless, and that conjoined with self-torture, painful, ignoble, and useless. Avoiding these two extremes the Tathagata has gained the knowledge of the Middle Way, which gives sight and knowledge, and tends to calm, to insight, enlightenment, nirvana."[30]

Such a way has helped him to be enlightened. *Tathagata*, as he calls himself, means "one has thus come." He came out of Hinduism which is founded on the assumption that humans have the divine potentiality to be liberated and thereby acquire some kind of divinity; either one becomes part of God or reaches God. The ways are directed from humans to Godhood. Buddha had already tried these paths and in comparison with these paths he claims that his Eightfold Path is the best one. Even though he acknowledges human potentiality to be liberated, he steers clear of the theistic facets of the Hindu ways. The justification of his claim is based on its success in aiding him to attain enlightenment; on experiential grounds. Instead of resorting to divine help he turns to self-help.

A Path of Self-Effort

In the Dhmmapada, Buddha states that, "You yourself must strive. The Blessed Ones are [only] preachers. Those who enter the path and practice meditation are released from the bondage of Mara [death, sin]."[31]

29. Ibid., 275.
30. Ibid., 274.
31. Ibid., 313.

Such striving accommodates every facet of human effort: physical, mental, moral, or spiritual. The activities of obtaining proper understanding, disciplining one's life-style, and insightful meditation that the Eightfold Path recommends could be taken as strategies of liberating oneself through human effort. In this sense the Buddhist way is essentially one of works.

If one could be liberated through self-effort, naturally there is no need for external help, especially a savior. The Dhammapada puts it this way, "Oneself, indeed, is one's savior, for what other savior would there be? With oneself well controlled the problem of looking for an external savior is solved."[32]

Even though early Buddhism did not look for an external savior, the success of the strategy of self-effort that it propagated depended on Buddha and his teachings.

A Path that Resorts to Buddha as Teacher

The formula of the "Three Jewels"—"I take refuge in the Buddha, I take refuge in the Doctrine (Dharma), and I take refuge in the Order (Sangha)"—is embedded in the Buddhist practice of faith. But, there are some questions, especially concerning the call to take refuge in the Buddha. If Buddha had insisted "Follow the dharma, not the person" how then could one recommend, "Take refuge in Buddha?" Moreover, if one takes Buddha to be a historical figure whose life came to an end at his death, how then could one take refuge in someone who is no longer alive? In order to find out how the Buddhists handle these issues we have to examine how they interpret the dictum, "Take refuge in the Buddha." Bhikku Bodhi, who represents the position of the early Buddhists, places the act of taking refuge in the Buddha as the first and momentous step in the path to liberation. He states:

> The first step in entering the Buddhist path is going for refuge to the Triple Gem, and the first of the three gems that we approach as refuge is the Buddha, the Enlightened One. Because the act of going for refuge to the Buddha marks the beginning of a new chapter in our life, it is worth our while to repeatedly pause and reflect upon the significance of this momentous step. Too often we are prone to take our first steps for granted. Yet it is only if we review these steps from time to time in a deepening awareness of their implications that we can be sure the following steps we take will bring us closer to our desired destination.[33]

Bhikku Bodhi is careful to point that the first momentous step is to find refuge in "Buddha the Enlightened One." For the early Buddhists, the Buddha is not god nor a personal savior. On the other hand, he is not just a benevolent sage, guru, or an expert in meditation. On the grounds of his own confession, Buddha is taken as the fully Self-Enlightened One (*sama sambuddha*), who is commissioned to teach. Tradition has it that after his enlightenment he was very hesitant to teach the way of liberation, until a deity, Sahampati, told him, "If you will only teach you will liberate countless beings

---

32. Ibid., 166.
33. Bodhi, "Taking Refuge," 23.

from the cycle of suffering."[34] The authenticity to provide teaching that would liberate people comes as a result of his possession of a full range of capabilities that enlightenment entails. It is this which makes the recluse Gautama Buddha a place of refuge. As Bodhi highlights, "The Buddha as refuge has no capacity to grant us liberation by an act of will. He proclaims the path to be traveled and the principles to be understood. The actual work of walking the path is then left to us, his disciples."[35]

Taking refuge in Buddha means following his teachings (dharma). The disciples, who took refuge in Buddha, were expected to follow his teachings, and not depend on him. They viewed Buddha as the teacher, whose guidance would enable a devotee to progress in the spiritual journey leading to enlightenment. But he is not savior.

Such an explanation of Buddha's identity as the enlightened teacher and the type of refuge that is involved no doubt helps us to understand how the early Buddhists of the Theravada tradition could reconcile the dictums, "Follow the doctrine, not the person" and "Take refuge in the Buddha." In taking refuge in Buddha's teachings one cannot avoid his emphasis on meditation (*samadhi*), which occurs as the last two stages in the Eightfold Path: right mindfulness and right meditation. It is meditation that ushers one into enlightenment. Hence his strategy is a meditative path.

A Meditative Path

Samadhi is the practice of concentration through right effort, mindfulness, and meditation. Since human craving is embedded in one's mental states, they need to be freed from such bondage. This takes us to the practice of *bhavana*, which literally means "mental development" and is commonly understood as meditation. Bhavana includes two types of trainings: concentration (samadhi) and wisdom (prajna). Two kinds of meditation were in vogue during this time. *Samatha-bhavana* aimed at mental tranquility while *Vipashyana-bhavana* aimed at development of insight that generates wisdom. There were techniques to practice *samadhi-bhavana* that could even generate trance-like states. Buddha himself acknowledged the usefulness of trances to provide mental tranquility, but he found that the mere mental tranquility that trances offered could not liberate him. He pointed out that they function only as stepping stones to the development of insight. Buddha achieved enlightenment when he practiced vipashyana meditation. This type of meditation enables the development of insight into one's own nature—the insight by means of which one may recognize and eliminate the cause of suffering. This was what he practiced for his own liberation and what he advocated.

The sole purpose of meditation in Buddhism is to enable the devotee to achieve enlightenment. Hence, mediation should neither stop at the level of concentration nor even mental tranquility through trances but provide the insightful wisdom (prajna) that liberates. This in Buddhism is Vipashyana meditation. Walpola Rahula, a reputed Theravada scholar and monk, clearly articulates the character and liberating function

34. Bercholz and Kohn, eds., *Buddha and His Teachings*, 18.
35. Bodhi, "Taking Refuge," 23.

of *vipashyana-bhavana.* He points out that the word meditation is a poor substitute for the term *bhavana,* which means "culture" or "development." According to Rahula, Buddhist bhavana is a mental culture that has to be cultivated. "It aims at cleansing the mind of impurities . . . and cultivating such qualities as concentration, awareness, intelligence, will, energy, the analytical faculty, confidence . . . leading finally to the attainment of highest wisdom (*prajna*) which sees the nature of things as they are, and realizes the Ultimate Truth, *Nirvana.*"[36]

Wisdom here may be understood as experiential wisdom rather than an intellectual proficiency. It is in the experiential wisdom that enlightenment occurs; the vipashyana-bhavana, the flash of insight, is a personal intuitive moment in which one sees the impermanence, egolessness, and suffering of existence.

Vipashyana meditation gives the seekers insight into the ultimate cause of their predicament and thereby delivers them out of it, and provides an effective means to enlightenment.

A Path that Targets Enlightenment

Enlightenment is the climax of the Buddhist quest, the ultimate bliss that Buddhists are seeking. One who attains it is called *arahat.* One may attain nirvana while living, but is still constrained by the limitations of existence. But when one who has attained nirvana dies, that person is free from such fetters and enters *Parinibbhana,* where there is no return to the crippling bondage of the cycle of rebirths (samsara).

Nirvana is not mere annihilation, even though described in negative epithets, like "blow-out." This is because it means the cessation of the life of samsaric suffering, and the illusions it carries with it. This is how Buddha described nirvana to his disciples: "Monks, there is a not-born, a not-become, a not-made, a non-compounded. Monks, if the unborn, not-become, not-made, not-compounded were not, there would be apparent no escape from this here that is born, become, made compounded."[37]

Nirvana entails the dying out of greed, anger, and illusions that beset human existence. To the question posed by King Milinda as to what nirvana is, Nagasena, a disciple of the Buddha, points out some of its qualities with the use of analogies. Just as a lotus is untarnished by water, nirvana is untarnished from evil dispositions. Just like medicine, nirvana kills the poison of evil dispositions, and acts as ambrosia for those suffering. Just like an ocean tosses dead corpses to the shore, nirvana pushes away evil dispositions; it is inaccessible to all evil dispositions like a mountain peak; just like a wish-fulfilling gem, nirvana satisfies every desire, causes delight, and is full of luster.[38]

Venerable Punaji highlights the positive impact of the negativity of nirvana thus:

> The final stage in the development of the path of Buddhism is depersonalization. This is when we are able to give up what has been personalized by seeing that there is nothing that we can call our own. When we see that all things are

36. Rahula, *What the Buddha Taught,* 68.

37. Woodward, *Minor Anthologies,* 98.

38. Rahula, *Way to Peace,* 82–83.

unstable (*anicca*), anxiety-producing (*dukkha*), and impersonal (*anatta*), we are free of all suffering. This is because there are no possessions or "self" to worry about. This depersonalization is that which makes an individual completely self-less. When this happens one can even face death without anxiety. This complete freedom from anxiety is the aim of Buddhism.[39]

Perhaps nirvana acquires its negativity because two negative claims are commonly associated with it: that at nirvana one realizes that there is "no-self" (anatta) and hence there can be nothing left of a person, after the physical and mental aggregates cease at death. Moreover, when one attains nirvana one also realizes things, being aggregates, are not permanent (anicca). In the nirvanic experience one does not confront a God or even become part of a cosmic reality. Nirvana is the experiential climax of the spiritual quest, when one realizes the nothingness of nothing that liberates the seeker to be freed from the human predicament, characterized as suffering (dukka).

If the Buddhist way of liberation is one that claims the adequacy of self-effort, depends on the efficacy of disciplined morality and mediation, took the liberated state to be negative "blowing out," and needs only an enlightened teacher, then Christ becomes irrelevant to the Buddhist quest. But it does not terminate with such a stance. The developments that took place eventually make Christ relevant to the Buddhist aspirations.

THE LATTER DEVELOPMENTS IN THE WAY OF THE BUDDHIST QUEST

A few hundred years after Buddha's death there arose several sects all claiming to be true to Buddha's teachings. These sects fall within two traditions: Hinayana and Mahayana. The distinction between them is not due to disagreement on the core doctrines of Buddhism but rather about the adequacy of the way to liberation that each presented. Mahayana (The Great Vehicle or the Wider Path) considers its path to be more accommodative and more efficacious as a salvific strategy than that of the Hinayanists. On the other hand, Hinayana views Mahayana as a return to theistic Hindu traditions, deviating from the path that Buddha proposed.

During the reign of King Asoka (276–232 BCE), the royal Buddhist benefactor, the Third Buddhist Council took place, where he declared that the Theravada teachings constituted the orthodox Buddhist doctrine. The country enjoyed peace and prosperity during his reign. Buddhism became theologically professional; monks and nuns lived in the seclusion of their comfortable monasteries, preoccupied with doctrinal studies and meditation. But, by the beginning of second century BCE, northwestern India became a prey to a succession of invaders—Bactrian Greeks, Scythians, Parthians, and a Central Asian tribe, known to Indian historians as Kushanas. This led to political upheavals and the social and economic fabric began to disintegrate.

Neither the ritualism of Hindu Brahmins nor Hinayana monastic meditation were able to meet the challenges of the times. Such practices could not relieve the people's anxiety or offer a practical way of liberation that was effective in such desperate

---

39. Punnaji, *Becoming a Buddhist*, 15.

conditions. Buddhism had to get out of the seclusion of monastic isolation and meet the hurting needs of the suffering masses. This is what Mahayana Buddhism attempted to do. Hence, Mahayana may be taken as a response to the inadequacies of Hinayana Buddhism, as a way of liberation. The new developments in Buddhism, such as the deification of the Buddha, the highlighting of the role of the bodhisattva, revisions of the path to liberation, and the re-characterization of nirvana figure prominently in the Mahayana Buddhism. These developments are noteworthy expressions of the Buddhist seekers to formulate a more adequate path to liberation; a strategy to render their quest for liberation more rewarding.

Mahayana Buddhism spread to China, Japan, Tibet, Mongolia, Korea, and Vietnam. It is difficult to identify those responsible for leading the developments of latter Buddhism. From the latter Buddhist scriptures we can discern that those who spearheaded Mahayana Buddhism did not claim to have initiated but rather to have continued the quest that Buddha initiated, by introducing some new and significant trends.

Plea for a Savior God

The early Buddhist way of liberation was essentially nontheistic. Buddha was resorted to and venerated as a teacher. But, people in utter desperation need more than a teacher, however enlightened he may be.

Early Buddhism views Buddha as a historical figure, who lived during a specific period. At death, he left his teachings, the dharma, as a guide. But there is a significant change in his personhood in latter Buddhism. In the Mahayana tradition, Buddha becomes a transcendental cosmic principle pervading the universe, manifesting in three aspects or "bodies" (*trikaya*): dharma body (*dharmakaya*) or "the body of own being"—the transcendent Buddha taken as the universal consciousness identical with absolute reality; "the body of bliss" (*sambhagayaka*)—the celestial aspect of Buddha, the heavenly Buddha who communicates in heaven with other buddhas and is the object of devotion; and the "appearance or transformation body" (*nirmanakaya*)—that by which the heavenly Buddha becomes human to liberate humanity at specific periods of time. Siddhartha Gautama is taken to be one such manifestation.[40] Buddha came to be viewed not merely as a teacher but as a transcendental being, who reveals himself through incarnations. Such a conceptual change in his personhood had a significant impact on how latter Buddhists characterized the way of liberation, which changed to become theistic. The deification of Buddha becomes evident in more than one way.

The belief developed that Gautama Buddha was an incarnation of a Buddha who had attained enlightenment long before he was born. Tibetan Buddhism, headed by the Dalai Lama, upholds such a view.[41] Early Buddhism claimed that the ultimate source of the authenticity of Buddha's path of liberation rested on his enlightenment

---

40. Oxtoby, *World Religions: Eastern Traditions*, 267; Fisher, *Living Religions*, 159.

41. Dalai Lama, *How to Practice*, 19.

in his earthly life, and the teachings generated from it. But, eventually, Buddhists took Buddha to be much more than the Enlightened Teacher. Perhaps, the practice of taking refuge in the Buddha acted as a catalyst in the deification of the Buddha in Mahayana Buddhism.

People started worshiping the Buddha. In some of the early Buddhist sculptures belonging to second and first century BCE, such as those of Bharhut stupa, worshipers are depicted as ecstatically prostrating themselves before the emblems of the Buddha like the wheel and the trident shaped symbol representing the Three Jewels. Gradually he came to be venerated through symbols associated with his anatomy. The footprint found on a mountain in Sri Lanka, popularly called Adam's Peak, became a place of Buddhist veneration. The Dalada Maligawa in Sri Lanka that houses Buddha's tooth has become a sacred place of pilgrimage for Buddhists. Eventually Buddha's images appeared in places like Mathura (in northern India) and Gandhara (in what is now northern Pakistan and eastern Afghanistan). The trend to glorify Buddha and elevate him above his teachings gradually started gaining ground. By the first century CE, whether due to the influence of Greco-Roman religious practices or the impact of Hindu idol worship, Buddha was deified and worshiped as an icon.

The ascendancy of Buddha is anticipated in earlier schools of Buddhism and is even evident in some Hinayana texts. For instance, Mahavatsu Sutra of the Mahasangika school describes Buddha as a supramundane being who appears in human form to meet human needs; an early Hinayana Pali texts calls him a great being (*Mahapurusa*).

People yearning for liberation need more than an enlightened teacher; people need a God. Hence, the deification of Buddha is not surprising. The Lotus Sutra presents a transcendent everlasting Buddha, able to manifest himself at any time, even to the common people, who lack spiritual wisdom.[42] Such a Buddha could no longer be a mere historical figure, but an everlasting, celestial, powerful, and compassionate divine being. The sutra calls upon Buddhists to view Buddha not merely as a historical figure but as a transcendent being. This indicates a significant change in Buddhalogy. The sutra emphasizes that if one is to successfully follow the Buddhist way of salvation, one has to resort not merely to an enlightened teacher, who lived and died at a particular period of time, but one who transcends time and space: "The Thus Come One (*tathagatha*), seeing the beings' desire for a lesser dharma, their qualities thin and their defilements grave, preaches to such persons saying, 'In my youth I left my household and attained anuttarasamyaksambodhi.' However, since in fact I achieved Buddhahood it has been a long stretch of time as this . . . It is merely by resort to an expedient device, in order to teach and convert living beings, to enable them to enter upon the Buddha Path, that I spoke such words as these."[43]

In contrast to the earlier Hinayana view of Gautama Buddha as an enlightened human being, latter Mahayana Buddhists began to view him as a divine being, motivated

---

42. Lai, "Three Jewels," 311.

43. Hurvitz, trans., *Scripture of the Lotus Blossom*, 238–39.

by compassion to liberate human beings. It is interesting that such an attempt to deify Buddha was between third century BCE and first century CE, during the time period of the incarnation of Christ.

Plea for a Vicarious Savior

With the accommodation of laity, Buddhism had to meet the needs of the common people. These were disturbing times. People were experiencing wars, foreign invasions, pillage, and poverty, resulting in the disintegration of society. Meticulous scriptural studies and sophisticated meditative practices in secluded monasteries were conducive to a clergy living in a peaceful, affluent society, but could not meet the spiritual yearnings of a hurting people who needed a way out of their troubles. The Hinayana monastic way failed to offer people a practicable path to relieve them in their time of desperation during the turbulent times.

This is where the bodhisattva finds a place in the Buddhist quest. The accommodation of bodhisattva made the Buddhist way of liberation more conducive to the tone of the times and more sensitive to the cries of the people. The latter Buddhist way of liberation could be described as the *Way of the Bodhisattva*. Hinayana Buddhism encouraged devotees to attain nirvana, through self-effort. One who attains nirvana was an arahat. But people began to realize that self-effort was not adequate to reach the goal; that people needed external help. Such a view became embedded in the Mahayana tradition. The Lotus Sutra claims that in contrast to the earlier goal of individual liberation that resulted in the follower of the Buddhist path becoming an arahat, there is a higher goal. This goal is to acquire the character of Buddha, the mind of Buddha that aspires to achieve enlightenment for the benefit of all sentient beings. Such a development had a significant impact on the depiction of the Buddhist way of salvation. The strategy of self-help yielded to that of mutual help, the strategy of self-effort gave way to resort to the assistance of bodhisattvas.

Bodhisattva means a person destined for or seeking enlightenment. In the early Buddhist Pali scriptures, the compound term, *bodhi-sattva* referred to a sentient being seeking enlightenment or one devoted to enlightenment. But in later Buddhist Mahayana scriptures, like the Sutra on Perfect Wisdom, the term receives a wider connotation. Bodhisattva refers to one who has altruistic intention of seeking the enlightenment of others rather than one's own. Bodhisattvas are potential arahats who, out of compassion for their fellow human beings, have delayed their own attainment of nirvana until they have enabled others to attain it. The replacement of the ideal of the arahat by that of the bodhisattva is one main distinction between the Hinayana and Mahayana Buddhism. Mahayana accommodates savior figures like Amida Buddha, Avalokitesvara (Bodhisattva of Compassion), Bhaisajyaraja (Medicine King), and Samantabhadra. They are supposed to transcend time and help devotees to attain liberation. Avalokitesvara is supposed to take different forms to enable devotees to attain nirvana (Lotus Sutra chapter 25). In fact, the Dalai Lama is believed to be an incarnation of the Bodhisattva of Compassion.

The development of the role of the bodhisattva vividly characterizes the change from self-effort to resort to "other-help" in the Buddhist quest for liberation. Mahayana attributes certain significant characteristics to bodhisattvas which render them efficacious in enabling the people to attain liberation.

First of all, bodhisattva is one who is committed to liberate others. The bodhisattva vow is soothing to a despondent people, since it assures them of what to expect from the bodhisattva. The vow runs thus: "Beings are infinite in number; I vow to save them all. The obstructive passions are endless in number; I vow to end them all. The teachings for saving others are countless; I vow to learn them all. Buddhahood is the supreme attainment, I vow to attain it."[44]

Such a vow gives the assurance that the bodhisattva is committed to liberate all human beings. Buddhism points out that people are caught up in the bondage of cycle of rebirths (samsara) due to lack of knowledge about who they really are and the nature of the world in which they exist. Hence, the Eightfold Path commences with proper understanding, which is developed through the other steps. Knowledge is indispensable for liberation. This vow assures that the bodhisattva will attain such knowledge, which would equip him to fulfill his commitment.

Second, in order to fulfill the bodhisattva vow, one needs to be motivated. Being compassionate to the suffering of people provides such motivation. A Mahayana sutra puts it this way:

> The bodhisattva is endowed with wisdom of a kind whereby he looks on all beings as though victims going to the slaughter. And immense compassion grips him. His divine eye sees . . . innumerable beings, and he is filled with great distress at what he sees, for many bear the burden of past deeds which will be punished in purgatory, others will have unfortunate rebirths which will divide [separate] them from the Buddha and his teachings, others must soon be slain, others are caught in the net of false doctrine, others cannot find the path [of salvation], while others have gained a favorable rebirth only to lose it again.
>
> So he pours out his love and compassion upon all those beings, and attends to them, thinking, "I shall become the savior of all beings, and set them free from their sufferings."[45]

The most popular bodhisattva of the Far East is Kuan-yin (Avalokitesvara) known to be most compassionate since he or she is committed to liberate all who are suffering and does not refuse anyone who seeks his or her aid. Ksitigarbha, also known as Earth-Store Bodhisattva, is the ultimate embodiment of altruism, by virtue of the vow he made to save all those tormented in hell. He has decided not to attain enlightenment until he liberates everyone in hell—until hell is empty.

Third, being compassionate is not enough. In order to fulfill the bodhisattva vow, one should have capacity to help others to be liberated. A bodhisattva needs supernatural powers. Mahayana claims that bodhisattvas could be humans with supernatural

---

44. Fisher, *Living Religions*, 164. (The Four Great Bodhisattva vows were compiled by Chih-I of the Tien-t-ai School of Mahayana Buddhism in 6 CE.)

45. de Bary et al., eds. *Sources of Indian Tradition*, 158.

powers or heavenly beings. They are seen as exhibiting qualities of the eternal Buddha, like wisdom and compassion. Kuan-yin (Avalokitesvara), the Bodhisattva of Compassion, is represented as having 1,000 hands depicting her almighty power.

Bodhisattva Avalokitesvara (Kuan-yan) at Buddhist Cham Shan Temple, Toronto, Canada

The feminine counterpart of Avalokitesvara is the revered deity of the Tibetan pantheon, the Green Tara Buddha. She is sought for protection and for deliverance from obstacles.

According to a popular legend, Avalokitesvara was once so moved by the suffering in the world that he shed tears. Out of one of these tears came forth a female Buddha, the Green Tara Buddha. Because of the merit she had accumulated, she was given the right to assume a human form. She preferred to take on a feminine form because she realized that there were many who gain enlightenment in male form and help human beings but there were very few female Buddhas.

People who realize their limitations naturally cry for superhuman help. The bodhisattva with superhuman powers is a response to such a cry.

Fourth, people living in a society of distrust need a person who is trustworthy. They would usually consider a person who does not waver in his or her commitment during challenging times as a trustworthy person. The following passage from a lost sutra called, "Meeting of Father and Son" (*Pitrputrasamagama*), exhibits the trustworthiness of the bodhisattva: "So the bodhisattva . . . is happy

Green Tara Buddha

even when subjected to the tortures of hell . . . When he is being beaten with canes or whips, when he is thrown into prison, he still feels happy . . . he cultivates and develops the consciousness of joy in his relations with all beings, and so he acquires a contemplative spirit filled with joy in all things . . . and becomes imperturbable—not to be shaken by all the deeds of Mara."[46]

Fifth, people in desperate situations need a helper who not only shows the way out, but also helps to get out in a tangible way. People, who are unable to help themselves, cry for someone to carry their burdens. In the Hinayana tradition, Buddha as the Master Teacher and other enlightened ones (arahats) could show one how to attain enlightenment but could not enable the seeker to attain it. This is where the help of the bodhisattva is essential. The bodhisattva does not merely provide the "how to" by pointing to the Eightfold Path, but takes a further step of enabling the seeker to attain liberation; the bodhisattva, unlike the arahat, delays entering into nirvana and helps others to attain it by transference of merit. People in a helpless predicament do not merely want to know how to be free but yearn for help that would free them from their predicament. Bodhisattva was a timely response to such yearning. In this sense, the bodhisattva becomes a vicarious savior, and many passages of the Mahayana scriptures indicate the solemn resolve of the bodhisattva to serve as a vicarious helper:

> All creatures are in pain, all suffer from bad and hindering karma . . . All that mass of pain and evil karma I take in my own body . . . Assuredly I must bear the burdens of all beings . . . for I have resolved to save them all. I must set them all free, For all beings are caught in the net of craving, encompassed by ignorance, held by the desire for existence; they are doomed to destruction, shut in a cage of pain . . . they are all on the edge of the gulf of destruction . . . I care not at all for my own deliverance. For I have taken upon myself, by my own will, the whole of the pain of all things living . . . I resolve to dwell in each state of misfortune through countless ages for the salvation of all beings . . . for it is better that I alone suffer than that all beings sink to the worlds of misfortune. There I shall give myself into bondage, to redeem all the world from the forest of purgatory, from rebirth as beasts, from the realm of death. I must so bring to fruition the root of goodness that all beings find the utmost joy, unheard of joy, the joy of omniscience.[47]

The Buddhists of the Mahayana tradition wanted a helper, who was seriously committed, sincerely motivated by compassion, trustworthy, endowed with supernatural powers, and would not merely show the way to liberation but carry their burdens and be their substitute. The bodhisattva met their plea.

Plea for Mercy

Accommodating bodhisattvas implies that people cannot liberate themselves, that they need "other-help." When one resorts to other help on account of one's helplessness,

---

46. Ibid., 168.

47. Ibid., 160–62. (The passage, cited in Shantideva's *Compendium of Doctrine*, containing citations from early Buddhist scriptures (Siksasamuccaya 278–83) indicates such a resolve.)

"grace" becomes relevant; people in desperate conditions feel their helplessness, and such a feeling generates a cry for mercy that could even lead to a plea for grace, depending of the degree of desperation.

According to Hinayana Buddhism's principle of karmic retribution, good and bad deeds produce corresponding happiness and suffering and the results return to the performer of the deeds. However, the belief that merit could be transferred gradually began to gain ground. The Mahayana tradition accommodates the transfer of merit from the bodhisattva to the devotees. Liberation is still based on the merit of works—the meritorious deeds of the bodhisattva. In Pure Land Buddhism, a significant development took place, especially when it reached Japan. The Pure Land sect originated in China in the fourth century CE, and is based mainly on the Indian Buddhist scriptures, Sukhavati-vyuha Sutras, which speak of the Western Paradise of Sukhavati, the Pure Land (*Jodo* in Japanese). To enter such a paradise, a personality called Amitabha (Amida in Japanese) comes into the picture. There are conflicting views as to who he is. Some believe that he is a heavenly being or one who has attained divine status. Legend has it that a king, Dharmakara, after hearing one of Buddha's sermons, had forsaken his throne and started on a journey to attain enlightenment. After years of tortuous discipline, Dharmakara, who had vowed that he would not attain Buddhahood until all sentient beings were saved, finally obtained Buddhahood. Then he was called Amitabha (Amida). He started calling all people, promising that they would be born in Pure Land by simply thinking of him. The resort to Amitabha (Amida) by the followers of the Pure Land sect best exemplifies such a way of liberation.

Honen Shonin, the founder of the Jodo sect (Japanese version of the Pure Land sect) and his disciple, Shinran Shonin, went to the extent of claiming that salvation was possible through faith alone. Such a faith required a childlike wholehearted repetition of the name of Amida. Shinran Shonin claimed that even a bad man could enter Pure Land, trusting Amida. He verbalizes the confession of the Buddhists thus, "We men are karma-bound so deeply that it is useless for us to attempt to undo the evil done. We can leave it to Amida to save us—and he will."[48] These Buddhists claim that total dependency on Amitabha is indispensable. They believe that he had resolved that all those who chant his name will be reborn in the Pure Land. Hence they recite *Namu Amida Butsu* (Hail Amida Buddha) with the hope that he will come to their aid. This seems to be a definitive plea for "grace." But is it a plea "grace" or for "mercy?"

The devotees of this school seek Amitabha's aid in order to be reborn in the "Pure Land" and eventually attain nirvana. In the idealistic Pure Land environment, no new negative karmic accumulations would be created and all existing ones would evaporate. Nirvana would be therefore just a short step away.

Plea for Eternal Life

Despite the enlightenment that early Buddhist nirvana provides, there is a negativity associated with it. It is described in such negative analogies as "a flame blown out," or

48. Corless, "Pure Land Piety," 264.

"seeing nothing." But, people need an assurance that there is a future for them; one that can be hoped for. The Pure Land sect provides that hope. Its gospel is that one can be reborn in a land of ultimate bliss, the Pure Land, through the enablement of Amida Buddha.

The description of the exquisite beauties of this heavenly place, where the faithful hope to go, provided a positive and refreshing view of enlightenment. Entering the Pure Land was not nirvana, but a stepping stone to it. Devotees realize that their stay in this heaven would not last long if based on their own meritorious deeds, as such deeds would be limited. They resort to Amida Buddha's aid, since his merit would be far greater than theirs; this would guarantee them a longer stay. They also believe that in such an ideal environment, no new negative karmic acts would accumulate and existing ones would evaporate. Nirvana would be therefore just a short step away. If life in Pure Land was so wholesome and rewarding, the subsequent nirvanic experience needed to generate something much better and more everlasting. We sense here the anticipation for not being just "blown out," but for a "life" of an entirely different order; a plea for eternal life—one that is qualitatively different from the present life.

Plea for a Tangible Nirvanic Moment

The early Buddhist depiction of nirvana in such negative terms as "coming to nothing" was rather a disappointment to the devotees, who wanted to experience a liberation that would generate some kind of optimism after following the strenuous Buddhist path. Description of nirvana in terms of "suchness" was an attempt to provide that sense of optimism to the liberated devotee. A Mahayana sect, *Vijnanavadin* school, proposed that at enlightenment one became aware of "suchness" (*tathata*), in which all phenomenal appearances were lost in the awareness of an ultimate being. The term thathata refers to the highest conception possible to describe "suchness"—it is something beyond human conception. Nirvana becomes the highest state of being, of becoming aware of and thereby connected to Pure Being, the Absolute, Buddha's Body of Essence. Thus the pessimism that colors the early Buddhist rendering of nirvana was replaced by one more positive.

Moreover, devotees want to experience nirvana as soon as possible. Early Buddhism prescribes an arduous path of self-effort for the devotee that demands proper understanding, moral conduct, and meditation. But, even after all this it would take several lifetimes to become enlightened. For this was the case even with Buddha. The Mahayana path is also a "slow path," since it would take three eons of rebirths to be enlightened. Hence in these traditions, one could never hope to be enlightened in one's lifetime. But, naturally people want to be assured of their enlightenment before they die. The Tibetan Tantric Buddhism meets this need. It provides an esoteric path called *Vajrayana* (based on the Diamond Vehicle Sutra) or *Tantrayana* (based on tantric practices). It claims that following such a path would allow enlightenment to occur within a single lifetime. The Tibetan devotees resort to the spiritual guidance and teachings of Dalai Lamas and also employ tantric practices. The present Dalai Lama's popular speeches and books are all based on the conviction that people can be freed from the problems that beset them and be enlightened in this lifetime. For instance, his book entitled, *How to Practice: The Way to a Meaningful Life*, is divided into a series of distinct steps that will lead seekers toward enlightenment. He accommodates tantra in his strategy. According to him, tantra blends imagination with meditation to generate a practice called "deity yoga." Such a practice calls the devotee to visualize himself or herself to be Buddha or a deity. It is the Dalai Lama's conviction that tantric practice enables one to achieve Buddhahood faster.[49]

Moreover, the traditional Buddhist emphasis on scriptural knowledge and moral propriety sometimes seems to overcloud the experiential aspect of the nirvanic moment. People do not want to know about the liberating moment, or even be preoccupied with the mechanics of meditation, but want to experience the nirvanic moment in an intimate firsthand manner. Zen/Chan Buddhism responds to this desire. Giving preference to directly experience the nirvanic moment, Zen advocates direct intuition of cosmic unity known as the Buddha nature. The direct way of experiencing that unity is *Zazen*, "seated meditation." Zen/Chan offers devotees the direct experiential assurance of the liberating moment.

The Mahayana, Tibetan, Tantric, and Zen/Chan facets of latter Buddhism contributed to make enlightenment (nirvana) positive and directly experiential, and feasible to attain within the lifetime of the devotees.

The metamorphosis that occurred in Buddhism makes Christ relevant to the Buddhist quest. Our next job will be to identity areas of such relevancy.

THE RELEVANCE OF CHRIST TO THE BUDDHIST QUEST

When trying to identify the areas of relevancy between Christ and the Buddhist quest, we have to keep in mind that the articulators of the Buddhist quest, commencing with Buddha, belong to a world where we cannot place Christ. The Buddhist quest originated and was articulated by humans. Buddha and the subsequent leaders of the sects of latter Buddhism, like Nagarjuna and the Dalai Lamas, are all humans. Christ, on the other hand, is God incarnate.

The humanity of Buddha is evident in his birth, his spiritual journey, his mission, and his death. The birth stories of Buddha and Jesus are similar in some ways. Both were conceived without normal human intercourse. Buddha's mother, though married, was under an oath of celibacy, while Jesus' mother was an unwed virgin. Buddha was born in a grove while Jesus was born in a stable. Angels or celestial beings appeared in the sky to announce their births, to shepherds in the case of Jesus and to a meditating sage in Buddha's case.[50] But the declarations concerning his birth, both by the deities and by Buddha himself, clearly indicate that he was a human being, even though acclaimed to be the "foremost among mankind." It is believed that prior to Buddha's birth, deities announced to his mother that she would be blessed with a son

---

49. Dalai Lama, *How to Practice*, 197.
50. Oxtoby, *World Religions: Eastern Traditions*, 223.

of great power. On other hand, Jesus was born Savior. The message given by the angel to the shepherds in Bethlehem ran thus: "Do not be afraid. I bring you good news of great joy that will be for all people. Today in the town of David a Savior has been born to you" (Luke 2:10–11). Jesus was born Savior of all humanity, while Buddha was "foremost among mankind," on the grounds of his enlightenment. Ananda mentions Buddha's declaration about himself after his birth thus: "I am the Highest in the world, I am the Best in the world, I am the Foremost in the world; this is the last birth; now there is no more renewal of being in future lives."[51]

The reason for Buddha's exuberance was that he was freed from the bondage of the cycle of rebirths (samsara). On the other hand, the angel informed Joseph that Mary would bring forth a son who would be called Immanuel, which means "God with us" (Matt 1:23). Buddha may be highest, best, or foremost among humans, but is not God incarnate.

The Buddhist scripture, Sutta Pitaka, records the poem of a Brahmin seer that foretells the coming enlightenment of Buddha. The seer states: "At a Sakyan city in the Land of Lumbini, a Being to be Enlightened, a Priceless Jewel, is born in the world of men for welfare . . . Foremost among mankind . . . "[52] Buddha was born to be enlightened and thereby to enlighten others. On the other hand, the comments and declarations, both angelic and human, surrounding the birth of Jesus highlight that he was God incarnate born as savior to save humanity.

Moreover, Buddha's quest originated in a spiritual crisis. The traumatic experiences that he had encountered distressed him and motivated him to find a solution to the human predicament. In his spiritual journey he tried the ways of liberation that were in vogue, ranging from tortuous asceticism to materialistic hedonism. After unsuccessful attempts to liberate himself, he sat crossed-legged under a tree, pledging to himself that he would not get up unless he found what he was searching for. Mara, the satanic tempter, became disturbed and tried to hinder Buddha from becoming enlightened. The tempter could be understood as the satan of Buddhism in the sense he represents craving which Buddhism views as the root cause of the suffering (dukka) of humanity. Mara was intent on hindering Buddha's enlightenment, but failed. Tradition has it that Mara first sent his daughters, whose names suggest greed and boredom. Then he sent his sons, whose names suggest fear and anger. As a last resort, he himself tried to tempt Buddha.[53] It is believed that Buddha defeated the tempter on the grounds of merit earned through virtuous deeds done in his past lives.

Buddha's temptation shows that he was struggling to be enlightened and that Mara tried his best to hinder it. On the other hand, Satan tempted Jesus by trying to deconstruct his identity. When he was baptized, after God the Father had acclaimed him as his beloved Son (Matt 3:17), Satan attempted to make Jesus doubt whether he was really God's Son. The temptation episode indicates that the tempter tried his best

51. Nanamoli, *Life of the Buddha*, 5.
52. Ibid., 6.
53. Oxtoby, *World Religions: Eastern Traditions*, 226.

to hinder Buddha achieving enlightenment. The tempter, on the other hand, could not hinder Jesus being saved, for he was born Savior. The tempter tried to make Jesus doubt his identity.

Buddha's teachings were founded on his enlightenment experience, while Jesus' teachings were based on the authority that came from his identity. Buddha never claimed to be God, while Jesus is God the Son. Buddha's teachings continue, but that Buddha died no one questions. In fact, Buddha himself encouraged his disciples to follow his teachings after his death. During his last hours he comforted his disciple Ananda, saying, "When the Blessed One is gone, you might think that the teacher is gone, that you no longer have a teacher. This is not true. The *Dharma*, the disciple, and the practice that I taught you will be your teacher after I am gone."[54]

The veneration of his tooth, hair, and other vestments drives home the point that he is no more. On the other hand, Jesus died and rose again; he and his teachings continue.

Buddha initiated the quest as a human being. The leaders who followed him were also very much part of humanity. Hence the Buddhist way has to be viewed as one that arose out of the spiritual anguish of human beings. Buddha provided a way of salvation on the grounds of his own enlightenment. It is true that Buddha claimed that his way was the best. Buddha recommended his path as the "Middle Path" in the context of the paths of liberation that were in vogue. All these paths were human attempts to attain liberation, based on the basic Hindu assumption that the human being is capable of reaching Godhood. Buddha categorized these paths into two groups: the hedonistic path of pleasure and the path of extreme asceticism. He placed his path as the "Middle Path" in comparison to these two extremes, and in comparison to these paths, it presents itself as the best path. But all these ways commence with the anguish of human beings and targeted to find a way out of such anguish, some of them attempting to reach God or attain godhood.

The Christian path, on the other hand, does not belong to this category of paths, since it is based on an entirely different assumption: that humans are not capable of reaching God on account of their sinful nature. Hence, the path of liberation had to be from God to humans. Jesus Christ, as God Incarnate, is not comparable to any of the paths, whether hedonistic, ascetic, or even "middle."

Jesus did not provide a way of salvation on the grounds of his own salvation. He does not provide a "way of salvation" but is himself the Way. He is a not a salvific strategy to be meticulously mastered but rather a person to be resorted to. The justification of the Buddhist path was based on the grounds that it had helped Buddha to attain enlightenment. Christ's recommendation is based not on his personal experience of salvation, for he did not need salvation, but on the grounds of his deity. The Christian way of salvation is based on the grounds of the personhood of Christ as God Incarnate.

Nevertheless, the Buddhist quest did not terminate with Buddha. There were significant developments that took place after his death. An examination of these

54. Bercholz and Kohn, eds., *Buddha and His Teachings*, 43.

developments shows how Christ becomes relevant to the Buddhist quest. In fact, the move from early to latter Buddhism points out the legitimacy of the claim that Jesus Christ could best satisfy the Buddhist quest for salvation.

What Buddhists really need for liberation from bondage is a transcendental absolute being that not only reveals itself but also incarnates. This is where Christ becomes relevant to the Buddhist quest for a divine incarnate.

The spread of Buddhism, especially in countries like China and Japan, witnessed new developments in the doctrine and practice of Buddhism. But these developments cannot be understood merely as contextualizations of Buddhism to cultures other than Indian; it was not just a tailoring of Buddhist doctrine to local taste. We could consider Buddhism in countries like China, Japan, and Tibet as further expressions of the Buddhist quest. The people of these countries were converted to Buddhism but they found it necessary to initiate and accelerate certain developments in its doctrine and practice to satisfy their quest.

The Buddhist way of salvation began as a nontheistic path based on individual self-effort. But the developments that took place after Buddha's death, especially in the Mahayana and Tibetan traditions, highlight the relevance of Christ to the Buddhist quest.

Buddha never claimed to be God. His identity was as a Master Teacher, who was able to guide those who follow him to the enlightenment that he had himself experienced. Buddha's claim to uniqueness as a teacher is found in his reply to a monk named Upaka.

> I have no teacher, and my like
> Exists nowhere in all of the world
> With all its gods, because I have
> No person for my counterpart.
> I am the Teacher in the world
> Without a peer, accomplished, too,
> And I alone am quite enlightened.[55]

Buddha's claim to be a unique teacher is on the grounds that he received enlightenment without the aid of any teacher. But that does not imply his divinity. He is "The Perfect One" on the grounds that his teachings were taken to be true. But they are true because they arise from and are justified by his own personal experience of enlightenment. There is no implication of divinity involved in such a claim.

There is a significant change in the personhood of Buddha in latter Buddhism; he is deified. As we have noted, Buddha as a transcendental cosmic principle manifesting in three bodies seems to envisage a trinitarian concept of a deified Buddha. He came to be viewed not merely as a teacher but as a transcendental being who reveals himself through his teachings and incarnations. What the Buddhists need is not merely a Master Teacher but a God, and that, too, a Savior God. They need a God who is transcendent, free from the fetters of the human existence, and not caught in the cycle

---

55. Nanamoli, *Life of the Buddha*, 40.

of rebirths. But one who is committed to help people to achieve enlightenment, by guiding them through his teachings and becoming a part of them through his incarnations. This is where God in Christ becomes relevant to the Buddhist quest. He fulfills the plea for a Savior God.

Buddhism commences as a way based on individual self-effort. The role given to the bodhisattvas in latter Buddhism carried with it a shift from self-effort to external help. Such a shift makes Christ relevant to the Buddhist quest. The claim that Christ can save humans is based on the conviction that human beings need "other help" since they cannot save themselves. The move from "self-effort" to "other help" confirms this Christian conviction. Moreover, the claim that only Christ can save is justified on the grounds that Christ has certain characteristics that makes him able and willing to save humanity. It is significant that some of the attributes rendered to bodhisattva indicate that Buddhists need a person like Christ to liberate them.

Buddhists place certain requirements on the personhood and mission of the bodhisattva. He should be seriously committed to save others, in fact all of humanity, and also motivated by compassion. A Mahayana sutra puts it this way: "He has compassion on the weak and does not dislike them. He gives the best food to those who are hungry. He protects those who are afraid. He strives for the healing of those who are sick. He delights the poor with his riches. He repairs the shrines of the Buddha with plaster. He speaks to all beings pleasingly. He shares his riches with those afflicted by poverty. He bears the burdens of those who are tired and weary."[56]

Ksitigarbha, also known as Earth-Store Bodhisattva, who vowed to postpone his attainment of Buddhahood until the last person in hell is liberated exemplifies such compassion.

Moreover the bodhisattva has to be trustworthy. When those who depend on him are faced with challenges, the bodhisattva should not forsake them. Christ on the cross exemplifies such trustworthiness. He endured the cross so that all humanity could be saved.

The bodhisattva had to be committed to help his devotees, sincerely compassionate toward them, and utterly dependable. Yet without the capacity to execute his salvific mission no one would resort to him; he needed superhuman power. The view that the human being has the potential to save not only himself but others on the grounds of Buddha nature inherent in every human gained acceptance in the Mahayana tradition. Such potential makes it possible for a human to have superhuman powers. Mahayana accommodates Dhyana Buddhas, who are heavenly beings helping humans to attain enlightenment. Amida (immeasurable radiance) who dwells in "the Happy Land" (Sukhavati) and Bodhisattva Avalokiteshvara ("the Lord Who Looks Down," also called Kuan-Yin, "the hearer of cries," in Chinese)[57] stand out as beings with superhuman powers willing to help humans. They receive the name *Mahasattvas*, meaning all-powerful helpers.

---

56. de Bary et al., eds., *Sources of Indian Tradition*, 169.

57. Ibid., 154.

Christ seems to ideally fit the model of the Mahayana concept of bodhisattva as "savior." Christ not only manifests supernatural powers from birth to resurrection but he himself is supernatural, for he is God Incarnate. Mahayanists trace the supernatural powers of the bodhisattvas to the very nature of their being; they are emanations of the Body of Essence. In other words, the Mahayanist doctrine highlights that in order for the bodhisattvas to have supernatural powers, they have to be supernatural in their very nature. Christ's supernatural powers are essentially connected with and a consequence of his divine nature, as God the Son.

Bodhisattva's serious commitment to help people, motivated by sincere compassion, and executed in a trustworthy manner through superhuman powers encouraged devotees to consider him as more than a guide to their enlightenment. They took him as their vicarious helper. We cannot fail to note resemblance to the depiction of Christ as the suffering savior (Isa 53:3–12). Some think that there was some Christian influence on Mahayana Buddhism, for Christian missionaries were active in Persia very early, and it became a center from which Nestorian Christianity was diffused throughout Asia. From the middle of the third century CE, Persian influence in Afghanistan and northwestern India was intensified with the rise of the Sasanian Empire and it was in these regions that Mahayana Buddhism developed and flourished.[58] But, just because similarities are found between two religions, one cannot jump to the conclusion that one has influenced the other. Perhaps, the Buddhist portrayal of the bodhisattva as a suffering savior could be taken as indicative of the fundamental cry for help of a suffering humanity for someone to vicariously share their suffering.

Hence, Christ seems to fulfill the requirements latter Buddhists want the bodhisattva to have in order for him to enable them to attain enlightenment. He should be a sincere, compassionate, trustworthy person who will take their place in their struggle to be "saved."

The plea for help to the bodhisattva developed into a plea for mercy, almost turning into a plea for "grace" in the Christian sense of the term. This is evident in the devotees of Amida. In and through reciting his name, they totally depend on Amida to enter the Pure Land. But, we need to remember that Amida is able to help them because of his good deeds. Moreover, their stay in the Pure Land depends on the merit Amida transfers to them, and their entering the final state of liberation (nirvana) is also determined by not accumulating bad deeds. The ideal conditions of the Pure Land deter them from accumulating bad deeds. Hence, liberation still is based on merited favor; it is really mercy rather than grace that is at work. But what they need is unmerited favor, which amounts to grace. Christ's gift of salvation on the grounds of grace satisfies such a plea. The liberation that Christ offers is based on unmerited favor.

Moreover the Buddhist devotees want to experience the enlightenment in their very lifetime and not in the distant future after several rebirths. The tantric methods adopted by Tibetan Buddhists, in particular, are meant for that. The Zen/Chan meditation offers the devotee the assurance of enlightenment on an experiential basis.

58. Ibid., 160.

Moreover the hope for eternal life that became prominent in the spiritual journey of latter Buddhists is a definitive reminder that people want to experience a wholesome life not merely in their lifetime but also eternally. The assurance of eternal life that Christ gives in this lifetime through his grace and the promise of eternal life that transcends death meet those innermost aspirations of the Buddhists. The Buddhist quest for enlightenment commenced as a way based on individual self-help, but latter developments indicate in a poignant manner that what the Buddhists really need is Christ.

7

The Hindu Quest

Through high philosophy or law, through the most exalted mythology or the grossest, through the most refined ritualism or arrant fetishism, every sect, every soul, every nation, every religion, consciously or unconsciously, is struggling upward toward God . . .[1]

THESE ARE THE WORDS of Swami Vivekananda, the reputed Hindu guru of modern times. His vibrant participation in Chicago's World Parliament of Religions in 1893 has had a significant impact in today's religious world. He brought Hinduism to the West in a manner palatable to contemporary religious thinkers. His attempt to substantiate the claims of Hinduism by reference to publicly accessible experience, as in the physical sciences, was very much in line with the developing trend of trying to make religion scientific. His preference for the methods of spiritual knowledge (*jnana marga*) and meditation (*raja yoga*) to attain liberation (*moksha*) led to the explosive infiltration of meditation in the West. His proposal not merely to tolerate but to accept all religions on the grounds that they contain elements of truth, gave an impetus to syncretic religious pluralism. But what is most relevant to our study is his claim that Hinduism, or for that matter every religion, is "struggling upward toward God"—that all humanity is involved in a quest for God.

Hinduism is a confusing conglomeration of sects, practices, rituals, doctrines, and worldviews. But amidst such diversity there is an underlying unity in that it expresses the quest of a people belonging to the Indian cultural soil but no longer bound to it. The series on World Spirituality has published two volumes on Hindu spirituality, placing Hinduism in two time periods.[2] The first volume deals with the classical period when Hinduism receives its identity through the formulation of doctrines and development of practices based on its scriptures. The second volume covers the postclassical period when subsequent developments occurred and still continue to occur

---

1. Vivekananda, *Complete Works*, 2:383.

2. Sivaraman, ed., *Hindu Spirituality*, vol. 1 and Sundarajan and Mukerji, eds., *Hindu Spirituality*, vol. 2.

in the practice of the Hindu way of life. Professor Sivaraman, the editor of the first volume, identifies a common trend that runs through the phases of Hindu history, both classical and post-classical. He characterizes this trend as a quest that involves a "turning around," a liberating "turn" from a life engulfed in the world toward fullness of life, variously called life eternal or life divine.[3] Such a characterization reinforces Swami Vivekananda's stance that Hinduism is essentially a salvific quest.

Hindus call their religion *Sanatama Dharma*, meaning "the eternal religion," since it does not have a founder or a specific date of origin. The word "Hindu" actually comes from the Persian *Sindhu*, which was the local name for the Indus River. Hence it refers perhaps to the way of life of the people who lived by the river Sindhu, associating the origin of Hinduism with the ancient Indus Valley civilizations of Mohenjo-daro and Harappa. But let us not get into territory fraught with historical uncertainty. Suffice it is to say that Hinduism, by whatever name we call it and whenever it originated, is essentially a way of life. As a way of life, we cannot expect it to be static. Through the centuries it has accumulated scriptures, doctrines, codes of conduct, institutions, rituals, pilgrimages, and festivals. These accumulations express the aspirations of Hindus for liberation or provide the ways and means to achieve them. This quest arises from the awareness that there is something drastically unsatisfactory with human existence. Hindus believe that humans, and for that matter all life forms including vegetables and animals, are caught up in a cycle of rebirths (*samsara*). This process of rebirth assumes that every life form is subject to an indefinite series of lives, an evolving as well as a devolving process of rebirths. The Upanisads, one of the main Hindu scriptures, uses certain similes to describe the cycle of rebirths. It states that just as a caterpillar draws itself together in a blade of grass to transform into another life form, and as a goldsmith takes a piece of gold and fashions out of it another form, so the soul gives up one body to adopt another.[4]

To be born human is itself an achievement, for the human soul has evolved to the point of being capable of sensing what the problem is and of finding ways and means to solve it. A human being can change his or her destiny, functioning under the parameters of the law of karma. According to this law, everything one does, whether in thought, word, or deed, determines one's destiny. One's actions could plunge one back into the chain of rebirths or enable one to be freed from it and experience liberation (*moksha*). The Hindu quest commences, then, with becoming aware of one's predicament of being engulfed in the enslaving cycle of rebirths. Through the adoption of certain ways (*margas*), one attempts to be freed from this bondage. When that occurs, the seeker attains "salvation" (moksha) and the quest ends. There is, of course, difference of opinion among the Hindus as to what causes them to be entangled in the cycle of rebirths and as to which ways are most effective in achieving liberation. Moreover, the descriptions of the liberated state (moksha) are not the same. Yet Hindus seem to

---

3. Sivaraman, ed., *Hindu Spirituality*, xvi.
4. Brhadaranyaka Upanisad IV, 4:3-4, in Smart and Hecht, eds., *Sacred Texts*, 193.

be in agreement concerning the need for liberation from the predicament in which they find themselves. This provides the motivation for their salvific quest.

The world and the human being figure prominently in the Hindu portrayal of the human predicament. "The world" refers mainly to the physical world but is not restricted to it. The world can also accommodate the intellectual, emotional, and social dimensions of human activity. The self pertains to the identity of the human being. It is the spiritual facet of the human being, the soul (*atman*). The human predicament arises as a result of a tension between the world and this self. Through the ages Hindus have been branded as advocates of renunciation of the world. A disheveled hermit tortuously practicing yoga in a godforsaken forest is a popular depiction of an ideal Hindu who has renounced the world and its pleasures. The hermits and swamis portray different degrees of renunciation. But does this adequately capture the Hindu view? If this is the case, many will be disqualified as Hindus.

For a Hindu, renouncing the world does not necessarily mean denying its existence and adopting an escapist, otherworldly mindset. Highlighting that the main goal of every human being should be to attain liberation (moksha), Hindus accommodate three other goals. They are expected to pattern their life based on moral standards (*dharma*). They should also aim to be productive, not merely materially but also socially and politically (*artha*). Kautilya's *Treatise on Material Gain* (*Artha Sastra*) is a classic presentation of this goal. The third goal is the sensual pleasure (*kama*) that one can experience through the fine arts, literary pursuits, and sex. A Hindu can enjoy in a wholesome manner what sex, art, and culture offer. Vatsyayana's Kama Sutra is a guide to matters especially related to sexual behavior. The accommodation of these three goals indicates that a Hindu does not advocate a totally ascetic otherworldliness, since these goals can only be accomplished in this world. For a Hindu, the world per se is not the problem. But to consider it as the one and only reality, be entangled in it, and thereby become world-centered, is what causes one to be in bondage. According to Hinduism, there is a reality (*Brahman*) that transcends the world. Hindus differ as to whether this reality is an ineffable, impersonal, spiritual cosmic force, or one that manifests itself in several deities or a specific god. But the Hindu quest for liberation is geared towards attaining that reality, however it is understood. The other three goals complement and do not replace the chief goal in life of attaining liberation (moksha).

The other factor that keeps a person in bondage pertains to one's identity. When one does not know who he or she really is, one is prone to acquire a false sense of personal identity. For the Hindu, a human being, though composed of body, mind, and emotions, does not receive his or her identity from such components. At the core of human personhood there is a soul (atman) that is essentially spirit. This is what gives true identity to a person; it is the real "I" of a human being. When one confuses this "I" with a sensuous being craving worldly pleasures or an intellectual genius captivated by its own capabilities, a false sense of identity results, an "I" that is egoistic at the core. It is this "I" that is problematic.

A Hindu does not deny the world and the self in a nihilistic sense, as if they are mere figments of imagination. Rather, it is a false view of them that brings about bondage. Such deception arises from what a Hindu calls *maya*. It causes one to take the world and its pleasures as the be-all and end-all of life and to develop an egoistic self that prides itself in being the master of its own destiny. Such a deception ultimately results in bondage, keeping a person caught up in the cycle of rebirths (samsara).

The Hindu quest is geared towards freeing one from such bondage. In order to accomplish this, Hinduism presents four main ways (*margas*). They are the way of works or deeds (*karma marga*), the way of devotion (*bhakti marga*), the way of spiritual knowledge (*jnana marga*), and the way of meditation (*raja yoga*). Sometimes meditation is taken to be part of the way of knowledge. Though these ways are different, they are not exclusive but mutually complementary. Today yoga and Transcendental Meditation have become popular, especially in the West, as practical disciplines to enhance physical and mental health. But in the Hindu context, these are not mere techniques of self-improvement but paths to liberation, just like the other ways (margas). Those who adopt these ways do not all share the same worldview; moreover, not all give equal weight to the different ways. The state of liberation (moksha) attained through these ways is also interpreted differently. Yet all these ways are salvific in intent. A Hindu who adopts one or more of these ways is involved in the quest for liberation.

Out of the multitude of Hindu systems that developed through the centuries, we can pick out six that developed between 500 BCE and 1500 CE. Even though we refer to them here as "schools," they should not be taken as structured theological schools or even organized sects, but rather as insightful viewpoints or visions (*darasanas*); *darasana* literally means vision or enlightened viewpoint. The six systems are *Vaishesika, Nyaya, Samkhya, Yoga, Purva Mimamsa*, and *Vedanta*.

Vaishesika is usually paired with the Nyaya system. The former provides the worldview in which the latter articulates the means to know the world and thereby be liberated. Vaishesika, literally meaning "particularity," characterizes the world that is taken to be self-existent and composed of the interplay of combining and recombining eternal and indivisible atoms. Human selves are also atomic in structure. At first, this view presented a pluralistic world ordered by the mechanistic combinations of atomic structures. It was essentially a nontheistic worldview. But with the passage of time, its adherents realized that the order of the world is not purely mechanistic but takes place by the power of a divine force, *Advishta*, which was eventually associated with an eternal cosmic soul. According to this school, ignorance of the true nature of the world causes bondage, hence liberation occurs only through acquiring true knowledge. The Nyaya school, founded by Gautama (not Gautama Buddha), provides a sophisticated logical system. Nyaya claims that true knowledge is derived through proper sense perception, inference, comparison of facts, and trustworthy testimony. Such knowledge liberates, while false knowledge leads to bondage. Adherents of Vaishesika apply Nyaya logical methods to obtain the knowledge that they hope will liberate them. Both schools highlight the way of knowledge (*jnana marga*) as the ideal path to liberation.

The Samkhya and Yoga schools could be similarly paired. Kapila, belonging to the seventh century BCE, is believed to have founded the Samkhya school. It represents a dualistic worldview, claiming that two independent categories of being constitute the world: matter (*prakriti*) and spirit/self (*purusa*). The human being is also a composite of these two elements: body (prakriti) and self (purusa). Such a self is spiritual in its makeup and gives identity to a person. Perhaps as a result of past karma it gets entangled in a body. This causes it to be ignorant of its true identity, to become captivated by the pleasures of the flesh and thereby be in bondage. Liberation of the soul is through extraction from the bondage of the body, which is matter.[5] Samkhya adherents strove to experience moments of insight, enabled through "higher intelligence" (*budhi*), to liberate themselves. Their preferred path of liberation was at first the way of knowledge (jnana marga), but they soon realized that higher intelligence could not deliver the necessary moments of insight because the human being is under the bondage of the body (prakriti). Hence one had to first subjugate the body. The Yoga system met that need. Yoga, as a practical discipline of the body and mind, has been in vogue among the Hindus from ancient times; it was given its classical form in the second century BCE by Patanjali in his work *Yogasutras*. Both Samkhya and Yoga schools attribute human bondage to the body, which causes the self to be ignorant of its true spiritual nature. What is distinctive about Yoga is that it provides a way to achieve control of the body and the fleshly mind. Its strategy, Raja Yoga, contains an eightfold series of steps that include physical and mental exercises leading up to a state of emancipation (*samadhi*). Yoga is not mere practical discipline to enhance the health of a person, but a way of liberation that combines the way of knowledge (jnana marga) and yogic meditation (raja yoga).

All six schools are taken to be orthodox in that they accept the authority of the Vedas, the most ancient Hindu scriptures. But the Purva Mimamsa school that originated with Jaimini in the fourth century BCE attributed a unique character and role to these scriptures. Purva Mimamsa means "ancient examination of the Vedas." According to this school, the authenticity of the Vedas does not depend on an author; they are neither divine revelations nor constructs of human spiritual insights. They are uncreated and eternal. One has to literally interpret them and follow what they say. According to this school, determining the literal meaning of the text and faithfully following what it prescribes enables one to be liberated from the cycle of rebirths. It is a literalism that is salvific in intent. Taking scripture to be the means of liberation even though it is not divinely authored gives the impression that the system was nontheistic. But eventually its adherents meticulously followed the prescriptions of scripture as an offering to a "Supreme God," believing that liberation would result.

Of all the six systems, Vedanta has had the most significant impact on Hindu doctrine and practice, so much so that Hinduism is often identified with it. Even though this school resorts to the epic Bhagavad Gita and the Brahma Sutras, its main scriptural source is the Upanisads, a collection of scriptures that followed the Vedas and elaborated on its ideas. Vedanta means the "end or concluding portions of the Vedas." The Vedanta school may be taken as a development and interpretation of Upanisadic

---

5. Oxtoby, *World Religions: Eastern Traditions*, 56.

themes that claims to be the best of all interpretations of these scriptures. According to this school, reality is one, referred to as cosmic spirit or consciousness (Brahman). The individual soul (atman) is identical with this cosmic unity. Liberation occurs mainly through spiritual knowledge, which enables the soul to realize its oneness with cosmic reality. Even while retaining this basic stance, however, Vedanta Hindus through the centuries have presented different versions of it. Badarayana (variously dated from the first to the fourth century BCE) was one of the first to articulate Vedanta's monistic stance. After him Gaudapada (seventh century CE), Sankara (ninth century CE), Ramanuja (twelfth century CE), and Madhva (thirteenth century CE) presented modified versions of Vedanta.

Sankara's view is called advaita (non-dualistic). He holds that reality is not two, but one. Moreover, being ineffable, it can be described only in negative terms: not this, not that (*netti-netti*). Besides this one reality all else, even though it looks real, is taken to be a product of illusion (maya). The individual soul (atman) is not different from Brahman. Liberation occurs when the veil of ignorance is lifted and one realizes that the individual soul is itself part of the cosmic spirit: that "atman is Brahman."

Such a way of liberation wrought through spiritual knowledge (jnana marga), though appetizing to Hindu intellectuals, was beyond the reach of most people. They needed a reality they could relate to, something personal. Eventually Sankara conceded that the ineffable *Nirguna Brahman* (one without attributes) could manifest itself with attributes as *Saguna Brahman*. This allowed people to conceive Brahman in terms of attributes such as power, justice, and compassion. Ramanuja, who came three hundred years after Sankara, revised Vedanta in two significant ways. His worldview may be described as qualified monism, in that he did not dismiss everything other than Brahman as illusion. For him the world and individual selves are real in that they are manifestations of the ultimate reality. Besides this, he conceived of Brahman not as an impersonal, ineffable force, but as a personal being with divine attributes, such as infinite knowledge, power, and love. At liberation one experiences the presence and fellowship of a personal being rather than being absorbed into an impersonal reality. In his commentaries on Bhagavad Gita and Brahma sutras, he proclaims the supremacy of Vishnu and emphasizes that devotion to Vishnu will lead one to liberation.[6] He is believed to have been a worshiper of Vishnu. Madhva, who followed Ramanuja, went a step further to claim that the ultimate reality Brahman and individual selves are separate. A soul is liberated through the aid of a deity, the wind god Vayu, son of Vishnu. At liberation, the individual self reaches the presence of the Supreme Reality, Vishnu, but does not lose its identity even though it is in close relationship with God. Madhva's stance may be best described as theistic dualism. These post-Sankara developments gave Vedanta a theistic flavor, suggesting a recognition that people need a personal God with whom they can relate.

All six systems articulate their respective ways of liberation based on the Vedas. There are also Hindu systems that resort to scripture other than the Vedas to base their

6. Ibid., 58.

way of liberation. Saiva Siddhanta may be taken as a good example. The Vedas, the Sanskrit Sivagamas, and the Tamil Thirumurais and Siddhanta Sastras are the main scriptures of this school. It claims that there are three realities: God (*pathi*), soul (*pasu*), and world (*pasam*). Pathi is identified as Shiva. Pasu collectively denotes an infinite number of souls. Pasam is the world that attracts and keeps souls in bondage. Souls, like God, are eternal and spiritual in makeup, but they need to depend on something to survive, either God or the world. When dependent on the world (pasam), they are in bondage. Liberation occurs when they become dependent on God, freed from the bondage of the world. Adherents of Saiva Siddhanta accommodate all the four ways (jnana, bhakti, karma, and yoga) to liberate themselves. At liberation (moksha) they claim that one experiences the joy and enlightened knowledge of being at the feet of God (*sat-sit-ananda*).

The Hindu quest for liberation cannot be adequately characterized without taking into account the resort to gods. Of the host of gods, three figure as a triune being: Brahma, the creator; Shiva, the destroyer of evil; and Vishnu, the preserver god of love and benevolence. These three constitute the Hindu trinity (*Thirumurthi*). The common belief is that these three are one in essence, that they are all manifestations of the Ultimate Reality (Brahman). Brahma, though one of the Trinity, is not very popular, and we can understand why. He, as creator of the world in the distant past, is not very relevant to the Hindus in their quest for liberation at present. On the other hand, Shiva and Vishnu help the seekers in tangible ways. Shiva wards off evil, and his son, the popular elephant god Ganesha, removes obstacles. Vishnu enables people to achieve liberation, especially through his incarnations, the most popular of which is Krishna. Hence the cults of Shiva and of Vishnu (Saivism and Vaishnavism, respectively) have quite an extensive following among the Hindus; most of the temples are dedicated to one of these two gods.

There are also millions of Hindu devotees of *sakti*, taken to be divine energy. When associated with Shiva, it is called Shiva-Sakti. Sakti takes the form of goddesses, usually as consorts to male gods. Perhaps it is in this way that Hindus consider God to be both male and female or to transcend gender divisions. Parvati (Durga) and Kali depict two facets of Shiva's spirit: his lovingkindness and his hatred for evil. Durga (Parvati), often represented as a beautiful woman with a gentle face, expresses Shiva's spirit of lovingkindness. Kali, on the other hand, is a fierce-looking woman, and depicts the spirit of divine anger at evil. Worshipers are careful to please Kali by avoiding evil acts, lest they be punished.

Hindus resort to sakti because it empowers them to overcome evil and illuminates them to know God. The spiritual teacher (*guru*) and a combination of ritual and spiritual practices (tantra) enable the devotee to attain liberation. Saktism is very much part of the Hindu quest, highlighting its spiritual makeup.

Hinduism may be confusing with its multifarious views concerning the world, humans, and their ultimate destiny. The mosaic of modes of worship, rituals, and festivals do not seem to follow a set pattern. But amidst all this there is an underlying common trend—a quest for liberation. This is what justifies the characterization of Hinduism as a quest.

Hinduism does not have an acknowledged founder. Most of the articulators of the Hindu quest, especially during its early stages, are either unknown or legendary. Hence it is more productive to explore the scriptural expressions of the quest rather than to decipher its articulators. This will be our next task.

SCRIPTURAL EXPRESSIONS OF THE QUEST

It was John Milton who, in his *Areopagitica*, pointed out that "books are not absolutely dead things, but do contain a potency of life in them to be as active as that soul was whose progeny they are."[7]

This is very true of the Hindu scriptures. They form a compendium of a variety of genres compiled through several centuries by different sectors of the Hindu populace. The Vedas, Brahmanas, Aranyakas, Upanisads, narratives like the epics (Bhagavad Gita and Mahabharata) and Puranas, the Code of Manu, the Agamas, and devotional hymns all figure prominently as sacred scriptures. But no Hindu is expected to be proficient or even familiar with all of them. In fact, the Hindu attitude towards scripture is eclectic. Even though the Vedas function as foundational scripture, Hindus tend to pick out texts that are conducive to their spiritual journey. These texts for them are not "dead things" but have life potency. However varied these scriptures may be in literary format, they express the quest for liberation not only to those who gave shape to them but also to those who emulate and abide by them. Hindus are able to orchestrate their quest through the texts of their choice. Through different literary modes, these texts give expression to the quest and provide doctrinal and practical guidelines for its enactment. For instance, the Brahmanas provide guidelines for ritualistic practices, while the Upanisads, philosophical in their expositions of Hindu doctrine, highlight the role of knowledge as the light that liberates. The following prayer exhibits this quest: "From the unreal lead me to the real, from darkness lead me to light, from death lead me to immortality" (Brhadaranyaka Upanisad 1.3.28). On the other hand, the epics and Puranas point out how devotion to a personal god is vital for release from bondage. Such a literary variety of scriptures enables Hindus to select what is best suited to them.

The Hindu scriptures fall into two main categories: *sruti* and *smriti*. In order to fully understand these categories, we need to take into account how each came into being. Sruti refers to a set of scriptures that resulted from people hearing, while smriti are scriptures that arose out of people remembering what was heard. Sruti means "what is heard." Hindus believe that the seers (*rishis*) of the distant past "heard." But what is it that they heard? Hindus call it speech or word (*vak*) that is not yet spoken or written. In its essence such speech is luminous in that it gives new insights when received. But it is not open to all; only the rishis are sensitive to it. When they receive it, it stirs in their minds and provides an illuminative insight about reality. The rishi is

---

7. Milton, *Areopagitica*, 6.

called a poet, a seer who is privileged to know something about the cosmic harmony (*rta*). These insights were transmitted orally through the generations by priests. The Vedas, Brahmanas, Aranyakas, and Upanisads belong to this category.

In a sense sruti may be taken as the revealed sacred literature. But such revelation was not from a personal god. It was an illumination that occurred when luminous speech was received by the rishis. Such speech is authorless and eternal. In fact, the Purva Mimamsa school of Hinduism proposes that the revelations received by ancient seers are eternal truths that do not even have an author. Swami Vivekananda claims that the scriptures were discovered by different sages (rishis) at different times.[8] Such a description is helpful in understanding how the ancient seers got their "revelations." Perhaps perturbed by calamities of life, these seers wanted to find a way out. In their quest, which probably involved ascetic forest living and self-inflicting yogic practices, they had certain exhilarating insights. Such insights, though not definitive revelations from a personal god, may be taken as pointing out that there must be a reality beyond the natural world. In fact, the concept of a personal god who communicates to humans evolved through the scriptures and was not presupposed by them. Being struck by the awesome powers of the elements of nature, the seers made these elements into gods or looked for a god who created and controlled them. The seers realized not only the need for a reality transcending the material world but also that this reality should be a personal god with whom they could relate. They acknowledged that, despite the efficacy of the traditional ways to liberation, they desperately needed god's grace and even divine incarnation. In this sense, these scriptures could fall under the orbit of that which Christians call "general revelation." On the other hand, the first statement of the Bible is "In the beginning God created . . . " (Gen 1:1). The Bible, as special revelation, assumes a personal God who communicates with humans by first creating them. But in Hindu sacred literature, the concept of a god relating on a personal basis with humans evolves only gradually.

Smriti literally means "memory," and refers to scriptures that took shape as a result of being remembered from generation to generation. They represent knowledge based on sruti but shaped by tradition. As a religious community lives through several centuries, interpretations and practices naturally accumulate, generating traditions. Such traditions played a significant role in the shaping of scriptures. The epics (that is, Bhagavad Gita and Mahabharata), the Puranas, the Code of Manu, the Agamas, and devotional hymns fall into this category.

Although Hindus take both sruti and smriti as authoritative scriptures, they give more weight to some scriptures than others, depending on their preferences. For instance, the Hare Krishna devotees take the epic Bhagavad Gita as their most authoritative scripture, since it highlights Krishna's incarnation.

Usually there is a tendency to identify scripture as written documents; the written word is given sacred status. But taking the Hindu scriptures merely as a body of written texts does not do justice to the Hindu view of scripture. The orality

8. Vivekananda, *Complete Works*, 1:7.

of the Hindu scriptures is pronounced, commencing with the Vedas and continuing through the later devotional poetic compositions. Sruti being "what is heard" expresses the oral nature of the scriptures. It was originally "heard" by seers and then transmitted orally by priests. The Vedic incarnations, the sacrificial formulas, and the chants in ritualistic practices, as stipulated in the Brahmanas, had to be recited orally. The dialogues in the Upanisads must be listened to rather than read. In Indonesia today the epic Ramayana is communicated effectively through puppet shows, shadow plays, and opera. The Puranas remind their listeners of the blessings they will receive when they recite what the scriptures contain. Hence the full impact of the scriptures on devotees in their quest for liberation occurs when they listen to and/or recite them. Orality characterizes Hindu scriptures both as expressing the quest and as providing guidelines for its enactment.

A cursory survey of the main scriptures will help us to better appreciate their role in the Hindu quest.

The Vedas, composed between 1500 and 800 BCE, are the oldest Hindu scriptures. Veda comes from the Sanskrit verb *vid*, which means "to know." Another name for the Vedas is *Brahmavidya*, which means "the knowledge that enables one to reach Brahma (God)." The Vedas are an anthology of four collections. The 1028 cryptic hymns of the Rg Vedas are mainly incantations to deities. The Sama Vedas consist of rhythmic chants to be used in sacrifices. The Yajur Vedas contain several prose passages giving guidelines for ritualistic practices. The Atharva Vedas provide charms, magical spells, and mantras to ward off evil.

The composers of the Vedas lived in the area of the Seven Rivers (Sapta Sindhu) in what is today Punjab in northwestern India and Pakistan. The reputed Indus Valley civilization of Mohenjo-daro and Harappa flourished in this part of the world between 2500 and 1500 BCE, but the Vedas were composed after 1500 BCE. There is speculation as to who their composers were. Some believe that they were Aryans who invaded India from Indo-Europe, while some think that they were Caucasian invaders. There is also the view that they originated in India and belonged to the remnant population of the fallen Indus Valley civilization. But whoever these composers were, their compositions, especially the Rg Vedas, were birthed in a world of social disruption and turbulence. The demise of the Indus Valley civilization had led to poverty and strife; the people who occupied the abandoned cities of Mohenjo-daro and Harappa built huts on top of the ruins. The Vedic seers came out of this world, and their desperation naturally motivated them to strive for a way out. The Vedas reflect this striving. The Rg Vedic incantations were a resort to numerous deities, while the Sama and Yajur Vedas orchestrated ways of pleasing these deities through sacrifices and rituals. The Atharva Vedas provided chants to ward off evil. The collective thrust of the Vedas was to provide a way of liberation.

The hymns of the Rg Veda were dedicated to deities personifying elements of nature: celestial, atmospheric, and terrestrial. Varuna the sky god and Mitra the sun god were celestial deities, while Indra the god of thunder and rain was the most popular atmospheric deity. Among the terrestrial deities, those most frequently sought were

Agni the fire god and Soma the god of liberation. The resort to these gods is significant. Awed by the order in the universe, the Vedic seers picked out Varuna the sky god as responsible for this order (rta). The devastation of the Indus Valley civilization is believed to have been caused by a killer flood or by foreign invaders, so Indra, the god of storm and war who conquered the demon Vitra, the personification of evil, became relevant to people who needed protection from such calamities. When the seers dedicated some 250 hymns to Indra, they were voicing the fears of the Vedic people.

Moreover, the resort to deities personifying elements of nature eventually led to the worship of a god who is the "Lord of all creation," named Prajapathi. The resort to such a god clearly shows that people needed someone who could not only control a specific element of nature but exercised lordship over everything.

To the question "What God with our oblation shall we worship?" the Rg Veda (x:121:10) responds thus: "Prajapati! Thou only comprehendest all these created things, and none beside thee. Grant us our heart's desire when we invoke thee; may we have store in riches in possession."[9]

Motivated by the beauty as well as the calamities of nature, the move to acknowledge a god who is lord over all may well be taken as an enactment of general revelation.

Sacrifice finds an important place in the Vedas and the Brahmanas. The incantations in the Rg Veda, supplemented by the chants and prescriptive guidelines given in the Sama and Yajur Vedas and the Brahmanas, highlight the vital role sacrifice played in Vedic times. There were no temples then; sacrifices took place on an open-air altar where fire was lit. This is where Agni, the fire god, becomes relevant. He consumed the sacrifices such as milk, butter, grain, and animals that the people offered, and carried them to the gods. He acted as the mediator between the people and the gods. The most important sacrifice that the Vedas and Brahmanas present is the Prajapati sacrifice, where Prajapati, the Lord of all Creation, sacrifices himself. The resort to sacrifice indicates that people desperately want to be in good relationship with what they consider to be god.

The search for a reality beyond the lesser gods who personify elements of nature is also evident in the hymn to creation in the Rg Veda. To the question of how the world originated, the Rg Veda (10:129) responded thus:

> Who verily knows and who here declares it,
> Whence it was born and whence comes this creation?
> The Gods are later than this world's production.
> Who then knows whence it first came into being?
> He, the first origin of this creation, whether he
> Formed it all or did not form it, whose eye controls
> This world in highest heaven, he verily knows it, or
> Perhaps he knows not.[10]

---

9. Griffith, trans., *Hymns of the Rg Veda*, 567.

10. Smart and Hecht, eds., *Sacred Texts*, 182.

The response is significant for its candid honesty. At a time when there were several myths attributing the origin of the world to gods, to claim that even gods are subsequent to creation shows courage. Moreover, to toy with the idea that there could be "one" who may or may not have created the world and who may not know how it all came about indicates genuine philosophical speculation. Such a speculative trend gains prominence in the later set of sacred texts, the Upanisads.

The Brahmanas, probably composed between 800 and 300 BCE, provide an exhaustive and detailed description of how to perform rituals and sacrifices, explaining the meanings of such practices. Each of the four Vedas has a Brahmana that deals with the practical side of what each Veda highlights. Eventually, such practices provided the guidelines for worship in temples.

Just as the Brahmanas provide guidelines for ritualistic practices, the Aranyakas enable the ascetics who retire to forests to attain liberation. They require guidelines of a different kind. Those who live in isolation cannot participate in ritual sacrifices performed communally. They need ways and means to cultivate their innermost nature. The Aranyakas provided guidelines that were esoteric.

The Upanisads is an anthology of more than one hundred texts, out of which fourteen figure as principal Upanisads. They were composed over several centuries from 900 to 400 BCE. The word Upanisad means "sitting devotedly nearby." The picture we get is of a devotee sitting beside a guru, receiving his teachings. The Vedas appear in the form of poetic utterances and cryptic statements, while the Upanisads are expository in their literary format. Dialogues occupy an important place in the expositions, which naturally open the door for discussion. But they are not mere theoretical speculations. They are fundamentally salvific in purpose; they articulated a way of liberation.

The dominant claim of the Upanisads is that reality is ultimately one: the "One" sought in the "Hymn to Creation" from the Rg Veda, quoted above. This "One" (Brahman) pervades the whole universe and yet is not material. Such a world view is best described as spiritual monism. The individual human spirit (atman) is very much part of this Cosmic Spirit; the problem is that the individual does not know it, and this ignorance is the cause of bondage. The solution lies in acquiring the right type of knowledge. The Upanisads provide a way to acquire such knowledge, that which enables the human spirit to realize its identity with the Supreme Spirit. To show the salvific role they play in gathering liberating knowledge about Brahman, the Upanisads provide an analogy: they are the bees that make honey from the flower that is Brahman. The act of collecting honey is taken as a brooding upon Brahman (Chandyoga Upanisad, 3.5.1, 2). Such liberating knowledge is acquired not through sense perception, but through spiritual insight enabled by meditation. According to the Upanisads, the identity between Brahman and atman is already there but obscured by ignorance (*avidya*). The Upanisads provide the knowledge that is able to remove the blindfolding ignorance and enable the devotee to attain liberation (moksha). Such knowledge receives the name Brahma-vidya/Atma-vidya in Sanskrit, a knowledge that reveals the identity of Brahman (Cosmic Spirit) and atman (the individual soul).

The Vedas, Brahmanas, Aranyakas, and Upanisads are the main sruti scriptures. All of them in their own way express the Hindu quest for liberation and the ways and means to achieve it. The ways of good works, devotion, spiritual knowledge, and meditation are all embedded in these scriptures. These are supplemented by a variety of other works of almost equal authority that fall into the category of smriti.

The epics, Mahabharata (the Great Story), Bhagavad Gita (The Song of the Supreme Exalted One), and Ramayana (The Story of Rama), show how narratives play a vital role in the life of the Hindu community.

Mahabharata, composed between 300 BCE and 300 CE, is believed to be the longest epic in the world of sacred literature. But it is not entirely a story. It contains expositions concerning politics, ethics, law, religious practices, etc. The epic presents the story of a feud between two related families, one characterized by vice and the other by virtue, that eventually leads the cousins to battle. When they are preparing for war, the god Vishnu incarnates as Krishna and comes to the aid of the virtuous Pandya family. He takes the role of a charioteer to the Pandya warrior Arjuna and enters into dialogue with him. Bhagavad Gita, an epic within an epic, commences at this stage and runs through eighteen chapters of Mahabharata. Due to Krishna's well-articulated advice, the initially hesitant Arjuna goes to war with his own cousins, convinced that it is wholly an act of devotion to Krishna. The Gita is an ideal example of how a narrative can motivate people to choose the way of utter devotional obedience to a personal god, Krishna, to attain liberation. Several Hindu sects, especially the Hare Krishna movement, base their way of liberation on the Bhagavad Gita. The epic needs to be taken not as a theological treatise to be analytically interpreted but as a devotional story that has salvific impact. The Gita points out, "One may cleanse himself daily by taking a bath in water, but if one takes a bath even once in the sacred Ganges water of *Bhagavad Gita*, for him the dirt of material life is altogether vanquished" (Gitamatmya 3)[11] For thousands of Hindus, reading and listening to the Gita is an act of worship rather than an exegetical exercise.

The third epic, Ramayana, composed between 200 BCE and 200 CE, is the story of a prince called Rama whose wife Sita is abducted by Ravana, the ten-headed demon-giant of Lanka. Ravana had obtained from the god Brahma a boon that he could not be killed by gods or demons; the only way to kill him was through human agency. Vishnu, the compassionate god, incarnates as Rama. With the aid of Hanuman, a monkey who could leap over oceans, Rama rescues Sita. Hindus deify Rama as Vishnu's incarnation and take the Ramayana as a story of liberation through divine intervention.

The epics are not mere antique legends but very much part of Hindu life. They are referred to as *itihasa*, which means "that is how it was." In a community where narratives motivate people to strive for liberation, inculcating hope by assuring them divine help, the distinction between myth and real history does not hold. These epics, originally composed orally, still continue to be communicated orally.

11. Prabhupada, *Bhagavad Gita*, 32. All quotations and citations from the Gita are from this translation.

The Puranas are also narratives, but they are shorter than the epics. There are eighteen main Puranas, compiled sometime between the second and the tenth century CE. They cover a variety of topics such as creation, the destruction and recreation of the universe, the genealogy of the gods, ways of liberation, etc. Their acceptability comes from the belief that they arise from a long tradition of spiritual insights of revered seers. They are popular, since as stories they are more interesting and easier to listen to than the cryptic verses of the Vedas. Moreover, they are accessible to the common people of lower castes and to women, who were forbidden even to listen to the Vedas. The articulation of the way of liberation in the Puranas has some significant features. The ideal that these stories portray accommodates spiritual release (mukti) as well as worldly enjoyment (bhukti), showing that Hinduism is not restricted to ascetic renunciation. The Puranic way of salvation is pluralistic in that it accommodates all the traditional ways. But the Puranas stress the need for divine help through incarnations (avatars) in order for humans to be liberated. Despite the diversity of their contents, the Puranas are very salvific in intent. Through their narrative and poetic modes, they play a vital role in enabling common people to become familiar with the ways of liberation.

For a Hindu, moral character and conduct are vital for liberation, whether it be through knowledge, good works, devotion, or meditation. The text that gives guidelines for proper conduct is the Code of Manu, compiled sometime before the second century CE. It contains regulations on matters such as marriage, diet, the duties of various castes, and sacrifices. The moral quality of life this code enables is not an end in itself but a means to liberation; it is also salvific in purpose.

Saivism refers to the theistic Hindu tradition that acknowledges Siva as the Supreme Lord. In addition to the above-mentioned scriptures, Saivism accepts twenty-eight Sanskrit Siva-Agamas. Doctrinal differences have split this tradition into two branches: Sanskrit and Tamil. The former accepts the Sanskrit Agamas. In addition to these Agamas, the Tamil branch includes in its sacred texts the twelve Tirumaras and fourteen Siddhanta Sastras, written in Tamil. Of the fourteen sastras, Meikanda Deva's Sivagnana Botham and his disciple Arulnanthi's Sivagnana Siddhiyar serve as the main expressions of the Tamil Saiva Siddhanta way of liberation.

The tantras provide the main scriptures for the mystical sector of the Hindu populace, who worship sakti, the divine energy. Hence Saktism is known also by the name Tantrism. It assumes that there is an affinity between the cosmic energy and the individual soul. In order to be liberated, the spirit (*kundalini*) that is dormant like a coiled-up serpent in an individual must be awakened. The tantras provide guidelines to escape the bondage of the body through yogic practices, mantras, and mystical modes.

This survey of the main Hindu scriptures makes clear that Hindus can hold different and sometimes even contradictory views on several matters. But the underlying thrust of these scriptures is to express the Hindu aspiration to be liberated and to propose ways and means to achieve this liberation. Our next task will be to examine the main features of the Hindu quest for liberation.

THE WAY OF THE QUEST

The quest for liberation in any faith community commences with the realization that there is something drastically wrong with human existence, that humans are in a predicament. The Hindus diagnose their predicament in terms of the cycle of rebirths (samsara). Such a cycle of rebirths occurs in a dimension where time is viewed as cyclic. A living creature that undergoes births and rebirths in cyclic time never reaches a final end. In fact, the end reached is nothing but the point where it first started its journey. Moreover, the whole process is controlled by the law of karma. The fruit of every action is determined by previous actions. The picture we get of the Hindu diagnosis of the human predicament appears at first sight to be utterly fatalistic. But the prognosis is positive. For a Hindu, to be born as a human is an achievement; it provides the occasion for liberation. The human soul has evolved through a series of rebirths to a state in which it is able to realize its own predicament and find ways and means to get out of it. Moreover, when it reaches human status, the soul has blossomed to show its real nature: that it is God or Godlike. The Vedanta school proposes that the human soul (atman) and the Universal Spirit (Brahman) are one. The human soul is not aware of its true identity and is thus in bondage. The Saiva Siddhanta school believes that the human soul is spirit and eternal, like God (*Pathi*), but tends to depend on the world (*pasam*) and hence is in bondage. But Hindus, whatever school they belong to, believe that humans are capable of getting out of their predicament. This conviction motivates their quest for liberation. The various paths of liberation are founded on this conviction. Our next task will be to identify the main features of the Hindu way of liberation.

The Hindu way is both nontheistic and theistic. Sankara best represents the nontheistic facet of the Hindu way. His commentaries on the major Upanisads, the Bhagavad Gita, the Brahmasutras of Badarayana, and his manual entitled Upadesa-Sahasri express his views. His non-dualistic world view is called Advaita Vedanta. For him, the one and only reality is Brahman and all else is illusion (maya). Such a reality is impersonal, infinite, unknowable, and incomprehensible. It can be described only negatively as "not this, not that" (netti-netti). The human soul (atman) is really not different in nature from the Ultimate Reality (Brahman); any idea of a difference arises out of ignorance (avidya), which causes bondage. The solution lies in knowledge (jnana), knowledge that is transformative in that it enables the human soul to become aware of its oneness with the Ultimate Reality. In this context, acquiring knowledge turns out to be the ideal way of liberation.

But people need a god, and moreover one who is personal and with whom they can relate. Even Sankara seems to have been sensitive to this need. He conceded that even though Brahman is one, there are two aspects to it. Brahman as *Nirguna* (devoid of attributes) transcends human comprehension. But Brahman as *Saguna* (with attributes) falls within the human conceptual realm and can be described as personal, almighty, eternal, and spiritual. Such a concession opens the door to accommodate personal gods manifesting various attributes of the ultimate reality.

Here we detect the development of the theistic facet of the Hindu way. Ramanuja (1056–1137 CE) and Madhva (1199–1278 CE) represent this facet. They both accept the core Vedantic claim that ultimate reality is one, but they concretize it in the image of a personal god, Narayana. Sankara's impersonal Brahman becomes a personal god with attributes and various manifestations. This god, addressed as Narayana, is for Ramanuja and Madhva identical with Vishnu, while another Vedantic adherent, Srikantha, identifies him with Shiva. The developments that occurred within the Vedantic tradition are also evident in other sectors of Hinduism. Saiva Siddhanta considers Pathi as the ultimate reality but takes it to be Shiva and not an impersonal cosmic spirit. The Hindus who adhere to the Puranas take the goal of their quest to be a personal god. Such developments indicate that the Hindu way of liberation is not merely nontheistic but very theistic.

Such a way may also be described as both philosophical and devotional. It is philosophical in the sense that it allows the use of rational speculation for transformative purposes. Sankara highlights the way of knowledge (jnana marga) for liberation. In his Upadesa-Sahasiri 4:5, he describes the liberating impact of knowledge thus: "The knowledge of one's identity with the pure Self, that negates the (wrong) notion of the identity of the body and the Self, sets a man free even against his will when it becomes as firm as the belief of the man that he is a human being."[12]

In Sankara's view, salvation happens when the human soul (atman) realizes its identity with the impersonal cosmic spirit (Brahman). But Ramanuja and Madhva who followed him take the ultimate reality to be a personal god, such as Vishnu or Shiva. When the ultimate reality is a personal god, the way of liberation demands a relationship between God and the human soul. But if the soul is altogether part of God or identical with God, it cannot relate to God; in order to orchestrate a relationship, the human soul needs to have an individuality of its own. Hence both Ramanuja and Madhva insist on the individuality of the human soul. They do not belong to the Advaita (non-dualistic) Vedanta that Sankara advocates. Ramanuja's version receives the name Visitadvaita (qualified monism). Individual souls are not illusions but finite forms through which the supreme reality manifests itself. When a human soul is liberated, it retains its individuality but becomes free from bondage in and through communion with the supreme reality, Vishnu. Madhva takes the human soul to be a reflection of God. Being spirit, it is similar to God, but is essentially dependent on God as a reflection depends on its archetype. Modern Hindu scholars like former President of IndiaRadhakrishnan, while associating with the Vedanta monistic tradition, affirm the reality of individual souls. Such individuality allows the human soul to relate to God.

But such a relationship can turn out to be nominal formality and hence detrimental to liberation. It is here that the way of devotion (bhakti marga) becomes relevant. Devotion (bhakti) is not a mere emotional attachment to a favorite deity but involves spiritual and whole-hearted commitment. Scriptures and gurus

12. Smart and Hecht, eds., *Sacred Texts*, 202.

provide knowledge about a deity and how to be devoted to it. Such guidance helps the devotee to make a well-informed decision that motivates sincere commitment. A devotee may carry out such devotion either through renunciation of the world and the adoption of an ascetic lifestyle or through communal channels. Temple worship, participation in rituals, festivals, and pilgrimages to holy places are popular communal expressions of Hindu devotion.

Bhagavad Gita most vividly depicts devotion as a way of liberation. Amidst the conflict between the two families, Vishnu incarnates as Krishna and plays the role of charioteer to warrior Arjuna, who is unable to decide whether or not to kill his own cousins. First Krishna assures Arjuna that a person's real soul can neither kill nor be killed, hence Arjuna need not be concerned about committing the crime of destroying life in battle. Then Krishna points out that the highest duty of a devotee is to be utterly devoted to him and that none of his devotees will perish. When Arjuna realizes that the charioteer is really Vishnu's incarnation, the hesitant warrior goes courageously to war. In this episode, devotion (bhakti) expresses itself as whole-hearted surrender to God and total obedience to his dictates. Bhakti as a way of liberation, highlighted by the Gita, has become widespread in the Hindu world. The devotional hymns of Manickavasagar, Nammalvar, and Andal are popular expressions of bhakti worship, especially among the Tamils.

The way of knowledge (jnana marga) is doubtless an integral part of the Hindu quest for liberation. It is appetizing to the philosophically-oriented Hindu intellectuals. But people's desperate need to relate to a personal god, worship him with love and adoration, and obey his commands is best met by the way of devotion (bhakti marga). The Hindu way accommodates both contemplative speculation and devotion as channels of liberation, and they are not to be taken as mutually exclusive; there are several high-quality Hindu intellectuals who are also sincere devotees.

The Hindu way is also both meditative and mystical. The popular forms of Hindu meditation are Yoga and Transcendental Meditation, while Siddha sakti worship and Tantric spirituality constitute the mystical aspect of the Hindu way.

All forms of Hindu meditation are geared toward liberation. They assume that humans have the potential to attain liberation. Yoga attempts to liberate people through a set of stringent exercises. Transcendental Meditation has become very popular, especially in the West. In a hectic world where people crave physical health and peace of mind, Transcendental Meditation is seen to be a popular cure. Perhaps it is popular because it can be practiced without undergoing the rigors of exercise that Yoga stipulates. Who likes to exercise!

In modern times Transcendental Meditation has been popularized by Maharishi Mahesh. It is based on a monistic view of reality, taking the human soul to be identical with the ultimate reality. Maharishi prefers to call this reality "Creative Intelligence," because when a transcendental meditation practitioner reaches the stage of being one with the ultimate reality, his or her intelligence is most creative. An examination of the process adopted in Transcendental Meditation is necessary to appreciate its nature and purpose. The following diagram will be helpful:[13]

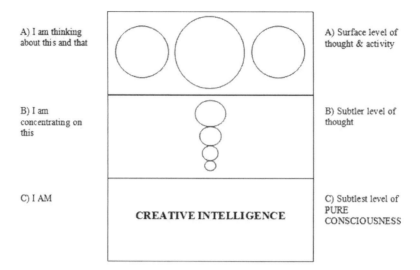

A) I am thinking about this and that

A) Surface level of thought & activity

B) I am concentrating on this

B) Subtler level of thought

C) I AM

CREATIVE INTELLIGENCE

C) Subtlest level of PURE CONSCIOUSNESS

As the diagram indicates, Transcendental Meditation takes the practitioner from the surface level of thought and activity to the subtlest level of pure consciousness. At the surface level one is caught up in the rat race of life and is restless, preoccupied with this and that. One is trying to think about a thing (the big circle) but is also thinking about other things (two smaller circles). At the second level, a person starts to concentrate on one thing. In the process of thinking about one thing, the thought itself becomes less and less pronounced in one's consciousness. The circle becoming smaller and smaller depicts this. A guru or a mantra could help one to concentrate. At the final subtlest level, even what was concentrated upon disappears. At this level, one has transcended thought itself. There are no circles in this cage. One is fully conscious but devoid of thoughts; one has reached that inner transpersonal reservoir of energy depicted as Creative Intelligence. In this transcendent state one realizes his or her oneness with the Ultimate Cosmic Reality, the "divinity" of Vedanta Hinduism.

Of all the mantras, the repetition of the word *aum* (or *om*) is claimed to be the most effective in transporting one to that transcendent state. Aum is said to phonically represent the Divinity that has no beginning or end. The recitation of aum catalyzes the divine vibrations latent in the one reciting it. Swami Vivekananda states well the phonic significance of *aum*:

> There are hundreds of words for God . . . But there must be a generalization among all these words, some substratum, some common ground of all these symbols, and that which is the common symbol will be the best, and will really represent them all. In making a sound we use the larynx and the palate as a sounding board. Is there any material sound of which all other sounds must be manifestations, one which is the most natural sound? *Om* (*aum*) is such a sound,

13. Kulathungam, "Christian Meditation," 35.

the basis of all sounds. The first letter, A (pronounced as in "all") is the root sound, the key, pronounced without touching any part of the tongue or palate; M (pronounced as "ma" in "maul" represents the last sound in the series, being produced by the closed lips, and the U (pronounced as in "put") rolls from the very root to the end of the sounding board of the mouth. Thus, "om" represents the whole phenomenon of sound-producing. As such it must be the natural symbol, the matrix of all the various sounds. It denotes the whole range and possibility of all the words that can be made.[14]

Through the recitation of such a mantra, Transcendental Meditation provides a way of liberation by transporting the practitioner to a level of consciousness in which one becomes aware of his or her true identity as part of the ultimate reality. It claims that concerted meditative effort can transport one into the realm of the "divinity" and thereby enable liberation. Hence TM is essentially salvific in intent.

There is also a mystical aspect associated with meditation, indicating that meditation by itself, even when practiced meticulously, is not adequate to liberate a person; one needs to resort to divine spiritual energy. People resort to gods believing that they have such energy. Sakti is the name given to this divine energy, usually categorized as feminine and taken as the consort of a deity. Saktism may then be described as a resort to the energy (sakti) of a god in order to gain his help. Saktism as related to the god Shiva exemplifies this strategy. Here sakti is Shiva's divine energy (Siva-Sakti). Shiva's consorts Durga and Kali personify this sakti. They are distinct from Shiva and yet inseparably connected to him, just like a man is connected to his wife. The wife knows her husband best; Shiva's consort knows him best. That is why Durga and Kali are popular Hindu goddesses. Saktism is evidence of a belief that humans need God's help for their liberation and the best resort is God's own power.

There are several ways a devotee is enabled by Shiva's sakti. A guru can connect one to sakti through his spiritual guidance or by giving a mantra to initiate one's spiritual journey. One can also follow the guidelines given in Tantric literature such as the Sivagamas and Saktagamas. The term tantra is derived from *tan*, meaning "to spread," and *trai*, meaning "to save." It is a way that accommodates both spiritual and ritualistic practices to achieve liberation. It uses *mantras, tantras, yantras, or mandalas* (diagrams or images) to activate the divine energy that is believed to be dormant in a human being, like a coiled serpent (*kundalini*). When this energy is activated through meditation, one reaches Shiva. A tantric text describes how sakti enables one to reach Shiva: "When one enters the state of Sakti [i.e., is identified with Sakti], there ensues the feeling of non-distinction between Sakti and Siva; then, one acquires the state of Siva [for] here, she (Sakti) is declared as the door of entrance [into Siva]."[15]

Reaching Shiva enabled by sakti, and with the aid of tantric practices, though mystical in many ways, shows clearly that Hindus acknowledge the need for God's power in order to reach and be liberated by him.

---

14. Vivekananda, *Complete Works*, 1:218–19.
15. Chakravarty, "Tantric Spirituality," 211.

The Hindu way is also both communal and ascetic. The Hindu populace is replete with ascetics, so much so that the world portrays Hinduism as otherworldly. The fact that the Aranyakas (forest books) provide guidelines for the practice of asceticism indicates that Hinduism takes asceticism as a legitimate means to attain liberation. Hinduism identifies four main stages in life's spiritual journey: bachelor student (*bramacharin*), householder (*grihasta*), forest dweller (*vanaprastha*), and ascetic renouncing the world (*sanniyasin*). The last two stages, though rarely observed, are highly respected. Moreover, the Hindu attitude to the material world as an illusion, locating human identity in one's spirit and degrading the body, contributes to the caricature of an ideal Hindu in the garb of a gaunt, disheveled hermit living in isolation. But such a portrayal of the Hindu way does not capture the whole picture. Communality figures prominently in the Hindu way. The significant place given to the role of the householder (grihasta) in the spiritual journey, and the emphasis on altruistic deeds, temple worship, pilgrimages, and festivals are all essentially communal. In a typical Hindu village, the temple is the hub of the community. Despite the divisive impact of the caste system on Hindu society, castes have enabled its orderly working for centuries. The Vedas identified four occupational groups, each having specific social duties: priests (Brahmins), performing ritualistic duties; kings, nobles, and warriors (*Kshatriyas*), guarding and ruling the community; farmers and merchants (*Vaishyas*), managing the economics of the society; and a group (*Shudras*) performing the most menial tasks. This structure enabled the community to function smoothly. Even though eventually these occupational groups became entrenched as castes based on a hierarchical order, each group performed their respective duties believing that past karma had determined their present state and that the faithful performance of their social duties would bear fruit in the future life. The caste system, though not to be condoned, has had a significant role in the communal life of Hindus.

Of all the Hindu festivals, Kumbha Mela best illustrates the meeting of the ascetic and the communal in Hindu practice. During this event, which lasts for months, millions congregate somewhere near Allahabad, where the Jumna River meets the sacred Ganges, to have a dip in the sacred spot. Huge processions of ascetics from various orders mingle with the community and discuss matters pertaining to religion and society. Their discussions eventually help in making revisions to standards of Hindu social conduct. Here we see how the ascetics help the community.

The Hindu way involves both human effort and divine enablement. The popular paths to liberation through knowledge, devotion, good deeds, and meditation exhibit human effort based on the assumption that humans are capable of liberation because of their inherent divine nature. The guidance given by gurus and seers (rishis), intercessory action by deities like Agni and Ganesha to higher gods, empowerment through divine energy (sakti), divine intervention through incarnation, and the plea for God's grace indicate how divine involvement enables humans to be liberated. Both facets of the way, human effort and divine enablement, are geared to one cardinal purpose: to facilitate liberation. A verse from the Upanisads continues to be the prayer of millions of Hindus:

> From the unreal lead me to the real
> From darkness lead me to light
> From death lead me to immortality.[16]

THE RELEVANCE OF CHRIST TO THE HINDU QUEST

The Hindu way of liberation seems complete and comprehensive, so much so that Christ appears redundant. Some relate Christ to Hinduism by accommodating him as an insightful teacher of spiritual truths, an exemplar of moral values, or even as one of their deities. But there seems to be a more conducive way of relating Christ to the Hindu world. Hinduism per se does not need Christ, but Hindus seem to seek someone very much like him. Some of the significant transitions that have occurred and continue to occur in the practice of Hinduism may be taken as indicators of certain aspirations that Christ seems to fulfill ideally. This makes Christ relevant to the Hindu quest.

The transition from a nontheistic to a theistic way of liberation, especially in Vedanta Hinduism, needs to be noted. Advaita Vedanta in its original version considered Ultimate Reality to be an impersonal, ineffable cosmic spirit. The move to characterize this reality in terms of a personal god makes Christ relevant to the Hindu quest. Gods as personifications of elements of nature have been in vogue since Vedic times; the storm god Indra, the sky god Varuna, and the sun god Mitra are typical examples. But when Sankara conceded that the Ultimate Reality, Brahman without attributes (Nirguna), could manifest itself as one with attributes (Saguna), he provided the groundwork for a new paradigm to view the gods. In such a context, they appeared as reflecting certain attributes of this Ultimate Reality (Brahman) rather than as mere personifications of elements of nature.

Among the thousands of Hindu deities, three command respect: Brahma, Vishnu, and Shiva. This group of gods (Thirumurti) is the Hindu version of God as a triune being. The three deities are equally divine, manifesting a single reality. In essence they are the same, but functionally they differ. Brahma as creator, Shiva as destroyer of evil, and Vishnu as compassionate protector, are all part of a single godhead but fulfill the different needs of Hindus. People need a God who will enable them to exist, destroy the evil that besets them, and protect them through compassionate acts. The Thirumurti provides the appropriate trinitarian model to meet these basic needs.

Moreover, such a triune godhead provides an appropriate framework to relate Christ to the Hindu quest. The functions attributed to Brahma, Shiva, and Vishnu exhibit certain aspirations that Christ, as second person of the Christian Trinity, could fulfill.

---

16. Brhadaranyakopanisa 1:3:28, in Padinjarekara, *Christ in Ancient Vedas*, 35.

The gods of the Hindu triune godhead, being more than mere personifications of elements of nature, transcend the world and humanity. Hence a mediator becomes necessary. The god Agni is a Vedic anticipation of such a mediator. Agni, as fire, transported the burnt offerings to the gods during sacrifices of the Vedic times. But the concept of a personal mediator god takes full shape among the devotees of Shiva. Hindus in their quest for liberation needed a god who would not tolerate unrighteousness but would destroy evil, and they found this in Shiva. But this in turn made them dread him, for his anger was evident when they failed to meet his high standards; tradition has it that the name Calcutta is a derivative of *Kali-Kata*, referring to the city that Shiva, in his righteous anger, had cursed through his consort Kali. To approach such a righteous god as Shiva, Hindus needed a mediator, and this they found in his eldest son Ganesha. This elephant-headed god is the most popular of all deities. He is the god who removes obstacles, intercedes on behalf of devotees, and mediates between them and his father Shiva.

Ganesha

The altar for Ganesha figures prominently in Hindu temples. His popularity shows that Hindus need a mediator who is easily approachable by them as well as closest to God. Jesus Christ as God's son ideally fulfills such a need.

The transition from people trying to reach God, on the one hand, to God trying to reach people, on the other, is also a significant indicator of the relevance of Christ to the Hindu quest. This move is best seen in the way Vishnu, of the Hindu triune godhead, attempts to help people in distress through his incarnations. The traditional paths of good works, knowledge, meditation, and devotion are all taken to be legitimate ways of liberation, but they are essentially attempts to reach God. On the other hand, Vishnu's incarnations are God's attempt to reach humans and free them from the problems that beset them.

There are ten recorded incarnations of Vishnu. The first three take the form of animals: fish, tortoise, and bull. The fourth is a man-lion, while the fifth is a dwarf (of the kind that figures in mythology as a sort of subhuman character). The rest are humans: Rama, Krishna, Buddha, and the future anticipated Kalkin. Krishna figures as the most popular incarnation; he has millions of devotees, and the Hare Krishna movement is a dynamic sector of the Hindu populace. The story of Krishna's incarnation is found in the Puranas and the epic Bhagavad Gita. One is not sure whether this incarnation is historical or legendary, but it is immaterial whether or not Krishna is a historical figure. What has to be noted is that the poetic narrative of his incarnation as given in the Gita expresses one of the deepest aspirations of Hindus. They need God to come down, become one with them, experience their calamities, and free them from their predicament.

Krishna appears as the charioteer of one of the five brothers, Arjuna, who is to fight on the virtuous side of a battle that would lead to killing his own cousins. Naturally, Arjuna is hesitant to become involved in such a battle, but for the virtuous to overcome vice, he has to fight. It is here that Krishna enters the stage. In order to make the hesitant Arjuna into a righteous warrior, Krishna makes certain strategic moves. After revealing his true identity, he presents the formula on which his incarnation is based and then, through his teaching, tries to convince Arjuna that fighting for the virtuous is justifiable. First he makes it clear that he is not just a charioteer but the supreme incarnation of the godhead: that he is both divine and human. His humanity is best seen in the Purana narratives where he shows himself as the cowherd boy mischievously playing with cowherd girls (*gopis*). In his identity, he no doubt resembles Christ in that he is both divine and human, but while Christ is the only incarnation of God, Krishna is the supreme incarnation, implying that there could be others. His formula of incarnation makes this clear. He proclaims:

> Whenever and wherever there is decline in religious practice, O descendent of Bharata, and a predominant rise of irreligion—at that time I descend Myself, to deliver the pious and to annihilate the miscreants, as well as to reestablish the principles of religion, I myself appear, millennium after millennium (Bhagavad Gita 4:7–8).

This formula makes it clear that Hinduism embraces multiple as well as recurrent incarnations. Vishnu incarnates whenever unrighteousness abounds. He protects the virtuous and destroys the evildoers and thereby establishes righteousness for a specific period of time. The positive impact of incarnation is limited to one sector of humanity: it is to save the righteous from the unrighteous. But Christ came to save all humanity, since in God's sight all humans are unrighteous. His incarnation is a one-time event and not recurrent.

Moreover, what stands out as distinctive is the way in which Krishna carries out his salvific mission. He convinces Arjuna that war is justifiable and motivates him to enter the battlefield. Krishna orchestrates his strategy through teaching that highlights the vital role played by the traditional paths in one's liberation: he emphasizes, in chapter 2 of the Gita, the necessity of correct knowledge about the world and the human being. In chapter 15 he points out that one cannot understand the nature of ultimate spiritual reality through sense knowledge of the material world, for it presents a warped view—just as a reflection of a tree appears upside down, branches below and roots pointing upwards. In order to get a correct view of reality, one needs suprasensory knowledge. Moreover, the human being is made up of the material body, which does not endure, and the soul, which is eternal (chapter 2:13, 16, 18, 20, 23). Hence the act of killing in battle does not amount to destroying the soul but rather releasing the soul from its body. Krishna tries to convince Arjuna that killing his vicious cousins amounts to a salvific act in that it enables them to be freed from the bondage of their evil bodily existence. Arjuna is reminded that when one engages in such an act without looking at the consequences but rather as devoted obedience to God (bhakti), it constitutes righteous action. Through such teaching Krishna motivates Arjuna to fight.

But it was Arjuna who fought. Krishna enabled him to fight and kill the enemies. There is no recognition of Krishna dying to save those he came to help. On the other hand, Jesus was born to die. In fact, his death figures more than his teachings and miracles as the means of salvation for humanity. His sacrificial death on the cross is central to his salvific mission. Krishna's incarnation shows divine enablement in the liberation of humans from the forces of evil, but such enablement is orchestrated mainly through his teachings that resort to the traditional ways of liberation based on human effort and knowledge. Hence Krishna's liberation still works within the paradigm of human effort. Its effectiveness is conditional on the quality of righteousness that people manifest through their effort. But Jesus' incarnation depicts divine involvement in the salvation of humanity that is not conditional on human effort. Jesus himself bore the sins of all humanity and offered himself as a sacrifice on the cross.

In one of his conversations with Arjuna, Krishna claims that he is the "sacrifice" (Bhagavad Gita 9:16). But there is no evidence that he sacrificed himself. The Bhagavad Gita mentions that in the end he dies as a result of an enemy shooting an arrow that pierced his only vulnerable spot, the sole of his foot, while resting in a forest. This cannot be taken as a vicarious sacrifice for sinners. Perhaps his claim to be a sacrifice was his attempt to identify himself as Prajapati, the Lord and Sustainer of all creation (Bhagavad Gita 9:16) who, according to the Vedas, sacrificed himself.

The Vedas refer to an event in which the god Prajapati is sacrificed, calling it the "Purusa-Prajapati" sacrifice (Rg Veda 10:90:1–16). The Brahmanas and the Upanisads provide additional material concerning it. It is believed to have taken place in the heavenly regions, before everything was created. Whether it really occurred or not, it has some significant features that allow us to relate it to Christ. Joseph Padinjarekara points out how Christ fulfilled the requirements of Hindu sacrifice, especially as described in the Vedas and Brahmanas.[17] Sacrifice has been practiced among Hindus from ancient times. Animal, even human sacrifices, and offerings of fruits and vegetables were attempts to gain peace with the gods. But in the sacrifice of Purusa-Prajapati, the one sacrificed is both god and man: Prajapati refers to God Almighty, and Purusa represents the perfect sinless human being. The sacrifice is conceived in the heart of God, in his love for humanity. The efficacy of the sacrifice is the shedding of innocent blood. The perfect God-Man, Purusa, meets this criterion. According to the Hindu scriptures, human beings came into being as a result of this sacrifice. But its ultimate purpose was to provide a way to liberation (moksha).

The resemblance of this sacrifice to what Christ accomplished on the cross is evident. But that does not warrant a conclusion that, in addition to the prophets of the Bible, ancient Hindu seers communicated God's plan of salvation through revelations

17. Padinjarekara, *Christ in Ancient Vedas*.

given under divine inspiration. Raimundo Panikkar seems to take such a stance.[18] The Vedas, or for that matter any scripture that predates the Bible, should not be taken as a prologue to the Bible just because there are some significant similarities. Such scriptures, though not part of what Christians regard as special revelation, may at best be accommodated within general revelation The insight highlighted by the story of the Purusa-Prajapati sacrifice is that the reconciliation of sinful humans with a holy God requires a sacrifice without blemish. Only a God-Man could be that. Perhaps such an insight may be an instance of general revelation.

In order to fully appreciate the significance of the Purusa-Prajapati sacrifice, we need to place it in the context of its occurrence. It takes place in the heavenly regions before all creation. The ancient seers are not recording a historical event, but speculating on what an ideal sacrifice should be; one that could bring about peace between humans and gods. What these seers sincerely aspired for is fulfilled in history through Christ's incarnation and sacrifice on the cross. The Hindu incarnations, even that of Krishna, do not adequately fulfill such aspirations. As noted earlier, Krishna's incarnation enabled some humans to overcome the forces of evil, but Christ through his death and resurrection overcame evil and saved humanity in a manner that adequately fulfilled the aspirations of the ancient seers.

The move from humanity's search for God to the initiative of God in reaching people eventually ended with divine incarnations having salvific intent. The Hindu seers articulated what the ideal incarnation should be: it should not only be God helping humans to overcome evil, but God himself vicariously saving humanity through sacrificing himself. This is what Christ did on the cross. Moreover, the anticipated incarnation, Kalkin, portrayed as one handling a flaming sword and riding on a white horse to put an end to an age fraught with evil (*Kali Yuga*) and establish divine rule naturally brings to mind Christ's second coming. It is he who fulfills the Hindu anticipation of a savior-god.

Closely connected with the resort to a God who reaches humans in their time of need is another move that makes Christ relevant to the Hindu quest: the transition from a way of works to a plea for grace.

The traditional paths to liberation are essentially strategies based on human effort. When the supreme reality turns out to be a personal God, "sin" is not mere spiritual ignorance but estrangement from God, who hates sin. In order to be reconciled with God, repenting of one's sins is required. Bathing in the holy River Ganges, going on pilgrimages to holy places, making offerings to deities, fasting, and participating in ritualistic practices bordering on self-torture are all meant to get rid of the guilt of sin and reconcile humans with God.

But amidst such multifarious practices there lingers a haunting feeling that something more is needed, something more than sincere and even tortuous human effort. This is where God's grace comes in.

18. Panikkar, *Unknown Christ*.

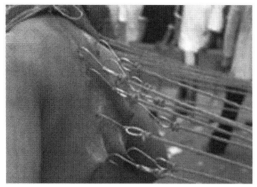

A Hindu devotee participating in the Kawadi Ritual

The plea for grace seems to arise in the least expected places. Sankara's way of liberation through knowledge does not really need God's grace. Sankara claims that liberation occurs when the human soul realizes its identity with the cosmic, impersonal spirit (Brahman). But what is startling is his personal life: he is believed to be one of the prominent devotional poets of India and is supposed to have sung moving pleas and praises to deities such as Shiva, Shiva's consort Durga and son Skanda, and Vishnu's incarnations Krishna and Rama. Perhaps the need for divine grace in his personal life compelled him to concede that the ineffable Nirguna Brahman should manifest itself as Saguna Brahman with knowable attributes eventually personified in gods whose grace could be sought.

His disciple Ramanuja considers devotion to god as the ideal way to liberation. But he realizes that such devotion demands much preparation, mastery of scriptural regulations, and disciplined practice. It is not for all. To a devotee who is unable to meet such stringent requirements, Ramanuja proposes Prapatti Yoga. According to this strategy a devotee allows God himself to act as the means of liberation. Through "burden-transfer" (*bhara-samarpana*) the execution and responsibility to attain liberation is surrendered to God, who fulfills it by grace.

A typical example of the plea for God's grace is seen in the prayer of Desika, a fourteenth-century follower of Ramanuja. His supplication runs thus: "Lord, I, who am nothing, conform to your will and desist being contrary to it, and with faith and prayer, submit to you the burden of saving my soul."[19]

Ramanuja's Parapatti Yoga, as articulated by Desika, appeals for God's grace in the face of human inability.

In order to seal the devotee's surrender to God and assurance of his grace, Ramanuja recommended a three-part mantra: *Aum-Namah-Narayana*.

Aum stands for the Supreme Reality (Brahman). Namah expresses the devotee's confession of utter helplessness, while Narayana refers to the divinity resorted to. In Ramanuja's case it is Vishnu. What the devotee needs is the assurance that God's grace has been bestowed; the mantra is intended to give that assurance. The assurance of salvation that God the Holy Spirit renders to a new believer in Christ is here perhaps attempted through the utterance of a mantra.

The plea for grace that Ramanuja's devotional Vedanta exhibited during the period of classical Hinduism continues to grow and spread through various sectors of post-classical Hinduism.

---

19. Vedanta Desika, "Nyasadasaka 2," in Raghavachar, "Spiritual Vision," 271.

Kashmir Saivism, which flourished in Kashmir between the eighth and eleventh centuries CE, explicitly appeals to the grace of the god Shiva. Based on the advaita (non-dualistic) view of reality as one, this school claimed that the supreme reality manifests itself at three levels: God (Shiva), sakti (his divine energy), and anu (individual souls). What makes this school noteworthy is its proposal that there is an ideal way to liberation, called the Non-Way (*Anupaya*).[20] What justifies such a name is that this understanding does not separate the way from its goal: the goal of liberation is Shiva, who also becomes the way. Through his divine energy (sakti) he enables the devotee to reach him. Kashmir Saivites appeal to such divine help to attain liberation. What they crave is for God to become the Way himself. Christ as the Way becomes very relevant to such an aspiration.

Two well-known South Indian Tamil poets, Manickavasagar and Nammalvar, also highlight the necessity of God's grace. Manickavasagar resorts to Shiva's grace, while Nammalvar appeals to Vishnu's grace.

Manickavasagar is believed to have relinquished his high position as prime minister during the reign of the Pandyan kings to become a poet reputed for his devotional poetry. His classic, *Thiruvasagam* (*Sacred Utterance*), highlights the importance of divine grace in one's quest for salvation. He believes that God wants to liberate all humanity. But three impurities deter humans from being liberated: the egoistic mindset (anava); the thoughts and deeds that arise out of such a mindset, including the notion that one can live without God (karma); and the bondage that these generate (maya). When one realizes the depravity in which one is caught up, there is a desperate plea for grace. The word "grace" occurs in nearly every stanza of Manickavasagar's opening poem of one hundred stanzas. His plea for grace is evident in stanza 83, which runs thus:

> I have no fear of births, but quake at the thought that I must die
> E'en heav'n to me were naught; for earth's whole empire what care I?
> O Siva wreathed with honeyed blossoms, "When shall come the morn.
> When Thou wilt grant Thy grace to me?" I cry with anguish torn.[21]

Shiva's Cosmic Dance at CERN, Switzerland

Manickavasagar is believed to have realized the absolute necessity of grace while worshipping the Dancing Shiva (*Natarajah*) in the famous Chidamparam Temple in South India; Natarajah means "the Lord of the Dance." The Dance of Shiva is one of the most popular Hindu icons. On June 18, 2004, an unusual landmark appeared on the premises of CERN, the

20. Baumer, "Four Spiritual Ways," 17–18.

21. Kingsbury and Philips, eds., *Hymns*, n.p.

European Centre for Research in Particle Physics located in Geneva: a statue of the Dance of Shiva, two meters tall. It highlighted the significance of Shiva's dance as a metaphor for the cosmic movement of subatomic particles observed and analyzed by CERN physicists. Since Fritjof Capra's attempt to draw a parallel between the dynamic world of creation and destruction orchestrated by Shiva and the findings of subatomic physics, the dance of Shiva has become a mythological depiction of the dynamics of subatomic matter. The metaphor of the cosmic dance seems to unify the world views represented by ancient mythology and modern physics. Despite the metaphysical implications of the dance, for Hindus it is essentially a pictorial allegory of Shiva's principal activities of emancipation (*anugraha*) by trampling under his feet the forces of evil and thereby maintaining harmony in the universe.

Manickavasagar's hymns encourage fellow Hindus to resort to Shiva's grace. Nammalvar, another poet, belongs to a group of Hindu seers known as *Alvars*. As the Tamil name indicates, they are the ones immersed in God's grace and love. Nammalvar also confesses his utter depravity and resorts to Vishnu, who manifests his grace through his incarnations. For Nammalvar, these incarnations are motivated by one supreme purpose: God's compassionate love to liberate helpless people. He articulates his plea for God's grace in his compendium of hymns, *Tiruvaimoli*. These two poets through their life experiences and their devotional songs have motivated many to appeal to God's grace.

Another *Alvar*, Andal, ideally represents a Hindu woman's devotion and plea for God's grace. Her devotional work *Thirupavai*, composed of thirty verses written in Tamil, describes the way of liberation in a way accessible to many. While many gurus have sought to awaken the souls of their followers from spiritual ignorance, *Thirupavai* attempts to awaken God himself to the need of bestowing his grace. Even though this work is utterly devotional, it does not advocate extreme asceticism. Sensual pleasure (kama), wealth (artha), and moral conduct (dharma) are accommodated in the way to liberation (moksha).

Resort to personal gods, devotional worship, and appeals to divine grace also find their way into Indian music (carnatic music) and dance. During the golden era of Indian music in the eighteenth and nineteenth centuries, one of the leading composers, Thyagarajah Pagavathar, made an interesting observation about good deeds. According to him, good deeds could at best give one a better life, but could not release one from the cycle of rebirths. He believed that devotionally loving God and fully depending on God's grace is necessary for such a release.[22]

The relevance of Christ to the Hindu quest is evident in more than one way. The transition from non-theism to the worship of a triune God (Thirumurti), who has not only created the world (Brahma) but also destroys evil (Shiva) and shows compassion through incarnation (Vishnu) shows the kind of God Hindus want in order to be liberated. Moreover, the popularity of Ganesha, the son of Shiva, as the mediator between humans and God is noteworthy. Hindus want a mediator that is not just a

22. Venugopal, "Spirituality of Carnatic Music," 456.

guru, hermit, or priest, but one who is God's own. Christ as God's son ideally fulfills the requirement. The transition from humans struggling to reach God, on the one hand, to God reaching humans by means of incarnations, on the other, brings out the desperate need of Hindus. They need a God who will give up his transcendence and reveal himself as a human, become one of them and thereby liberate them. Christ, in giving up his life on the cross for humans, ideally responds to such a need. The plea for grace, founded on the conviction that humans are helpless to liberate themselves despite their laudable efforts, makes Christ relevant. The fact that one can be saved by faith in Christ through grace seems to be the answer to the Hindu plea for grace.

Even though Mahatma Gandhi did not fully endorse Christianity, he had a special appreciation of Christ and his sacrificial death on the cross. Gandhi took the cross to be a supreme example of *satyagraha*, the act of overcoming evil through truth and sacrificial love. In fact, two Christian hymns were his favorites: "When I Survey the Wondrous Cross" and "Lead, Kindly Light, Amidst the Encircling Gloom." The second hymn formed part of his funeral at his own request. These two hymns aptly epitomize the motivating factor and the goal of the Hindu quest. The Hindu quest's plea is to be led by the "Light" to the "Wondrous Cross."

8

The Sikh Quest

God is only One
His Name is True
He is the Creator
He is without fear
He is inimical to none
He never dies
He is beyond births and deaths
He is self-illuminated
He is realized by the kindness (grace) of the True Guru (Japuji, stanza 1).[1]

T HIS IS THE PRAYER a devout Sikh makes every morning. Guru Nanak, the founder of Sikhism, uttered this prayer when he encountered God and was called to be his messenger. The prayer expresses two vital facets of the Sikh quest. Its goal is God, whose name is True, and the way to reach him is through the kindness (grace) of the guru.

Some hesitate to include Sikhism among the world's major religions. Having originated as late as sixteenth century CE, it does not receive the respect of age. Its adherents constitute a very small section of the world's religious population. Moreover, most Sikhs are clustered in a specific region of India: Punjab. Some view Sikhism as merely a reform movement of Hinduism, while others consider it to be a blend of Hinduism and Islam. But to relegate Sikhism to such a secondary status does not do justice to the Sikhs, who consider themselves as belonging to a legitimate faith community. Their turbans, attire, and uncut but well-groomed hair make them a distinguishable religious community. For them, Sikhism is a way of life that fulfills their innermost spiritual aspirations. They believe that such a way was given to them by divinely inspired gurus, commencing with Guru Nanak. The above-mentioned prayer is uttered with the conviction that resorting to the God of Truth through the help of the gurus is not a strategy borrowed from Islam or Hinduism, but rendered to them

1. Doabia, *Sacred Nitnem*, 19. All quotations from Sikh scriptures in this chapter are from his translation, unless otherwise stated.

through the spiritual insights of the gurus. Those who share such a conviction came to be known as Sikhs. The word *Sikh* in the Punjabi language means "disciple." A Sikh is a disciple of God, guided by gurus.

"Guru" is a pivotal concept that is basic to the understanding of the Sikh quest. The concept of guru has been very much part of Indian religious culture from ancient times. The word guru literally means one who brings light amidst darkness: *Gu* meaning darkness and *Ru* meaning light. The Sikh quest is orchestrated through the guidance of the gurus. For the Sikhs, a guru is not an ordinary teacher or a prophet or even just a saintly poet. He is a spiritual torch endued with the *jyothi* (light) that illuminates the path to God; the path of liberation. Adi Granth, the sacred Sikh scripture, compares the guru to a ladder, boat, raft, and ship to highlight the guru's role as one who enables a seeker to reach his or her destination.

Sikhs acknowledge the following as their gurus; their pontificate is as follows:

1. Guru Nanak	Founder to 1539 CE
2. Guru Angad	1559 to 1552
3. Guru Amardas	1552 to 1574
4. Guru Ramdas	1574 to 1581
5. Guru Arjan	1581 to 1606
6. Guru Hargobind	1606 to 1645
7. Guru Har Rai	1645 to 1661
8. Guru Harkrishan	1661 to 1664
9. Guru Tegh Bahadur	1664 to 1675
10. Guru Gobind Singh	1675 to 1708
11. Guru Granth Sahib	1708 to present

The tenth guru, Gobind Singh, designated the Sikh sacred text Adi Granth to serve as the guru for the Sikhs after him. Hence there are ten human gurus and one scriptural guru. But Sikhs claim that, even though there are several gurus, the carrier of the divine message is really one. The gurus who succeeded Guru Nanak mention him as the real composer of their hymns. Hence Sikhs claim that Nanak, operating through the successive gurus, is the carrier of God's message. In a culture where the doctrine of rebirth was a given, Guru Nanak being born as nine successive persons is conceivable. Moreover, the present guru, Adi Granth, is essentially a compendium of the hymns of the gurus; it is the collective voice of the gurus. Keeping in mind the Sikh view of the guru as "one soul in several bodies" giving light amidst darkness, let us look at how the gurus express and articulate the Sikh quest.

Guru Nanak, the founder of Sikhism, was born in 1469 in Talwandi, now known as Nankana Saheeb (named after the Guru) in Pakistan, west of Lahore. Since his hymns contained in the scriptures, Adi Granth, reveal more his spiritual aspirations than his life story, we have to depend on sources beyond the scriptures to know about his life. Scholars tend to depend on eighteenth and nineteenth-century historians and on Mughal court records to sketch his life story.[2]

In order to fully appreciate the impact of Guru Nanak's mission, we need to situate him in the context of his time and the place where he lived, north India.[3] This was a locality where Hindus and Muslims intermingled and in the process fought against each other. But amidst such tensions there developed a pacifist tradition that attempted to reconcile the communities in conflict by directing them to a transcendent being. Such a tradition received the name *Sant*, the etymology of which could be traced to the Sanskrit word *sadhu*, meaning a holy ascetic or a seeker of truth. Those who belonged to this tradition were saintly seekers of truth. The Sant tradition evolved out of the Hindu Bakti movement that resorted to Vishnu and his incarnation Krishna, Tantric Yoga that was geared to the devotion of Shiva, and Islamic Sufism that strove to experience mystical union with Allah. Guru Nanak came out of such a world and these movements had a significant impact on him and his mission.

Nanak was from a devout Hindu family. His father, Kalidas Chandrana, also known as Mehta Kalu, was an accountant of crop revenue for the village of Talwandi. Nanak's mother was Tripta Devi and he had an older sister, Nanaki. His parents were keen that he should succeed in life both academically and financially. His father tried his best to place him in various occupations and business ventures but was not at all successful. The son was seeking something beyond book learning and lucrative jobs. He was a reflective dreamer who relished the company of Hindu and Muslim seers. In 1488 CE he was sent to his sister Nanaki at Sultanpur Lodhi where he got a job as a storekeeper. He married Sulakhni and had two sons. No doubt his storekeeper's job helped him to support his family but was too mundane to be spiritually rewarding. Hence, he became preoccupied with spiritual matters and neglected the duties his job required of him. He partnered with a Muslim friend, Mardana, and organized groups to participate in nightly devotional hymn singing. They made frequent retreats to the forest to meditate. A significant spiritual crisis in his life occurred when he was thirty years old. In one of his meditational jaunts to the forest he had a spiritual experience that drastically changed him from a restless wanderer to a guru with a mission. Such an experience made him aware of a supreme transcendent being who is the creator of everything and who is devoid of enmity and beyond racial and religious prejudice. He realized that liberation could be attained only through reaching him. Such an encounter gave him a divine mandate to proclaim that there is no Hindu, there is no Muslim; that all are equal in the sight of this supreme being. He realized that his mission was to go into the world and teach mankind. He executed his mission mainly through his devotional hymns. His voluminous collection of hymns contains poetic prayers and supplications for God's grace. They became effective channels to spread his gospel.

2. Mcleod, *Textual Sources*, 17. See also, Mcleod, "Essay on Sikhism," 21; Singh, *Fundamentals of Sikhism*, 22–30.

3. Biographical details of Guru Nanak and the gurus who followed him are primarily from the following sources: Singh, *Faith and Philosophy*, 10–21; Singh, *Fundamentals of Sikhism*, 21–61; Singh, *Encyclopaedia of Sikhism*, 88–91.

Devotees made these hymns their own in their quest to liberate themselves. In fact, Nanak's response to the divine call that he received on that significant day has become the *Mul-Mantra* (root supplication), the above-stated prayer that Sikhs repeat in their daily morning devotions.

In the following years, Nanak traveled extensively to almost every part of India and even to Sri Lanka, Afghanistan, Tibet, Iran, and Mecca. Two events that took place during his travels clearly illustrate Nanak's view of God. When visiting a mosque in Mecca, Nanak had stretched out to sleep in a colonnade. A Muslim reproved him for having his feet pointed towards Kabbah, the holiest shrine of the Muslims located in Mecca. Nanak's response is noteworthy. He asked the Muslim critic, "Then turn my feet in the direction where God does not dwell."[4] Nanak's response indicates his view of God as being omnipresent and not restricted to a specific location. Hence for him the Muslim ritual of praying while facing Mecca appeared to be meaningless. In his visit to Hardwar, one morning he saw a large crowd of people bathing in river Ganges, the holy river for the Hindus. They were throwing water towards the east in the direction of the sun. He asked them why they were doing this. They replied that they were throwing water in the direction of the sun where they believed that their ancestors were, millions of miles away. Hearing this Nanak started to throw water in a westerly direction. Naturally the Hindus were surprised and asked him why he was throwing water in such an untraditional manner. Nanak replied that he was doing this to water his field in Punjab, located in the west. The Hindus could not understand how the water could reach the fields of Punjab. Nanak's reply was, "If my water won't reach my field just a few hundred miles away, how will your water reach your ancestors millions of miles away?"[5] Such a response reveals his skeptical stance on ritualistic practices so popularly prevalent among the Hindus. No doubt he believed with them that humans are caught in the cycle of rebirths (*samsara*) and release from such bondage is and should be the goal of the spiritual quest. But the way to liberation for him went beyond rituals.

Wherever he went, he tried his best to reconcile the Hindu and Muslim communities. His attire combined both the Hindu and Muslim styles. He pointed out that the way to liberation had to be resort to God, who he called "True Name." Perhaps such a designation was to highlight the character of God as truth as well as to transcend partisan names such a Vishnu, Shiva, or Allah. When people accepted his message he organized faith communities.

After several years of traveling, he settled down in the Punjab village of Kartarpur as guru of a community of disciples. Meditating on the Divine Name (*nam simran*), singing devotional hymns (*kirtan*), facilitating the fellowship of believers through communal worship and participating in meals in a common kitchen (*langar*), and active involvement in social services were characteristic features of this community.

4. Oxtoby, "Sikh Tradition," 181.

5. Singh, *Fundamentals of Sikhism*, 28.

Nanak died at the age of seventy. His conviction that a guru is absolutely needed for people to be liberated led him to appoint a guru to succeed him. The new guru was not one of his sons but one who was very close to his heart and dedicated to his message. The new guru was Angad Dev, whose name means "godly person who is very part of him." The articulation of the Sikh quest for liberation that commenced with Guru Nanak was continued and developed by a series of nine human gurus and then through the sacred scripture, Adi Granth.

Some gurus merit special attention. Guru Anjad Dev (1504–1552), was a worshiper of the Hindu goddess Durga before he became a disciple of Nanak in 1532. Guru Angad developed and popularized the Punjabi Gurmukti script that eventually became the script of the Sikh scriptures. Hindu priests played a dominant role in the religious life of the people because of their knowledge of Sanskrit, the language of the Hindu scriptures that was used in the performance of rituals. Guru Anjad Dev initiated a process which eventually provided Sikhs a sacred text, Adi Granth, written in a language other than Sanskrit, one which the common people of Punjab could understand and hence not depend on the mercy of the Hindu priests. He also extended the langar (the common kitchen) by personally administering it.

Guru Amardas (1479–1574) was appointed the third guru when he was seventy-three years old. He successfully propagated Sikhism by organizing the community into regions and appointing a devout Sikh to be in charge of each region. He trained missionaries to spread Sikhism in different parts of India. As a social reformer, he courageously fought against some of the social evils of his time. The caste system stratified society and degraded some people as untouchables. He made the langar an integral part of Sikh religious life by ensuring that his disciples, whether rich or poor or high or low caste, had their meals together. Thereby he tangibly demonstrated that Sikhism advocates social equality. He is believed to have emancipated women from the tortuous Hindu practice of *satee*, the burning of widows on the funeral pyres of their dead husbands. His services to the community highlight that the Sikh quest for liberation was not through ascetic renouncement of the world but through active involvement in the affairs of the world in order to rid it of some of its evils.

Guru Amardas appointed Ramdas (1534–1581) as the fourth guru. Guru Ramdas is known for the construction of a pool, the location of which later came to be known as Amritsar or the "Pool of Immortality," which is one of the sacred places for the Sikhs. He was a talented musicologist who contributed 638 hymns to Adi Granth.

Guru Arjan Dev (1563–1606) completed his father's project of building the Shri Darbar Sahib, popularly known as the Golden Temple at Amritsar. Today this is the holiest temple for the Sikhs. In addition to this, his most significant contribution was the compilation of the Sikh scripture, Adi Granth (the First Book). He collected the hymns of Guru Nanak and those of three succeeding gurus as well as of several saintly poets. The holy book was ceremoniously opened in the Golden Temple at Amritsar on August 30, 1604. Due to Guru Arjan's efforts, Sikhs came to have a holy book which they could call their own. Moreover, they had a holy place where they could go on pilgrimages. Naturally these developments helped in the spread of

Sikhism. Many Hindus and Muslims embraced Sikhism. Not surprisingly, people preferring Sikhism to Hinduism and Islam created hostile reactions. Until this time, Sikhism enjoyed imperial patronage. Cordial relationships prevailed between the gurus and the Mughal emperors. Emperor Humayun had called Guru Angad to his headquarters. Guru Amardas was friendly with Emperor Akbar, who came to pay his respects and according to custom participated in the common meal at the langar. Guru Ramdas was also friendly with Emperor Akbar and persuaded him to remove oppressive taxes on non-Muslims. But intolerant of the Sikh evangelistic infiltration into Muslim territory, the Mughal emperor Jahangir ordered that unless Guru Arjan Dev converted to Islam, he would be executed. Upon his refusal to abandon his faith, he was tortuously put to death. Such a gruesome death motivated Sikhs to take a militant stance to defend their faith. The sixth guru, Guru Arjan Dev's son Hargobind, spearheaded this militant move.

After seeing his father brutally tortured to death in 1606, Guru Hargobind took the stance that defending one's faith cannot be merely spiritual warfare but should accommodate temporal, even militant methods. On the day of his installation as guru, he began wearing two swords representing the spiritual (*peeri*) and the temporal (*meeri*) facets of Sikhism. This practice eventually led to the artistic construction of *khanda*, the emblem of Sikh identity. He also started building Akat Takht, the highest seat of temporal authority, opposite the Golden Temple, the spiritual center of the Sikh community. Both these innovations highlight the Sikh strategy of propagating and defending its faith through spiritual as well as temporal means.

Guru Tegh Bahdur (1621–1675), the ninth guru, was a brave soldier. He defended not only his faith but gave his life defending freedom of faith for all people. When the Muslim emperor Auranzeb had ordered the Kashmir Brahmins to convert to Islam, they appealed to Guru Tegh Bahdur Saheeb, He informed the emperor that the Brahmins would convert to Islam if he could be persuaded to accept Islam. Failing to convert the guru, the Muslims tortured and killed him.[6] Even though the guru did not himself believe the ritualistic practices of the Brahmins, he upheld their right to follow their own religion.

Guru Gobind Singh (1666–1708), the tenth guru, played a significant role in articulating the Sikh quest. During a time when Sikhs had no legal rights and were subjected to forcible conversions and their temples were burnt, Guru Gobind Singh tried his best to uplift an oppressed people to a place of dignity. Realizing that the Sikhs needed to belong to a community in order to articulate their faith, he organized them into a strong brotherhood called the *Khalsa*. Wherever he went, he set up communities of disciples who worshipped together and ate from a common kitchen (langar) when they congregated. Guru Gobind developed Nanak's strategy further and organized the Sikhs into a disciplined communal unit that could not only worship and fellowship together but could also defend their faith with courage. Guru Gobind Singh expected those who belonged to the Khalsa to be saint-soldiers. Such an organization

6. Ibid., 55–61.

not only enabled the Sikhs to survive the challenging times but also motivated them to articulate their quest for liberation in a more active, even aggressive manner. The Khalsa showed the Sikhs the value of working as a courageous body of believers to practice their faith in the midst of violence and bloodshed.

Guru Gobind Singh shared the conviction of Guru Nanak and his successors that the guru plays an indispensable role in enabling Sikhs to reach God and thereby be liberated. Before his death, Guru Gobind Singh made a significant decision. He installed Adi Granth, the Sikh holy book, as the eternal guru after him. Up to this point, the Sikh gurus were all saintly human beings, but Adi Granth is a compendium of devotional hymns of the gurus as well as saints (*bhagats*) from the Hindu and Islamic communities. Guru Gobind's decision gave the Sikhs a guru for all times.

The quest that Guru Nanak initiated was further articulated by the nine gurus who succeeded him. Founded on their spiritual experiences and insights, they formulated a way of liberation—a way that aims at reaching God, the "True Name" through the Guru's help. After the tenth guru, Sikhs resort to their sacred book, Adi Granth, as the Guru. Our next task will be to find out the vital role it plays in the Sikh quest for liberation.

THE SCRIPTURAL EXPRESSIONS OF THE QUEST

The principal sacred text for the Sikhs is Adi Granth. They venerate it as their final and eternal guru and call it Shri Guru Granth Saheeb (the revered book that is the guru). This sacred book is called Gurbani, which means "Guru's word." The term *bani* is also called *shabad*, which in Sikhism refers to the divine word that is contained in the guru. Since God revealed the bani through the guru, Sikhs view bani as the guru and guru as the bani. Even though the contents of Adi Granth are taken as divinely inspired, it is not verbally dictated by God. Gurus creatively structured their thoughts, which they believed to be given under divine inspiration in the form of hymns. Hence one cannot view Adi Granth in the way Muslims view the Quran. Sikhs take Adi Granth as being the living presence of the guru embodied in sacred text. The Sikh quest for liberation is geared toward reaching God through the guru's grace. Adi Granth, as guru, is therefore vital to the attainment of such a goal. There are several ways Adi Granth expresses the aspirations of the Sikh devotees and enables them to attain liberation.

Guru Granth was initially compiled by the fifth guru, Arjan Dev, in 1604 and completed by the tenth guru, Gobind Singh. It is essentially a devotional book consisting of 5,894 hymns arranged in 31 musical measures (*ragas*). Of these hymns, 2,216

Reading of Adi-Granth

176

are by the gurus: Guru Nanak, Guru Arjan Dev, Guru Amar Das, Guru Raam Das, and Guru Gobind Singh. The hymns of thirty other saintly poets also find a place in the sacred book; fourteen Hindus, five Muslims, and eleven bards.

The character of its contents indicates the intent of its composition. The text contains no historical narratives or biographical details. It does not explicate doctrine nor prescribe a specific code of conduct. The sacred book is essentially exalted poetry and the theme that runs through the text is "that of the individual's longing for the Ultimate Reality, which is molded into poetic symbolism of great aesthetic delicacy and beauty."[7] Guru Granth's conclusion, called the Mundavani, highlights the artistic efficacy of the sacred scripture as a means for liberation.

> On the platter lie arranged three delicacies
> Truth, contentment, and contemplation . . .
> All who eat them, all who savor them
> Obtain liberation.[8]

The food that the sacred scripture offers has to be eaten and savored and not analytically dissected. Such savoring is made possible when devotees recite and listen to its devotional hymns and thereby identify themselves with the longing for liberation that the hymns express. The text functions in a similar way to the Psalms in the Bible.

The Guru Granth Sahib is essentially a compendium of devotional hymns arranged in musical measures (ragas). In order to receive what they these hymns seek to offer, one has to sing them. The literary forms and musical measures of the hymns have been carefully selected so that all could identify themselves with the aspirations the hymns express. When compiling Adi Granth, Guru Arjan Dev rejected musical measures that were too exuberant or too melancholy. He did not allow musical measures that were restricted to specific social groups like families, sons, and daughters. He was careful to exclude poetry that had the slightest flavor of discrimination of caste, sex, etc. He used the popular literary expression of his time, the metaphor of bani, which all could appreciate. When the devotees sing these hymns or listen to them being sung, they relate to the sentiments they express in a manner that mere reading and analyzing a piece of prose writing is unable to deliver. Some hymns articulate certain aspirations, especially the quest to be liberated from the bondage of being caught up in the cycle or rebirths (samsara). Other hymns present ways to be freed from such bondage. For instance, the first hymn in Guru Granth Sahib, "Jap," believed to be authored by Guru Nanak, outlines the spiritual journey a devotee needs to take to reach God and thereby be liberated. For a devotee wanting to reap the full benefits of the sacred text, it is not enough to merely exegete it and find out what it means. One cannot enjoy a song by merely analyzing its words. The sacred book is essentially Guru's voice presented musically.

In accommodating the devotional hymns of Hindu and Islamic poets, Guru Granth facilitates people outside the Sikh faith community to express their aspirations

7. Singh, "Spiritual Experience," 548.
8. Ibid.

through literary forms and expressions with which they are familiar. The Hindu poets who figure in the sacred text come from different cultural and literary backgrounds. The Hindu poets Kabeer, Ramanand, Ravdas, Soordas, and Sain were from Utara Pradesh; Sadhna from Sind; Surder from Punjab; Jaidev from Bengal; Namdev, Trilochan, and Paramand from Maharashtra; Peepa and Dhanna from Rajasthan; and Beni was a popular poet from north India. The hymns from the Muslim poets were from Baabaa Fareed, Bheekhan, Satt, Balwand, and Mardaana.[9] Accommodating poets from other religious backgrounds exemplifies the catholicity of the Sikh sacred scripture. But that does not mean that Sikhism asserts that all religions are the same. The hymns of the poets from other religions have been carefully selected. All these hymns align with the underlying theme of Guru Granth: the human longing to be liberated could only be satisfied by a resort to God, the Ultimate Reality and through the guru's grace. The hymns, whether by Sikh, Hindu, or Islamic poets, all resort to such a reality.

Moreover, the sacred text accommodates authors from different castes and social status. Kebber was a weaver, Naamdev a calico-printer, Dhanaa a farmer, Sadhna a butcher, Ravdas a shoemaker, and Sain a barber.[10] In a Hindu society, where caste system was sacrosanct, to make room for people so low in the social order to be co-authors with Peepa, a king, and Trilochan, a Brahmin, shows what Adi Granth wants to highlight: that human longing for liberation is open to all and that all could resort to God.

Gobind Singh's decision in 1708 to name Adi Granth as his successor for the Sikh community had significant repercussions. Up to this time, the gurus were all human beings. The efficacy of their guruship was naturally affected by the challenges they faced and the calamities that came upon them. Some were even assassinated. Adi Granth, being a book, is a guru beyond these challenges. When Guru Gobind Singh made Adi Granth succeed him as the guru and called it Guru Granth Sahib, it turned out to be much more than a sacred book. It presented itself as divine word (*shabad*) functioning as the embodiment of the guru who is indispensable for one to reach God and thereby be liberated. The view that the sacred book is the very embodiment of the guru is best expressed in an eighteenth-century compendium of Punjabi poems:

> This (the Granth) you must accept as an actual part, treating its letters as hairs of my body. This truly is so. Sikhs who wish to see the Guru will do so when they come to the Granth. He who is wise will bathe at dawn and humbly approach the sacred scripture. Come with reverence and sit in my presence. Humbly bow and hear the words of Guru Granth.[11]

Wherever there is a significant number of Sikhs there will be a temple. They call it Gurdwara, which means gateway to the guru. The main reason they go to their temple is to worship God through the enablement of the guru. The present guru being their sacred book, it gets a central place in their temples. The Golden Temple,

---

9. Singh, *Fundamentals of Sikhism*, 66.

10. Ibid.

11. Para Singh Padam in Oxtoby, *World Religions: Eastern Traditions*, 193.

the Sikh cathedral, has four doors from four directions, all leading to the altar where Guru Granth Sahib is enshrined. All worship is centered on it. The manner in which it is venerated in the Golden Temple provides the model for Sikh worship in other Gurwardas.

Guru Granth Sahib (Adi Granth) in Gurwardara

The sacred book takes on a personhood of its own and becomes venerated. In fact, Guru Arjan Dev's acts of veneration during the installation ceremony in the Golden Temple in 1604 exemplifies this. He walked barefoot in the procession that took the holy book to the temple and slept beside it on the temple floor every night

Every morning when the Guru Granth is installed on the altar in a Gurwardara, the devotees stand with bowed heads. Guru Granth is placed on an elevated stand below a canopy which carries the monogram *Ik Onkar*, which in Punjabi language means "One God." Such a God could be experienced in a personal way, through the help of Guru Granth, which being God's word has a personhood of its own. Colorful cushions are used to support the sacred book. The officiating reader (*granthi*) sits on a lower level and occasionally waves a ceremonial whisk (*channi*). This follows the ancient Indian custom used to honor monarchs. Those who enter the Gurdwara remove their shoes, cover their heads, and prostrate before the sacred book. It is reverently opened every day for devotees to listen to it. It is not kept open unless it is being read. At nights it is closed and laid in a comfortably cushioned bed. Rituals like ringing of bells, worship of idols, and ceremonial use of lamps or fire that characterize worship in the Hindu temples do not figure in the Gurdwara. The veneration rendered to Guru Granth poignantly points out that for the Sikh devotees it is more than a sacred book; it is their guru whose grace they implore. Hence it is treated as one with divine personhood.

The treatment of the sacred book as a person is also evident when we look at the way Sikhs attempt to receive a blessing from it. They treat it not as a theological document to be analyzed through exegetical methods but as one that could speak to them—one they could listen to and hear its voice. The orality of the Sikh scripture has to be kept in mind in order to appreciate its role in the spiritual quest of the Sikhs. They believe that even reading it is ennobling. The practice of reading Guru Granth Sahib on a continuous basis on certain assigned days in the Gurwardaras is based on the conviction that merely hearing what the scripture says bears fruit. One popular way the scripture is consulted is to open it at random and read whatever passage one comes upon. The passage that comes up is called *Hukam*; it is God's message the guru is giving to the devotees for a particular day or occasion. This practice is believed to have started with the fifth guru, Arjan Dev who opened and read a specific passage from Adi Granth on the occasion of its ceremonial dedication. Such a practice indicates that for the Sikhs scripture is not a just book about sacred matters in written language but a living person who is sensitive to the needs of people and communicates with them on a daily basis. The Hukam is the response to such a need; it is Guru's message given through the scripture.

There are some other popular Sikh scriptures but they are not placed on par with Guru Granth Sahib. Dasam Granth is a compilation attributed to the tenth guru, Gobind Singh. In addition to containing his autobiography; it has a long prayer, "Jap Sahib." Some Sikhs include it as part of their morning devotions along with Guru Nanak's shorter prayer ("Japji"). The hymns of Gurdas Bhalla and Nand Lal Goya are also approved for recitation in worship. Another significant religious text among the Sikhs is the Janam Sakhis, which contains life stories, especially those of Guru Nanak. This body of literature indicates the impact of narratives in a religious community. Some of these stories tend to glorify Guru Nanak but people like to listen to life stories and tend to believe them even though they may be exaggerative. Nevertheless, Sikhs give a unique place to Guru Granth, mainly because it is not only a sacred scripture but also a devotional expression of the guru for the Sikh faith community, the guru whose grace is needed for liberation. Our next task will be to look into what characterizes the Sikh way of liberation.

THE WAY OF THE QUEST

Khanda is the emblem that best exhibits the core features of the way of the Sikh quest, as executed through the Khalsa (the Sikh brotherhood). The khanda is made up of three symbols: the double-edged sword at the center (which is also called khanda), circled by a chakra (*qouit*) and both being flanked by two swords (*kirpans*). The double-edged sword confirms the Sikh belief in one God who wields sovereign power over both life and death and administers divine justice as well as demolishes all evils that

Sikh *Khanda* Emblem

beset mankind. The chakra, a circle without a beginning or an end, exhorts Sikhs to acknowledge the manifestation of God in his creation. Hence the Sikhs are called upon to treat the world with compassion and look after it. The two swords represent those originally worn by Guru Hargobind signifying the spiritual and temporal leadership of gurus. The emblem highlights that the Sikh way is God centered, not restricted to a particular race or caste but encompassing the whole world and adopting both spiritual and temporal means to achieve liberation.

God plays a central role in the Sikh way of liberation. In fact, Guru Nanak prefers to call the Sikh way, *Naam-Marga* (the path of Naam); *Sat-Naam* refers to God as "True Name." The path of liberation is not only a path to God but a path of God. God is indispensable to the efficacy of the path. Such a proposal comes in the context of the Hindu way that places considerable weight on the devotee. Through devotion (bhakti), knowledge (jnana), good works (karma), or mediation (yoga) a devotee is expected to attain liberation (moksha). On the other hand, the Sikh way, though not belittling the efforts of the devotee, points out that God is vital to the way both as its object as well as the means to liberation. Both Sikhs and Hindus believe that humans are caught up in the cycle of rebirths (samsara) conditioned by past acts (karma). But Sikhs make it a point to emphasize that God's help enabled through the guru is absolutely necessary for one to be freed from karmic bondage.

Who is the God of the Sikhs? Sikhs believe that God transcends time, is omnipresent, and eternal, but that does not mean that humans cannot relate to him. He may not be anthropomorphic but that does not mean that he is an impersonal deity, indifferent to human concerns. God as "the Name" has an identity of its own, as "Truth" he is real, and as "the Word" he is communicable. Adi Granth is God's word communicated through language. The first hymn in Guru Granth Sahib, attributed to Guru Nanak, opens with the assertion of the existence of a Supreme Reality (*Ikk Oan Kar*). *Oan* is the Punjabi equivalent of the Sanskrit word for the Supreme Being, *Aum* (*Om*). When a Hindu devotee pronounces the word Aum, he or she not only acknowledges that there is a supreme reality (Brahman) but believes that one could participate in it in an experiential manner. Guru Nanak used Oan in place of Aum to refer to the Supreme Reality in order to highlight that it could be experienced in a personal way. The Sikh way of liberation commences with the conviction that a devotee could experience God, even though he is transcendent and ineffable. How is this possible?

The Sikh worldview does not degrade the physical world as an illusion. God and the world are not antithetical. The world is very much part of God but not in a pantheistic sense. The world is God's creation and reflects his characteristics. In the light of such a positive stance concerning the physical world, the Sikh way of liberation does not advocate renouncing the world but actively participating in it without getting entangled in its "sins." Human existence in the world is authentic and significant. In the quest for liberation the devotee becomes aware of the greatness of the God in and through the world that is his handiwork. This is somewhat similar to the Christian view of God's general revelation in and through his creation, which impels a Christian to be in the world yet not be part of it.

Such a positive stance concerning the world naturally prevents the Sikh devotee from degrading the human body and considering it as a mere appendage to the soul, hindering it from reaching its full potential. For the Sikh the body is an integral part of the human being, and divinity resides in a human, taken as soul and body. Hence the Sikh way of liberation does not start with ascetically renouncing the world and tortuously degrading the body, as is popular in some Hindu circles. Both the physical world and the human body reflect characteristics of the divine. The Sikh way encourages the devotees to be engaged in activities of the world, to look into themselves and decipher the divine potentiality in them. They need not search for God in some realm out there; the hero really lies in them. The journey begins with the acceptance of the reality of human existence and the realization of human potentiality, but for the successful completion of the journey, God's help is a must. This is where "grace" clicks in. Sikhism orchestrates grace through the guru.

As the Sikh morning devotional prayer indicates, it is through guru's grace humans know God and are thereby liberated. For the Sikhs the guru is the one who sheds the liberating light amidst the bondage of darkness and thus becomes indispensable in the way of liberation. The guru manifests in different forms that are not really exclusive of but complementary to one another. God, Guru Nanak followed by the nine human gurus, and the sacred book, Guru Granth Sahib, are the three forms of Sikh guruship.

God is the guru of all gurus. For Sikhs, God is no doubt transcendent, indescribable, and formless. Yet they strive for the mystical presence of God in the way Guru Nanak claimed that he had experienced divine presence in his transformative spiritual encounter. The names given to God in Sikh devotional hymns reveal their striving to experience his liberating presence. They designate God as timeless person (*Akal Purah*), true creator (*Sat Kartar*), true teacher (*Sat Guru*), and most emphatically True Name (*Sat Naam*). In the Indian, as in the Hebrew, world, "name" reveals the identity of a person. God designated as "True Name" reveals his identity, that his essence is truth. Sikh worship is geared to "remembering the Name" (*nam simran*) with the deep conviction that such remembrance would provide an occasion conducive to experience liberation.

The second main form in which guruship manifests is through human gurus commencing with the founder Guru Nanak. According to the Sikhs, God in his grace vested in Nanak "guruship" that would enable people to be liberated. They believe that the nine gurus who followed him are more than just his disciples; they are Guru Nanak reincarnated. Hence when they listen to the messages of the gurus, they take it is as a message from essentially one guru whose guru is God.

But how do the present Sikhs get the message of the gurus who are dead and gone? This is where the sacred book comes in. When Gobind Singh, the tenth guru, was about to die he ordered that guruship should no longer be designated to a human being but reside in Adi Granth, the sacred scripture, which was given the honorific title of Guru Granth Sahib. Sikhs take it as the most complete guide for their liberation. They remind themselves of Guru Gobind Singh's declaration of Adi Granth's dominant role, by their congregational singing which runs thus:

> Command came from the Timeless One
> And the Khalsa Panth was established.
> All Sikhs are commanded
> To recognize the Granth as the Guru.
> It is the Visible body of the Masters
> Those who wish to meet the Lord
> May see him therein.[12]

For the Sikhs, resorting to the Guru takes precedence over ritualistic practices on the grounds of the scriptural injunction, "One fasts, practices religious observances, and atonement, one visits the river banks and pilgrim centers all over the earth, but he alone is saved who takes refuge with the Guru."[13]

Nevertheless, Sikhs acknowledge that all do not follow its guidance. They identify two kinds of people. There is the self-willed person who turns toward oneself (*manmukh*) and hence is caught up in the bondage of the cycle of rebirth (samsara). On the other hand, there is the person who is turned toward the Guru and remains in harmony with his divine word (*gurumukh*). It is this one who eventually gets liberated.

There are three steps that Guru Nanak gives in the Guru Granth Sahib to enable one to be transformed from a self-willed (manmukh) into a guru-willed person (gurumukh).Guru Nanak condenses the precepts into a simple maxim which runs thus: "*sunia, mania, mani kita bhau.*"[14] The first step is to hear what the Guru is saying (*sunia*). As we have already noted, Sikhs place a great emphasis on hearing the scriptures. The second step is to pay heed to what they have heard (*mania*). This is where faith comes in. Since God is ineffable, placing confidence in his word is a matter of faith. Faith here is not a mere intellectual assent to scriptural dogmas but a conviction in the God of the scriptures. The third step stipulates that much more than hearing God through the scriptures and having faith in him, one should cultivate a passionate love of the divine name that is taken to be God (*mani kita Bhau*). Unlike the Vedanta version of Hinduism that renders a significant role to spiritual knowledge (jnana) and contemplation (dhyana), the Sikh way, perhaps influenced by the Hindu Bhakti movement, makes love of God indispensable for liberation. Sikhs acknowledge that spiritual knowledge and contemplation are vital but according to them, it is the passionate love for God that motivates a devotee to reach him. Guru Granth Sahib provides an effective channel for cultivating this devotional motivating love (*prana*). Several of the hymns in Guru Granth Sahib are psalms that express one's love for the God, whose name is truth. When the devotees listen to and participate in singing these hymns, they naturally become captivated by the passionate love for God and this motivates them to reach him despite the challenges they face in their spiritual journey. The hymns they sing are from the Guru Granth Sahib and composed by the gurus and saintly bards in their quest to be liberated. Hence in singing these hymns they are actually getting the help of the Guru. Without the guru's help salvation becomes

12. Singh, *Encyclopaedia of Sikhism*, 9.

13. Ibid., 88.

14. Sivaraman, *Hindu Spirituality*, 536.

impossible. This is why the Sikhs implore for guru's help in the daily morning devotions. The Raag Bhairao section of Guru Granth Sahib vividly describes the salvific role of the Guru. It runs thus:

> The Guru is Divine; the Guru is Inscrutable and Mysterious. Serving the Guru, the three worlds are known and understood . . . Without the True Word of the Shabad you shall never be released, and your life shall be totally useless . . . The Yogis, the householders, the Pandits, the religious scholars, and the beggars in religious robes—they are all asleep in egotism . . . In this Dark Age of Kali Yuga, glorious greatness is obtained through the Lord's Name.[15]

In order to appropriate Guru's grace, the Sikh community of faith plays a vital role. When the tenth guru Gobind Singh designated guruship to reside in the sacred book (Guru Granth Sahib) he made it a point to state that the collective wisdom of the community is absolutely necessary to fully appropriate the help of the Guru. This community, Khalsa came to be referred as *Khalsa Panth* which means "path" or "way" orchestrated communally. All Sikhs do not belong to the Khalsa. Only those baptized Sikhs called *Amrit-dharai* are members of the Khalsa. But Sikhs in general acknowledge its vital importance in their spiritual journey. The Khalsa gives identity to the Sikh community and provide the ideal way to follow the precepts of the guru and thereby be liberated. Hence the Sikh way could be described as a communal way in contrast to the ascetic isolationistic way so popular among Hindus, Buddhists, and Jains.

The way the Khalsa came into being reflects its character and the role it plays in the Sikh faith community. That the faith of a community should express itself in communal action even leading up to martyrdom was very much part of the spirit of Khalsa, even before it was formally installed. Guru Nanak initially articulated such a strategy when he defended the innocent Hindus against the atrocities of Babar, by calling for communal action.[16] Each guru who succeeded Guru Nanak made his contribution to develop the spirit of communal action. The tenth guru Gobind Singh gave a final stamp to such a developing trend by installing the Khalsa in 1699 CE, and thereby gave a distinct identity to the Sikh community of faith.

Guru Gobind Singh did not want to merely establish a religious institution but a dynamic body that would be effective to defend the Sikhs in the turbulent times of his day as well as be an effective channel to help the devotees in their quest for liberation. For that he realized the Khalsa should have the correct leaders. He asked five Sikhs to come forward and give their heads to him. This was in keeping with Guru Granth Sahib's stipulation, "If you aspire to taste the elixir of love, then come to me prepared to die. Walking on this path of love, hesitate not in giving your head."[17]

Seeing the willingness of these five Sikhs to give up their lives for the faith, Guru Gobind Singh appointed them as the leaders of the Khalsa and called them *Panj*

---

15. Guru Granth Sahib (Khalsa Consensus Translation). This is acknowledged by Sikh scholars as an authentic translation in abridged form.

16. Rahi, "Unyielding Spirit," 34.

17. Singh, *Fundamentals of Sikhism*, 70.

Piyaaray (the five cherished ones). In a world of atrocities and assassinations, what was needed was an aggressive corporate model for defending the Sikh community and allowing the Sikhs to achieve their spiritual aspirations. The Khalsa, led by the five soldier-saints, served as that model.

Even though membership in the Khalsa is open to all, the process of becoming a member is not easy. One is admitted into the Khalsa through an initiation ritual called the baptism. Those receiving baptism are asked to sip consecrated sweetened water (*amrit*). It is said to resemble the nectar offered to Guru Nanak when he had the spiritual experience that changed his life. A Khalsa Sikh is called *Amrit-Dhari* (nectar bearing). But in order to become an Amrit-Dhari, one has to first of all be committed to the Sikh doctrines and the way of the liberation that it offers. Such a commitment is exhibited in the attire which depicts a saint-soldier. The five components of the attire are popularly called the five "K's" of Sikhism.

Kesh denotes uncut hair and beard. Unshorn hair is taken to indicate both physical and spiritual strength. *Kangha* is a comb placed in the as a reminder that hair has to be combed; strength needs to be disciplined. Guru Gobind Singh is believed to have made the wearing of the comb compulsory. Through such an order he prevented Sikhs matting their hair as was the practice among Hindu ascetics. While the matted hair (*jata*) symbolized renunciation in Hindu circles, kangha symbolized orderliness and discipline among the Sikhs as useful citizens. *Kirpan* is a steel dagger or sword that depicts a soldier equipped to fight for the faith. *Kara* is steel bracelet worn around the wrist which could serve as a weapon of defense or as an article of identity of a Sikh as part of the Khalsa. *Kacha* is a pair of shorts showing that the Khalsa Sikh is ready to serve the community. Such attire has sometimes become controversial because of its militant appearance. But we have to understand the context in which such a kind of attire was initially advocated. During the time of Guru Gobind Singh when Sikhs were persecuted, and when their faith was being challenged, they had to be defend themselves and their faith. Hence they had to be soldier-saints. In the history of Sikhism, the members of the community have had to face situations that were not conducive for their survival to say the least. This naturally necessitates aggressive action. But that does not warrant us to dismiss the Sikh faith as a religion of the sword. There is spiritual underpinning to the Sikh attire. The Khalsa way is essentially a way of communal effort. But such an effort is founded on the conviction that it cannot succeed without God's help. The Khalsa greeting, "*Waheguru jee kaa Khalsa. Waheguru jee kee Fateh*" illustrates this well. It means that Khalsa the Pure One is of the Lord who is wonderful/great (*Waheguru*). When Sikhs greet one another in this manner, they remind themselves that victories wrought in and through the Khalsa belong to the Lord; whatever happens occurs because of God's enablement. This is where the Sikh way that appears to be militant turns out to be one that resorts to God's help.

The Sikh way of liberation is God centered, guru enabled, scripture guided, world-oriented, and orchestrated communally. Essentially it is way that depends on God's help. Sikhs acknowledge that God's "grace" is necessary even to begin the spiritual journey. Then "grace" becomes indispensable for a devotee to ultimately be liberated from the bondage of the cycle of rebirths and to encounter God whose name is Truth. God is the object as well as the means for liberation. Such an emphasis on God's "grace" allows us to find out how Christ is relevant to the Sikh quest. This will be our next task.

THE RELEVANCE OF CHRIST TO THE SIKH QUEST

The Sikh way exhibits certain characteristics that make Christ relevant to the Sikh quest. In his commentary on the Sikh sacred texts, Harban Singh Doabia points out that "according to the Sikh religion, the real object of human life is to attain salvation, that is union with Almighty God and to liberate one's soul from the punishment of continuous births and deaths."[18]

The very fact that Sikhism claims that humans strive for salvation makes Christ relevant to the Sikhs, for Christ came to save humans. The quest for salvation arises when people realize that they are in a predicament. Christianity characterizes such a predicament in terms of sin—that which separates humans from God. No doubt Sikhs describe the human predicament as being entangled in the cycle of rebirths (samsara). But they go a step further and point out that being separated from God as the core cause for human bondage. Since salvation for them is "union with Almighty God," anything that causes separation from God puts one into bondage. "Sin" in the Sikh context is not mere ignorance of one's spiritual identity or craving that arises from a false sense of self but excluding God from one's life. A human being is born with divinity, according to God's will, but tends to depart from him. The third guru's hymn puts it this way: "When it pleases God, a child is born and then the family loves it. Afterwards, the love for God is departed and *maya* controls him. *Maya* is that influence by which God is forgotten, worldly love is born, and the mortal gets attached to secular things and pleasures" (Anandu Sahib stanza 9).

Such a description indicates that "sin" that puts one in bondage is to be understood in terms of one's relationship with God; it is that which separates one from God. No doubt, there is no concept of the Christian concept of original sin. One is not sinful by nature; one falls into sin. But Sikhs acknowledge the devastating effect of sin. It causes one's love for God to dwindle and thereby causes one to be separated from God and become entangled with the worldly. The Sikh striving to bridge the gap between the sinner and God makes Christ relevant to the Sikh quest. For in taking upon himself on the cross the sin of all humanity, Christ bridges that yawning gap.

How do the Sikhs attempt to bridge that gap? Even though one is separated from God by the destructive influence of maya (mammon), Sikhism claims that one could get out of such bondage. Guru Nanak proclaims, "Those who love God with the grace of the Guru will find Him, even in the midst of *Maya*" (Anandu Sahib, 29).

18. Doabia, *Sacred Nitnem*, 313. Note that subsequent scriptural citations placed within brackets are from this book.

Such a positive prognosis is made possible by two key factors that the Sikh way of salvation highlights: God and grace. "There is only One God. He is obtained by the grace of the True Guru" (Anandu Sahib, 1). It is precisely at this point that the relevance of Christ becomes evident.

Sikhism claims that only God can save, since He is immune from a temptation that entails sin. "God is the Nourisher of the World, God is Giver of Salvation, God cannot be lured by temptation" (Japu Sahib, 94, 95).

From the Sikh perspective, except God, the whole world is under the grip of maya. "The world lies asleep under the influence of mammon and superstition and it passes its night (time) in sleep" (Japu Sahib, 125). The Sikh resort to God as the only one who could save indicates what Sikhs require of a savior. He cannot be part of the maya-stricken world and humanity. He has to be sinless. Hence, only God can be that one. The Christian claim that Christ is the Savior is founded on the conviction that he is God and hence sinless. But, it is right here that Christ becomes controversial to the Sikhs. They do not accept that God could incarnate as a human. Hence, Christ cannot be God incarnate. If so, he is then part of humanity and is also under the influence of maya. Then he does not have the capacity to save. The Sikh response to Christ as Savior ultimately hinges on whether he is God; hence he becomes the "stumbling block."

Sikhs acknowledge that God's Names are countless (Japuji 19). Nevertheless, they pick out "True" as the name that best denotes his identity. When the scriptures claim, "God as well as His Name is True and those who repeat His Name are True" (Japuji 4), there are two significant features attached to God's Name: God and his name are the same and it is only through God's name that one achieves salvation. For the Sikhs, God is Truth and Truth is God. Like God, "Truth" is eternal (Japuji 27).

Like God "Truth" is the highest of the high (Japuji 24). The Sikh emphasis on God as "Truth" provides a window to introduce Christ to the Sikhs. When Jesus Christ was comforting his disciples before his departure, Thomas, his doubting disciple asked him, "'Lord, we don't know where you are going, so how can we know the way?' Jesus answered, 'I am the Way, and the Truth, and the Life. No one comes to the Father except through me. If you really knew me, you would know my Father as well. From now on, you do know Him and have seen Him'" (John 14:5–7).

Here Jesus claims that he is not only the Truth but also God. When he tells his disciples that anyone who has seen him has seen God the Father, his claim to divinity is obvious. Preposterous though it may sound to the monotheistic Sikh mindset that cannot accept God as incarnate, what Christ claims of himself is precisely what the Sikhs stipulate God to be: he is Truth.

Moreover, it is through God's "True Name" one achieves salvation. Uttering God's name in sincerity has salvific value. The transforming impact of God's name is well said in this scriptural passage, "The True Name (*Nam*) is my support. The True Name (*Nam*) which satisfies all my hungers is my mainstay. God's Name (*Nam*) which has taken abode in my house (within my body and mind) has fulfilled all my ambitions and has bestowed upon me peace and bliss" (Anandu Sahib 2).

By hearing the name of God, the blind see the way to salvation, which is the way to God (Japuji 11). Not only sins but also diseases are destroyed by hearing the name of God (Japuji 11). True knowledge about the world and God the unfathomable becomes possible through God's name (Japuji 8, 11). One can be free from the fear of death through God's name: "On hearing (your name) the messengers of death leave off" (Rahras (i) Sahib 15). Death cannot touch or come near one who is hearing God's name (Japuji 7). A devotee absorbed in God's name is relieved from the fear of births and rebirths (Kirtan Sohil 4). Those who repeat, listen, and enshrine in their hearts God's name are made pure; a mortal becomes a saint (Anandu Sahib 17; Japuji 8). Hence, God's name plays a vital role in the Sikh way of salvation. Through God's name Sikhs believe that one's sins and sicknesses be destroyed, be freed from the fear of death, be transformed, and could reach God, the source of salvation. Hence, singing God's name finds a prominent place in Sikh congregational worship. The Sikh quest could be aptly described as a cry to God to save through his name.

Jesus Christ could well be that name! He is God and Truth. Through his death and resurrection sin and sickness loses its grip on humanity. Those who trust him even though they may die will live eternally. Hence they need not fear death (John 11:25). It was Peter, the disciple of Jesus, who declared before the Jewish Sanhedrin that there is no other name under heaven given to humans, by which they could be saved (Acts 4:12). Both Jews and Sikhs naturally find it difficult to accept Jesus Christ as God's True Name, for that would imply that he is God. The point of controversy lies in the claim that Jesus, though human, is still God. But, despite such a tension, the Sikh stipulation that only God whose Name is True can be the Savior makes Christ relevant to the Sikh quest. Such relevance becomes more poignant when we look into the vital role that the Sikh way of salvation renders to "grace."

In the Hindu world where rituals, pilgrimages, ascetic practices, chants, idol worship, and good deeds were considered effective means of attaining liberation, the priority given to grace by Guru Nanak and his successors is noteworthy. The Sikh articulation of the role of grace in the way of salvation arose out of the Hindu context. Guru Nanak's Hindu parents, especially his mother, had a great impact on him during his early years. Hindus present four main ways to attain liberation (moksha): way of knowledge (jnana marga) devotion (bhakti marga), good deeds (karma marga) and meditation (yoga). These ways work within the parameters of the law of karma. According to which every act whether it be in thought, word or deed has consequences. Guru Nanak claimed that grace is absolutely necessary for salvation within such a conceptual framework. While not totally denying the efficacy of such ways, he proposed that they are not in themselves adequate for salvation; that God's grace is a must.

In the first hymn of Guru Granth Sahib, "Jap," Guru Nanak outlines five stages through which a devotee has to go through in order to be liberated. They are the regions of good deeds (*sharam khand*), divine knowledge (*gyan khand*), intuition and true wisdom (*saram khand*), divine grace (*karam khand*) and the region of truth (*sach khand*) (Japuji, 33–37).

What has to be first noted is that in presenting the spiritual journey that leads to reaching God, Guru Nanak does not totally exclude the traditional Hindu ways. For instance, in the realm of good deeds (*dharam khand*) he takes the world to be the arena where good deeds pleasing to God could be done. A devotee is not to ascetically renounce the world but be actively engaged in the world serving humanity, without becoming worldly in mindset. In the realm of divine knowledge (*gyan*) and true wisdom (*saram*), a devotee acquires an understanding of God, sacred scriptures, and divine matters that would help in liberation. Here we find the Sikh version of the Hindu way of knowledge (jnana marga). But Guru Nanak is careful to point out that mere theoretical knowledge is inadequate. One has to be motivated by love for God and cultivate faith in Him. This is where we see the Hindu way of devotion (bhakti marga) at play in the Sikh path of liberation.

But it is the last two stages of a devotee's spiritual journey, the realm of grace (karam khand) and of truth (sach khand) that makes the Sikh way stand out particularly in the Hindu world. Guru Nanak places these two stages in the same stanza (Japuji 37). Perhaps this is to highlight how the realm of grace is so close to the realm of truth, which is God. Without grace one cannot reach God and thereby be liberated. "There is only one God. He is obtained by the grace of the True Guru" is the recurrent reminder in Sikh sacred literature (Japuji 1; Rahras (i) Sahib 2, 7; Kirtan Sohila 1).

"True" is no one but God. He is the Guru of all gurus and he was the Guru Nanak's guru. God communicated and bestowed his grace on Guru Nanak and through him to the nine successive gurus. At present the sacred scripture, Guru Granth Sahib, is the guru, whose grace the Sikhs have to resort to be liberated.

Both Hindus and Sikhs believe that life passes through several births and rebirths and that liberation is possible only when one reaches human status. This is achieved through past deeds in accordance with law of karma. Coming from a Hindu background Guru Nanak accepts this, but goes a step further. He claims, "Mortal obtains human body as a result of good deeds but he reaches the gate of salvation with God's kind grace" (Japuji 4). Divine grace becomes necessary when humans are helpless. Guru Nanak confesses his helplessness, when he cries out to God, "You, the Creator, I am nothing; If I (attempt to) do something, nothing comes out of it" (Rahras (i) Sahib 1). In fact, he commences his presentation of the five stage spiritual journey with the acknowledgement of human helplessness. He states that "It is not within man's power to gain understanding of divine knowledge or God's meditation. It is not within man's power to find the method of freedom from the world's bondage" (Japu 33). Since humans are helpless, human effort without God's grace is worthless.

This is how the Sikh scriptures state it:

> (Men) may take baths at places of pilgrimage, exercise acts of mercy, control their passions; perform acts of charity, practice continence, and perform many more special rituals. (Man) may study the Vedas, the Puranas, and the Holy Quran and other books of the religions of all times, countries and places. (Men) may live only on the air and practice continence and thousands of such rituals

and ceremonies. Even then all (these) methods are worthless and of no account, without meditation upon the love for God (Savaiye 4).

According to Sikhism, it is the sincere love for God that results in resorting and devotionally repeating his name that results in the bestowal of divine grace. Those who reach the realm of grace (karam khand) become detached from the grip of maya (mammon) and meditate only on God's True Name. Then God showers his grace (Japu 37). When this happens, one is captivated by divine happiness since "all pains and sins are cut (washed)" (Anandu Sahib 7). Hence, it is only through divine grace that one reaches the final realm, the realm of truth. It is in this final stage that one reaches God and is thereby liberated. One can appreciate the veneration Sikhs give to their scripture, Guru Granth Sahib. Taken as God's word containing divine wisdom it acts as the guru on earth to enable the Sikh devotees to attain liberation.

Guru Granth's claim that liberation cannot be merely through good deeds, rituals, and pilgrimages to holy places, but through faith in God whose Name is True and by divine grace may be taken as foundational to the Sikh way of salvation. It is of interest to note that Guru Nanak (1469–1539) was a contemporary of Martin Luther who proclaimed to the Christian world that salvation is by faith through grace and not by works. While Martin Luther's proclamation challenged the Roman Catholic theology of salvation, Guru Nanak's proposal challenged the ritualistic good works oriented Hindu way of human liberation. But Christ makes the difference between the two proposals. The Sikhs in accordance with Guru Nanak's recommendation resort to God and His grace through devotionally appealing to his name. Their supplication is well said thus:

> O my Great and True Guru, (O) true worshipper of God,
> I make one supplication before you
> I am an insect and a worm,
> I have sought your shelter;
> Kindly bestow upon me the Light of your Name . . .
> The Light of the Name of the Omnipresent God (Rahras (i) Sahib 5).

The Sikh quest is characterized by this sincere supplication: an appeal to "The Light of the Name of the omnipresent God" to bestow his grace. Perhaps Jesus Christ who claimed to be the light of the world is the name they are seeking. A Sikh by the name of Sundar Singh, depressed by the death of his mother and brother, frustrated with the religious formalism of his day, and angered by the aggressive evangelistic tactics of foreign Christian missionaries, burned the Christian New Testament and was at the point of committing suicide. He tells his story:

> Though, according to my ideas at that time, I thought that I had done a good deed in burning the Gospel, yet in my unrest of heart increased and for two days after that I was very miserable. On the third day, when I felt I could bear it no longer, I got up at three in the morning and after bathing, I prayed that if there was a God at all; he would reveal Himself to me, and show me the way of salvation, and end the unrest of my soul. I firmly made up my mind that, if this prayer was not answered, I would before day light go down to the railway, and

place my head on the line before the incoming train. I remained till about half-past four praying and waiting and expecting to see Krishna or Buddha or some other *Avatar* of the Hindu religion; they appeared not, but a light was shining in the room. I opened the door to see where it came from, but all was dark outside. I returned inside, and the light increased in intensity and took the form of a globe of light above the ground, and in this light there appeared, not the form I expected, but the Living Christ whom had counted as dead. To all eternity I shall never forget His glorious and loving face and the few words He spoke: "Why do you persecute me? See I have died on the Cross for you and the whole world." These words were burned into my heart as by lightning and I fell on the ground before Him. My heart was filled with inexpressible joy and peace, and my whole life was entirely changed. Then the old Sundar Singh died and a new Sundar Singh, to serve the Living Christ, was born.[19]

The new Sundar Singh who was later acclaimed as Sadhu Sundar Singh came to be one of the most well known Christian evangelists of the Indian subcontinent. What makes him significant to us is that he ideally exemplifies how Christ can fully satisfy the Sikh quest for salvation. His powerful sermons, outreach ministries, books, and most of all his life reflect how Christ can provide and equip a desperate seeker a life that is so wholesome and fruitful.

In response to the question as to how best one could obtain God's grace, Guru Nanak stated: "In the ambrosial hours of the morning, recite His True Name, and sing His glories" (Japuji 4). Coming from a Sikh family, Sundar Singh followed Guru Nanak's advice and prayed in the early hours of the morning. In all probability he would have repeated the "True Name" for that is the only supplication he would have been familiar with. The response to that desperate supplication was Christ. In the context of the Sikh supplication to God to "bestow the Light of His Name" Christ coming as light to the Sikh Sundar Singh is significant. Sadhu Sundar Singh's encounter with Christ may well be seen as an enactment of Christ's fulfillment of the Sikh quest for salvation.

19. Singh, *With and Without Christ*, 100–102.

9

The Islamic Quest

AFTER SEPTEMBER 11, 2001, much of the world associates Islam with terrorism and brands Muslims as fanatical terrorists ready to be martyred for Allah, dragging along with them a host of innocent victims. Such an image highlights the stereotype of Islam as a militant religion, a view that has existed since its origin. Muhammad's raids on Quraysh caravans, Bedouin tribes, Jews, and Byzantines may have contributed to such a view. During the Crusades Muslims were depicted as warriors of the antichrist trespassing into Holy Lands and blocking the silk route to China. When the Holy Roman Empire was threatened by the Islamic Turks, Islam was branded as a rabid religion of the sword. The modern era saw Western powers colonizing the Middle East, Africa, and Asia. This resulted not only in the exploitation of the natural resources of these countries but also threatened the religious and cultural heritage of their people. This naturally led to a backlash that expressed itself in several ways. In the Hindu Indian subcontinent it came in the form of Gandhi's peaceful yet provocative satyagraha movement. In the Muslim countries the backlash expressed itself more radically in what is now called "Islamic Fundamentalism." The inflammatory political proclamations, suicide bombings, plane hijackings, revolutionary riots, and unwanted bloodshed all done in the name of Allah caused the world to christen Islam a religion of terror. Paranoid political powerheads and pious religious propagandists proclaim with passion that the evil that besets humanity today is Islam.

Nevertheless, Islam is a religion of peace. It strives for peace through submission to God. The word "Islam" is derived from the Arabic root *slm,* which means, among other things, peace.[1] Why is such an endeavor of peace stereotyped as a dreaded religion of war, or even terror? Part of the reason lies in Islam itself, its preoccupation with *jihad.* There is much controversy both within and outside the world of Islam over the nature and justification of jihad. But, before jumping to hasty conclusions, it is best to view jihad in its proper context.

Jihad in Arabic means "striving," but whether such striving is purely an internal spiritual struggle or an external endeavor, even involving warfare, is a matter of

---

1. Rizvi, *Shi'ism.* 1.

controversy. What is significant is that jihad, in whatever form it shows itself, enables us to characterize Islam as a dynamic quest.

The goal of Islam as a faith community is to achieve peace, not only at a personal level, but also at a communal and even global level. That such peace is attainable only through total submission to God is the core conviction of Islam. But such an ideal is not easily attainable in a corrupted world where human beings revolt against God and one another. This calls for a willingness to strive (that is, to perform jihad) and even to sacrifice one's own life. The Quran, the sacred scripture of Islam, points out that, "Those who believe fight in the cause of Allah. And those who reject Faith fight in the cause of Evil (*taghut*). So fight ye against the Friends of Satan: feeble indeed is the cunning of Satan" (4:76).[2] The Arabic term *taghut* functions here as a metaphor to describe the nature of evil. Just as water has a tendency to overflow, the forces of evil tend to overflow their rightful limits, trespassing into territories outside their own. The impetus to strive (perform jihad) is basically defensive arising out of a determination to ward off the onslaught of evil.

The Islamic worldview identifies two underlying forces that are in conflict with each other: good and evil. God is the source of all good while Satan, the fallen angels, and the evil spirits (bad *jinns*) are working against the forces of good. The onslaught of evil is evident at personal, communal, and even global levels. At a personal level, jihad turns out to be an internal spiritual warfare against the baser elements of human nature. But when Muslims are threatened as a community, they are called upon to defend themselves. Even though most resort to peaceful modes of defense, some do take up arms. Defensive action, whether peaceful or militant, is justifiable. Jihad turns out to be "just war." Muslims do not use the term "holy war" to describe jihad. In fact, such a term originated with the crusaders who wanted to render divine legitimacy to their fight for land and trade routes. There are certain passages in the Quran which stipulate when warfare could be justifiable. The Quran states "Fight in the cause of Allah those who fight you. But do not transgress limits; For Allah loveth not transgressors" (2:190). That jihad is justifiable when Muslims feel oppressed for their faith is highlighted thus: "To those against whom War is made, permission is given [to fight] because they are wronged—and verily, Allah is Most Powerful for their aid" (22:39). Whether jihad occurs at a personal level involving an internal spiritual struggle or at a communal level due to the injustice wrought against a faith community, whether enacted through peaceful negotiations or militant action, the motivating factor is a feeling of being oppressed.

Such a feeling of frustration that the world has not treated Muslims with fairness, that they have been misunderstood, misinterpreted, slandered, exploited, and even persecuted has motivated much of Muslim politics and provocative actions. Such an emotive impulse may be described as the "anger of Islam," not taking "anger" in a derogative sense. It is multifaceted, deep-rooted, spiritual at its core, and taken to be justifiable; it is a righteous anger. It is such an anger that motivates jihadic activity and

2. All quotations are from Ali's *The Holy Quran: Text, Translation and Commentary.*

permits one to describe Islam as a quest—a quest to strive against the evil that besets those who belong to God.

We could trace the "anger" to several sources. Muhammad ideally exemplifies as one impelled by it. He was born during a time described as the age of ignorance (*jahiliyyah*), an age of polytheistic religious pluralism, idol worship, ritualism, corruption, and moral depravity. Mecca was a city of idols. Kabbah, the reputed Black Stone shrine, housed more than three hundred gods. Business magnates of the Quraysh tribe managed Kabbah and received considerable income from pilgrims who flocked to the shrine every year. These magnates lived in comfort on the offerings of pilgrims.

It was in such a world Muhammad was called to proclaim that "God is one." There were already some advocates of monotheism, most notable of which was an Arabic movement called Hanifism led by reputed leaders like Zayd ibn Nawfal. But since they had a deep veneration for Kabbah, they were not a real threat to it. Hence they were tolerated in Mecca. What makes Muhammad's call to worship one God a threat to Quraysh business magnates was that he went a step further to openly discredit idol worship by planning to destroy the gods of Kabbah. Nevertheless, being merely a prophet in Mecca and that, too, without many followers, he could not accomplish his plan immediately. But in 622 CE, when he was invited to rule Yathrib (later Medina), a significant transformation occurred in him and his mission. He was now not only a prophet but the ruler of Yathrib. As its ruler, he had the wherewithal to defend his faith and propagate his message through political strategies, economic maneuvers, and even militant action. His decision to declare Medina a sanctuary city (*haram*) was a direct challenge to the religious and economic hegemony of Mecca. Medina now became both a pilgrimage site and a center for trade. This proved to be a threat to the Quraysh magnates whose main source of income was Mecca's Kabbah. After capturing Mecca in 630 CE, Muhammad made his way to the Black Stone shrine and destroyed its idols, and named it the "House of God."[3] He claimed that his god, Allah, was the one worshipped by Jews and Christians. He reminded his fellow Arabs that God had established for them the same religion that was given to Noah, Abraham, Moses, and Jesus (Quran 42:13). For Muhammad, such a religion not only claimed that God is one but also rejected idol worship and demanded a life of high moral standards. Hence, his monotheistic mission not only undermined the Quraysh business operation of the Kabbah but also challenged their lifestyle of exploiting pilgrims. His monotheistic message was a deliberate attack on the idol worship of Kabbah and the Quraysh management of it. It is no surprise that the Quraysh magnates could not tolerate him and were determined to put an end of him and his message. His "anger" is located right here. He had to strive against the Quraysh onslaught in order to defend and propagate his message. The several caravan raids on Quraysh traders and the battles of Badr (624 CE), Uhud (625 CE), and Kandaq (627 CE), leading up to the conquest of Mecca (630 CE), constitute the first Islamic jihadic quest to make a polytheistic idol worshiping people submit to one God. If one views Muhammad's militant moves without tak-

3. Aslan, *No God but God*, 106.

ing into account what motivated him, he would appear to be a ruthless man of war. But it was the onslaught of the evil of polytheism manipulated by Quraysh magnates that made him take up arms. In such a context, he could be viewed as a true jihadist involved in a just war.

The Jewish nation is another source of Islamic "anger." In Muhammad's lifetime, such anger festered first in Medina. When he migrated to Medina, the Jews were already there. Some were migrants from Palestine and Syria, while there were also Arabs who had converted to Judaism. Along with some Bedouin tribes, Jews occupied the most fertile lands in Medina. They almost monopolized Medina's economy in that they were involved in its most lucrative trades: dates, wine making, and jewelry. Conflicts between the Jews and the new Gentile immigrants were bound to arise. Muhammad and his followers came to settle in their newfound land. But, since land and resources were limited, feuds were inevitable.

But the underlying cause of the tension between these communities goes beyond conflict over land and trade. Muslims feel that they have been treated unfairly by the Jews both religiously and politically.

Muhammad claimed that the God of the Jews is the same God who gave him his prophetic message. In fact, the term "Allah" is a contraction of the Arabic word *al'ilah* that means "the God." From the Muslim perspective, Muhammad becomes the climax of God's revelation that commenced with Abraham (Ibrahim). Of the several prophets recorded in the Quran, he finds a significant place. He was the first prophet to whom God revealed that he is one. Since Abraham, a line of prophets, including several mentioned in the Bible, highlighted the oneness of God, and Muhammad climaxed this message.

Muslims consider themselves as the children of Abraham. For them, Ishmael is Abraham's firstborn, not Isaac (Gen 22:2). According to the Middle Eastern marital customs of that time, a mistress became a wife only when she conceived. Hagar conceived first and hence she became Abraham's first wife. Since Ishmael was born first and was circumcised first (Gen 17:23), he is Abraham's legitimate firstborn. God's promise to and provision for Ishmael also has to be taken into account. The name Ishmael means "God hears," indicating that God had not forgotten Ishmael. As a response to Abraham's appeal on behalf of his son, God covenanted with him. He declared "And as for Ishmael, I have heard you: I will surely bless him; I will make him fruitful and will greatly increase his numbers. He will be a father of twelve rulers, and I will make him a great nation" (Gen 17: 20). Abraham circumcised Ishmael and thereby met the covenant requirement. When Hagar was chased away from Abraham's household and was alone in the desert and her thirsty son Ishmael cried for water, God heard his cry. He provided water through a well. Along with this provision God confirmed his covenanted promise that he would make Ishmael a great nation (Gen 21:17–19). Moreover, God did not forget Ishmael but was with him in his growing years (Gen 21:20). Muslims identify the site where God provided water to Ishmael as *Zamzan*. This is one of the sacred sites they visit during their annual pilgrimage to

Mecca (*hajj*). It reminds them of their roots as a nation provided for and blessed by God. Muhammad's lineage is traced to Ishmael.

On the other hand, Jews claim that they are the children of Abraham on the grounds that Isaac is the firstborn, and the blessings that accompany the firstborn go to Isaac and his descendants. Muslims consider this as a concerted effort to degrade Ishmael and his descendants by modifying the scriptures, the Torah. It is this sense of frustration that ignites the "anger of Islam" against the Jews and provides the grounds for jihadic activity, whether peaceful or militant, against the Jews. Such activity commenced with Muhammad and still continues.

At first, Muhammad tried to win over the Jews by presenting himself as a prophet reiterating Abraham's monotheistic message. He took some positive steps to try to live in peace with the Jews and tried to convince them of the wisdom of joining with the Muslims to confront Quraysh, the common enemy. He accommodated them, along with the Christians, as part of the monotheistic community of faith. He encouraged his followers to pray in the direction of Jerusalem. He imposed an annual mandatory fast, popularly known as Ramadan, during the month of the Jewish Day of Atonement (*Yom Kippur*). He adopted several Jewish dietary rules and encouraged his followers to marry Jews, as he himself did (Quran 5:5–7). But these reconciliatory measures did not succeed. In 624 CE he changed the direction of prayer (*qiblah*) from Jerusalem to Mecca, where the Black Stone shrine, Kabbah is located. The month of the fast, Ramadan, was no longer the month of Yom Kippur, but the month when Muhammad received his first revelation. Having failed in his reconciliatory attempts, he resorted to force, which led to several battles with the Jews.

One can understand why these reconciliatory measures changed to provocative aggressive maneuvers. Reconciliation cannot work when there is a deep-rooted sense of frustration festering in the Muslim psyche: that Muslims as a faith community have been denied their rightful place in God's plan and provision. They believe this is no fault of God, but attribute it to what they perceive to be the concerted efforts of the Jews—such as meddling with their own scriptures (Torah) for their own advantage, trespassing into Muslim territories, and exploiting the Muslim economy. Such "anger" prompted Muhammad to be involved in jihad against Jews and it still continues. The Palestinian chief Yasser Arafat's address to his nation on December 18, 2001, when a Palestinian youngster was killed by Israeli forces in a Gaza Strip battle, runs thus: "We will defend the Holy Land with our blood and with our spirit. We do not wear uniforms; we are all military. We are all martyrs in paradise."[4]

Muslims feel that they have been treated unfairly by the Jews, both in the religious and political realms. Hence, the Islamic quest to establish peace through submission to Allah needed to include a defense against the Jewish onslaught.

The Muslim struggles against the Quraysh, the Jews, and presently against what is perceived as the Americanized Christian West seem to arise from Islam's anger—a fear that Muslims who have been mistreated so far would be exploited in the future.

---

4. In Caner and Caner, *Unveiling Islam*, 27.

It is such an anger that motivates the Muslim jihadic quest, whether it be peaceful or militant. David Cook points out that, "One of the factors binding globalist radical Muslims together is the shared belief that the entire world is united in a concerted effort to destroy Islam."[5] He cites the so called tradition of Thawban as giving divine sanction to such a belief. The tradition runs thus:

> The Messenger of God said: The nations are about to flock against you (the Muslims) from every horizon, just as hungry people flock to a kettle. We said: O Messenger of God, will we be few on that day? He said: No, you will be many in number, but you will be scum, like the scum of a flash-flood, without any weight, since fear will be removed from the hearts of your enemies, and weakness (*wahn*) will be placed in your hearts. We said: O Messenger of God, what does the word *wahn* mean? He said: Love of this world and fear of death.[6]

Perhaps such a tradition instigates paranoia among some Muslims to resort to aggressive militant action in the name of Allah.

In order to achieve peace (*salam*), total submission to Allah is a must. Anything that hinders the seeker to realize such an ideal, whether it is personal or communal, internal or external, religious or political, has to be resisted. Just because such a striving sometimes accommodates militant action, one cannot brand Islam as merely a religion of war and violence. The Muslim populace is divided over the issue concerning the use and justification of militant methods. But the Islamic world seems to agree on one thing: that its quest to realize the ideal of achieving peace through submission to Allah must involve striving against the forces that work against it. Such a striving is jihadic. Most Muslims advocate peaceful striving although some resort to militant methods.

Moreover, since historically such a striving has been interwoven with politics and economics, popular opinion brands Islam as a religion that promotes dictatorial governments propagating militant action. Karen Armstrong identifies an inherent paradox in religious life in that "It seeks transcendence, a dimension of existence that goes beyond our mundane lives, but that human beings can only experience this transcendent reality in earthly, physical phenomena."[7] It is but natural for religious history to be intertwined with political conflicts, and as she points out, this is evident in Islam. In her view, politics for Muslims are what Christians would call a "sacrament": the arena in which Muslims experience God and which enables the divine to function effectively in the secular world.[8] In the Islamic world the spiritual quest is distinguishable but not separable from its political expressions.

Muhammad's confrontations with the Quraysh and Jews illustrate how Muslims articulate their faith through political strategies. But, we should not become too preoccupied with their political involvements that are often exaggerated by the media and

---

5. Cook, *Understanding Jihad*, 136.

6. Ibid., 137.

7. Armstrong, *Islam*, x.

8. Ibid., xii.

thus miss their underlying deep-rooted spiritual quest. The various sects and splinter groups within Islam clearly show how the sacred and the secular, the pious and the politician, the civilian and the soldier, are so intertwined in the Islamic quest.

The Sunni sect commenced as a response to an administrative challenge which Muslims faced after Muhammad's untimely death; they needed a successor to the prophet. They had to come up with a plan that would enable them to adhere to the prophet's teachings as well as maintain the political structure he had created in Medina. They created the office of the caliph to succeed Muhammad, not as prophet, but as the rightly "guided one." He was expected to give leadership to the Islamic community not only on religious but also on social, political, and military matters. He resorted to the Quran that records the revelations Muhammad received as well as to the *Sunnah* and *Hadith* (or *ahadith*). The Sunnah depicts the events of Muhammad's life and his practices, while the Hadith contains his sayings and decisions on crucial matters. The caliphs who spread and consolidated Islam after Muhammad were: Abu Bakr (632–634 CE), Umar (634–644 CE), Uthman (644–656 CE), and Ali (656–661 CE). Abu Bakr, the first caliph, was a father-in-law of Muhammad, one of his first converts and closest companions. Abu Bakr established Islam in the Arabian Peninsula through political maneuvers and military moves. He preserved Muhammad's prophetic message through facilitating the writing of the first version of the Quran. Umar, his successor, extended the Muslim empire by conquering Syria, Iraq, Egypt, and Persia. Jerusalem also submitted to Muslim control during his time. Even though known to be a just and merciful caliph, he was murdered by a Persian slave. Uthman, the third caliph, codified the Quran into its final form. When Uthman was killed by rebels, Ali, Muhammad's son-in-law and cousin was selected to become the fourth caliph, but was assassinated in 661 CE. Since that time, Islam has been divided between the followers of Ali (Shi'ites) and the Sunnis.

Those who accepted the leadership of the caliphs came to be known as Sunnis. They take the Quran as the highest authority, giving a significant place to the Sunnah. For them, the consensus of the community (*ijma*) plays a significant role. In fact, they accept the legitimacy of the appointment of caliphs on the grounds that they are selected on common consensus. Sunnis instituted Islamic law (*shariah*). Living according to shariah is salvific in intent in that it would bring about a society fully submitted to Allah and thereby generate peace. Such a strategy relates the religious with the political.

The split between the Sunnis and the Shi'ites commenced with a controversy that appeared to be political but was religious at its core. After Muhammad's death a group of his close companions selected Abu Bakr as the caliph by common consensus. Some Muslims contested such an appointment. They believed that the legitimate leader should be from Muhammad's household and be selected through divine direction, rather than by common consensus. In their view, Ali met both these requirements. He was Muhammad's cousin and son-in-law, and was designated as successor by Muhammad under divine direction at a place called Ghadir.

Shi'ites developed a mode of leadership that substituted the imam for the caliph. Ali was acclaimed as the first imam. Shi'ites recognize a series of twelve or seven imams, starting with Ali. These imams give divine guidance in all aspects of the life of the community. The last imam, Mahdi, is believed not to have died, but is in hiding in a spiritual state, giving guidance to the devotees. Shi'ites anticipate his return, as a messianic figure, to establish Allah's kingdom on earth. They strive to create conditions that would be conducive to Mahdi's return. Some of these strategies may even include jihadic warfare against peoples and powers they perceive to be against the realization of such an ideal.

The sense of frustration that the world has not treated Muslims fairly is sometimes directed at sectors within Islam itself. This is best seen in Shi'ism. Hamid Dabashi calls Shi'ism a religion of protest that was born and bred as a protest over the appointment of Abu Bakr instead of Ali as Muhammad's successor. Dabashi identifies a paradox in Shi'ism in that it thrives when it is combative but loses its strength when it succeeds and is in power; that it is paradoxically only in power when it is not in power.[9] He cites Iran, Iraq, and Lebanon as sites that best illustrate the paradox of Shi'ism.

It is in such a context that we can understand why Shi'ites insist on having a theocratic state based on Islamic law (shariah). In their view, it not only provides the ideal political arena for its citizens to submit to Allah, but also acts as a means to correct the injustice wrought on them and ultimately bring about God's rule on earth. Ayatollah Khomeini issued an announcement on April 3, 1979 declaring the establishment of the Islamic Republic of Iran as a theocratic state under the caption, "This is the First Day of God's Rule."[10] On the same day, in a radio-television announcement, entitled "The Deprived will dominate the Arrogant" he declared how Iran, founded on Islamic principles, would become a nation under God.[11] Such a claim indicates that what impelled the setting up of the theocratic state of Iran was the feeling of being "deprived," an expression of the Islamic "anger." The way out was a strategy that combined the religious with the political.

Sufism represents a mystical facet of Islam. The Sufi movement is not a distinct sect; Sunnis as well as Shi'ites may be Sufis. Sufism is a response to the legalism in Islam. The Islamic strategy of submitting to God through obeying the Islamic law (shariah) and the traditional Islamic practices could lead to religious formalism devoid of personal experience. Sufis strive to submit to Allah not in a legalistic way, but to have spiritual experiences through meditation, trance-oriented dances, chanting Allah's names, and fasting. Sufi Islam does not have a systematic theology but proposes a way to commune with Allah in a personal manner. Each Sufi group has a spiritual guru (*shaik*) who mentors his disciples (*fakirs*) on a distinctive path (*tariqa*) to reach Allah. When one reaches the highest point in the spiritual journey, one becomes almost one with Allah. Such a claim generates a pantheistic view and hence seems to conflict with

9. Dabashi, *Shi'ism*, xii–xiv.

10. Khomeini, "First Day of God's Government," 265–67.

11. Khomeini, "Deprived Will Dominate the Arrogant," 5–9.

the orthodox Islamic view of a transcendent God. But the Sufi striving to be one with Allah shows how Muslims crave for a personal relationship with God.

Along with the Sufis and the Sunni and Shi'ite sects, there are several other sects that also need to be taken into consideration in order to get the full picture of the Islamic quest.

The "Nation of Islam" is essentially an Afro-American movement. Its official name is "The World Community of Al-Islam in the West" and it was founded in Michigan around 1930 by Wallace Dodd Ford, who was influenced by Noble Drew's teachings. Drew claimed the African-Americans were of Arabic heritage and that they were originally Muslims but were presently under white domination. The white man turned out to be the "devil" and the goal was to establish a separate Muslim African nation. Ford's disciple, Elijah Muhammad, was responsible for the expansion of the sect. His son, Wallace Muhammad, attempted to reform the sect and make it conform to orthodox Islam. The claim of black superiority and the demand for a separate African-American Muslim state were dropped. The Sunnis attempted to accommodate this sect. But a splinter group led by Louis Farrakhan founded an Islamic movement highly motivated by African nationalism. The Nation of Islam is a typical example of how the Islamic quest could be motivated by a feeling that Muslims are treated unfairly, in this case by the white man, and how Muslims have to adopt political means to achieve religious aspirations.[12] Malcolm X's life and mission exemplifies this. He rose as a public figure, resorting to Islam partially as a result of a television documentary entitled, "The Hate that Hate Produced." He was a victim of the despair the blacks experienced during his time, and he found that Islam was most conducive to get out of such a predicament.

The Wahhabi movement grew as a radical version of Sunnism. It was founded by Muhammad ibn Abd al Wahhab (1703–1792) who wanted to reform Islam. Wahhabis opposed anything that went against the doctrine that God is One. Hence, they condemned the use of the name of prophet, angel, or imam in prayer. Practices such as venerating Muhammad's birthplace or grave, and the Black Stone in Mecca were taboos to them. They insisted on interpreting the Quran literally and advocated an aggressive notion of jihad. For them warfare is between those committed to Allah and infidels who worship gods other than Allah. They represent the most radical form of the Islamic quest. They highlight verses from the Quran (for example, surah 9:29; 8:13–17; 4:101–2; 4:89) and the Hadith to support their stance that Muslims should aggressively fight against infidels (*kafirs*). They seem convinced that fighting in the cause of Allah will give them direct entry to paradise.

The Alawites, founded by Nucair Namin Abdi, is a splinter group of the Shi'ites operating mainly from Syria. According to them, Ali was not merely a prophet, second only to Muhammad, but also divine in essence. In addition to the traditional Five Pillars, they recognize jihad as a struggle against Ali's enemies, and devotion to Ali as part of their religious practice. What the Alawite movement highlights is that Muslims

---

12. Whitie, *Inside the Nation of Islam*, 9.

need someone more than a prophet; someone who is superhuman, someone to venerate and fight for.

The Nusairiyyah sect operates mainly in Syria, developed on the Alawite notion of Ali. The Nusairis claim that Ali is Allah in flesh. The Alawite and Nusairiyyah sects indicate that what the Muslims need is not merely a prophet, but one who could incarnate from the superhuman realm. Is it Christ that they are looking for?

The Ahmadiya movement that originated in Pakistan is one of the fastest growing Islamic sects. It was founded by Mirza Ghulam Qadini (1835–1908) in Punjab. His claims about himself became controversial. First he claimed to be a writer, then a revivalist, then the promised Messiah, and finally the prophet of Allah. Claiming to be prophet after the final prophet naturally caused orthodox Muslims to consider Ahmadiyas heretics. What the Ahmadiya movement highlights is that Muslims were looking for prophetic guidance after the final prophet.

Islam may well be described as a multifaceted dynamic quest—a striving (jihad) that is both religious and political, moral and militant, individual and communal, local and global. Let us take a look into the life of the man who articulated the quest.

PROPHET MUHAMMAD, ARTICULATOR OF THE QUEST

Muhammad's life is a story of one immersed in a quest that came out of a crisis that he and his fellow Arabs experienced. Such a crisis was much more than political, social, or economic. It was spiritual at its core.

Information about his life and mission comes mainly from the Quran. Even though it does not give vivid biographical details, it highlights his role as prophet. It gives us insight into some of the spiritual episodes in his life. The Quran records revelations that he had over a period of twenty-two years, often in response to or in the context of a crisis or challenge pertaining to him or his community. About one hundred years after his death some of his followers compiled his practices (Sunnah) and sayings (Hadith), which provide information about how he lived and what he said on several matters. During the eighth and ninth centuries, Muslim historians began writing about him. The first historian was Muhammad ibn Ishq (760 CE). He was followed by Muhammad ibn Umar al-Waqdi (820), Muhammad ibn Sa'd (845), and Abu Jarir at-Tabari (923). These historians provide a comprehensive reconstruction of Muhammad's life and times. But they belonged to a world that did not make a clear distinction between fact and legend. Nevertheless, the legends in these historical accounts have a symbolic value. They indicate how people came to view Muhammad with the passage of time.

Muhammad was born in the city of Mecca in Arabia in 520 CE. The child was named Muhammad, which in Arabic means "the praised one" or "praiseworthy." His second name Ahmad means "one who praises God most of all." His father Abdullah had died before his birth and his mother died when he was six years old. As an orphan he grew up mainly under the care of his uncle, Abu Talib, a merchant by profession.[13]

---

13. Biographical details primarily from: Naqvi, *Manual of Islamic Beliefs*; Dar Rag Haqq's Board of Writers, *A Glance at the Life of the Holy Prophet*; Armstrong, *Muhammad*; Lari, *The Seal of the Prophets*.

Muhammad was from the Banu Hashim clan of the Quraysh tribe. The Arabian society was made up of several independent tribes, which were further divided into clans. There was a time when the tribal system worked well and gave Arabia stability and prosperity. But during his time the system had deteriorated. Each tribe plundering the other was the way of desert life. His own tribe, Quraysh, was in fact the master exploiter. The old communal spirit had been replaced by a market economy that encouraged ruthless competition; the rich became richer, while the others felt exploited, lost, and disoriented.

The religion of the day was also not conducive to a stable communal life. Each tribe had its own tribal god. Idol worship was predominant, especially in Mecca's Kabbah that housed a host of idols. These gods were not committed to the welfare of the people. They needed to be pleased with rites and rituals rather than venerated through proper moral living.

It was in such a world that Muhammad grew up. Arabia, especially Mecca, was in the grip of a political, moral, and, more fundamentally, spiritual crisis. He was sensitive to and reacted against the disease of his day. At the age of twelve he accompanied his uncle on a caravan trade tour to Syria. There, a Christian monk named Bahirah saw in the child a future spiritual leader.[14] When Muhammad was twenty-five, he met Khadija, a wealthy and successful businesswoman, fifteen years his senior. Impressed by his trade skills and honesty, she married him. They were happily married for twenty-five years and had six children. Only Fatima, the youngest daughter survived. She married Ali, who later became the leader of the Shi'ite sect.

Despite his success in life, Muhammad became increasingly troubled not only by the political turmoil and exploitation of his own tribe, but also with the strife and spiritual bankruptcy of the Arabian society. He called the spirit of his age *jihiliyyah*. In his view, jihiliyyah was not a mere "time of ignorance" referring to a specific historical era but rather a mindset that gave rise to violence, strife, and moral depravity—a worldview that allowed everyone to selfishly pursue their own plans.[15] Amidst the tribal conflicts, caravan raids, and social anarchy there was a sense of frustration, a spiritual restlessness among the Arabs. They came to realize that their gods, unlike the God of the Jews and Christians, were not seriously concerned about people. Even their High God, originally a sky deity, was distant from people and their problems. In fact, some Arabs believed or wanted to believe that their God was the same as the God of the Jews and Christians. But, if that was the case, why had such a God sent no Arabian prophet? Were they a people left out of God's plan?

It was such an anguish that forced Muhammad to spend long and lonely hours of fasting and prayer on Mount Hira. Here was a man who was convinced that the Arabian problem was spiritual at its core. Such a conviction led him into a spiritual quest in search of the God who would care for him and his people. The revelations that commenced on Mount Hira in 610 CE and continued for several years ultimately gave

---

14. Dar Rah Haqq's Board of Writers, *A Glance at the Life*, 26–27.

15. Armstrong, *Muhammad*, 19.

him the confidence he needed and motivated him in his spiritual journey. The first revelation, on what became known as the "Night of Power" (*layat-al-quadr*), came in the form of a command:

> Proclaim [or Read]
> In the name
> Of thy Lord and Cherisher
> Who created . . .
> Proclaim! And thy Lord
> Is most Bountiful . . . (Quran 96:1, 3).

Muhammad was not exuberant when he first heard such a command. His reaction included doubt, hesitancy, mental agony, and even convulsive physical pain. It took his wife Khadija and her Christian cousin, Waraq ibn Nawful, to assure him that what he had heard was from the God he was yearning for and that God had not given up on him or his people. Whenever he had a revelation it affected him physically and mentally. One can understand such a reaction. He realized that he was very much part of the problem. He took the divine dos and don'ts that were revealed to him as applicable not only to his community but also to him and sincerely appropriated the message. Hence, he not only articulated the Islamic quest for "salvation" but fully participated in it.

But proclaiming "There is no God, but Allah" in a decadent, polytheistic Quraysh-dominated community was no easy matter. During the first three years he confided his teachings only to members of his family and close friends. His first converts included his wife, Khadija; Zayid ibn Harith, his faithful servant; Sayyidina Abu Bakr, a leading merchant; Sayyidina Ali, his future son-in-law; and Sayyidina Uthman, another close friend. Eventually, in the fourth year after his revelation on Mount Hira, he went public in his mission. His first sermon on Mount Safa and subsequent preaching in marketplaces were powerful and provocative. His message was a downright condemnation of idol worship. This naturally infuriated the Quraysh, who saw him as a threat to their lavish mode of living. The militant conflicts with the Quraysh constitute the first episode of Muhammad's struggle (jihad).

The year 620 CE was catastrophic in the prophet's life. He lost his uncle and benefactor, Abu Talib, as well as his devoted wife Khadija. He was also completely frustrated with the poor response to his message. During this critical year, two events occurred that had a significant impact on his life and mission.

The first one was his extraordinary spiritual experience popularly called "The Night of Ascension" (*layat-al-mi-raj*) or the "Night Journey." It is believed that one night, when Muhammad was asleep in Mecca's shrine Kabbah, he was miraculously transported to Jerusalem and, from there, right into the presence of God, journeying through several heavens. The Quran refers to such an event thus:

> Glory to (Allah)
> Who did take His Servant
> For a journey by night

From the Sacred Mosque
To the Farthest Mosque
Whose precincts We did
Bless—in order that We
Might show him some
Of Our Signs for He
Is the One who heareth
And seeth (all things) (Quran 17:1).

Although the Quran does not identify the "Sacred Mosque" or the "Farthest Mosque," tradition associates the "Sacred Mosque" with Kabbah and the "Farthest Mosque" with the site of the Temple of Solomon in Jerusalem at or near which now stands the Dome of the Rock. A Hadith describes in detail his ascent through several heavens, encountering important prophets of the past like Adam, Abraham, Moses, Joseph, and John the Baptist, Jesus, and finally into the very presence of Allah. Such an event is cited to indicate his closeness with God.[16] The Dome of the Rock was eventually built to mark the location in Jerusalem from which, according to tradition, he ascended to heaven.

Such a momentous event at a time when Muhammad was so depressed greatly impacted his life and mission. The fact that he not only met the great prophets of the past but was also in the very presence of Allah, gave him the confidence he so desperately needed and his community a new identity. Muslims

Dome of the Rock as seen from Mount Scopus

were no longer a God-forsaken community, but one headed by a prophet who had been in the presence of God. The event transformed the hesitant prophet into an aggressive apostle, ready to spread his message beyond Mecca.

During the same year, another event occurred that gave him the wherewithal to execute his vision. Six Arabs from a group of hamlets called Yathrib invited Muhammad to their part of the country, not merely as prophet but also as ruler. Eventually, in 622 CE, he along with some seventy Muslim families migrated from Mecca to Yathrib, later named in his honor as Medina, the city of the prophet. This migration, *Hijrah*, marks the beginning of the Muslim calendar.

16. Smart and Hecht, eds., *Sacred Texts*, 167–71. The *Hadith* from al-Suyut's al-La-ali-masnū'a underscores the closeness of the prophet to God while the *Hadith* from al-Baghawi's Masabih al-Sunna elaborates his encounters with past prophets.

In Medina, Muhammad was not only a prophet but also its political head. Such a role naturally involved him in political and military activities. He had many difficult tasks ahead of him: settling the Meccan refugees, fostering cordial relationship between Muslims and non-Muslims of Medina, and consolidating the Muslim community of Medina. First he built a mosque and established a Muslim brotherhood. Then he established a state with a constitution geared toward making people submit to God and thereby live in peace. But such an establishment ignited conflicts. The Quraysh and Jews considered his endeavor a threat. Hence, he had to resort to military action. In 630 CE, his conquest of Mecca, the Quraysh stronghold, and his cleansing Kabbah of its idols, gave him the satisfaction that he had achieved his ideal, at least to an extent. But, after such a high point in his prophetic-political career, his health began to deteriorate. After his last pilgrimage to Mecca, he died on June 8, 632 CE. As soon as the news of his death spread, people assembled near his house. Some refused to believe that their holy prophet who had seen God could die. His friend and disciple, Abu Bakr, assured the crowd that Muhammad was dead since all humans eventually die.

Muhammad always identified himself as the "Messenger of God." What makes him remarkable is that he faithfully conveyed Allah's message. The Quran is his accomplishment. The most crucial event in his life was the Night of Power, when he received the first of the series of revelations, which later were codified in the Quran. If not for the Night of Power, there would have been no Night of Ascension, the night when he ascended to heaven. The authenticity of Muhammad's prophethood totally rests on his receiving the Quran, following it to the letter, and communicating it faithfully to his followers. Islam takes him to be the seal of the prophets on the grounds that he fully followed and communicated the most perfect revelation of God. Our next task will be to examine Quran's role in the Islamic quest.

SCRIPTURAL EXPRESSIONS OF THE QUEST

> In the name of Allah, Most Gracious, Most Merciful.
> Praise be to Allah The Cherisher and Sustainer of the worlds;
> Most Gracious, Most Merciful;
> Master of the Day of Judgment.
> Thee do we worship, And Thine aid we seek.
> Show us the straight way
> The way of those on whom
> Thou hast bestowed Thy Grace,
> Those whose (portion)
> Is not wrath
> And who go not astray (Quran surah 1, Al-Fatihah).

This is called Al-Fatihah (The Opening). It is not the first revelation Muhammad had but was given to him in the fourth day after his first revelation. Being placed as the opening chapter of the Quran is significant. This prayer makes a plea to be shown the "straight path." Muslims repeat this prayer at least five times a day. The rest of the Quran is a response to the plea that this prayer expresses. The Quran provides the way to walk the "straight path" that Muhammad meticulously followed and those after him are striving for.

The Quran consists of 114 chapters (*surahs*) subdivided into verses (*dyas*). The chapters have not been arranged in the order in which they were revealed. They fall under two main groups: Meccan and Medinese surahs. Muhammad started his mission in Mecca, where he lived for twelve years, and then migrated to Medina, where he continued his mission as a political head. Eighty-eight surahs belong to the Meccan period, while twenty-six were revealed to him in Medina. Interestingly the surahs are not arranged in that order. Some latter Medinese surahs, like surah 2, precede the Meccan surahs. Hence, the Quran should not be read as a history book, even though it contains some information about the life and times of the prophet.

Moreover, the Quran is not a doctrinal treatise, even though it contains the core doctrines of Islam. The book does not explain the doctrines topic by topic. They figure in different parts of the book as prescriptive guidelines in the context of issues and struggles which Muhammad and his community faced at specific times. For instance, in the context of a polytheistic idol-worshiping community, the Quranic proclamation, "There is no God, but Allah" was more than a doctrinal statement. It was a command that, if disobeyed, would lead to damnation. Hence, reading the Quran as a book on systematic theology will not be helpful.

The Quran is much more than a written document. The first word of Muhammad's first revelation is *iqra*, meaning "read," but not silent reading, rather "recite" or "proclaim aloud." It is the imperative tense of the Arabic root word, "recitation." The first command "Proclaim (Read) in the Name of Thy Lord and Cherisher . . . " (Quran 96:1) indicates that Muhammad was expected to recite what was revealed to him; *Qur'an* means recitation. He obeyed the command and proclaimed the Quran to his followers, who in turn conveyed it to others. To a great extent, the Quran's spiritual impact lies in being a sonoral revelation. Muslims believe that the Quran's psalmody has itself the power to generate a spiritual rapture, even if one does not know Arabic, the language of the Quran. The recitations of Quranic formulas and quotations are seen to be effective in the edification of the believer. The poetic format, especially the Meccan surahs, facilitate devotional recitation.

Quran's written format also has a part to play in the book's spiritual impact. The reputed Islamic art of calligraphy was really developed to exhibit the resplendent character of the Quranic language, the beauty of God's word. This is the Muslim confession of faith, the *shahadah* in calligraphic form. It states "There is no God but Allah and Muhammad is His messenger." The beauty of the calligraphy is meant to highlight the aesthetic aspect of the divine word.

Shahadah in calligraphic form

For the Muslims, the Quran both in its sonoral and calligraphic form is much more than a written document. Hence, analytic exegesis of it through the popular semantic and syntactic tools cannot capture its visual and sonoral impact. Nevertheless, its efficacy does not reside merely in its literary or artistic quality but fundamentally in it being divine word. Since God's word is inseparable from God, the very presence of the book is taken to be divine, which is why Muslims treat the Quran with such reverence.

As the revealed Word of God, the Quran receives a personhood that resembles Jesus Christ in some ways. The Quran is foundational to Muhammad's prophethood and is logically and temporally prior to it. The Quran as the "Mother of the book" (43:4) implies that it existed before it was revealed to Muhammad, that the revealed version is a copy of its heavenly archetype. This gives it an incarnational character similar to that of Jesus Christ. Just as Christ is God's eternal word incarnated, Muslims claim that the Quran is Allah's eternal word incarnated through the agency of angel Gabriel.

Muslims give certain names to the Quran which further indicate its personhood. It is called *al-Huda,* meaning guide and *Dhikar Allah,* meaning "the remembrance of God," which indicates its role as Allah's reminder. It is referred to as *Wahy,* meaning revelation. Muhammad is not God's revelation, but the Quran is. Many passages of the Quran point out that it is God's revelation and Muhammad its recipient. It declares, "The Quran is no other than a revelation revealed to him [Muhammad]" (Quran 52:4, see also 53:19; 41:5; 18:110). The Quran's most important role is to reveal to Muhammad and through him to all humanity the one and only True God. In order to convey such a revelation, Muhammad first had to be equipped. The early Meccan surahs contain passages that are meant to encourage and give Muhammad the confidence he needed. This passage exemplifies such encouragement:

> O thou wrapped up [in a mantle]
> Arise and deliver thy warning?
> And thy Lord
> Do thou magnify
> And thy garments
> Keep free from stain
> And all abomination shun
> Nor expect, in giving
> Any increase [for thyself]
> But for the Lord's [Cause]
> Be patient and constant (Quran 74:1–7).

Such exhortations enabled the hesitant prophet to become not only the accomplished proclaimer of Quran's message, but also one who meticulously followed its guidance. Muhammad's accomplishment was the Quran. The Islamic world revolves around the Quran. The soothing of its voice, the beauty of its calligraphic appearance, the power of its guidance in providing the "straight path" to liberation, and its intimate connection with Allah as his incarnated Word make it much more than a sacred scripture. Perhaps such a characterization of the Quran bears resemblance to Christ as God's incarnated Living Word.

Sunnah and Hadith are secondary to the Quran. They are not additional revelations. They enable Muslims to understand the Quran better as well as emulate the prophet in his deeds and sayings. Muhammad b Ishma'il al Buhkari (810–870 CE) and Muslim b al-Nisabuti (817–875) are believed to have compiled collections of Hadiths, entitled Sahih al-Burhari and Sahih al-Muslim. Subsequently, the Muslim community recognized four other collections of Abu-Dawid, Ibn Majah, al-Tirmidhi, and al-Nasi. Hadith collections could be classified into two main categories, the prophetic Hadith and the divine or sacred Hadith.[17] The former deals with legal and moral matters and provided the basis for shariah law, while the latter consists of pious exhortations and reflections, which provided the scriptural source for Sufi mystical practices. Hadith for the Shi'ites include not only the sayings of Muhammad but also those of the seven or twelve imams, beginning with Ali.

Muslims consider the Quran as their best source to guide their spiritual journey and Muhammad as the one who perfectly followed the path of salvation that the Quran presents. Our next task will be to look into the way of salvation that the Quran presents and Muhammad ideally exemplifies.

THE WAY OF THE QUEST

"Show us the Straight Path"—this is the Islamic plea for salvation. "Salvation" in Islam is freedom from the predicament which one gets into as a result of "sin." Muslims believe that humans are born sinless but have the freedom to commit sin. The underlying sin is not submitting to the one and only true God, Allah. The way of salvation that Islam presents is to guide people to avoid sinning, submit to Allah, and thereby achieve peace (*salaam*) while on earth and enter paradise after death.

What are popularly known as the Five Pillars of Islam exhibit best the Islamic way. They are not mere doctrines to be believed, but duties to be performed. These obligations are:

1. *Shahadah*: The declaration of faith, to testify that "There is no god, but God (Allah), and Muhammad is His Messenger."

2. *Salat*: The ritual daily prayer performed five times a day.

3. *Zakat*: Annual tithe or poor tax to help the poorer sector of the community.

4. *Sawm*: Fasting during the month of Ramadan.

5. *Hajj*: Pilgrimage to Mecca.

Muslims strive to submit to Allah through practicing these pillars. They may be taken as essentially jihadic in nature; they orchestrate the striving of seekers to free themselves from the predicament in which they feel trapped. In this sense, jihad in whatever form it appears is taken to be salvific in intent. Seyyed Hossein Nasr claims

17. Oxtoby, *World Religions: Western Traditions*, 408–9.

that, "From a spiritual point of view all the Pillars of Islam can be seen as related to jihad. The fundamental witnesses (*Shahadah*), 'There is no divinity but God' and 'Muhammad is the messenger of God' are not only statements of truth as seen in an Islamic perspective but also weapons of the practice of inner jihad."[18] He points out that the very form of the first letter of the shahadah, *la illaha*, when written in Arabic calligraphy, is like a bent sword.[19] Hence, we could well accommodate jihad as another pillar of Islam.

The way, as orchestrated through these pillars, exhibits certain significant features.

God-Centered

All these pillars work within a theistic paradigm. They are useless as salvific strategies if God is left out. The first pillar, shahadah, begins with the confession, "There is no god but God (Allah)." This signifies Islam's cardinal doctrine of God: *tawhid*, which literally means "making one." It refers to the act of affirming God as One, as absolute indivisible unity and entirely unique. All divine attributes flow from this fundamental truth (tawhid) about God. Islam's stance against any form of polytheism has been and still is its definitive declaration that God is one and only one.

Islam, no doubt, accommodates Jesus as a prophet but not as God. Accepting Jesus as God would amount to claiming that there is a god beside the one and only God, which amounts to the unpardonable sin, *shirk*. This is precisely why Muslims are unable to accept Jesus as God. For them such an inclusion pollutes the essential truth about God, his oneness. Hence, the Christian claim that God is three in one (Trinity) becomes most controversial.

Such a controversy really hinges on the conflict between two mathematical systems, Greek and Arabic. The debate between a Nestorian patriarch, Timothy I (780–823 CE), and Mahdi, the third Abbassid caliph (775–785 CE),[20] ideally exhibits the underlying reason for such a controversy.

Timothy I, though unknown today, played a significant role in his time. He was from a wealthy Christian family and was well-educated both in theology and Greek philosophy. He studied at "The Mother of Patriarchs and Bishops" school, located in the famous Adriabana monastery in Bet Abba (south of Masul, Iraq). His studies there gained him proficiency not only in Arabic but also in Greek philosophy and hermeneutics.[21] He is believed to have translated the works of Aristotle into Arabic. Mahdi was an eminent Arabic Muslim scholar. Their educational backgrounds exposed them to two different mathematical systems, Greek and Arabic. The tension between these systems is evident in their debate over the concept of God.

The debate between Timothy and Mahdi occurred towards the end of 781 CE or early 783 CE, and is supposed to have lasted for two days. On the second day,

18. Nasr, *Islam in the Modern World*, 46.
19. Ibid.
20. Mingana, "Debate," 11–12.
21. Norris, "Timothy I of Baghdad," 133.

Mahdi asked Timothy what he thought of Prophet Muhammad. Timothy responded by placing Muhammad in the line of prophets who proclaimed that God is one and condemned idol worship. Then Mahdi posed the question that epitomizes the Islamic contention of the Christian concept of God: "If God is one, how can he be three?"

Timothy commenced his apology thus: "I believe in one God in three, and three in one, but not in three different Godheads, however, but in the persons of God, God's Word and His Spirit. I believe that these three constitute one God, not in their person but in their nature."[22] But Mahdi could not accept this. According to him, claiming that God is three precludes the claim that there is only one God. If there are three, how can they be one? We can understand Mahdhi's reaction; in the Arabic number system, the number three is third in the number series that commences with number one. But Timothy's response comes out of his use of the Greek (Pythagorean) number system in which numbers are spatial units, and number one is the basic unit represented as a dot. When extended it is two, a straight line, and when further extended and enclosed it turns out to be three, which is represented by a triangle. Hence, number three is really number one enclosed. For Timothy, number three (triangle) is the complete and perfect number and it is still one. Adopting such a number system, Timothy claims that number one is the cause of all numbers, but unlike the Arabic system, it is not the first in the series of the number series. He applies number one to God without any reference to the beginning of a number series. He also applies to God "the number three without any implication of multiplication or division of Gods, but with a particular reference to the Word and the Spirit of God, through which heaven and earth have been created."[23] For him, when God is described as "one in three" it enables one to understand the God as Father, Son, and Spirit rather than counting the number of Gods. Here he is merely following the Greek view of mathematics to understand reality and not to count it. But for Mahdi, the number one is the first in the series and number three is a plural number. Hence, he categorically states, "The number three denotes plurality, and since there cannot be plurality in Godhead, this number three has no room at all in Godhead."[24] On the other hand, Timothy maintains his position that God is one in three and that three does not denote plurality. The debate seems to have reached a dead end. Perhaps that is why Mahdi changes the topic of discussion and calls on Timothy to provide biblical support for claiming God is "three is one." This Timothy does. The debate exhibits the continuing controversy between the Islamic and Christian view of God, one that arises from a conflict of two mathematical systems.

For Muslims, the affirmation that God is one is not a mere doctrinal statement. It is very much involved in their spiritual journey from start to finish. It is the very first words a newborn baby hears and the last that are spoken by or to the dying. When uttered with sincere conviction, such an affirmation transforms the seeker

22. Mingana, "Debate," 11–12.

23. Ibid.

24. Ibid.

into a devotee who has begun to walk in the "straight path" that leads to liberation. Prayer, fasting, almsgiving, and pilgrimage to Mecca generate from this confession. It forms part of daily prayers and constitutes the call to corporate prayer heard in mosques. It is on the lips of the Sufi mystic engaged in spiritual striving, as well as in the chant of the militant fighter for Allah. Such words give martyrs the hope that paradise would be their reward, even though they are treated unfairly and put to death. Perhaps, it was such a hope that motivated Saddam Hussein to utter these words as he walked to be hanged.

The God that the shahadah affirms is the Creator, Sustainer, and Lord of the Universe (Quran, surah 1), and the one who treats humans with compassion. Almost every surah of the Quran begins with the assertion, "In the Name of Allah, Most Merciful, and Most Compassionate." This compassionate God is also just and every human has to face his judgment one day. The Quran has more than eight hundred verses concerning the impending day of judgment. The fear of the day of judgment motivates Muslims to resort to the master of the day (surah 1), and follow the "straight path." The way of liberation enacted through the pillars of Islam is God-centered, in that they are all God-given, orchestrated to make one submit to God, and thereby face God's final judgment with confidence.

Prophet-Guided

The second part of the shahadah runs thus, "Muhammad is His Messenger." Prophethood is central to the Islamic way of liberation. It claims that God, through the ages, has related to people through prophets. According to Muslims, Islam commences with creation, predating Muhammad. They view Adam, before he disobeyed God, as an ideal Muslim. He obeyed God and hence enjoyed a peaceful life in the Garden of Eden. But, when he disobeyed God, the problem started. Islam does not view humans as being sinful by nature. They are born in a natural state of purity or innocence (*fit rah*). Adam's sin is not carried over by succeeding generations. According to the Quran, no one can carry another's burden of sin (35:18). People commit sin following the example of Adam. Disobeying God results in the loss of peace. Hence, the quest for peace aims for submission to the one and only true God. Humans have the potential to submit to God's will and law, but they tend to go astray. In his mercy, God sends prophets to restore them to what they should be under the will of God. Such a restoration enacted through prophetic guidance is essentially salvific in intent. God reveals his will, guides, counsels, and enables people to submit to him. He even warns and chastises them so that they will not go astray.

A prophet's worth lies in his message. It should be God-revealed, and it has to be effectively and faithfully conveyed both through word and deed. Muslims claim that Muhammad met these requirements. Allah revealed the Quran to Muhammad verbatim in the Arabic language. Since Muhammad was illiterate, the Quran was not his literary creation of Allah's ideas; it is Allah's speech, uttered through Muhammad's lips. Progressive revelation stipulates that what is revealed last is the best. Since Muhammad is the last in the series of prophets, the message revealed to him is taken to be the best. Muhammad's divine encounters equipped him for a prophetic mission to proclaim to humanity a way of salvation. The Islamic world claims this way of salvation is the continuation and perfection of God's plan to save humanity—a plan that commenced with Abraham, continued through a series of several prophets, including Moses and Jesus, and climaxed in Muhammad.

Moreover, there should be substance in a prophet's message, in that it should meet the needs of the people who hear it. What they need is not merely to know that God is one, just, and merciful, but that he provides a definitive way to submit to him and thereby be liberated. Muslims take pride in the fact that Muhammad faithfully conveyed that way through his preaching and lifestyle. He became the ideal model of perfect submission to God. Even though the Quran does not contain many details about the way he lived, the Sunnah and Hadith inform Muslims about how the prophet really lived and made vital decisions. They try to emulate him in the hope that they will acquire what he achieved—peace (salam) that results from total submission to Allah. The prophet conveyed the message by practicing what he preached. Hence, for Muslims, Muhammad is the messenger of Allah, the Seal of the Prophets. The Quran highlights the vital role he plays in guiding people to follow the "straight path" thus: "Those who follow the Messenger, the unlettered Prophet, whom they find mentioned in their own (scriptures), in the Law and the Gospel—for he commands them what is just and forbids them what is evil; he allows them as lawful what is good (and pure) and prohibits them from what is bad (and impure); He releases them from their heavy burdens that are upon them, so it is those who believe in him honor him, help him, and follow the Light which is sent down with him. It is they who will prosper" (Quran 7:157; see also verse 158).

In the above passage the phrase "in their own scriptures" refers to the Jewish Torah and Christian Gospel. Muslims interpret this verse as a claim that both Moses and Jesus anticipated Muhammad. Moses's statement that God will send a prophet just like him (Deut 17:15) is taken to refer to Muhammad. Jesus' promise of another comforter (John 14:16) is taken to refer to Muhammad.[25]

For Muslims, the "way of salvation" depends on prophetic guidance and Muhammad is the prophet that fully renders it and ideally models it.

Devotion-Ritualized

The other pillars which follow the confession (shahadah) show how those committed to the confession put that commitment into practice. Such a practice is not haphazard but set in order through rituals: a ritualized practice. This is best seen in the way Muslims exhibit their devotion through prayer. Failure to pray is not merely an offense against God but one that goes against human nature. It is instinctive for a human to adore great beings and God is the greatest; when one prays, one is true to his or

---

25. Ali, *Holy Quran*, 1127, footnote 389.

her nature and thereby is able to achieve one's aspirations,[26] the core aspiration being liberation through submission to God. Islam accommodates two kinds of prayer: individual informal prayer (*du'a*) and obligatory ritualized prayer (*salat*). The latter is the second Pillar of Islam. Salat means "to bow" or "bend." Such prayer consists of several postures such as bowing and falling prostrate, and is done five times a day facing Mecca's Kabbah. Before praying one must wash parts of the body which are exposed to dust or smog. This ritual, called absolution (*wudu*), signifies out that praying to a holy God should not be taken lightly; one has to be clean outside to be cleansed inside. For this reason, those who are ill and women who are menstruating cannot participate in salat. In addition to this obligatory prayer, there are also formalized prayers for special occasions like childbirth, marriage, and funerals.

Fasting (*sawm*) is also a form of ritualized devotion and takes place during the month of Ramadan. Muhammad instituted it as a ritual after his emigration to Medina. We can understand why he had to formalize fasting. In a world of competing gods, making offerings which pleased them turned out to be more lucrative than fasting and praying. In fact, fasting in arid deserts was suicidal to the nomadic Bedouin tribes. Muhammad prescribed fasting to his followers as it was done by those before them (Quran 2:183). This could refer to the Jews. At first the Muslim fast coincided with the Jewish Yom Kippur, and only later was changed to fall in the month of Ramadan. Then the fast became a ritual that commemorated God's revelation to Muhammad. The event enabled the participants to pay heed to the prophet's instructions and follow them more diligently. By providing an occasion that is conducive to following prophetic guidance, fasting serves a salvific purpose.

Muslims worship at the Kabbah in Mecca

The most spectacular pillar is the annual pilgrimage, hajj, when Muslims from around the world congregate in the holy city of Mecca. Every Muslim, if able, should

---

26. Abdalati, *Islam in Focus,* 55.

travel to Mecca at least once. It is a devotional event, orchestrated through several rites and rituals. Worship at the Kabbah, the Black Stone shrine, occupies a central place in the pilgrimage. Before entering the shrine, pilgrims must cleanse themselves and dress in simple white garments. The host of devotees all dressed in white devotionally circling the Black Stone dramatically exhibits the Muslim conviction that in God's presence there is no distinction between male and female, black and white, rich and poor.

The seven counter-clockwise circumambulations (*tawif*) of the Kabbah symbolize the unwinding of oneself from sin. Even though some devotees kiss the Black Stone, they do not worship it. This is really an orbiting prayer walk directed to Allah. They walk crying out, "At thy service, O Lord, at thy service."

The circling of the Kabbah is no doubt the climax but not the end of the pilgrimage. There are other rituals following this. Pilgrims run seven times between two hills, *Safah* and *Marwah,* re-enacting Hagar's desperate search for water for her thirsty son, Ishmael. Then the pilgrims take a drink of water at the well of *Zamzan* to remind themselves that just as God met Hagar's quest for her son's need, he will meet their needs.

Pilgrims then travel to Mount Arafat where Muhammad preached his last sermon. Here they participate in a very significant prayer, called "standing" because they pray while standing from noon to sunset in the manner Muhammad stood and delivered his final sermon.[27] The prayer is a plea asking Allah to forgive their sins and prepare them to face the impending dreaded day of judgment.

After this, the pilgrims go to Mina, believed to be the site of Abraham's sacrifice of Ishmael, and where the prophet uttered his last words during his final pilgrimage to Mecca.[28] Here they throw seven stones against three pillars that represent Satan. This ritual is meant to enable them to resist the devil, just as Ishmael is supposed to have thrown stones at the devil to resist his temptations.

The final ritual is the sacrifice of an animal, in remembrance of Abraham's sacrifice of the ram that God gave to replace the sacrifice of his son, in this case Ishmael. This ritual also commemorates the Muslim festival of the sacrifice (*Eid-al-Adha*) associated with the day of resurrection. The sacrificial rite marks the end of the pilgrimage and gives the pilgrims some assurance of being purified.

Hajj for the Muslim pilgrims is not a pleasure trip to the sacred city, but an arduous pilgrimage to seek Allah's mercy, to seek his forgiveness for the sins accumulated throughout life. Hajj is the best illustration of the Muslim quest to be freed from their sins through a ritualized devotional journey.

Prayer, fasting during Ramadan, and hajj pilgrimage are essentially all devotional rituals. Muslims, whether they pray, fast or go to Mecca, carry out these rituals meticulously with the hope that this will enable them to submit to Allah and thereby be liberated. It is devotion ritualized for salvific purpose. But, such an endeavor has also a moral underpinning.

27. Caner and Caner, eds., *Unveiling Islam*, 129.
28. Ibid.

Moral-Conditioned

Rituals tend to become mere formalities, which turns the way of salvation enacted through such rituals into empty religiosity. As a preventive measure, the Quran emphasizes that there should be a moral basis for ritualistic practice, one that involves right beliefs and morally motivated action. The Quran points out that righteousness is truly believing in Allah and not ritualistically turning towards the east or west when praying (Quran 2:177).

The Islamic concept of morality centers on God. A human being's ultimate responsibility is to God and to live according to what he pleases. Since God is both just and merciful, the human response should meet the demands of such a God, a response that is not merely having right beliefs but also exhibiting proper conduct and a response that shows itself in action that bears the character of Allah. The same verse of the Quran goes on to point out that those who believe in Allah and his messengers should strive, "To spend your substance out of love for Him, for your kin, for orphans, for the needy, for the wayfarer, for those who ask, and for the ransom of slaves; To be steadfast in prayer and practice regular charity, to fulfill the contracts which ye have made; and to be firm and patient" (Quran 2:177).

The Quran emphasizes that one who confesses the shahadah should also share his wealth, care for the needy, and defend the rights of slaves; one should not only pray steadfastly but also practice charity and be honest in keeping contracts. Such a blend between sincere belief and proper moral conduct, and between prayer and charity, would naturally prevent one from falling into empty ritualistic formalism. The pillars are not mere rituals but positive moral obligations. Islam also stipulates certain other preventive or precautionary measures. For instance, one should avoid consumption of intoxicants (Quran 2:219; 4:43; 5:93–94), products of swine and certain other birds and animals (2:172–3; 5:4–6), all forms of gambling (2:219; 5:93–94), sexual relations out of wedlock, and immodest dressing (23:5–7; 24:30–33; 70:29–31). Hence the "way of salvation" enacted through the pillars is a morally-oriented ritual strategy.

Community-Oriented

For Muslims, "salvation" is essentially communitarian. When Muhammad migrated from Mecca to Medina, there was a significant transformation in his mission. In Medina he was no longer a lonesome prophet trying to persuade individuals to submit to Allah, but a political head with authority. As a ruler of Medina, his goal was to make the whole community come under the rule of Allah. The constitution that he created for Medina was to make it a theocratic state. The peace (salam) that would result from a state submitting to God would naturally be communal in scope. This was what the prophet envisioned.

In such a context, the pillars serve as communal activities. When Muslims pray five times a day (salat) they pray as a community. Even though each mosque may have its own prayer sessions, there is uniformity in the schedule of the sessions, prayer postures facing Mecca, and in the content of the prayers. These uniformities enable

Muslims to feel that they all belong to one community, praying to the same God. Muslims around the world fast in the same month of Ramadan. The stipulations about when to start and finish the fast, how to fast, and what to do when fasting are the same for everyone; the Ramadan fast is a communal activity. Giving a portion of one's income (zakat) obviously has a communal impact. The money given is to help the poor in the community (Quran 2:184). The pilgrimage to Mecca (hajj) exhibits best the communality of the Islamic way. Pilgrims from every corner of the world congregate in Mecca, Islam's holiest city. Divisions such as gender, race, rank, culture, and class become invisible when identically dressed pilgrims participate in the same rituals. Penitent pilgrims circumambulating the Black Stone and praying to the same God is the most spectacular communal event of Islam. After his own pilgrimage, Malcolm X commented: "I have never seen before such sincere and true brotherhood practiced by all colors together."[29]

Shahadah, no doubt, is a confession that arises out of personal conviction. Nevertheless, such a confession initiates one into the *ummah*, the Muslim counterpart to the Christian church. The ummah is the nucleus of the Muslim community and serves as the means to enable society to submit to God and thereby become a community of peace (salam). The main purpose of the other pillars is to assist believers to effectively function in and through the ummah.

Effort-Enabled

Islam claims that Allah will show mercy provided people make the effort. Prayer, fasting, pilgrimage, almsgiving, living according to moral standards, and jihadic activity are all types of human effort that could qualify one to receive his mercy. The Quran contains a covenant between Allah and his devotees that clarifies the nature and role of jihad in the Islamic quest:

> Allah has purchased of the believers
> Their persons and their goods
> For theirs [in return]
> Is the Garden [of Paradise]
> They fight in His Cause,
> And slay and are slain:
> A promise binding on Him
> In Truth, through the Law,
> The Gospel, and the Quran
> And who is most faithful
> To His covenant than Allah?
> Then rejoice in the bargain,
> Which ye have concluded:
> That is the achievement supreme (Quran 9:111).

According to this verse, when believers give up their wealth and lives for the sake of Allah, he assures them of life in paradise.

29. Aslan, *No God but God*, 150.

The salvific role of jihad highlighted by this verse is further developed in the Hadith. Some of the earliest Hadith compilations provide some information on jihad's salvific role. Abdallah Ibn al-Mubarak, in his eighth-century compilation *Kitab-al-Jihad,* records how Muslims viewed warfare during the period of conquests after Muhammad's death. He cites three types of believers. The first is the true believer who is killed fighting for Allah and is given a prominent place in the "camp of God." The third type, on the other hand, is the hypocritical believer who is killed and enters hell. But the second type is the repentant devotee who seeks to expiate his sins fighting for God. Here, the sword along with a repentant spirit wipes away sins. This type highlights the redemptive aspect of jihad, that "the sword wipes away sins."[30] The same Hadith states, "Being killed in the path of Allah washes away impurity; killing is two things: atonement and rank [in heaven]."[31]

Another motivating factor to fight for Allah is the apocalyptic and messianic vision that is associated with jihad. The Quran indicates that the trials and tests that people experience are part of Allah's plan to prepare them for paradise, separating the true from the hypocritical believers (3:140–2).

The Quran repeatedly warns of the impending day of judgment. The Hadith describes several events that would happen as the day approaches. Out of these apocalyptic signs three stand out. First will be the appearance of *Dajjal* (the Muslim Antichrist), who will try to make the entire world submit to him. Second is the appearance of *Isa* (Jesus). Muslims do not believe that Jesus was crucified, but claim that he was taken up to heaven and that he will return to slay Dajjal, with Allah's empowerment. Third is the appearance of the long awaited Muslim Messiah, Mahdi. According to Shi'ites, he went into a state of spiritual hiding and as an unseen imam he guides his people and enables them to defend the faith. This messianic figure will return from hiding and appear at the proper time. Murtaza Lakha puts it this way:

> The last Imam will be concealed from the people and his reappearance will be delayed for so long that people will begin to doubt his existence. He will not reappear until the last days of the world, when it will have been filled with sin and injustices. Then he, on the command of Allah, will reappear and change the face of the world. He will wipe out injustices and sins and replace them with truth and justice. Prophet Isa [Jesus] will descend from the heavens at that time and both of them will spread the name of Allah from one end of the earth to the other.[32]

The hope of Islam is that ultimately all humanity will come under the submission of Allah. Mahdi along with Isa (Jesus) will be instrumental in fulfilling this hope. But, since all will not readily submit to Allah, Muslims feel it is necessary to fight the forces that obstruct the coming of Allah's kingdom. Passages from the Quran and Hadith are cited to give support to what believers ought to do until Mahdi appears: "And fight

---

30. Abdallah Ibn al-Mubarak in Cook, *Understanding Jihad*, 15.

31. Ibid.

32. Lakha, *The Twelfth Imam*, 8.

them on until there is no more tumult or oppression, and there prevails justice and faith in Allah" (Quran 8: 39).

This, and similar verses, call on believers to fight for Allah; to participate in jihad. Whether this includes militant action is a matter of controversy. In this context, jihad acquires an apocalyptic function. It facilitates the return of Mahdi by means of fighting those people and forces that obstruct the establishment of God's rule. Such a rule will come into effect when sharia, the Islamic law, is implemented. But since it is perceived to conflict with the norms of human rights, there is bound to be conflict. This is evident in states like Afghanistan, Saudi Arabia, and Nigeria where sharia's implementation has become contentious. In such a context, implementing sharia becomes very much a part jihadic activity to facilitate the return of Mahdi.

Hence, jihad has two main roles to play: salvific and apocalyptic. First, it enables the participants to be rid of their sins and enter paradise without facing the day of judgment (Quran 9:111). Second, jihad prepares the grounds for Mahdi to appear and establish Allah's kingdom (Quran 8:39–40).

The instructions, entitled "The Last Night,"[33] given to the participants of 9/11 highlight the salvific and apocalyptic roles that jihad plays. The directions were meant to assure these individuals that they were not involved in merely a militant action but a life-changing spiritual encounter—one that would have a lasting impact on their own lives as well as on the Muslim community at large. First of all, they had to fully commit themselves to fight for Allah. They had to swear to one another that they would keep their commitment (directive 1). Then they had to know their plan of action well, anticipating the strategies of the enemy (directive 2). In order to execute their plan of action effectively, they had to pray steadfastly and devotionally recite the Quran, especially surahs 8 and 9 (directives 4–6). They should not waste time, but need to purify their hearts, obey God, and do what was pleasing to him (directive 7). Quran 9:111 assures a place in paradise for the fighter for Allah, thus: "Let your breast be open, tranquil to the bounty of God, because it is only a few minutes before the happy, satisfying life and the eternal Paradise begins in the Company of the prophets . . ." (directive 8).[34]

They were reminded that when difficulties arose: "This is nothing but God's test in order to raise the level [of your martyrdom] and to expiate your sins. You can be certain that there are only minutes left until the merit will be clear—with God's permission—of that great reward from God (directive 9).[35]

When confronted with death, the participants were asked to remember Quran 2:249, which gives the assurance of God's support and that no one would be able overcome them.

While Quran 9:11 points out the salvific aspect of jihad, Quran 8:39 highlights its apocalyptic function. It commands believers to fight against anti-Allah forces, in the

33. Cook, *Understanding Jihad,* 196. A translation of the hijackers' last night's preparation letter appeared in the *New York Times* on September 29, 2001 and is included in Cook's book as appendix 6, "The Last Night."

34. Ibid., 196.

35. Ibid., 197.

hope that their struggle would facilitate the final total annihilation of evil. When they come to the point of death, the directive states: "Let your last words be 'There is no god but God and Muhammad is His Messenger.'"[36] Such a confession assures them of paradise when they face death. No doubt, many do not consider such an enactment of jihad legitimate. But those who adopt it see it as an effective mode of human effort to gain Allah's mercy and thereby enter paradise.

The "Straight Path" that Muslims aspire for is a way of salvation that is God-centered, prophet-guided, ritualized-devotion, moral-conditioned, community-oriented and based on human-effort, involving jihadic striving. Hence, those who follow it acclaim it as the best way.

Acclaimed the Best Way

Progressive revelation claims that what is revealed last is the best. Muslims believe that the final revelation of the way of salvation came to Muhammad through the Quran. God revealed that he is one first to the prophet Abraham (*Ibrahim*); then to Moses (*Musa*) was revealed that God is just. His love was revealed through the prophet Jesus' (*Isa*) life of compassion. Finally, a way to submit to this one and only just and loving God was given to Muhammad.

Islam acknowledges the Jewish original scrolls of Abraham, the Torah as given to Moses, the Psalms of David, and the Gospel of Jesus (*Injil*) as legitimate pre-Quranic revelations. But, Muslims do not accept the current versions of these scriptures as accurate representation of the original versions. For instance, presenting Isaac instead of Ishmael as the firstborn son and thereby claiming Isaac's descendants to be the children of Abraham, is viewed as a Jewish revision of the original Torah. Moreover, the inclusion of Jesus' crucifixion and resurrection in the Gospels is seen as an attempt on the part of Christians to deify Christ. On the other hand, Muslims claim that the Quran, being preserved in its original form, is most reliable: the final and best scriptural revelation. By making Muhammad the culmination of prophethood and the Quran the completion of divine revelation, God has given to humanity the best way of "salvation."

But the salvation that Jesus offers is taken to be the only way. Claiming that a way is the best way is not the same as claiming it to be the only way. Addressing the Jewish Sanhedrin, Peter states: "Salvation is found in no one else, for there is no other name under heaven given to men by which we must be saved" (Acts 4: 12). Such a weighty claim leads us to discover how Christ is relevant to the Islamic salvific quest.

THE RELEVANCE OF CHRIST TO THE ISLAMIC QUEST

Despite the sporadic feuds that crop up between Muslims and Christians, there has been an intimate relationship between these two faith communities through the years. Several passages in the Quran refer to Christ and Christians, and in fact, one passage encourages Muslims to have a cordial relationship with Christians. It runs thus: "And

36. Ibid., 202.

nearest among them in love to the Believers wilt thou find those who say 'We are Christians' because amongst these are men devoted to learning, and men who have renounced the world, and they are not arrogant" (5:82).

The fact that the Quran encourages Muslims to live "nearest in affection" with Christians should motivate both faith communities to find ways and means to cultivate that affection. The Quran points out that Muslims should live in harmony with Christians because they have been devoted learners, neither worldly-minded nor arrogant. Perhaps the Quran is here referring to the Abyssinian Christians who welcomed the persecuted Muslims when they fled from Mecca. The Quran goes on to say this about Christians: "And when they listen to the revelation received by the Messenger; thou wilt see their eyes overflowing with tears for they recognize the Truth" (5:83).

Such a response of some Christians to Islam is indicative of the affinity between these two faith groups: an affinity that becomes more pronounced in the way Islam treats Christ. The Quran cites him eighty-seven times and one whole chapter (surah 19: Maryam) is devoted to him. Islam acknowledges his miraculous conception, virgin birth, being endowed with God's spirit, his miracles, and as the "Word of God" to his people. He ascended to heaven and will return in the last days to kill the antichrist and judge humanity. But Islam does not accept that he died on the cross and rose again. The Quran states: "That they said [in boast], 'We killed Christ Jesus, the son of Mary, the Messenger of Allah.' But they killed him not, nor crucified him, but so it was made to appear to them . . . " (4:157).

Denial of the cross naturally implies that Muslims do not accept what Jesus accomplished on the cross to save humanity. For them, he is no more than a "Messenger of Allah" (Quran 4:171) and not the Son of God (Quran 9:30). Even though Islam gives such a prominent place to Jesus, he is not accepted as Savior. But, it is precisely at this point that he becomes relevant to the Islamic quest,one that wants to be salvific but without a savior.

When relating Christ to Islam, comparing him to Muhammad does injustice to both. They belong to entirely different paradigms. Muhammad is the "Seal of the Prophets" but never God. On the other hand, Jesus is the Savior God. In fact, Islam traces Muhammad's identity as prophet to Jesus' prophetic reference that after him God will send another counselor (John 14:16). Christians take this to refer to the Holy Spirit, while Muslims claim that it refers to Muhammad, citing the Quran which states, "And remember Jesus, the Son of Mary said: I am the messenger of Allah . . . giving glad tidings of a Messenger to come after me, whose name shall be Ahmad . . . " (61:6). Ahmad, meaning the praised one, is one of the names given to Muhammad.

The Quran renders five roles to Muhammad as prophet (33:45–46). He comes as a witness, bearer of good news, warner, one who calls people to repentance, and as a lamp spreading light. Just as all prophets, he was a witness to and conveyor of spiritual truths to the people of his time. These roles place him in the ranks of the prophets, who are all human. As bearer of good news, he conveyed to people the way to be freed from their predicament. On the other hand, Jesus is the Good News; he is the way of salvation. Muhammad is called to warn people and call them to repentance, just as

John the Baptist warned people of their transgressions and called them to repent. But he made it a point to tell people that he was not the Christ (Matt 3:11). Muhammad is called upon to function as a lamp, to spread the light. But he is not the light. On the other hand, Jesus is the Light of the World (John 8:12: 9:5).

Muhammad would not have wanted anyone to venerate him. However, his spiritual escapades, political achievements, and exemplary lifestyle had a significant impact on how he came to be perceived in the Muslim world. What he experienced during the Night Journey from Mecca to Jerusalem and from there to heaven was enough for Muslims to believe that he was much more than a prophet. His followers wanted one who had a special relationship with Allah—one who not only served him on earth but also experienced heaven, his abode. The Night Journey fulfilled that aspiration. Muhammad had a firsthand glimpse of heaven. But, on the other hand, heaven was nothing new to Jesus; it was his home, his Father's house. He came from there and he went back to prepare a place for those who accepted him as savior (John 14:1). Muhammad's followers desired him to be a citizen of both earth and heaven. Christ fulfills this to the fullest.

The Quran presents Muhammad more as Allah's messenger than a mediator. But with the passage of time Muslims began to ascribe to the prophet the functions of a mediator and intercessor. This trend was perhaps influenced by an ancient Iranian belief that a propitiator was needed to mediate between heaven and an alienated world.[37] In fact, there is a belief, especially among the Shi'ites, that on the final day of judgment that will occur near the Dome of the Rock in Jerusalem, Muhammad will act as an advocate. Ascribing the role of mediator to him provides a reference point to relate Christ to the Islamic quest. The role of Christ as mediator and advocate is pronounced in Christianity (Gal 3:20; Heb 8:6). The Muslim call for a mediator suggests Christ's relevancy.

The Islamic "way of salvation" demands of the devotee a life of moral integrity. Muhammad showed himself as a powerful political head respected for his moral integrity. He soon became the model of moral integrity that his followers emulated, one whose conduct and teachings exhibited the Quranic injunction of perfect submission to Allah—"the living Quran." Following his example came to have a salvific purpose; it was not to merely make devotees good people but to enable them to have a wholesome life in this world and the next. The Sufi mystics went even further in suggesting that one could aspire to experience God's presence just as Muhammad did on his Night Journey, to assimilate divine qualities by getting in tune with his spirituality. They revere him as the mediator, the creative light on earth, who enables them to see the divine light, similar to the way Jesus is viewed as the light that shines in the darkness of this sin-ridden world (John 1:3–5).[38]

Even though Muhammad's message is more significant than his person, people came to exalt him. Legends concerning his birth, youth, ministry, and death gained

---

37. Brown, *Nearest in Affection*, 6.

38. Ibid., 5.

sacred status, especially in folk Islam. His birth became portrayed as miraculous—that when the prophet was born many wonders occurred in the sky and on earth. The Persian tyrant monarch Anushiravan's palace, an edifice of eternal dictatorial monarchy, trembled.[39] Muhammad's tomb in Medina became a sacred place of pilgrimage. This progressive veneration of Muhammad indicates that people needed more than a prophet, one they could idealize as the perfect person and in order to be liberated. Perhaps it is someone like Christ they are looking for.

Even though prophethood ended with Muhammad, there was still a need for spiritual guidance, especially during changing times and contexts. The community needed a successor who could give such guidance.

The question of succession was not so much who, but what type of person should succeed the prophet. Abu-Bakr was chosen as caliph by common consensus. However, Ali's supporters contended that common consensus could not choose the person needed for the job. They attributed the cause of a series of catastrophes the community underwent to the caliphs. For Shi'ites, caliphs were not the type to give leadership to the community. The Shi'ites call their leaders imams rather than caliphs. The Shi'ite umamate is based on two principles: *nass* and *ilm*. Nass refers to the special gift bestowed by God upon a chosen person from Muhammad's family. Muhammad articulated the first nass in Ghadir, when by divine direction he chose Ali as his successor. Hence, Ali, chosen by divine direction rather than common consensus, is considered the legitimate successor. The second principle is *ilm*, which means that the imam is possessor of divinely-inspired knowledge. Such knowledge enables him to lead the community in all matters. Such knowledge also carries with it the esoteric function of interpreting the mysteries of the Quran. This type of person, *wilayah*, has to be free from error and sin, and most near to God.[40] Such a characterization of the imam indicates that Muslims are asking for a guide who is near to God, a closest friend of God who knows his thoughts, infallible, and free from sin. Christ meets all these requirements.

When Muhammad's son-in-law was chosen caliph, his followers rejoiced that at last the community had a legitimate leader. But their hopes were shattered. He was assassinated in 660 CE by dissenters among his own supporters. Mu'awiyah from the Umayyad clan proclaimed himself as caliph. The civil war did not end with Ali's death, but continued, first led by his elder son al-Hassan. When Mu'awiyah died, his son Yazid became the next caliph. Then al-Hussayn, Ali's second son, was invited to lead the protest against Imam Yazid. This protest resulted in al-Hussayn's tragic death on October 10, 680 CE at the hands of the Umayyads at Karbala. Hussayn's severed head was displayed to the crowd by Yazid's troops. The manner in which Muslims responded to this brutal event is noteworthy. This tragedy motivated the followers to consolidate themselves as a distinct sect, as Shia, the party of Ali. Moreover, the response to the pathos of the event shows how Christ becomes relevant to the Islamic salvific quest.

39. Dar Rah Haqq's Board of Writers, *A Glance at the Life*, 20.

40. Tabataba'i, *Shi'a*, 10–11.

With the passage of time, the hatred against the brutal killer turned into penitence shown to the victim. About four years after the massacre, a group of Muslims calling themselves penitents gathered at Karbala with their faces blackened and their clothes torn to mourn the death of Hussayn. This expression of grief was meant not merely as homage to Hussayn, but as an act of atonement for their failure to aid him. It was an act to display publicly their guilt, and their mourning was a means of absolving themselves of their sin: an act of repentance for their sin.[41]

Karbala made an indelible mark on how Muslims view humans. For Shi'ites, Karbala's sin did not stop with the event but continues to mar all humans. The popular Shi'ite saying, "Every day is Asura, every place is Karbala" brings out the pervasive nature of the sin that Karbala generates. Asura is the tenth day, the date the event occurred, while Karbala is its location. The annual enactment of penitence that the Karbala event exhibits indicates that those gripped by the guilt of sin need much more than prophetic guidance. They need a savior. This is where Christ clicks in.

The significance of Hussayn as one who sacrificed his life gave rise to a doctrine of atonement through sacrifice that involves shedding of blood. The concept called *aza* (mourning) eventually became expressed through rites and rituals. Every year, Shi'ites commemorate Karbala through lamentations, passion plays, and mourning processions in which participants beat their chests, flog their backs with whips, and shed their blood. Such rituals are carried out with the conviction that Hussayn, who sacrificed himself, would intercede on their behalf and rid them of their sins. They repeat with contrition, "A tear shed for Hussayn washes away a hundred sins."[42] For such penitents, Karbala is their "Garden of Eden" where humans fell into sin. This sin cannot be erased except by one who sacrificed himself on their behalf; Hussayn's sacrifice becomes indispensable for their atonement. Christ on the cross fulfills such a need.

"Salvation" in Islam is personal and communal. In order to achieve such a goal, prophetic guidance climaxing in Muhammad is indispensable. But the question arose as to how such guidance could be given after Muhammad's death. It is in this context that the concept of Mahdi developed in Muslim theology, meaning "one who divinely guides."

According to Shi'ites, even though Muhammad is the final prophet, there is a need for divine guidance. Beginning with Ali, divinely appointed imams meet this need. The Shi'ite "Twelvers" sect claims that the office of imam passed from Ali down to the eleventh imam, Askari. His son and successor Muhammad Abul-Qasim was taken from the world in his childhood. Since then he is in a state of spiritual hiding (*ghaybah*) and will appear during end times as *Imam-Mahdi* to establish Allah's kingdom of peace and righteousness. He is called the "Hidden Imam." The anticipation of the appearance of a messianic figure, though popularized by the Shi'ites, was not confined to them. Some orthodox Sunnis also believe that at the end of time Allah will send into the world one that will destroy evil and establish his kingdom. They too call

41. Aslan, *No God but God,* 178.

42. Ibid., 179.

him *Imam-Mahdi*, the one guided right by Allah. Even though they reject the Shi'ite version, they accommodate Mahdi as a messiah-myth that renders hope for the future. Whether Mahdi is myth or real, he performs a significant role in the Islamic quest for salvation. The anticipation of the appearance of the Hidden Imam provides the believers strength for today and hope for tomorrow.

Since ten out of the eleven imams were martyred, Allah in his wisdom has placed Mahdi, the twelfth imam in hiding. He functions mostly in concealment. Whenever Islam is in jeopardy, he protects the believers and thus defends their faith. When Islamic scholars are confronted with issues, he provides them with much needed illumination and guidance. He helps the faithful and strengthens the weak. Several citations in Shi'ite sacred literature show how the Hidden Imam protects, illumines, and empowers the believers, and thereby defends their faith.[43] Shi'ites consider the Mahdi as the "Chief of the Age" (*qa'im al-zaman*) who is able to communicate his will to believers. The belief in the Hidden Imam's active participation in the events of the world, especially in the affairs of the faith community, characterizes the Shi'ite worldview. In order to receive Mahdi's help, believers are expected to sincerely and affectionately remember him, make supplications for his help, and be loyal to him. Shi'ites view the future with the conviction that the Hidden Imam will return at the end of time and establish Allah's kingdom. That a community that has suffered centuries of unfair exploitation by powers within and outside Islam would resort to a messiah figure is understandable—one who would not only right the wrongs but also establish a world order founded on divine justice. In his address to the sixtieth session of the United Nations General Assembly in New York on September 14, 2005, His Excellency Dr. Mahmood Ahmadinejad, President of Iran, articulated the messianic hope thus:

> From the beginning of time, humanity has longed for the day when justice, peace, equality and compassion envelop the world. All of us can contribute to the establishment of such a world.
> When that day comes, the ultimate promise of all Divine religions will be fulfilled with the emergence of a perfect human being who is heir to all prophets and pious men. He will lead the world to justice and absolute peace.
> O mighty Lord, I pray to you to hasten the emergence of your last repository, the promised one, that perfect and pure human being, the one that will fill this world with justice and peace. O Lord, include us among his companions, followers and those who serve his cause.[44]

The Iranian president's prayerful wish epitomizes the aspirations of a significant section of the Islamic community, a people who live and work with the conviction that the Hidden Imam empowers them to defend their faith. The anticipation of his appearance motivates them to endure the injustices wrought against them.

It is precisely in such a context that Christ becomes relevant to the Islamic community. What the Muslims long for is someone who is able to help them overcome the forces of evil, without being a victim to them—a messiah who will usher in a world

43. Lakka, *The Twelfth Imam*, 16–38.
44. Ahmadinejad, "Address," para. 42–44.

of peace and justice. The role of Mahdi as Hidden Imam protecting, illuminating, and empowering believers is comparable to the way the Holy Spirit functions in the lives of people. Both are invisible. Muslims compare the Hidden Imam to the sun which gives light and heat even though it may be hidden by clouds. Jesus compares the Spirit to the wind: "The wind blows where it wishes, and you hear the sound of it, but cannot tell where it comes from and where it goes" (John 3:8). Muslims resort to the Hidden Imam because, although human, he is God empowered. They long for divine help. The Holy Spirit, being God himself, ideally meets the Muslim longing. Moreover, Mahdi as the anticipated messiah may of course be "the perfect and pure human being" as the president of Iran puts it. But, Christ being much more than a perfect human being ideally fulfills the Muslim longing; he is God incarnate, not merely God-empowered. But the problem resides right here. Islam does not accept the deity of Christ.

Muslims attribute a character and function to the Quran that makes Christ relevant to the Islamic quest in a special way. God and God's word, though distinguishable, are inseparable. God's word is as divine as God. Muslims take the Quran to be the actual word of Allah revealed in Arabic to Muhammad. Allah, and not Muhammad, is the author of the Quran. Allah makes it clear that he has given the Quran in the Arabic language so that Muhammad could understand (Quran 43:2–3).

For Muslims, the Quran is more than a sacred text, in that it did not come into being when revealed to Muhammad but had existed eternally in Allah's presence as the "Mother of the Book" (Quran 43:4; see also 3:7; 13:39). As Allah's incarnated word it was given to Muhammad. It and not Muhammad is the Islamic counterpart of Jesus (Word made flesh). Muhammad was the *rasul* (apostle) who spread the message. Just as Christ came to fulfill and not abrogate the Mosaic law, the Quran is taken as the fulfillment of previous scriptural revelations. The Quran puts it thus:

> It is he [Allah] who sent down
> To thee [step by step]
> In truth, the Book
> Confirming what went before it;
> And He sent down the Law
> [Of Moses] and the Gospel [of Jesus]
> Before this as a guide to mankind . . . (3:2–4).

Muslims accommodate Jews and Christians as "People of the Book" because they believe that these faith communities received their scriptures from the same source, "The Mother of the Book." For Muslims, Quran being the accurate copy of the original book is its fullest revelation.

Jesus came into this world as savior. The good tidings the angel proclaimed to the shepherds were that "Jesus the Savior is born" (Luke 3:11). For Muslims, the Quran is good news for it contains the "way of salvation" (Quran 2: 25; 5:19; 16:89; 48:8). "Salvation" for them is through divine guidance. Allah is described as *Rabb*, which means nourisher, cherisher, or sustainer. It signifies fostering of a thing in such a manner as to make it attain step by step to its goal of perfection.[45] Allah, as Rabb, has guided humans through prophets and the Quran revealed to Muhammad provides the best guidance.

The Quran states:

> Verily this Quran
> Doth guide to that
> Which is most right [or stable]
> And giveth the glad tidings
> To the Believers who work
> Deeds of Righteousness
> That they shall have
> A magnificent reward
> And to those who believe not
> In the Hereafter [it announceth]
> That We have prepared
> For them a Penalty
> Grievous [indeed] (17:9–10; see also 10:38–41)

The call to Muslims to put their whole trust on the Quran resembles the call to Christians to believe on the Lord Jesus Christ for their salvation (John 3:16–18). Both the calls are based on the conviction that the way one responds to the Quran or Jesus determines one's destiny.

The Quran is comparable to Christ in its salvific role as the guide to one's liberation. But there is a significant difference between the two. Christ is a person, in fact, a divine person. The Quran is attributed features that pertain to a person, such as guide and reminder of God. It is treated with such veneration that Muslims hesitate to place it on the floor, underline it, or make notes on it. Despite such veneration, it is still scripture. It is no doubt Allah's word but is still essentially sacred scripture. Apostle John states that Jesus "In the beginning was the Word, and the Word was with God, and the Word was God" (John 1:1). But he makes it a point to state that the "Word" is essentially a person; a "he" and not an "it." He puts it this way: "*He* was in the beginning with God. All things were made by *Him*, and without *Him*, nothing was made. In *Him* was life, and the life was the light of men" (John 1:2–4).

The Quran as God's fullest revelation (*wahy*), essentially reveals God's will to humans. On the other hand, Jesus is not merely revelation of God's will but God himself. He is God incarnated in human flesh, while the Quran is God's will in scriptural format. Jesus pre-existed in the Godhead before he was born on earth, while the Quran pre-existed as "Mother of the Book" in God's presence.

The Quran for the Muslims is divine, infallible, and satisfies their salvific quest to the fullest. It is Allah's incarnated will that provides the "way of salvation" for humanity. In fact, Muhammad's spiritual journey commenced with the descent of the word of God upon him. If not for this descent, Muhammad would not have ascended to heaven on the Night of Ascension. Such an ascension becomes the model of the

---

45. Elmi, "Word of God and Revelation," 279.

Islamic salvific quest, an ascent that involves human effort, even striving (jihad) in an evil world. Reconciliation of the "sinful" with Allah depends on both human effort and divine response. God's mercy is conditional on human effort. The Quran describes Allah's response to human effort thus: "But my Mercy extendeth to all things. That [Mercy] I shall ordain for those who do right, and practice regular Charity, and those who believe in Our Signs" (7:15b).

Even though Allah's mercy extends to all, to appropriate his mercy one must live up to the standards set by him. The Quran goes on to claim that even the Jews and Christians are welcome to receive God's mercy, if they follow Prophet Muhammad, who is mentioned in their respective scriptures (Quran 7:157). Muslims consider that Moses prefigures Muhammad and anticipates him, on the grounds of the biblical statement: "The Lord thy God will raise up unto thee a prophet in the midst of thee, of thy brethren, like unto me" (Deut 18:15). Muhammad gave the world sharia (law), similar to the law Moses gave to the Jews, through the commandments. When the *Injil* (Gospel) states that Jesus promised another comforter will come after him (John 19:16), Muslims claim that the reference is to Muhammad and not to the Holy Spirit. Muslims expect both Jews and Christians to note what their own scriptures reveal about Muhammad and follow his prophetic guidance. In other words, Muslims contend that when "people of the book" accept Muhammad as portrayed in their own scriptures, then Allah's mercy will extend even to them.

The Quran highlights the character of Allah as most merciful. Every surah in the Quran (except the ninth) commences with the statement, "In the Name of Allah, Most Gracious (*Rahmain*), Most Merciful (*Raheem*)." It is repeated at the beginning of every act of worship. But, can the term Rahmain be translated as "most gracious?" In the Arabic language, the word Rahmain is one of the adjectival forms rooted from the word *Rahmah*, which means mercy. Raheem is also rooted from Rahmah. By using two different forms of adjectives, the Quranic text highlights that Allah is "the most merciful." Such a literary practice is very common in Arabic poems and literature. Hence the Arabic words, Rahmain and Rahim translated as "Most Gracious" and "Most Merciful" are both intensive forms of different aspects of Allah's mercy.[46] From the Muslim perspective, the Arabic intensive is better suited to express Allah's merciful character than the superlative degree in English. The latter implies a comparison with others showing mercy, while the Arabic intensive forms highlight that Allah's mercy is unique; no other beings possess such "mercy." Such mercy may imply pity, long-suffering, patience, forgiveness, compassion, and protection that the sinner desperately needs. For this reason the attribute Rahmain (Most Gracious) is not applied to any others but Allah, while the attribute Rahim (Merciful) is a general term and may be applied to anyone who shows mercy.[47] It should be noted that even the Arabic term Rahmain (Most Gracious) is an intensive form of the attribute of mercy: the mercy that only Allah possesses. But the Arabic term *Neamah*, which means "Grace,"

---

46. Thanks to Ashraf Beshara who assisted me in exegeting these terms.

47. Ali, *Holy Quran*, 14. See Ali's note 19 commentary on surah 1:1

is missing from the Quranic description of Allah. He is described as most and uniquely merciful (Rahmain) but not one that shows grace (Neamah).[48] There is a significant difference between the attributes of mercy and grace. God's grace is very much like his mercy. Both arise from a heart of love and compassion that is sincerely concerned with sinful humans. But grace is prevenient. It precedes all human decision and endeavor. It is God who takes the initiative. The whole point of grace is that it does not start with humans. It starts with God; it is not earned or merited, it is freely and lovingly given to those who have no resources or deserving of their own.[49] The enactment of God's grace is best seen in the experience of Saul the persecutor who was dramatically changed to Paul the apostle on the road to Damascus. He testifies that "By the grace of God I am what I am, and His grace toward me was not in vain . . . " (1 Cor 15:10). On the other hand, in the Islamic perspective, Allah's mercy in its most intensive form (Rahmain) is a response to human effort; when the sinner takes the initiative, Allah shows his mercy. Human effort, through good deeds and proper conduct, however laudable it may be, cannot hope to meet God's perfect standards. Hence, he has to show mercy to compensate the inadequacy of human endeavor. The devoted Muslim faithfully confesses his faith (shahadah), prays at least five times a day, fasts during Ramadan, gives alms, and tries to go on a pilgrimage (hajj) to Mecca at least once. The penitent Shi'ites beat their chests and whip their backs in commemoration of the Karbala tragedy. The spiritual Sufis go into meditation, trances, and dances. The radical jihadists fight and give their lives for God. The Muslim world is replete with such activities, all meant to obtain Allah's mercy, and all salvific in intent. The penitent devotees, realizing the inadequacy of their efforts, cry for Allah's mercy. Perhaps what they are really crying for is God's grace, not merely his mercy. This is where Christ becomes most relevant to the Islamic salvific quest. The Quran opens with the plea:

> Thee do we worship
> And Thine aid we seek
> Show us the straight way.
> The way of those on whom
> Thou has bestowed Thy Grace (1:5–7).

The plea is to show the "straight way," which is often the narrow or the steep way. The Quran talks about two highways of life. One is the popular and easy way of rejecting God that ultimately ends in hell. The other way is the narrow or steep way which people shun but that which liberates the sinner (90:10–20). It is the way that involves human effort that generates God's mercy. Christ also refers to two ways, one the wide and popular way that leads to destruction and the other the narrow way that leads to life (Matt. 7:13–14). He identifies himself as the way (John 14:6) and the only way of salvation (Heb 9:8; 10:20). Six times in the book of Acts the Christian faith and community are designated as "the Way" (Acts 9:2; 19:9, 23; 22:4; 22:14, 22), with reference to Christians as "followers of the Way" or those who belong to Christ, the Way. In both

48. See footnote 46.

49. Hughes, "Grace," 480.

Islam and Christianity, the way to life is narrow and not popular. Islam describes it as a "steep way" (Quran 90:11–12), implying the one who takes that path is traveling up, from the sinful state to Allah. On the other hand, Christ claims "I am the Way . . . No one comes to the Father except through me" (John 14:6). Here Jesus refers to God as his own Father. He employs a household term showing that he and God belong to the same family. He points out to his disciples, "If you had known me, you would have known my Father also . . . He who has seen me has seen the father . . . I am in the Father and the Father in me . . . " (John 14:7–11). These are weighty words, especially coming from a Jew. They highlight the deity of Christ as God the Son. This would mean that salvation through Jesus the Way goes from top to bottom, from God to sinners. The way of salvation originates in God the Father's heart of love and is enacted by the sacrificial life and death of God the Son.

> For God so loved the world that He gave His only begotten Son, that whoever believes in Him should not perish but have everlasting life (John 3:16).

Since God himself takes the initiative, salvation is not conditional on human effort. In the Christian context, sin incapacitates humans; human effort, however laudable it may be, cannot deliver the goods. That is why God demonstrates his own love towards helpless humans in that while they were still sinners, Christ died for them (5:8). Hence, salvation is not conditional upon human effort but rather on human response. In order to be saved, one needs to respond to God the Father's unconditional love in allowing his Son to die on the cross as a substitute for one's sin. Such a response calls for committing oneself to Jesus the Way and depending fully on his grace.

Both Muslims and Christians want to be freed from their perceived predicament and both turn to God for liberation. Muslims resort to God who is "most merciful." Allah shows his mercy to the Muslim who makes a sincere effort to live according to the way revealed to Prophet Mohammed. Allah's mercy depends on and is a response to the quality of the human effort. One cannot be absolutely sure whether such effort is adequate to earn Allah's mercy. Such an assurance is missing because Allah's mercy is dependent on human effort. On the other hand, one who takes refuge in a God's grace need not be concerned about the adequacy of his or her effort. The assurance that one who accepts Christ as savior receives is not dependent on one's effort but rather on God's grace. Human effort through good deeds and conduct is really a response to, rather than a means to, obtain God's grace. God himself provides the assurance to the sinner who comes to Jesus, not on the grounds of the quality of one's effort, but entirely by his grace.

It is precisely this assurance that the Muslim devotee craves. Praying five times a day, fasting during Ramadan, giving alms, travelling to Mecca, and confessing the creed (shahadah) until one takes his last breath are all meant to earn Allah's mercy. The strenuous spiritual endeavors of the Sufi mystics are geared to bring their baser nature under captivity and allow them to experience Allah in an intimate manner. The Sufi method is essentially a way to reach God through human spiritual effort. The militant maneuvers associated with 9/11 no doubt are condemned by the majority of

Muslims. Nevertheless those who participated in them considered them to be jihadic and not mere militant violence. Those who view jihad as fighting for the cause of Allah that entails forgiveness of sins and entry to paradise, even without facing the dreaded day of judgment, cite the Quran and the Hadith to support such a stance. The Quran points out the atoning impact of martyrdom thus:

> Let those who fight
> In the cause of Allah
> Who sell the life of this world
> For the Hereafter
> To him who fighteth
> In the cause of Allah
> Whether he is slain
> Or get victory
> Soon shall We give him
> A reward of great [value] (4:74).

The following Hadith narrated by Abu Huraira states that Allah guarantees entrance into paradise for the one who dies in jihad:

> Allah's Apostle said: "Allah guarantees to the person who carries out Jihad for His Cause, and nothing compelled him to go out but the Jihad in His Cause, and belief in His words, that He will either admit him into Paradise or return him with his reward . . . (Hadith 9:93:549; also see Hadith 9:93:555).[50]

No doubt such divine assurances motivate some devoted Muslims to become suicide bombers and crash on concrete edifices. But, such acts of martyrdom provide at best only the hope of heaven and not the assurance; the martyr has to wait until death to know of his or her fate. Since all these, whether religious or political, spiritual or violent, are essentially human efforts, one cannot be really sure of salvation. Even Muhammad, the ideal exemplar of the Islamic way of salvation is believed to have confessed at the point of his death, "By Allah, though I am the Apostle of Allah yet I do not know what Allah will do to me" (Hadith 5:266).[51]

Muslims seem to strive for a way of salvation that is not merely based on God's mercy and dependent on human effort but one that is enabled though God's unmerited favor: his grace—a way that is not merely directed by prophetic guidance but enabled by divine incarnational intervention. The way enacted by God himself in Christ and appropriated through his grace seems to ideally meet the aspiration of Muslims. But Christ and him crucified is the stumbling block!

50. Caner and Caner, eds., *Unveiling Islam*, 295–96.

51. Ibid., 32.

10

The Aboriginal Quest

ABORIGINAL OR INDIGENOUS PEOPLE constitute quite a variety of cultures, world-views, religious beliefs, and economic and social structures. They live in different parts of the world stretching from Australia to North America. The Native Indians, more recently called the First Nations of North America, the forest people (Bambuti) and mountain tribes (Ik) of Africa, the Buryats of Russia, the Aborigines of Australia, the Maori of New Zealand, and the Veddahs of Sri Lanka are some of the better known aboriginal communities.

It took the world centuries to acknowledge aboriginals as a religious community. The Parliament of Religions accommodated indigenous people as delegates only in 1993. In one of its sessions, the delegates pointed out that, "One hundred years ago during the 1893 Parliament of World Religions, the profoundly religious Original Peoples of the Western Hemisphere were not invited. We are still here and struggling to be heard for the sake of our Mother Earth and our children."[1]

Such a comment voices a sense of utter disappointment, even bitterness among the aboriginals that the world at large does not recognize them as a religious community, or even as a people. Brainwashed by the evolutionary perspective on human history, many consider aboriginals to be subhuman savages. Perhaps it was such a bias that prompted K. T. Preuss to locate the origin of religion in what he labeled "primitive stupidity."[2] Nevertheless, our approach is founded on the conviction that even though some of these aboriginals may have been illiterate, they were not subhuman. They were at one time illiterate in that they did not communicate through written language, and their history was not recorded in writing. Their ways of life may have been quite different from those of the rest of the world, but that does not mean they were subhuman. They were as human as the rest of humanity. They may be prehistoric, but not prehuman.

It is understandable that the religious world was and perhaps still is hesitant to include the religion of the aboriginals into the family of organized religions. No

---

1. "Declaration of Vision," 8.
2. Carmody and Carmody, *Ways to the Center*, 22.

doubt the aboriginals do not present a codified system of beliefs articulated through written scriptures. They may not have reputed founders, well-structured ecclesiastical institutions, towering temples, or impressive cathedrals. But we cannot dismiss their religiosity as primitive just because they are not structured like organized religions. It does not mean that these communities were devoid of the quest that characterizes the devotees of the religions of the world. The quest of a community does not depend on how structured its religion is. The quest does not characterize a religion but the people who belong to a faith community. On the grounds of their humanity, we can identify a quest among the aboriginals to free themselves from their perceived predicament.

This predicament may not be articulated through the kinds of sophisticated theological concepts and institutional structures that organized religions exhibit. But that does not mean that the aboriginals are not beset by problems or were not so in the past. For instance, the earliest humans, believed to be hunters in land or sea, had to strive to survive. They had to protect themselves and their children from sickness, disease, animals, and natural disasters. Birth, sustenance, and death were catastrophic events in their life journey. No doubt they resorted to practical means of survival such as hunting, protecting themselves through basic tools, and cultivation of their lands, but their recourse to free themselves from besetting problems went beyond such practical strategies. Their ways of life indicate recourse to something beyond themselves: a transcendent, unseen being that supports and animates everything.[3] This is where they exhibit a deep-seated aspiration of the kind that justifies characterizing their belief system as a quest. It is the suspicion that the earliest humans worshiped a supreme heavenly being, a high god, that led Mircea Eliade to refute the popular evolutionist view of the history of religion: that religions evolved from primitive animism, to polytheism, and then to monotheism.[4]

No doubt colonization, racism, pressure from missionaries, cultural assimilation, capitalistic commercialism, and exploitation of the natural environment by global consumerist economies have seriously affected indigenous peoples. But despite such challenges they are still very much a part of the human populace and want to be recognized as a distinct faith community. Peter Iverson's book, *We Are Still Here*, is indicative of such a resolve.

There are some barriers we need to cross when trying to get a better understanding of the religiosity of the aboriginals. Their world is so complex and variegated that generalizations about it turn out to be half-truths. Hence the observations we make are not to be taken as applying universally to the indigenous world.

Through the ages indigenous traditions have been threatened in several ways. As a result some traditions have disappeared, while some have long been practiced in secretive isolation. For instance, some of the teachings of the Aborigines of Australia have been underground for hundreds of years. Through the centuries there has also been a blending of Aboriginal practices and beliefs with other religious traditions such as Buddhism,

---

3. Bowler, *The Sense of God*, 44–65; Oxtoby, *World Religions: Eastern Traditions*, 471–85.
4. Eliade, *Patterns in Comparative Religions*, 38–40; Eliade, *Myths, Dreams and Mysteries*, 66.

Islam, and Christianity. For instance, the Veddahs, the Aboriginals of Sri Lanka, have been mostly assimilated into Buddhism. The traditional aboriginal homeland that falls north of the Sahara in Africa is now predominantly Islam, while the part that falls south is mainly Christian. Islam and Christianity have greatly infiltrated indigenous beliefs and practices on that continent.[5] In North America numerous Native Indians not only converted to Christianity but intermarried with whites and became known as the Métis. There has also been a popular trend to blend Christian doctrine with Native Indian traditionalistic views. But even though such assimilation occurs, some aboriginals still continue to adhere to their traditional ways. It is rather difficult to decipher what is authentic aboriginal practice and what is imported from other religious traditions.

Religion in the aboriginal world was and still is not a distinct dimension of society. aboriginal spirituality permeates all aspects of life. The aboriginals claim that their whole culture and social structure is infused with a spirituality that cannot be separated from the rest of the community's life. Moreover, the life and activities of such people are essentially communitarian rather than individualistic. For instance, the Native Indian Green Corn Ceremony, the Snake Dance, the Sun Dance, and the sacred pipe performances are essentially communal ceremonies, whether of a tribe, clan, or family. In a context where the sacred is not distinct from the secular, such collective activities express not only the social but also the spiritual aspirations of the whole community. Some aboriginal communities have structured hierarchical social institutions that, in the modern context, would fall under the secular rather than the religious category. But in the aboriginal context such taxonomy does not apply, since the two are seamlessly blended.

In order to identify the quest of the aboriginals, the Native American Indian community seems to be an ideal exemplar. But in picking out this community, one has to be careful not to make sweeping generalizations. Some but not all features that characterize Native American spirituality are applicable to other aboriginal communities. Moreover, even within the Native American religious community, there is great diversity. Perhaps the relative isolation of different tribes scattered over a vast continent for centuries has allowed the evolution of diverse beliefs and practices among these tribes. Despite such differences, there are certain commonalities that seem to exhibit a concern for the supernatural. Resort to an invisible being, veneration of the earth and elements of nature, contact with spirits, meticulous observance of taboos, visions, and a resort to the help of spiritual specialists like shamans and/or medicine men seem to be practiced by a significant sector of the Native American populace.

The Native American Indian community also ideally exhibits the recent aboriginal resurgence. Many Native Indians have turned to their traditional religion in order to get back to their roots. The deep hurts that they have experienced at the hands of some religious groups have naturally forced aboriginals to react against anything white or western. We are all aware, for example, of the horrors that took place in the residential schools. But such reactive resurgence is not a mere return to orthodoxy or

---

5. The following are effective literary presentations of the indigenous impact on Islam and Christianity, respectively: Kane, *Ambiguous Adventure* and Achebe, *No Longer at Ease*.

traditional societal structures and practices. Even though motivated to a considerable extent by the frustrating discontent of the community concerning its status in the American sociopolitical arena, the resurgence is spiritual at its core.

The pan-tribal movement called the Ghost Dance exemplifies the spirituality of the Native American resurgence. The Ghost Dance is a cult assuring Indians that, if they go back to their old ways and participate in a trance-like dance, they can defeat the whites and renew their spiritual heritage.[6] In recent times another religious movement called the Peyote religion has gained ground. It began in 1890 CE and came to venerate *peyote* as a sacramental food. *Pe-yo-tl* is a spineless, dome-shaped cactus (*Lophophora williamsii*) having button-like tubercles. It is native to Mexico and the southwestern United States, and is chewed fresh or dry as a narcotic by certain Native American peoples. It is also called *mescal*.[7] This sect advocates the practice of a ritualistic sacrament involving the use of peyote, with singing, drumming, and praying. Peyotists belonging to many tribes founded the Native American Church in 1918; it was a concoction of Christian and Native Indian beliefs and practices. Even though both traditional Native Indians and orthodox Christians oppose such a blend, this church has flourished covertly. Now incorporated as the Native American Church, the Peyote sect has secured for Indians the legal right to practice the peyote sacrament.[8] "Pan Indianism" is also a recent and growing movement that encourages a return to traditional beliefs and seeks to create a common Native Indian religion. It typifies to a great extent the spiritual thrust of the contemporary aboriginal resurgence. These recent movements among the American Indians indicate that the resurgence is not a mere political protest movement but a spiritual quest.

The Native Indian "Great Spirit Prayer" poignantly exhibits the spiritual overtones of such a resurgence:

> Oh Great Spirit,
> Whose voice I hear in the winds,
> And whose breath gives life to all the world.
> Hear me. I am small and weak;
> I need your strength and wisdom.
> Let me walk in beauty and make my eyes ever behold
> The red and purple sunset.
> Make my hands respect the things you have made
> And my ears sharp to hear your voice.
> Make me wise so that I may understand the things you have taught my people.
> Let me learn the lessons you have hidden in every leaf and rock.
> I seek strength, not to be greater than my brother but to fight my great enemy—myself.
> Make me always ready to come to you
> With clean hands and straight eyes,
> So when life fades, as the fading sunset
> My spirit may come to you without shame.[9]

6. Carmody and Carmody, *Ways to the Center*, 49–50.

7. Schaefer, "A Biblical Look," 24.

8. Carmody and Carmody, *Ways to the Center*, 50.

9. "Native American Prayer," n.p.

Sioux Prayer to the Mystery, 1908

The belief in a High God or Great Spirit, sometimes called the Sky God, is popular among these people. Sioux Indians call it *Wakam Tanka* (Creator or Great Maker). Algonquins call it *Gitchi Manitou* (Supreme Being). The Inuit believe in a great spirit called *Sila* who supports the world and speaks through storms, snow, and rain; this being also goes by the name Great Mystery. The above prayer acknowledges a transcendent being who gives life to the entire world and is the resort of humans in need. Moreover, those who participate in such a prayer have a great appreciation of nature, which inspires them to acknowledge a creator God. Perhaps such an acknowledgment of a divine being, impelled by the appreciation of nature, could be taken as an instance of general revelation.

Nevertheless, a regard for the beautiful artifacts of nature as infiltrated and orchestrated by the Great Spirit is indicative of a pantheistic worldview. These people venerate nature and take care of it devotionally. A Winnebago wise saying, "Holy Mother Earth, the trees and all nature are witnesses of your thoughts and deeds," expresses this veneration.[10] Even though the world is divinely created and orchestrated, the participants in the above prayer recognize forces that could beset them. Such forces may be not only external but also internal; as the prayer states, the great enemy could be "myself." This recognition that the human predicament is caused by humans themselves, and moreover arises from the interplay of spiritual factors, naturally motivates the participants to resort to a being they designate as "High Spirit." The plea to obtain this being's aid, so as to be freed from forces that beset them and eventually face death with confidence, characterizes the aboriginal quest.

Our next task will be to look into the ways in which the aboriginal quest is expressed.

EXPRESSIONS OF THE QUEST

Scriptures, especially in written form, play a significant role in expressing the quest of most religious communities. aboriginals do not have such scriptures. But that does not mean that there is no linguistic expression of their quest. aboriginal traditions are mostly conveyed orally, and specifically through narratives, particularly myths. Seldom do we find doctrines expressed in propositional format through codified scriptures. Such traditions have been preserved and communicated orally through narratives that are often updated and modified as a result of subsequent dreams and

10. Hopfe, *Religions of the World*, 38.

visions experienced by individual aboriginals. In order to understand these oral, often dramatized narratives, one has to go beyond grammatical exegesis and immerse oneself in the cultures of the communities so as to become familiar with the message of their metaphors and oral gestures.

Myths and Stories

In a scientific world, myths are often branded as superstitious stories of subrational people. The demarcation between the rational and the mythical is perhaps a Greek legacy that has impacted much of Western thought. But such a demarcation does injustice to the aboriginal mindset. The myth is never intended to stipulate beliefs set in propositional form justified through rational arguments. The myth is not a normative code but essentially a narrative. Its impact lies not in its historical accuracy or logical consistency but in its relevance to the people. As Karen Armstrong puts it, a myth is "something that had in some sense happened once but that also happens all the time."[11] The myth in the aboriginal context is not to be merely believed but should also motivate one to act. Such a motivation comes not through meticulous analysis of the story. The oral enactment of the story through the ages prompts both those who tell and those hear it to believe in its message and act according to it. Hence dramatic telling of the myth was and is a characteristic communal event that gives expression to the inner aspirations of the aboriginals while also prompting them to carve out certain preferred ways to achieve these aspirations. In order to identify the aboriginal quest, we need to look into these narratives as well as other avenues of expression.

Even though many aboriginals acknowledge a High God, such a God is believed to be impersonal, distant, and unapproachable. Originating around the end of the Ice Age and persisting since the Mesolithic is a myth that makes reference to a golden era when relations between heaven and humans were harmonious.[12] But somehow or other such a relationship was disrupted. According to some myths this High God was close to humans in the distant past, but since they disrespected him in some way, he was forced to withdraw. Hence there was a need to resort to mediators. Mother Earth and the elements of nature, including both trees and animals, serve as the mediators between humans and the High God. aboriginals consider elements of nature to be not dead matter but living spirits. aboriginal cultures, both nomadic and agricultural, insist that humans are to live close to nature, since it is kin to them. They are animistic in that they believe not only animals and birds but also so-called inanimate elements, such as trees, rocks, and rivers, to be actually alive. Nevertheless, they go a step further in proposing that the High Spirit lives and manifests itself in all the elements of nature and that, hence, nature should be treated with utter veneration. The elements are like the High Spirit in that they have a will of their own and can either help or harm humans. Hence these elements, whether trees or animals, must be appeased in order for them to give humans the help they need in order to be freed from their problems.

11. Armstrong, *Case for God*, xi.
12. Carmody and Carmody, *Ways to the Center*, 26.

Aboriginals are not monotheists in that they do not see the world as created and sustained by a supreme personal God, like Allah or Jehovah. They are also not strict polytheists in that they do not view the world as being under the discretion of a pantheon of gods. Their way of life necessitates utter dependence on the elements of nature, such as earth, forests, streams, seas, and animals, which for them are infused with spirits akin to the distant High Spirit. Hence their salvific quest expresses itself in ways and means to please these spirits. The totem and the rituals associated with it ideally illustrate such an expression.

Totems

Totem Pole

Aboriginal society is essentially tribal. Its quest is, therefore, often orchestrated through the tribe. This is where totem becomes significant. Totemism may be taken as an expression of the tribal aboriginal quest, especially among the Aborigines of Australia and the Native Indians of certain areas of North America. Webster defines "totem" as a natural object, usually an animal that serves as a distinctive, often venerated emblem or symbol of a tribe, clan, or family. It is a means of personal or spiritual identity. According to Native American tradition, nine animals usually figure at different stages in one's life journey, but one animal is involved throughout life. This is taken to be the totem animal.

Totemism is rooted in a deep sense of kinship between humans and other creatures of nature. This is evident in the manner in which a totem is chosen. If one wants to select a totem—say, an animal—one resorts to genealogy to find out whether such a totem has figured in the family history of the person concerned. One may also resort to the zodiac sign assigned to one's birth date; Native Americans have an animal assigned to each zone of the zodiac. One could also identify the totem through dreams, visions, prayers, trances, and meditations. Aboriginals resort to these methods in order to determine their affinity with a particular creature that could serve as their totem. Such an affinity is vital for the totem to perform the role of a mediator effectively, not only for individuals but also for a tribe. Animal totems are very popular. They can be land animals such as a bear or deer, water animals such as a beaver or crab, flying animals such as a bat or eagle, reptiles such as a snake or lizard, insects such as bees or butterflies, and even dragons. A totem serves as the emblem of the tribe in that it is responsible for its origin and character. For instance, a tribe that takes the bear as its emblem believes that the bear is the prime ancestor of the tribe and is intimately connected with its survival. The tribe is believed to possess the features of bearlike ferocity and strength, and tribe members believe that when they die they take the form of a bear. They also believe that the bear protects and frees the tribe from calamities and enables them to have a better life. Tribe members may not eat or kill the bear except in self-defense or when it serves as a sacrificial animal. Then the participants in the sacrifice eat the meat of the bear believing that it will benefit them spiritually and bind the tribe closer. Totem animals serve as embodiments of the personality traits that aboriginals strive to emulate; by focusing on the attributes of the totem, tribe members seek to internalize its virtues. The totem also facilitates visions that can transform lives and, in this context, serves as a means of "saving" and protecting not merely individuals but the family, clan, or tribe it represents.

Totemism has both a social and ritual dimension. On the social side, a group's totem is that which binds the tribe. Based on the belief that marriage between people of the same totem will cause dissension, the Australian Aboriginal rules stipulate that a marriage partner should be selected from outside the totem group. On the ritual side, the members of a tribe are forbidden to kill and eat their totem animal except on special ritual occasions. So intimate is the relationship between the tribe and the totem that the totem object is venerated with the greatest courtesy and reverence.[13] Ceremonies venerating totems carved or painted on a totem pole are popular in some aboriginal communities.

This brings us to the role rituals and ceremonies play in expressing the aboriginal quest.

Rituals and Ceremonies

For aboriginals, ceremonies and rituals play a vital salvific role; they serve as a means of contact with the spirit world and thereby freedom from the people's predicament. Since the High God or Great Spirit is so distant from the world of humans, there is a need for mediators. aboriginals resort to the spirits to get in touch with the High God. Since these spirits can be benevolent or malevolent, humans must appease the good ones and ward off the evil ones. Ceremonies and rituals enable humans to make the correct partnership between humans and spirits. Such ceremonies and rituals involve fasting, dancing, bathing, and observance of certain taboos.

Dancing is one of the most popular elements of these ceremonies. It is a means of contacting the spirits and obtaining their help in order to prepare the tribe for a successful hunt, agricultural season, or war. Usually the whole community participates in such an event. The dance is accompanied by songs, chants, drumming, and the shaking of rattles.

The Sun Dance is a very popular dance performed annually during the midsummer months and usually lasts from four to eight days. It has spiritual significance both for the individual and the community. The participants dance to the sound of drums and singing around a center pole, often a tree such as cottonwood. The dance

---

13. Smart, *Religious Experience of Mankind*, 35.

represents the quest of the participants to facilitate a harmonious relationship with the spirit world, especially with the Great Spirit, and thereby be endowed with spiritual strength to ward off the evil spirits. The tree represents the Great Spirit. It is freshly cut and ceremoniously raised to the center of the dancing circle.

Dancers experience pain, especially when piercing their bodies; such gruesome acts are based on the belief that a "flesh offering" (torturing the body) is integral to the success of the prayer. Through their own efforts, which often include torturous acts, dancers seek to be purified so that they will be in communion with the spirit and so obtain the spiritual power that acts as a medicine to live a wholesome life. The spiritual relationship, which includes the endowment of spiritual power, purification, and communion between the dancers and the Great Spirit, is both individualistic and communal. Dancers participate in the sweat lodge with the intention of self-purification, experiencing as they do so visions that provide assurance of the spirit's favor.

In the final part of the Sun Dance ceremony, the dancers circle the tree four times, each time touching it with their palms. Following the fourth touch the dancers lean against their ropes, seeking their own Sun Dance vision. The other members of the tribe are not mere onlookers, but are involved in deep prayer, seeking their own visions. The dance is both individualistic and communal, and is essentially salvific in intent.

The sweat lodge ceremonies serve a variety of purposes. They are used as a ritual to heal the sick, to be purified spiritually, or as an arduous activity to appease the spirits. These ceremonies take place in total darkness in a sweat lodge, which is a small structure made up of a frame of saplings covered with skins, canvas, or blankets. At the center of the lodge, a hole is dug into which hot rocks are placed; water is thrown on the rocks to generate hot mist, while a small flap opening is used to regulate the temperature. As many as a dozen people can be accommodated in some lodges.[14] The medicine man chants and prays repetitiously, invoking the spirits. The pipe ceremony usually forms a part of the proceedings as well. What must be noted is that all the purposes of the sweat lodge are interrelated and have a spiritual thrust. No doubt sweating in the lodge is painful, but the ceremony is not meant simply to make the participants suffer. The suffering is intended to purify them and thereby prepare them to be liberated. Hence these ceremonies are also an expression of the salvific quest of the participants.

Hunting has been one of the main occupations of aboriginals. In fact, calling it an occupation is a misnomer, as hunting for aboriginals is much more than killing for food. Rituals precede and follow hunting. After an animal like the bear is killed during a successful hunt, a ritual treatment of the animal follows in order to appease its spirit and appeal to other animals to be willing to be killed in the future The belief is that failing to do so will cause the animal's spirit to be angry, which would in turn result not only in bad luck at hunting but also in a rift between the hunters and the spirit world.

---

14. Schaefer, "A Biblical Look," 17.

Dancing, sweat lodge ceremonies, and hunting are essentially ritualistic practices with salvific import.

Shamans and Medicine Men

Narratives, totems, rituals, and ceremonies are no doubt significant expressions of the aboriginal quest. But in order for them to be effective, those who participate in them resort to people with special spiritual powers, people who can access the sacred or the High Spirit. Shamans, medicine men, and diviners function in such a role. Shamanism is believed to have developed in Africa and Europe during the Paleolithic period and spread to Siberia and eventually to North America and Australia. The term *shaman* means "one who knows." The shaman not only knows his tribe but also knows the spirit world and how to communicate with it. The *angakut* or shaman now plays a central role in aboriginal religious practice, although in some North American Indian tribes this office is referred to by other names. As the spiritual leader of a tribe, the shaman is able to interpret the causes of sickness, hunting mishaps, and calamities such as untimely death or infertility. He is not just a magician. Mircea Eliade observes that, "He is believed to cure like doctors and to perform miracles of the fakir type, like all magicians. But beyond this he is psych-pomp, and he may be also a priest, mystic and poet."[15] Eliade finds that this type of shaman figures prominently in hunting and pastoral societies like Siberia and Central Asia. The view that humans once lived and enjoyed a wholesome life and then an event occurred that caused them to fall from such a state, is a common belief among many aboriginals. In his examination of Shamanism, Eliade discerns shaman's unique ability of enabling people to regain their condition before the "fall out of sacred time," through mystical experiences which betray a nostalgia for paradise, the desire to recover the state of freedom and beatitude before the "fall."[16] In this respect a shaman may be taken as a key figure helping aboriginals in their salvific quest. In order to function in this role, the shaman is supposed to have a death and resurrection encounter. This occurs particularly during his initiation, when spirits are believed to dismember him, strip off the flesh from his bones, and then put him back to life. In and through such a death to life experience, he is believed to become a new person, elevated above human nature, and able to communicate with the spirit world, especially with the High God.[17] He enters into a trance through the orchestration of drum beating and chanting, allowing his spirit to leave his body and traverse distances to determine the causes of mishaps, and free those stricken with sickness and demonic control. The shaman works within a conceptual framework in which time is not linear but exists simultaneously on different planes. Cyclic movements, such as those of the seasons, earth, and moon, and even life, characterize such a view: life is understood as the "circle of life." Birth, life, and death are cyclic. The shaman's role is to help and heal the members of his community at each stage of this circle of life. This is made possible

15. Eliade, *Shaminism*, 4.

16. Elaide, *Myths, Dreams and Mysteries*, 66.

17. Ibid., 66, 82–83.

when the shaman is able to connect with the spirit world. In the Peruvian Amazon Basin and north coastal regions of Peru, healer shamans known as *curanderos* are very popular. They use a herb called *ayahuasca* for both physical and psychological healing; in recent times these shamans, also called *ayahuasqueros,* have become very popular among Western seekers. The core aspiration of the aboriginals to align themselves with the spirit world and thereby free themselves from the calamities of life finds expression in their resort to shamans.

Aboriginals also resort to "medicine men," who can be male or female. They function in different roles: as the spiritual leader, physician, astrologer, seer predicting the future, interpreter of dreams, teacher, keeper of confidential information, and one who is intimate with spirits. They perform certain rituals to enable success in gambling, hunting, trapping, and farming. Through these rituals they can also cast spells on people that cause them to fail in these activities and even harm and kill them. They call upon the spirits both to heal and to harm people.

Shaman from Amazonian forest, Peru

Medicine men often make use of medicine bags, which are made to protect people from evil, give them physical and spiritual strength, and even increase their political power. The ingredients of a medicine bag are usually kept very secret; only the medicine man handling the bag knows what is in it. Different combinations of ingredients, such as feathers of birds, especially the eagle, bear claws and gall, otter noses, fish gall, animal bones, intestines, fat, skulls, fur, bats, freshwater clams, dried birds, frogs, snakes, turtles, roots, bark from trees, dried dog feces, certain rocks, and salt are found in these bags. In order to be effective in their profession, the medicine men must protect themselves from evil spirits and cleanse themselves physically and spiritually. They use a variety of things to cleanse themselves. Sweetgrass, sage, pine needles, the stalks of a variety of grass called "raven stick," fungus growths found on rotting stumps, and *kenekenik* (dried red willow bark) are common cleansing agents. They ignite one or more of these and bathe themselves in the smoke. They also use the sweat lodge to cleanse themselves both physically and spiritually.[18] After such cleansing they attempt to contact the spirit world through ritualistic ceremonies that involve chanting, repetitive prayers, drumming, dancing, blowing on pipes, and offerings to the spirits. The purpose of such offerings is to secure health, wealth, and success, or even to articulate a curse on someone. Though the activities of the medicine man seem to cover more areas than those of the shaman, both are mainly involved in helping their people communicate with the spirit world and enlist its help in order to liberate themselves. The main function of both shamans

18. Schaefer, "A Biblical Look," 13–14.

and medicine men in the aboriginal world is to enable people to be liberated; they act as salvific agents.

Even though aboriginals do not have codified written scriptures, their myths, totems, rituals, ceremonies, shamans, and medicine men provide effective ways not only to give expression to their quest but also to achieve its objectives. This brings us to a description of the way of their quest.

THE WAY OF THE ABORIGINAL QUEST

Aboriginals throughout the world, including the North American Native Indians, do not constitute a homogeneous religious community. They are made up of various clans and tribes who are culturally diverse. They live in isolation in different parts of different continents, having faced, and still facing, several challenges. Some of them have even been challenged with regard to their identity as a people group and their right to live in their own lands. Amidst such a mosaic multiplicity of aboriginals, we can nonetheless discern a salvific quest, the quest of a people who find themselves caught up in a predicament and striving to orchestrate a way out of it. This way has some distinctive features.

A Way that Resorts to a Higher Being

The aboriginal way commences with venerating earth and nature, but goes beyond it by resorting to a Higher Being. African aboriginals describe such a being as "All-Powerful One," "Creator," "One who is met everywhere," and "the One who exists by himself: The High."[19] Among the North American Sioux Indians, this being is known as Waka, among the Algonquin, Orenda, and among the Inuit, Sila, who communicates with humans through storms, snow, and rain. The Iroquois, who originally occupied the eastern part of the North American continent extending into Canada, believe in a powerful "Great Spirit" (*Ha-wen-e-yu*) who rules and administers the world. The core aspiration of these aboriginal peoples is to remain in harmony with this being. They believe that such harmony will enable them to have an abundant life, generate tribal harmony, and bring success in their hunting, fishing, or farming. But disasters like droughts, ruined crops, hunting failures, storms, sickness, defeat in tribal wars, and premature death make them realize that there is something fundamentally wrong, something that cannot be attributed to "Mother Earth" or the elements of nature, for these are divinely ordained. They come to the realization that the root cause of such calamities lies in themselves: their disharmony with the flow of the cosmic Higher Being. In their view, such waywardness has spiritual roots. The Iroquois, interestingly, trace the existence of evil in this world to the brother of the Great Spirit, *Ha-ne-go-ate-gah*, which means "evil minded." In their view, both the Great Spirit and his evil brother have invisible agents constituting a lower class of spiritual beings, either good or evil. The evil brother and his lesser invisible evil agents are in the business of enticing

19. Fisher, *Living Religions*, 52.

humans to live in disharmony with the Great Spirit.[20] In the context of this worldview, the conflict between good and evil spirit beings explains the root cause of the human predicament. In order to get out of such a predicament, the aboriginal people need to be involved in a type of spiritual warfare.[21] They must first of all choose between the Great Spirit and his evil-minded brother, and then resort to the Great Sprit. They believe that the soul is immortal; that they will be judged by the Great Spirit at death, and punished or rewarded. Fear of this judgment motivates them to live a life that is morally clean.

Taboos play a significant role in this endeavor. Many taboos may be taken as indicative of the belief that the higher being demands purity, but the purity that is demanded is not always clearly moral; it may include physical or hygienic cleanliness. However, we must keep in mind that in this worldview, there is no distinction between the moral and the physical. For instance, contact with a dead body or a menstruating woman is taken to be impure, both hygienically and morally. Some taboos act as means to keep oneself both physically and morally pure, and thereby facilitate cordial relationship with the higher being. This in turn enables one to be liberated.

A Way that Links the Human with the Spirit World

When the High God is viewed as transcendent and aloof from humans the concept of a mediator between the two becomes necessary. Aboriginals resort mainly to animals, birds, trees, and humans to mediate. The aboriginal worldview does not make a marked distinction between the animal, plant, and human kingdoms, since all of the beings in them are spiritual at the core. Hence there is an underlying affinity among them. In view of this fact, when the aboriginal individual, family, clan, or tribe selects an animal, plant, or bird as a mediator, they believe it to be capable of such a function because it is akin both to them and to the higher being. Moreover, when a shaman or medicine man is picked out as the mediator, the selection is based on the conviction that he is able to communicate with the spirit world. This is why a shaman, even before he gets into the ecstatic trance that transfers him to the spirit world, purifies himself in the sweat lodge. Such purification not only protects him from the evil spirits but also enables him to have intimate contact with the spirit world and ultimately with the higher being. But such mediation, whether effected through a plant, bird, animal, or human being, is orchestrated through an arduous and meticulous enactment of rituals.

A Ritualistic Way

The aboriginal way is a very ritualistic way that depends on ceremonies in which the community participates. Such ritualistic ceremonies usually include songs, chants, and dances, but they are not mere entertainment. Rituals are many and varied, but

---

20. Ruvolo, "Summary of Native American Religions." See also Carmody and Carmody, *Ways to the Center*, 47.

21. Ibid.

most of them have a spiritual undertone and salvific purpose. Myths enable those who hear the myth to do what it calls for, and rituals are meant to internalize the message of the myths so that it is practiced. Karen Armstrong points out that, in the ancient world, "without ritual, myths made no sense and would remain as opaque as a musical score, which is impenetrable to most until interpreted instrumentally."[22]

Ritual ceremonies also play a vital role in the journey of life of aboriginals in the form of rites of passage connected with the cycle of birth, puberty, marriage, and death. Since each of these is taken to be the threshold to a new stage in life, help from the spirits becomes a necessity. Rituals are supposed to please these spirits, secure their help, and thereby enable the people to face each new chapter in life with confidence. Some of the North American Indian rituals and ceremonies also aim at generating life-impacting visions. For instance, when a young aboriginal needs a vision at a critical stage in his life, he resorts to the vision quest ritual. This ritual enables him to receive a vision of the spirit that will help and guide him as he attains adulthood, and as such it plays a significant role in the life of both the young man and his family or tribe. The vision he receives in the practice of the ritual gives him a new identity as a spiritually equipped adult and obligates the family or community to recognize him as such. Rituals in the aboriginal community are meant to provide the practical means for an individual, family, or community to make contact with the spirit world, achieve harmony with the higher being, and thereby enjoy a life freed from the onslaughts of evil spirits.

The resort to a higher being, dependency on mediation, and ritualistic practices are all geared to free the aboriginals from the predicament in which they perceive themselves to be and give them an abundant life. This is precisely where Christ becomes relevant to the aboriginal quest.

THE RELEVANCE OF CHRIST TO THE ABORIGINAL QUEST

Noah Augustine, a Mi'kmaq Indian, responds to Christianity thus: "Rather than going to Church, I attend a sweat lodge; rather than accepting bread and toast from the Holy Priest, I smoke a ceremonial pipe to come into Communion with the Great Spirit; rather than kneeling with my hands placed together, I let sweetgrass be feathered over my entire being for spiritual cleansing and allow the smoke to carry my prayers into the heavens. I am Mi'kmaq and this is how we pray."[23]

Augustine prefers his religion to Christianity on the grounds of ritual. One can understand his preference. He comes from a religious tradition that gives a significant role to ritualistic practice as a means to satisfy one's spiritual aspirations. He finds that experiencing the sweat lodge, smoking the ceremonial pipe, and being feathered with sweetgrass is more rewarding than going to church, partaking in the Mass, and penitently praying. What must be noted is that he takes the Christian rituals to be of the same type as aboriginal rituals. These Christian practices, though ritualistic in some

---

22. Armstrong, *Case for God*, xii.

23 Augustine, "Grandfather was a Knowing Christian."

sense, do not fall into the same category as aboriginal rituals. The latter are a means to obtain the favor of the spirit world; they serve as a means of liberation. On the other hand, the Christian rituals are not taken as a means to liberate oneself. Salvation in Christianity is a free gift from God. Hence these rituals are a response to God's grace through Christ. Of course, they can become empty formalities in the absence of a relationship with Christ. It is Christ who satisfies, not the rituals. Perhaps part of the reason for Augustine's lack of interest in Christ lies in the way Christianity was presented to him; there is always the possibility for Christ to be buried under the meticulous performance of rituals. Mere "Churchianity" that involves pharisaical praying or meticulous observance of the Lord's Supper without knowing the Lord of the supper naturally amounts to empty ritualistic performance. In any case, Augustine's preference for indigenous over Christian rituals shows that he is depending on the rituals to satisfy his quest; he is truly questing. When one prefers Gatorade over water, it does not mean that one is not thirsty. The aboriginal preoccupation with rituals indicates an underlying salvific quest. This cannot be satisfied through rituals either indigenous or Christian, but only by appropriating God's gift of salvation through Christ.

The sacrifice of animals, grain, and sometimes even humans has been practiced in many religions. But sacrifice seems to be very rare in Native Indian religions. Perhaps this is due to the belief that the life of animals, plants, and humans are sacred since they are believed to be spirit-infused. But when the totem animal of a tribe is killed, the act is taken to be a sacrifice of the animal for the members of the tribe, and its meat is taken with trepidation and thanksgiving. Such a practice is to honor the animal that gave its life for the tribe, an "acknowledgement of the tragic fact that life depends upon the destruction of other creatures."[24] This practice shows that long before Christ's sacrificial death, people seem to have had some insight into the significance and efficacy of sacrificial death. The totem animal's death for the sake of the tribe seems to foreshadow what Christ, the Lamb of God, did for all humanity.

Purification is one of the vital stages in the spiritual journey of an aboriginal. Rituals and ceremonies connected especially with the sweat lodge are meant to purify a person both externally and internally. The cleansing that occurs to the body when one sweats in the lodge pertains to the external. Sickness in this context is taken to be not merely a bodily ailment but a spiritual defect. It is caused by evil spirits polluting a person, hence the remedy is purification. Rituals are also used as an offering to secure the help of good spirits in order to ward off the attack of evil spirits. Such purification rituals are meant to heal the sick, provide spiritual cleansing, and receive a new name and thereby a new identity as a purified person. Receiving a new name stands for a personality overhaul that is spiritually based. Offering to the good spirits in order to ward off evil spirits is essentially a spiritual confrontation. The readiness of the aboriginals to undergo the torturous experience of the sweat lodge indicates how much they yearn to be purified. They realize that such purification is vital to achieve harmony with the spirit world and be freed from their predicament. It is here that

24. Armstrong, *Case for God*, 6.

Christ can fulfill their yearnings. For Christ on the cross took upon himself the sin and sickness of all humanity, including that of the aboriginals (Isa 53:4–5), and through his name, and the faith that is made possible through him, brings healing to the sick (Acts 3:16). When an aboriginal enters the sweat lodge, he or she is yearning for a new name and a new identity entailed by the spiritual overhaul accomplished through purification. This is what Christ provides through his grace. When a person is in Christ, he or she is a new creature, born again (2 Cor 5:17); one's sins are all forgiven and is purified" (1 John 5; 7). Jesus gives that person a new name and a new identity (Rev 2:1). Moreover, one need not sweat in the lodge in order to please the good spirits and ward off the evil ones; Jesus on the cross crushed Satan, the source of all evil and the chief among evil spirits. When we submit ourselves to God and resist the devil with the power of Christ, the devil flees (Jas 4:7). When we put on the full armor of God (Eph 6:11), we are not only well protected from evil but also have the weaponry to fight the enemy. For Christ who is in us is greater than any power in the world (1 John 4:4). Remarkably, long before Christ, these people in such remote areas of the world were yearning for what Christ accomplished on the cross with the same yearning that characterizes the people of every faith community.

The search for mediators is another area where Christ becomes relevant to the aboriginal salvific quest. The resort to a mediator, whether it is a totem animal, bird, or plant, a shaman or medicine man, is mainly in order to obtain help so as to be freed from one's predicament and attain a fuller, more satisfying life. In hopes of achieving this objective, aboriginals resort to mediators who meet two requirements. First, they must be kin to humanity. For aboriginals, not only shamans and medicine men but also totem animals, birds, and plants are their ontological kin. All are akin in that they are all spirit-infused. Secondly, these mediators should be adequately equipped to make contact with the spirit world, ward off the evil spirits, and eventually reach the higher being who is the source of salvation. The aboriginals believe that their totems, as well as the shamans and medicine men, meet these criteria. What is significant is that Christ, being both human and divine, ideally meets the aboriginal specifications. But whereas shamans and medicine men must purify themselves in order to accomplish their task, Christ, being sinless, does not need to purify himself. He is fully equipped on account of his humanity and divinity to accomplish the task of mediation.

What happens to a person after death has not been a popular preoccupation of aboriginals. They have been concerned mainly with confronting the challenges of this life. There has been no well-developed doctrine of life after death; some aboriginals believe in reincarnation, while others believe that humans return as ghosts, or that people go to another world. But Native Indians seem to have a lingering fear of the dead and have many taboos with regard to treatment of the dead. These are meant to prevent the dead troubling the living. Indians seem to believe that when a person dies, one part of the soul that gives life dies with the body, while the other part wanders around until it enters the land of the dead. Often offerings such as food and drink or even living sacrifices are made to appease the wandering soul and persuade it to enter the land of the dead.[25] With the passage of time, whether or not due to the impact of Christian eschatology, other concepts concerning life after death found a place in aboriginal religions. During the late nineteenth century, the Ghost Dance cult presented an eschatology that is worth noting.

Known as the messiah to his followers, Wovoka (who also went by Jack Wilson), was a Paiute mystic from western Nevada who lived from about 1856 to 1932. After he claimed to experience a vision during an eclipse of the sun in the late 1880s, Wovoka began to weave together various cultural strains into the Ghost Dance religion, which spread among many tribes across the American west. He proclaimed that the earth would soon perish and then come alive again in a pure, aboriginal state. Whites would vanish, leaving Native Americans, both living and dead, to live in a land of material abundance, spiritual renewal, and immoral life; an eternal existence free from suffering. Wovoka's prophecies stressed the link between righteous behavior and imminent salvation. Salvation was not to be passively awaited but welcomed by a regime of ritual dancing and upright moral conduct. Wovoka also discouraged the practice of mourning because the dead would soon be resurrected, demanding instead the performance of prayers, meditation, chanting, and especially dancing, through which one might briefly die and catch a glimpse of the paradise to come.[26] Such eschatology indicates a concern not only for this life, but life after death. Aboriginals also seem to realize that how they live their life before death determines their life after death, and that they need to resort to a messiah to enable them to live in a way that will lead to a life of a different and superior order, an ideal life in an ideal world. This is what Christ came to accomplish: to give eternal life.

This survey of aboriginal religiosity, though cursory, brings to light certain significant points of interest. First of all, just because it is prehistoric and preliterate, does not make aboriginal religiosity primitive or ignorant. In fact, long before the concept of a transcendent being developed in the so-called sophisticated religions, aboriginals had a fairly clear notion of such a being in their High God. Moreover, their resort to shamans and medicine men as mediators to communicate with such a being and be freed from their predicament, their insistence on purification, their ritualistic totem animal sacrifices, and their resort to messiahs to assure them of a fuller life after death, all seem to suggest that, like other religious communities, the aboriginals also were, and still are, searching for Christ.

25. Hopfe, *Religions of the World*, 51.

26. Public Broadcasting Service, "New Perspectives on the West: Wovoka"; Last of the Independents, "Wounded Knee: The Ghost Dance."

11

Now What?

EVEN THOUGH RELIGION MAY be characterized as a quest, the human quest is not to be reduced to the quest of religions. The people who associate themselves with religions are no doubt involved in a quest. They are trying their best to find a way out of the predicament in which they perceive themselves to be. The Confucian "Way of Deliberating Tradition," the Taoist "Way of flowing with Tao," the Buddhist "Middle Path," and the Islamic "Way to peace (Salam) through submission to Allah," are typical examples of people from various faith groups involved in such a quest striving to find a way out. But, the quest was there before the rise of organized religions and will continue even if our contemporary scientific world sees their demise. The rationale for such a claim arises from the very makeup of human beings. In a sense, no religious endeavor, whether rudimentary or sophisticated, is merely a product of human ingenuity impelled by sociological, economic, political, or even theological factors. To deny such a claim is to pluck out of human personhood its core characteristic, that which distinguishes humans from all other living creatures. Every human being is made in God's image. Despite the fact that God's image has been distorted, the image is still there. A broken mirror will reflect a distorted image, but it is still an image. Our reflection of God's image is there as long as God does not give up on us, and he never does. We may even break the mirror and thus not see the image. But that does not mean the image is gone; what is needed is a new mirror! An image's identity lies in its reflection of the original; it is intended to reflect the original. The human being, as God's created image, is geared to reflect God. The religious quest exhibits the effort of humans to reflect the divine as best as possible in whatever way they conceive it.

But care should be taken not to reduce the quest to an instinct or biological disposition. It was Charles Darwin who popularized such a perspective on human religiosity. His argument was based on analogical reasoning. He compared human religious devotion to that of a dog's instinctive devotion to its master.[1] The comparison was possible for he worked within an evolutionary paradigm that took the difference

---

1. Darwin, *Origin of Species*, 470.

between the dog and the human being to be one of degree; one is more evolved than the other, and the behavior of both could be explained through laws of biology.

Building on Darwin's view, several biologists and psychologists have attempted to explain away human religiosity in terms of biological and neurological predispositions. Richard Dawkins, a British evolutionary biologist and popular science author, is a reputed propagandist of such a strategy. Based on his view that evolution is gene-centered, he proposes that "meme," a word he coined, is the cultural counterpart of the biological gene.[2] Using this concept, he attempts to describe how evolutionary patterns might be extended to explain the spread and development of cultural ideas. He describes meme as a cultural entity, a fundamental idea, or unit of information that one may consider as a replicator. He claims that people can view certain cultural entities as replicable since humans have evolved as efficient imitators, as copiers of information and behavior. Just as genes propagate themselves through eggs or sperm, memes propagate themselves from person to person through imitation. This provided him a framework for a hypothesis of cultural evolution analogous to gene-propagated biological evolution. The analogy between genes and memes allowed him to claim that religious devotion is an instinctive behavior caused by a "God meme."[3] Biologists and behavioral psychologists, developing on Dawkin's view, have been and are still trying to provide a physiological basis for human religiosity. Blackmore's *The Meme Machine* is a typical example of such an attempt. Any human activity, whether it is literary, scientific, or religious no doubt has a biological basis, since it involves the brain. But the question is whether human religiosity can be reduced to a mere instinct that drives people to be deceived into believing in God. In trying to provide a biological basis for religious behavior, Dawkins dismisses religion as "God Delusion" in his book of the same name.[4] His endeavor is a typical example of the reductionist strategy that may be formulated thus:

> In attempting to understand something, say "X," one selects a method that seems most appropriate (in some cases the only one available) way of understanding "X." When such a method, say "M," turns out to be successful in that it has delivered or could deliver, if adequately developed, a satisfactory understanding of "X," call it "U," then a further claim is made: that on the strength of "M," "X" is nothing but "U;" that "X" is nothing but one understands or could understand "X" to be through a method or set of methods, "M."[5]

The strategy pertains to two conceptual realms: the methodological and the ontological. The articulation and assessment of method M to understand X belongs to the methodological realm, while the claim that X is nothing but what is understood through M (U) is ontological in nature. When adopting such a strategy, methodology seems to determine ontology. The problem of the strategy lies in its reductionist aftermath. One

---

2. Dawkins, *The Selfish Gene*, 11, 19.

3. Kelly, *Out of Control*, 360.

4. Dawkins, *The God Delusion*.

5. Kulathungam, "Scientific Understanding and Christian Faith," 25.

is entitled to claim that X has been or could be understood through a method. But on the strength of such a methodological accomplishment, to make the further claim that X is nothing but what is or could be understood through a method, amounts to reducing the ontological to the methodological by providing a methodological criterion for an ontological claim. Such a strategy reduces the analysis to merely a methodology, and based on the success of a method, disregards the ontological claim. Rodney Stark and Roger Finke identify such a fallacy when they point out that some social scientists claim that if the actions of those who believe could be explainable through natural laws, then their faith is nothing but naturalistic phenomenon.[6]

In order to understand human religiosity, Dawkins draws an analogy between gene-centered biological and meme-centered cultural evolution. He notes that life evolves by the differential survival of replicating entities. In *The Extended Phenotype* he describes natural selection as the process whereby replicators propagate each other. Interpreting animal behavior in terms of natural selection, he claims that gene is the principal unit of selection in evolution. Taking human religiosity as a facet of animal behavior leads him to conclude that religious behavior can best be understood in terms of meme analogous to the gene.[7] On the grounds of his methodological accomplishment, he proclaims that human religiosity is nothing but meme-driven instinctive behavior. In this, one is attempting to provide a methodological criterion for an ontological claim. Religious people, whatever their religion may be, take the "God" they resort to, whether it be one or many, personal or impersonal, immanent or transcendent, as real. To deny such a reality, on the grounds that human religiosity is nothing but meme-driven instinctive behavior, glaringly exhibits the reductionist fallacy.

To the question as to how memes propagate and transmit themselves in religious communities, Dawkins resorts to viral infections. He reduces religions to "mind parasites" and the God meme to an infectious "virus." He points out that the faith of religious people is one of the world's great evils, comparable to the smallpox virus but harder to eradicate.[8] But why is it harder to eradicate such faith than the deadly smallpox virus? History records several onslaughts against religion and many prophetic proclamations regarding its imminent demise. But religion is still with us. Human religiosity is much more than instinctive behavior. It exhibits itself essentially as a quest—a quest to be freed from the predicament in which humans see themselves, a quest that resorts to a reality, "God," to get out of such a predicament. Such a quest is incurably dissatisfied with and even revolts against anything less than what it seeks for.[9] Such a quest cannot be reduced to mere propagation of memes from person to person through instinctive imitation, nor can it be eradicated through viral medications.[10] It is very much part and parcel of human personhood. It is global in scope, both in time and space, and

6. Stark and Finke, *Acts of Faith*, 20.

7. Dawkins, *The Extended Phenotype*.

8. Dawkins, "Is Science a Religion?" para. 1.

9. Radhakrishnan and Moore, *A Source of Indian Philosophy*, 92.

10. Dawkins, *The Selfish Gene*, 192.

can be destroyed if and only if all humanity is eradicated. A human being made in God's image cannot but quest for God. Only God can satisfy such a quest. It is in such a context that a savior like God in Christ becomes relevant to the quest of humanity.

The history of religion is replete with people trying to diagnose the predicament in which they perceive themselves to be and find ways and means to get out of it. The Vedic seers, the Upanishadic thinkers, Buddha, Lao-Tzu, Confucius, Guru Nanak, and Muhammad are some who have figured prominently in such a quest. We have so far tried to determine how Christ is relevant to the quest of specific faith communities, like Hindu, Sikh, and Islam. But from a cumulative perspective, there are some factors that further indicate how Christ is uniquely relevant to the human quest.

Chapter 2 presented Christ as one who is not part of the quest, and who is well-equipped to satisfy those involved in the quest because of his unique personhood. Our journey through the lives of the prominent leaders of the various faith groups shows us how sincere their quest was, how insightfully they diagnosed the cause of the human predicament, and how masterfully they articulated their respective ways of liberation. Karl Jaspers described the individuals who spearheaded the revolutionary religious movements of the Axial Age (800–200 BCE) as "paradigmatic personalities."[11] Such a description could apply to the articulators of the quest of most of the faith groups we have surveyed. These personalities exemplify what a human being could or should be; they are archetypal models. People tried to emulate them with the hope of attaining what they had achieved. But these paradigmatic figures, though endowed with superhuman powers, were still humans. Even though some of them, like Buddha and Confucius, eventually came to be deified, they never claimed divinity. When Upanisadic thinkers, like Sankara, claimed that humans are essentially divine, they did not place themselves in a special social class to be worshiped as God. All these figures, however prominent and venerated they may be in their respective communities, were essentially part of the human religious quest. The story of their lives tells us that every one of them faced a crisis, realized that they were in a predicament, and attempted to trace its cause and find a cure for it.

In order for a cure to be effective, the sickness first has to be diagnosed correctly. Only then can the cure be prescribed as the proper medicine for the sickness. It is in the diagnosis of the sickness of humanity that the Axial Age becomes significant. Karl Jaspers demarcates 800 to 200 BCE as the Axial Age, but picks out the sixth century as the pivotal period of this age.[12] This period saw the rise of new religions, such as Buddhism and Jainism in India. Lao-Tzu and Confucius gave Chinese religions an identity of their own as Taoism and Confucianism. Vedic Hinduism received a theological overhaul through Upanisadic thinkers like Sankara. Greek philosophical speculation blossomed, spearheaded by Milesian thinkers like Thales and Anaximander. Hebrew prophets such as Jeremiah and Ezekiel conveyed a message to the people of Israel that, although not well received by them, needed to be proclaimed at that time.

---

11. Jaspers, *The Great Philosophers*, 99–105.
12. Jaspers, *The Origin and Goal of History*, 6.

Zarathustra's ancient monotheistic teachings were reorganized and reformed in Persia. It is most significant that these developments covered a large geographical area, extending from the Mediterranean to China. They came out of completely diverse cultures and were spearheaded by individuals who did not know one another. Yet there was a commonality underlying these developments. Though they could be described as religious, they were not theistic in that they did not give much prominence to God or gods. Buddha and Mahavira, the founder of Jainism, proposed a way of liberation based on self-effort rather than dependence on gods. Confucius and Lao-Tzu articulated a politico-religious strategy that provided a way of life that facilitated the Chinese to free themselves from the turbulence of their time. Greek philosophy was more concerned with cosmological than theological issues. Upanisadic Hinduism no doubt acknowledged the divine but placed it within the human. According to Vedantic thinkers like Sankara, humans had to realize the divinity in them rather than worship it as a transcendent being. Only Zoroastrian reformers and Hebrew prophets could be taken as theistic, in the sense that they worked with the conviction of a transcendent God. Hence, we cannot choose the belief in God or gods as the underlying common denominator. But these so-called religious movements, whether they were theistic or nontheistic, acknowledged that there was something rotten in the state of humankind, and that the core cause for this lay in the human being and not somewhere else. The leaders of these movements came out of a world where several gods and elements of nature were worshiped. These amoral and anti-moral gods competed against one another and expected their devotees to please them through offerings and sacrifices. Devotees feared to displease them and thereby suffer the consequences. The catastrophic natural disasters were traced to the violent actions of angry nature deities like sun and rain gods. But the articulators of the Axial Age sidetracked such a diagnosis of the human predicament. They pointed out that the core reason humans were in bondage lay within themselves—their moral failure and spiritual deficiency. This they proposed to be the "sin" that besets humanity.[13] It is described in different ways. Buddha identifies this "sin" as human craving. Lao-Tzu thought of it as swimming against the life-giving flow of Tao. Upanisadic thinkers traced it to spiritual ignorance which caused a false sense of identity. But all these paradigmatic religious leaders agreed on one thing: the cause for the human predicament lies in the character and conduct of the human being—the "sin" in the human. How did these leaders, coming from such diverse cultures and countries, reach this common conclusion?

We noted earlier that general revelation also has an internal aspect; one could have insights about the divine not only by looking out at the world and its wonders, but also by being sensitive to the dictates of one's conscience. The Bible states that those who are not aware of God's law could still follow the requirements of the law enabled by their conscience, which shows them that their actions are right or wrong (Rom 2:14–15). These paradigmatic figures realized that the character and conduct of their community, including themselves, was morally defective, and this was causing them

13. Stark, *Discovering God*, 20.

to be in bondage. They seemed to have reached this conclusion not on the grounds of any preset universally accepted moral code, for they had none. Their conscience was the determining factor.

It is significant that the leaders of the Axial Age gave insight into the cause of the human predicament by being sensitive to the dictates of their own conscience. This is an ideal example of the working of the internal aspect of general revelation. Moreover, such a diagnosis pointed out that it is human "moral deficiency," "spiritual bankruptcy," "sin"—call it whatever you wish—that is causing the problem. It is precisely at this point that Christ becomes relevant to the Axial Age.

If the Axial Age had traced the cause of the human predicament to the anger of amoral gods, or the devastative actions of divinities that personified elements of nature, or the devotee's failure to practice rituals properly, then Christ as the cure for such a problem would not be very appropriate. But the religions of the Axial Age identified the cause as being "sin" that pertains to human moral failure or spiritual deficiency. Hence, in order to eradicate the cause, one had to deal with the human being. The connection between human "sin" and "salvation" became evident. The various ways of salvation proposed by Hindu gurus, Buddha, Lao-Tzu, and Confucius were all meant to find a way out of "sin" that pertains to the human being. It is here that Christ as Savior may be introduced as the one who could cure the sickness of humanity.

But before bringing Christ into the picture, we need to take into consideration certain significant developments in the concept of "sin" that, in fact, had their roots in the Axial Age. During the sixth century BCE, when the world at large saw the blossoming of new religions and the reformation of older religions, the Hebrew prophets conveyed difficult messages to the Israelites concerning "sin" and its "cure."

The biblical Old Testament prophets Jeremiah, Ezekiel, and Daniel belonged to the sixth century, and lived during extremely turbulent times. The Israelites came under Babylonian captivity following the siege and destruction of Jerusalem in 586 BCE, with many people being taken to foreign lands. But more than the challenges they faced as a nation in exile, they had a serious problem that directly concerned them as human beings. These prophets pointed out, in rather harsh terms, that the people were caught up in "sin." "Sin" according to the prophets was not mere moral failure or spiritual deficiency but that which separates or alienates people from God, who is holy and righteous. For instance, the prophet Jeremiah called his people backsliders thirteen times and transgressors against God Jehovah fifty-three times. He called the people to repentance (Jer 7:2–7) and pleaded with them forty-seven times to return to the Lord. The seers of the Axial Age identified "sin" as pertaining to the human being's moral character and conduct, but the prophets went a step further. They made it clear that sin alienates people from the one and only true and holy God, Jehovah. Noticing that some Jews were involved in idol worship, the prophets made a scathing attack these practices. Jeremiah proclaimed a prophetic statement in Aramaic Greek, the only verse in the book of Jeremiah that is not in the Hebrew language. This verse highlights the fate of gods worshiped as idols: "These gods who did not make the heavens and the earth will perish from the earth and from under the heavens" (Jer 10:11). One may wonder why it is only this statement in Aramaic Greek while the rest of the book of Jeremiah is in the Hebrew language. Perhaps it was meant to show people outside the Jewish world the disruptive impact of idol worship. Jeremiah and the prophets definitively pointed that such idol worship broke the relationship between God and people, whether they were Jewish or not. "Idol" in this context is not a mere image or sculpture, but that which attempts to substitute for God; it could be a system of belief, a ritualistic practice, a cultural tradition, a religious organization, an edifice, or even a profound theological stance. In trying to bridge the gap between humans and God, these prophets made a direct connection between human "sin" and "transcendence"— a "transcendence" that referred to a personal, holy, and righteous God who desired humans to relate to him so they could have a wholesome life.[14] "Sin" is that which disrupts the relationship between such a God and humans. Hence, the prophets made a passionate plea to the Israelites to repent and return to the Lord. Such a plea also contained a positive prognosis in that it proclaimed the coming of a Messiah who would ultimately be the cure for sin-ridden humanity. Jeremiah prophesied that the Lord would raise the Messiah from the house of David and that he would be a king who would reign wisely and do what was right (Jer 23:5). The foreshadowed Messiah could well refer to Jesus Christ, for he came from the house of David (Matt 1) and one day in the future, the kingdom of the world will become the kingdom of the Lord Jesus, who will reign forever (Rev 11:15).

It is most significant that there seems to be an underlying connection between the pivotal sixth century of the Axial Age and the Christ event. The Hebrew prophets, as well as the seers of the various religions outside the Jewish world, diagnosed the human predicament in terms of something that pertains to the human being, whether it is taken as moral failure or revolt against God. The various religious founders and reformers made sincere efforts to find a way out. Such a strategy still continues. Through sincere efforts, humans try to reach "god," whether that "god" is a personal transcendent being or a cosmic impersonal spiritual force or something resident in the innermost part of the human being.

The Persian Sufi mystic Bayazef Al-Bastami (804–874 CE) made an insightful comment about his spiritual journey: "For thirty years I sought God until I recognized that God was the seeker and I the one sought."[15] Such an insight gives us the appropriate conceptual framework to relate Christ to the human religious quest, especially to that of the faith groups we have surveyed. As a result of the spiritual crisis their leaders experienced, they sought a way out; they sought to reach their "god." On the other hand, God in Christ sought humanity. God is the seeker and humans are the sought. The cure came as a result of divine rather than human diagnosis and prognosis.

A cure can tell us something about the nature and seriousness of a sickness. For instance, when an orthopedic surgeon suggests that knee replacement surgery is the best option, the patient realizes what is really wrong with the knee. The patient's

---

14. Schwartz, "The Age of Transcendence," 1–7.

15. Schwartz, *The Other Islam*, 44.

diagnosis of the problem as muscle pain has to give way to the surgeon's diagnosis. The cure that the surgeon proposes is indicative of the nature of the sickness. Christ, as cure for humanity's sickness, tells us something of the nature and seriousness of the sickness. Christ is God incarnate. If he had to give up his glory, become part of humanity, and carry its sin on the cross, it means that humans are critically sick. The high cost of the cure indicates the seriousness of the sickness. The fact that God in Christ had to sacrifice himself shows the gravity of the sickness of sin.[16] The seriousness of sin is seen not so much in the method of Christ's execution on the cross, however brutal it may be, but that God in Christ was executed. It is not what happened at the cross but who happened to be on the cross that matters.

If God had to become the cure for the sickness of humans, it means that they are incapable of curing their sickness. The incapacitating effect of sin renders the rationale for the claim that the whole of humanity is inherently sinful (Rom 5:12–21). The Bible describes humans as being dead in sin (1 Cor 15:22; Eph 2:1). The Old Testament talks about sin's grip on humans (Ps 51:5), but it is Paul of the New Testament who elaborates on it. Why so late? Christ as the cure had to be revealed in order for humans to truly understand the crippling effect of sin. The aggressive and costly nature of the cure, seen in Christ's horrific death on the cross, was a powerful pointer to cause humans to realize how sick they are in "sin." Perhaps this is an instance of God's revelatory strategy through "divine accommodation."[17] Christ on the cross, dying for humanity's sin, shows clearly that humans desperately need divine help; human effort, however efficacious it may be, cannot cure the sickness of sin. His agony on the cross stands out as the catastrophic crisis of his life, although it was really not of his making. It was brought about by the sin that plagues all humanity. "He himself bore our sins in his body on the tree, so that we might die to sin and live for righteousness; by his wounds you have been healed" (1 Pet 2:2). Christ on the cross becomes the cure for humanity's disease, the way out of the human predicament.

Moreover, such a cure is enacted only by God without any human help. In order to appropriate such a cure and thereby be freed from the sickness of sin, the only avenue is "grace." Like many theological concepts, "grace" has a variety of meanings and nuances. The character and role of grace has been a matter of controversy even within Christianity. Without becoming entangled in the polemics of grace, we want to discover how divine grace liberates sin-ridden humanity.

The incapacitating impact of sin on humans makes all their attempts to free themselves through various ways, such as good deeds and religious practices, inadequate. It is precisely at this point that divine grace becomes absolutely necessary. Humans desperately need divine help enacted through grace. Such grace is God given and made possible by God the Son, Jesus Christ. It is grace of God in Jesus Christ (Rom 5:1–2; Gal 5:4).

---

16. Stott, *Cross of Christ*, 91–93.

17. Stark, *Discovering God*, 6.

First of all, such grace is not cheap. It cost God in Christ an incarnation, a crucifixion, and a resurrection to make possible the grace that would save humanity (Titus 2:11–14). Moreover, such an enactment of grace was not an afterthought. God had planned for the salvation of humans long before their fall into sin—in fact, even before the beginning of time (Titus 1:2).

God's grace through Jesus Christ is a spontaneous unmerited gift of divine favor—favor that is totally undeserved by humanity. The most appropriate response to such grace is faith—a faith that stands on the strength of God's grace alone and does not depend on deeds and devotion, however good they may be (Eph 2:8). Hence, faith is really trust in God and his grace.

Some of the ways of "salvation" that we surveyed exhibit a passionate plea for "grace." But such a plea for "grace" has to be understood in its proper context. The ways of salvation of the faith communities we examined were all articulated by seers and prophets who were part of the religious quest. These were all attempts to find a way out of the predicament the articulators perceived humans to be in; they all commenced with the human. The plea for "grace" arose from the hearts of people who were in desperate need of superhuman help. There is no doubt that such a plea was sincere. Nevertheless it was initiated by humans. On the other hand, the "grace" that is involved in the way of salvation that Christ provides is God initiated.

Moreover, the methods of liberation like good deeds, ritualistic practices, devotion, meditation, fasting, prayer, and spiritual knowledge are all based on the assumption that humans have the capacity to liberate themselves, at least to some extent. Such liberation is geared to culminate in attaining enlightenment (nirvana), escaping from the cycle of rebirths, (samsara), in realizing one's identity with cosmic reality (Brahman), in experiencing the blissful presence of God (Sat-Sit-Ananda), in achieving the peace (salam) that comes from total submission to Allah, or entering a paradise called "Pure Land" in the western sky. But in the meticulous practice of these methods, the devotees realize that they need something more; these strategies, however efficacious they may be, seem to be inadequate. No doubt they have a contribution to make in one's liberation, but one can never have an "assurance of salvation." There will always be a lingering doubt whether one's good deeds and religious practices are enough. Hence, the plea for "grace" arose out of the conviction that human effort is good but not good enough for one to be liberated. It must be noted that such a plea is really one for "mercy" and not for "grace" in the Christian sense of the term. The "grace" that figures in a paradigm which is founded on the conviction that human effort, though inadequate, is helpful for one's salvation is really "mercy."

Mercy plays a significant role in most religions. Islam addresses Allah as the "most merciful." Virtually every chapter in the Quran begins with the proclamation, "In the name of the All-Beneficent and Most Merciful." Early Buddhism, though nontheistic, describes Buddha as a compassionate being, whose mercy is evident in his passionate plea to his associates to follow the path he followed to attain liberation. The introduction of bodhisattvas in latter Buddhism makes "mercy" prominent in the Buddhist way of liberation. Bodhisattvas are compassionate beings who show their mercy by transferring their merit to those struggling to liberate themselves. Bhakti Hinduism portrays God as being all-loving, whose mercy could be acquired through sincere devotional worship. The Chinese resort to the popular goddess of mercy, Guanyin. The Hindu self-torture and offerings to gods in temples and shrines, the Muslim fasts during the month of Ramadan, the Sufi devotional dances, and the strenuous pilgrimages to holy places are all ideal examples of the human plea for "mercy." But we should not confuse such "mercy" with "grace"; they belong to entirely different paradigms. The "mercy" here is really merited divine favor. Human effort through good deeds and religious practices still has a part to play in human liberation. Since human contribution is felt to be inadequate, there is a plea for "mercy." "Mercy" is that which makes human effort adequate. On the other hand, "grace" is God initiated and is undeserved blessing freely bestowed on humans; it is unmerited divine favor.

The Bhakti school of Hinduism and the Pure Land Mahayana Buddhist sect have a concept of "grace" that seems to come closest to the Christian concept. But these two religious sects also belong to the paradigm that works on the conviction that human effort is at least partially instrumental in liberation. The Bhakti school came out of Ramanuja's theistic Vedanta. Ramanuja claimed that the worship of Vishnu, who he referred as Isvara, plays a significant role in one's liberation. Vishnu is the god who incarnates, and one of his incarnations is Rama. The Bhakti school resorts to Rama as the Savior. But how does he save? The school presents two ways. According to one group called the "Monkey school," just as a baby monkey clings to its mother, a devotee has to cling to Rama through devotional acts and good deeds. The other Bhakti school, called the "Cat school," claims that just as a kitten is carried by its mother, a devotee is carried by Rama and that all the work is done by Rama on behalf of the devotee.[18] Cat's school's way of salvation seems to suggest that it is by "grace," in this case Rama's grace, that one is liberated, and not by human effort. But on whom does Rama shower his grace? Rama is one of Vishnu's incarnations. Vishnu incarnates whenever unrighteousness abounds in the world and helps the righteous to overcome the unrighteous. According to Hinduism, the law of karma determines the destiny of every human being. One's deeds determine one's mode of existence. One joins the righteous based upon his or her good deeds of the past. Hence Rama's help of the righteous is really merited favor; it is conditioned by the good deeds of the righteous. Hence, the Bhakti Cat school presentation of Rama's "grace" is really Rama's "mercy." His mercy is confined to the "deserved" and not to all.

The plea for grace is also evident in the Latter Buddhist *Jodo Shin-Shu* sect, popularly known as the Pure Land sect. Amida Buddha, its central savior figure, vowed after his enlightenment that he would create a Pure Land, a paradise, and make a way for all to enter it. He realized that most needed help to attain enlightenment (nirvana). The rigorous meditative and moral path that orthodox Buddhism advocated was too difficult for most people. The Pure Land sect provided an easier way. A seeker first enters the Pure Land, which serves as a stepping stone to attain enlightenment

---

18. Otto, *India's Religion of Grace*, 57–58.

(nirvana). To enter this Land, Amida Buddha provided a sacred name, *Namu Amida Butsu*, shortened to *Nembutsu*. He granted this name as a gift to all, to be repeated with faith and gratitude, which would provide the assurance of entrance to the Pure Land. The creed of the sect is "We rely upon Amida Buddha with our whole heart for enlightenment in the life to come." Such a way seems to resemble closely the Christian way. Just like Christians resort to Christ, Buddhists resort to Amida Buddha. Merely repeating the sacred name, Nembutsu, without undergoing the rigors of meditation and arduous ritualistic practices, one may enter the Pure Land, the gateway to ultimate liberation. At first sight, it appears to be a way based on "grace," understood as unmerited favor. But we must note two features about this way. First, when Buddhists resort to Amida Buddha, they take refuge in the merit he has acquired through works, rather than to him as a person. The name Nembutsu denotes the embodiment of all the merit, the highest values and qualities he acquired in his long period of meditation and disciplined moral life. It is really the appropriation of Amida's merit, acquired through his good deeds, that allows the devotees to enter the Pure Land. Second, since the Pure Land is a paradise of supreme bliss devoid of any possibility of acquiring bad karma, the chances of devotees attaining enlightenment is increased, since in the Pure Land one is free from the temptation of doing bad deeds and returning to the cycle of rebirths. To enter the Pure Land, the devotees repeat the sacred name, depending on the good deeds of Amida. To then attain enlightenment, they depend on the avoidance of bad deeds which the Pure Land makes conducive. Hence, the merit of human effort is still very involved in the way of Jodo Shin-Shu. The "grace" that Amida Buddha renders comes out of the merit he has acquired through ages. Life in the Pure Land facilitates ultimate enlightenment by providing an environment conducive to avoidance of bad deeds. Hence the "grace" that is offered is merited favor, or "mercy."

"Mercy" is asked for on the grounds that human effort is felt to be inadequate or defective. Yet such effort is taken to be instrumental in liberation. "Grace," on the other hand, is given without stipulating human effort as a requirement; it is unconditional. Two very similar parables arising from two entirely different times and worlds are helpful to understand how "mercy" differs from "grace." The parable of Lost Son comes from a sacred Buddhist text, Lotus of the Good Law,[19] and the other is Jesus' parable of the Prodigal Son, as given in the Bible (Luke 15:11–32). Both stories are about a son who forfeited the privileges of his sonship and was separated from his father. The son in the Christian story squanders his patrimony in riotous living, while the son in the Buddhist story fails to acquire wealth, disappointing his father. Both leave their father's household, but eventually return to their fathers. In the Buddhist story, the son does not recognize the father but the father recognizes his son and desires him to become part of the family once again. Nevertheless, he makes his son undergo a long period of humble probationary service, working as a servant before raising him to the position he merits by his birth. On the other hand, the prodigal son in the Christian story squanders all that was given to him and later comes to his senses and returns to

19. de Bary et al., eds., *Sources of Indian Tradition*, 162–63.

his father. He confesses to his father that he is no longer worthy to be called his son and pleads with his father to show him mercy and make him one of the servants in the household. Instead, the father wholeheartedly welcomes him back as his son into the family and dresses him in fine clothes. Placing a ring on his finger, he declares with joy that his son who was dead is alive again. During the period of probationary service, the son in the Buddhist story gradually recognizes his father and faithfully performs his menial duties with the hope of gaining his father's favor. Ultimately his father shows him favor based on the son's performance as a servant—favor based on the merit of works. The son in the Christian story expected to gain his father's favor through working as a servant, while the father instead showed favor that was not based on merit. He accepted his son just as he was; it was unmerited favor or "grace." The son pleaded for mercy but was given grace. Favor within the framework that accepts the merit of works cannot be anything except merited favor. No doubt it is mercy that comes out of a loving and compassionate heart, but still does not amount to grace, which is unmerited favor. It is such "grace" that motivated former slave-trader John Newton to write the popular hymn, "Amazing Grace." In the same way that the father received his son just as he was, the grace of Jesus Christ saves anyone, in whatever condition he or she may be.

Christ seems relevant to the human religious quest in more than one way. He, being God incarnate even though fully human, is not part of the human quest. His way of salvation is both divinely orchestrated and humanly articulated in a manner humans can relate to. Christ did not save humanity while residing in his heavenly home. He came and dwelt among humans. It is a way where God seeks humans rather than humans seeking God. Moreover, the world at large was made aware even before the advent of Christ that the human predicament is caused by "sin" in the human. Such a diagnosis was pinpointed by the seers and prophets of the Axial Age. Furthermore, the cost of the cure indicated the seriousness of the disease. God the Son had to give up his glory and die for the sin of all humans on the cross. Christ, through his accomplishment on the cross, provides the cure for the disease. Moreover, anyone can appropriate the cure that Christ provides, for it is given on the grounds of unmerited favor: grace. This is why Christ is so relevant to the human quest.

Placing Christ in such a pivotal position in the quest of humanity demands a conceptual framework that commences at the grassroots level rather than one that is preoccupied with comparing religions as being true/false, better/best, or valid/invalid. The world is orchestrated by systems of belief, worldviews, and codes of conduct that are sustainable without Christ. Some of them were prevalent even before the advent of Christ. The pre- and non-Christian religions, some sects within Christendom, religiosities like the New Age movement, and nontheistic movements like secular humanism and atheism would all fall under the above-mentioned category. But the human religious quest is not confined to these. They may, of course, express the quest, but it really pertains to the people behind such systems. The quest that Jesus Christ satisfies is located in the people and not in the systems they orchestrate. The system is what results when the quest is wrestled with, articulated, and clothed in the language of a culture; it is the crystallization of aspirations that results through filters of society. As such, even Christianity is the product of an engagement of a culture meeting with Christ. Christianity as a system cannot be the answer to the quest but Christ could be. The people who, through such systems, seek to find a way out of the predicament in which they perceive themselves to be show definitive signs of needing him.

Moreover, when trying to relate Christ to the quest, one is sometimes tempted to separate the sheep from the goats, the super spiritual from the carnal, the elect from the damned, and the Christian from the non-Christian. Often the criteria of demarcation between such categories arises from warped theology, pharisaic perspectives, and even cultural biases. The world is non-Christian only in a historical sense. It is already in God's plan and purpose. God so loved the world—the entire world—that he gave his only begotten Son (John 3:16); it is the whole world for which Christ died. It is true that many, even within Christendom, have not accepted him and stubbornly refuse to do so. But, even they are within the saving work of Christ, not outside the ambit of his grace. Hence, those who have not yet accepted him are not enemies of the faith but family members in the making. Charles Wesley's hymn points this out well:

> The world He suffered to redeem;
> For all He hath the atonement made;
> For those that will not come to Him.
> The ransom of His life was paid.[20]

The relation we are trying to make between Christ and humanity has been established by Christ himself, by his death on the cross for all humanity. God the Son came to die so that he could satisfy the quest of sinful humanity. Perhaps, the world has best captured the point of the cross when it dismisses Christ on the cross as either a stumbling block or foolishness (1 Cor 1:18–23). Such a dismissal is not because Christ was illegally judged and murdered brutally on the cross. There are several who have gone to the gallows through illegal process and have died more tortuously than Christ. Those of the monotheistic mindset claiming that God is one and only one find accepting Jesus as God a stumbling block to their faith. The fact that God, who is eternal and almighty, could be killed is utter foolishness to the wisdom of the world. What makes Christ on the cross so controversial is the fact that he is God the Son. Such an act was absolutely necessary to satisfy the quest of humanity beset by the incapacitating impact of sin. This book commenced by citing Saddam Hussein's plea on his way to the gallows as exhibiting the quest of human beings striving to free themselves from the predicament in which they find themselves. It is such a quest that Christ fulfills; it is this which makes Christ relevant to the human quest. The picture below was painted by Salvador Dali in 1951, based on the sixteenth-century painting, St. John of the Cross. It is an ideal depiction of the relevance of Christ to the human quest. The absence of nails, crown of thorns, and blood highlights that it is not what happened at the cross but who happened to be on the cross that really makes the cross relevant to the human quest for salvation. There were two thieves who were also crucified with Jesus

---

20. Wesley, "Father, Whose Everlasting Love," 140.

but it is he who makes the cross at the center significant. In fact, the response of the two thieves to Jesus expresses humanity's response to what he offers; one thief hurled insults at him, while the other appealed to him at the point of death. Several grueling things happened to him at the cross and these have significance. For instance the Bible states that "by his stripes we are healed" but when understanding such a statement, we should place the stress on "his." In this picture, Jesus looks down from the cross, symbolic of God's infinite love and concern for helpless humans.

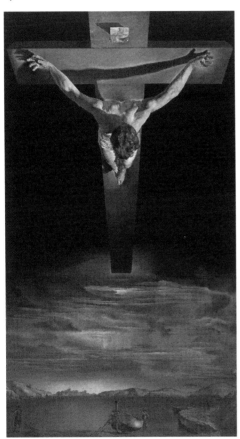

Christ on the cross (Christ of St. John of the Cross by Salvador Dali, 1951)

If Christ is so pivotal to the quest of humanity, those who are committed to him have an awesome task. Since the whole world is in God's purpose and plan of salvation, it is not surprising that he is at work in the lives of people, whether they are aware of it or not. Since Jesus died for the sin of all humanity, he is earnestly seeking to bring all to experience the salvation he has wrought. God is at work drawing people to Christ. In fact, when Christ is introduced to a person, one should remember that God has already been at work in the life and struggles of that person.

Sometimes a person outside the Christian world is equipped with the faith that brings him or her to Christ. Jesus said to a Roman centurion, who in Jewish eyes would be branded a Gentile pagan, "Truly, I say to you, not even in Israel have I found such faith" (Matt 8:10). Those of us who have lived with non-Christians can bear testimony to the faith that some of them exhibit. It is not surprising that spectacular miracles occur in most unexpected places, in so-called "pagan" quarters. But that does not mean that faith that comes from non-Christian and even Christian sources always makes one accept Christ. Once a rich young man came to Jesus to find out how he could inherit eternal life. When Jesus told the rich man to give up his wealth, he went away disappointed. His faith in wealth made him reject Christ. But the Bible states that Jesus loved him (Mark 10:17–23). Even those who reject him come under the embrace of his love. How God works in the lives of each person cannot be described in the same way. The process by which people find Christ does not have a set pattern.

It is hoped that such a presentation of Christ would encourage people of other faith communities, and even those who do not belong to any such community, to give some consideration to this person who occupies such a significant place in the quest of humanity. Just as one who is thirsty pauses with relief at the sight of water, anyone who is searching needs to find out whether Christ is relevant to their quest. The fact that Christ is well-equipped to satisfy the human quest on the grounds of his unique personhood and sacrificial death does not mean that "saviors" beside him are of absolutely no value in the salvific endeavor of humans. Their significance lies in the fact that their aspirations manifested in the articulation of their respective ways of salvation indicate how relevant Christ is to them. Our journey through the lives and mission of these "saviors" shows their role in articulating the way of the quest of humanity.

The quest of humanity clearly indicates that people are thirsty for a better quality of life both here and hereafter. It is in this context that the Bible ends with these words: "The Spirit and the Bride say 'Come!' And let him who hears say 'Come!' Whoever is thirsty let him come, and whoever wishes let him take the free gift of the water of life" (Rev 22:17).

Bibliography

Abdalati, Hammudah. *Islam in Focus*. Plainfield, IN: American Trust Foundation, 1996.

Abedi, Mehdi, and Gary Legenhausen, eds. *Jihad and Shahadat: Struggle and Martyrdom in Islam*. Houston: Institute for Research and Islamic Studies, 1986.

Achebe, Chinua. *No Longer at Ease*. New York: Fawcett, 1969.

Ahmadinejad, Mahmood. "Address by H. E. Dr. Mahmood Ahmadinejad, President of the Islamic Republic of Iran at the Sixtieth Session of the United Nations General Assembly." In *Islamic Republic of Iran Permanent Mission to the United Nations*, September 14, 2005: n.p. Online: http://www.iran-un.org/index.php?option=com_content&view=article&id=210:-sep-14-2005-address-by-he-dr-mahmood-ahmadinejad-president-of-the-islamic-republic-of-iran-at-the-sixtieth-session-of-the-united-nations-general-assembly-&catid=41:general-assembly&Itemid=54.

Al-Ghazali. *Inner Dimensions of Islamic Worship*. Translated by Muhtar Holland. Leicester, UK: Islamic Foundation, 1995.

Ali, Abdullah Yusuf, trans. *The Holy Qu'ran: Text, Translation and Commentary*. Brentwood, MD: Amana, 1989.

Andrews, C. F. *Sadhu Sundar Singh: A Personal Memoir*. London: Hodder and Stoughton, 1939.

Anselm of Canterbury. *Proslogion*. In *Anselm of Canterbury: The Major Works*, edited by Brian Davies and G. R. Evans, translated by H. H. Charlesworth. New York: Oxford University Press, 1998.

Armstrong, Karen. *Buddha*. New York: Penguin, 2004.

———. *The Case for God*. Toronto: Vintage Canada, 2010.

———. *Islam: A Short History*. New York: Modern Library Chronicles, 2000.

———. *Muhammad: A Prophet of our Time*. New York: HarperCollins, 2006.

Arnold, Edwin. *The Light of Asia*. Chicago: Donohue, 1879.

Ashokananda, Swami. *Meditation Ecstasy and Meditation: An Overview of Vedanta*. Calcutta: Advaita Ashrama, 1990.

Aslan, Reza. *No God but God: The Origins, Evolution, and Future of Islam*. New York: Random House, 2005.

'Ata ur-Rahim, Muhammad, and Ahmad Thomson. *Jesus, Prophet of Islam*. New York: Tahrike Tarsile Qu'ran, 2002.

Augustine, Noah. "Grandfather was a Knowing Christian." *Toronto Star*, August 9, 2000.

Baldock, John. *The Essence of Sufism*. London: Arcturus, 2004.

Baldrian, Farzeen. "Taoism: An Overview." In *The Encyclopedia of Religion*, edited by Mircea Eliade, 292–99. New York: Macmillan, 1987.

Baumer, Bettina. "The Four Spiritual Ways (Upaya) in the Kashmir Saiva Tradition." In *Hindu Spirituality: Post Classical and Modern* 2, edited by K. R. Sundarajan and Bithika Mukerji, 3–22. New York: Crossroad, 1997.

Bercholz, Samuel, and Sherab Chödzin Kohn, eds. *The Buddha and His Teachings*. Boston: Shambhala, 1993.

Berry, Thomas. "Individualism and Holism in Chinese Tradition: The Religious Cultural Context." In *Confucian Spirituality* 1, edited by Tu Weiming and Mary Evelyn Tucker, 39–55. New York: Crossroad, 2003.

Bickersteth, Edward Henry. *The Trinity: Scripture Testimony to the One Eternal Godhead of the Father, and of the Son, and of the Holy Spirit*. Grand Rapids: Kregal, 1959.

Blackmore, Susan. *The Meme Machine*. New York: Oxford University Press, 1999.

Bloom, Irene. "Practicality and Spirituality in the Mencius." In *Confucian Spirituality* 1, edited by Tu Weiming and Mary Evelyn Tucker, 233–51. New York: Crossroad, 2003.

Bloomfield, Harold H., et al. *TM: Discovering Inner Energy and Overcoming Stress*. New York: Delacorte, 1973.

Bodde, Derk. "Myths of Ancient China." In *Essays on Chinese Civilization*, edited by Derk Bodde et al., 64–76. Princeton: Princeton University Press, 1981.

Bodhi, Bhikku. *The Buddha and His Dhamma*. Kandy, Sri Lanka: Buddhist Publication Society, 1999.

———. *The Buddha and His Message: Past, Present and Future*. Kandy, Sri Lanka: Buddhist Publication Society, 2001.

———. "The Buddha's Teachings." In *The Buddha and His Teachings*, edited by Samuel Bercholz and Sherab Chodzin Kohn, 61–65. Boston: Shambhala: 1993.

———, ed. *In the Buddha's Words: An Anthology of Discourses from the Pali* Canon. Somerville, MA: Wisdom, 2005.

———. *The Noble Eightfold Path: The Way to End Suffering*. Kandy, Sri Lanka: Buddhist Publication Society, 2010.

———. "Taking Refuge in the Buddha." In *Toronto Buddhist Maha Vihara Journal*, Vesak Issue (May 1993).

Boltz, Judith Magee. "Lao Tzu." In *The Encyclopedia of Religion* 8, edited by Mircea Eliade, 452–66. New York: Macmillan, 1987.

Bowler, John. *The Sense of God: Sociological, Anthropological and Psychological Approaches to the Origin of the Sense of God*. Oxford: Clarendon, 1973.

Brown, Stuart. *The Nearest in Affection: Toward a Christian Understanding of Islam*. Geneva: WCC Publications, 1994.

Burnett, John. *Early Greek Philosophy*. New York: Meridian, 1964.

Campbell, Joseph, and Bill Moyers. *The Power of Myth*. New York: Doubleday, 1988.

Caner, Ergun Mehmet, and Emir Fethi Caner. *Unveiling Islam: An Insider's Look at Muslim Life and Beliefs*. Grand Rapids: Kregel, 2002.

Carmody, Denise L., and John T. Carmody. *Ways to the Center: An Introduction to World Religions*. 4th ed. Belmont, CA: Wadsworth, 1993.

Cavey, Bruxy. *The End of Religion: An Introduction to the Subversive Spirituality of Jesus*. Oakville, ON: Agora, 2005.

Chadwick, Henry. *Alexandrian Christianity*. Philadelphia: Westminster, 1954.

Chai, Ch'u, and Winberg Chai. *Confucianism*. Woodbury, New York: Barron, 1973.

Chakravarty, H. N. "Tantric Spirituality." In *Hindu Spirituality: Post Classical and Modern* 2, edited by K. R. Sundarajan and Bithika Mukerji, 209–31. New York: Crossroad, 1997.

Chan, Wing-Tsit, trans. *A Source Book in Chinese Philosophy*. Princeton: Princeton University Press, 1963.

Ching, Julia. *Chinese Religions*. London: Macmillan, 1993.

———. *Confucianism and Christianity: A Comparative Study*. Tokyo: Kodansha, 1977.

———. "East Asian Religions: Taoism." In *World Religions: Eastern Traditions*, edited by Willard G. Oxtoby, 418–36. Toronto: Oxford University Press, 1996.

Ching, Julia, and Hans Kung. *Christianity and Chinese Religion*. New York: Doubleday, 1989.

Chittick, William C. *A Shi'ite Anthology*. Qum, Iran: Ansariyan, 1989.

Clark, Andrew D., and Bruce W. Winter, eds. *One God, One Lord: Christianity in a World of Religious Pluralism*. Grand Rapids: Eerdmans, 1992.

Clooney, Francis X. *Comparative Theology: Deep Learning Across Religious Borders*. Chichester, UK: Wiley-Blackwell, 2010.

Conjubilant With Song. "Trinity Sunday." Blog entry, May 18, 2008. Online: http://conjubilant.blogspot.com/2008/05/trinity-sunday.html#links.

Cook, David. *Understanding Jihad*. Berkley: University of California Press, 2005.

Cooper, Anne, ed. *Ishmael My Brother: A Biblical Course on Islam*. Bromley, UK: Evangelical Missionary Alliance, 1986.

Corduan, Winfried. *A Tapestry of Faith: The Common Threads Between Christianity and World Religions*. Downers Grove, IL: InterVarsity, 2002.

Corless, Roger J. "Pure Land Piety." In *Buddhist Spirituality: Indian, Southeast Asian, Tibetan, Early Chinese*, edited by Takeuchi Yoshinori, 242–74. World Spirituality Series 8. New York: Crossroad, 1994.

Cua, A. S. "The Ethical and the Religious Dimensions of Li." In *Confucian Spirituality* 1, edited by Tu Weiming and Mary Evelyn Tucker, 252–86. New York: Crossroad, 2003.

Dabashi, Hamid. *Shi'ism: A Religion of Protest*. Cambridge, MA: Belknap, 2011.

Dalai Lama. *How to Practice: The Way to a Meaningful Life*. New York: Atria, 2002.

———. *Mind in Comfort and Ease: The Vision of Enlightenment in the Great Perfection*. Boston: Wisdom, 2007.

Daniel, Kunjumon. *A Christian Response to Islam*. Sulthan Bathery, India: PrintXpress, 2004.

Dar Rah Haqq's Board of Writers. *A Glance at the Life of the Holy Prophet of Islam*. Translated by N. Tawheedi. New York: Mostazafan Foundation, 1989. Online: http://www.al-islam.org/glance/.

Darwin, Charles R. *On the Origin of Species by Means of Natural Selection*. 1st ed. London: John Murray, 1859. Online: http://darwin-online.org.uk/content/frameset?itemID=F373&viewtype=text&pages eq=1.

Dawkins, Richard. *The Extended Phenotype: The Long Reach of the Gene*. New York: Oxford University Press, 1999.

———. *The God Delusion*. Boston: Houghton Mifflin, 2006.

———. "Is Science a Religion?" *Humanist* 57/1 (January/February 1997) 26–27. Online: http://www.thehumanist.org/humanist/articles/dawkins.html.

———. *The Selfish Gene*. 2nd ed. Oxford: Oxford University Press, 1989.

de Bary, William M. Theodore, et al., eds. *Sources of Indian Tradition*. Vol. 1. Records of Civilization, Sources and Study 56. New York: Columbia University Press, 1958.

———, et al., eds. *Sources of Japanese Tradition*. Vol 1. New York: Columbia University Press, 1958.

"Declaration of Vision Towards the Next 500 Years: From the Gathering of the 1993 United Indigenous Peoples at the Parliament of Religions, Chicago, Illinois." *Turtle Quarterly Magazine* (Fall-Winter 1994) 8. Online: http://ili.nativeweb.org/dovision.html.

Demarest, Bruce. "General and Special Revelation: Epistemological Foundations of Religious Pluralism." In *One God, One Lord: Christianity in a World of Religious Pluralism*, edited by Andrew D. Clark and Bruce W. Winter, 189–206. Grand Rapids: Eerdmans, 1992.

Denny, Frederick M. *An Introduction to Islam*. 2nd edition. New York: MacMillan, 1994.

Dhammananda, K. Sri. *What Buddhists Believe*. Taipei, Taiwan: Buddha Educational Foundation, 1993.

Doabia, Harbans Singh. *Sacred Nitnem: Containing the Divine Hymns of the Daily Prayers by the Sikhs*. 18th ed. Amritsar, India: Singh Brothers Maisewan, 1995.

Doniger, Wendy. *The Hindus: An Alternative History*. New York: Penguin, 2009.

Eastman, Roger, ed. *The Ways of Religion*. New York: Harper and Row, 1975.

Eber, Irene, ed. *Confucianism: The Dynamics of Tradition*. New York: Macmillan, 1986.

Eliade, Mircea. *Myths, Dreams and Mysteries*. Translated by Philip Mairet. New York: Harper and Row, 1967.

———. "On Prehistoric Religion." In *History of Religions*, edited by Mircea Eliade, 14:2, 140–7. New York: Macmillan, 1974.

———. *Patterns in Comparative Religion*. New York: Sheed and Ward, 1958.

———. "The Quest for the Origins of Religion." In *History of Religions*, edited by Mircea Eliade, 4:1, 154–69. New York: Macmillan, 1964.

———. *Shamanism: Archaic Techniques of Ecstasy*. Princeton: Princeton University Press, 1964.

Elmi, Mohammad Jafar. "Word of God and Revelation: A Shia Perspective." In *Catholics and Shi'a in Dialogue: Studies in Theology and Spirituality*, edited by Anthony O'Mahony et al., 278–89. London: Melisende, 2004.

Elwell, Walter A., ed. *Evangelical Dictionary of Theology*. Grand Rapids: Baker, 1984.

Fernando, Ajit. *The Christian's Attitude Toward World Religions*. Wheaton, IL: Tyndale, 1987.

Fideler, David. *Jesus Christ: Sun of God: Ancient Cosmology and Early Christian Symbolism*. Wheaton, IL: Quest, 1993.

Fingarette, Herbert. "A Confucian Metaphor: The Holy Vessel." In *The Ways of Religion*, edited by Roger Eastman, 234–39. New York: Harper and Row, 1975.

———. *Confucius: The Secular as Sacred*. New York: Harper, 1972.

Fisher, Mary Pat. *Living Religions: An Encyclopedia of the World's Faiths*. 4th ed. Upper Saddle River, NJ: Prentice-Hall, 1999.

Fredericks, James L. *Faith among Faiths: Christian Theology and Non-Christian Religions*. New York: Paulist, 2001.

Gaiman, Neil. *Coraline*. New York: Harper Collins, 2002. Online: http://browseinside.harpercollinschildrens.com/index.aspx?isbn13=9780380807345.

Gandhi, Mohandas K. *Autobiography: The Story of My Experiments with Truth*. Translated by Mahadev Haribhai Desai. New York: Courier Dover, 1983. Online: http://entersection.com/posts/934-mohandas-k-gandhi-on-his-experiments-with-truth.

Goldziher, Ignaz. *Introduction to Islamic Theology and Law*. Edited by Bernard Lewis. Translated by Andras Hamori and Ruth Hamori. Modern Classics in Near Eastern Studies. Princeton: Princeton University Press, 1981.

Graham, Billy. *Peace With God*. New York: Doubleday, 1953.

Graham, William. *Beyond the Written Word: Oral Aspects of Scripture in the History of Religion*. New York: Cambridge University Press, 1987.

Griffith, Ralph T. H., trans. *The Hymns of the Rig Veda*. Benares, India: E. J. Lazarus, 1920.

Guru Granth Sahib (Khalsa Consensus Translation). Section 28: Raag Bhairao. Online: http://www.hinduwebsite.com/sacredscripts/sikhscripts/guru928.asp.

Hamada, Louis Bahjat. *God Loves the Arabs, Too*. Jackson, TN: Hamada Evangelistic Outreach, 1990.

———. *Understanding the Arab World*. Nashville: Thomas Nelson, 1990.

Hamer, Dean H. *The God Gene: How Faith is Hardwired into Our Genes*. New York: Doubleday, 2004.

Haruji, Asana. "Offerings in Daoist Ritual." In *Daoist Identity: History, Lineage, and Ritual*, edited by Livia Kohn and Harold D. Roth, 274–94. Honolulu: University of Hawai'i Press, 2002.

Hazm, Abu Mohammad Ali-ibn. "The Conduct of Life and the Healing of Souls." In *Introduction to Islamic Theology and Law*, by Ignaz Goldziher, edited by Bernard Lewis. Princeton: Princeton University Press, 1981.

Heath, Thomas. *A History of Greek Mathematics*. Vol 1. New York: Dover, 1981.

Henry, C. F. H. "Revelation." In *Evangelical Dictionary of Theology*, edited by Walter Elwell, 944–48. Grand Rapids: Baker, 1984.

Hesse, Herman. *Siddhhartha*. Translated by Hilda Rosner. New York: New Directions, 1951.

Hick, John. *God Has Many Names*. Philadelphia: Westminster, 1980.

———. *An Interpretation of Religion: Human Responses to the Transcendent*. New Haven: Yale University Press, 1989.

———, ed. *Myth of God Incarnate*. Philadelphia: Westminster, 1977.

———. "Religious Pluralism and Salvation." In *The Philosophical Challenge of Religious Diversity*, edited by Philip L. Quinn and Kevin Meeker. New York: Oxford University Press, 1999.

Hill, William J. *The Three-Personed God: The Trinity as a Mystery of Salvation*. Washington, DC: Catholic University of America Press, 1982.

Hiroshi, Maruyama. "Documents used in Rituals of Merit in Taiwanese Daoism." In *Daoist Identity: History, Lineage, and Ritual*, edited by Livia Kohn and Harold D. Roth, 256–73. Honolulu: University of Hawai'i Press, 2002.

Hodgkinson, Brian. *The Essence of Vedanta*. London: Arcturus, 2006.

Hopfe, Lewis M. *Religions of the World*. 5th ed. New York: Macmillan, 1991.

Hughes, P. E. "Grace." In *Evangelical Dictionary of Theology*, edited by Walter A. Elwell, 480. Grand Rapids: Baker, 1984.

Humphreys, Christmas. *Buddhism: An Introduction and Guide*. Harmondsworth, UK: Penguin, 1951.

Hurvitz, Leon, trans. *Scripture of the Lotus Blossom of the Fine Dharma (The Lotus Sutra)*. New York: Columbia University Press, 1976.

Hutchison, John A. *Paths of Faith*. New York: McGraw Hill, 1975.

Irwin, Lee, ed. *Native American Spirituality: A Critical Reader*. Lincoln: University of Nebraska Press, 2000.

Iverson, Peter. *We are Still Here: American Indians in the Twentieth Century*. American History Series. Wheeling, IL: Harlan Davidson, 1998.

James, Andy. *The Spiritual Legacy of Shaolin Temple: Buddhism, Daoism, and the Energetic Arts*. Boston: Wisdom, 2004.

James, E. O. "Prehistoric Religion." In *Historia Religionum: Handbook for the History of Religions 1: Religions of the Past*, edited by Claas Juoco Bleeker and Geo Widengren, 442–94. Leiden: Brill, 1969.

Jaspers, Karl. *The Great Philosophers: The Foundations, The Paradigmatic Individuals: Socrates, Buddha, Confucius, Jesus; The Seminal Founders of Philosophical Thought: Plato, Augustine, Kant*. Edited by Hannah Arendt. Translated by Ralph Manheim. London: Harcourt, Brace and World, 1962.

———. *The Origin and Goal of History*. Translated by Michael Bullock. New Haven: Yale University Press, 1953.

Jayatilleke, K. N. *Facets of Buddhist Thought: Six Essays*. Kandy, Sri Lanka: Buddhist Publication Society, 1984.

Jones, E. Stanley. *Christ at the Round Table*. Toronto: McClelland and Stewart, 1928.

Kaltenmark, Max. "Lao-Tzu." In *God's Light: The Prophets of the World's Great Religions*, edited by John Miller and Aaron Kenedi, 311–44. New York: Marlowe, 2003.

Kane, Cheikh Hamidou. *Ambiguous Adventure*. Translated by Katherine Woods. New York: Collier, 1969.

Kasahara, Kazuo, ed. *A History of Japanese Religion*. Tokyo: Kosei, 2002.

Kaur, Rajinder. *God in Sikhism*. 2nd ed. Amritsar: Shiromani Gurdwara Parbandhak Committee, 2003.

Kawaski, Ken, and Visakha Kawasaki. *Jataka Tales of the Buddha: An Anthology*. Vols. 1–3. Kandy, Sri Lanka: Buddhist Publication Society, 2010.

Kelly, J. N. D. *Early Christian Doctrines*. Revised ed. New York: Harper and Row, 1978.

Kelly, Kevin. *Out of Control: The New Biology of Machines, Social Systems and Economic World*. Boston: Addison-Wesley, 1994.

Khomeini, Ruhollah. *Islam and Revolution: Writings and Declarations of Imam Khomeini*. Translated and annotated by Hamid Algar. Contemporary Islamic Thought. Berkeley, CA: Mizan, 1981.

———. "The Deprived Will Dominate the Arrogant." In *Islam and Revolution: Writings and Declarations of Imam Khomeini*, 5–9. Berkeley: Mizan, 1981.

———. "The First Day of God's Government." In *Islam and Revolution: Writings and Declarations of Imam Khomeini*, 265–67. Berkeley: Mizan, 1981.

Kim, Heup Young. *Christ and the Tao*. Eugene, OR: Wipf and Stock, 2006.

Kingsbury, Francis, and G. E. Philips, eds. *Hymns of the Tamil Saivite Saints*. Calcutta: Association Press, 1921.

Kitagawa, Joseph M. *Religion in Japanese History*. New York: Columbia University Press, 1966.

Koch, Rudolf. *Christian Symbols*. With Fritz Kredel. Translated by Kevin Ahern. San Francisco: Arion, 1996. Online: http://catholic-resources.org/Art/Koch-ChristianSymbols.htm.

Kohli, Surindar Singh. *Grace*. Amritsar, India: Singh Brothers, 2001.

Kohn, Livia, and Harold D. Roth, eds. *Daoist Identity: History, Language, and Ritual*. Honolulu: University of Hawai'i Press, 2002.

Kohn, Sherab Chödzin. *A Life of the Buddha*. Boston: Shambhala, 1993.

Kruger, C. Baxter. *The Great Dance: The Christian Vision Revisited*. Jackson, MS: Perichoresis, 2000.

Kulathungam, Lyman C. D. "Buddhist Elements in the Logic of Saiva Siddhanta." *Saiva Siddhanta* 13/2 (1975) 35–46.

———. "Christian Meditation: Doubts and Hopes." In *Eastern Journal of Practical Theology* 6/2 (Fall 1992) 22–37.

———. "Scientific Understanding and Christian Faith." In *Faculty Dialogue* 25 (Fall 1995) n.p. Online: http://www.iclnet.org/pub/facdialogue/25/kulath25.

Lai, Whalen. "The Three Jewels in China." In *Buddhist Spirituality: Indian, Southeast Asian, Tibetan, Early Chinese*, edited by Takeuchi Yoshinori, 275–341. World Spirituality Series 8. New York: Crossroad, 1994.

Lakha, Murtaza. *The Twelfth Imam*. London: Tyrell, 1993.

Lari, Sayyid Mujtaba Musavi. *God and His Attributes: Lessons on Islamic Doctrine*. Translated by Hamid Algar. Pontomac, MD: Islamic Education Center, 1989.

———. *The Seal of the Prophets and His Message*. Translated by Hamid Algar. Pontomac, MD: Islamic Education Center, 1989.

Bibliography

Last of the Independents. "Wounded Knee: The Ghost Dance." Online: http://www.pbs.org/weta/thewest/people/s_z/wovoka.htm.

Lawrence, Bruce. *The Qur'an: A Biography*. Vancouver, CN: Douglas and McIntyre, 2006.

Lee, Jung Young. *The Trinity in Asian Perspective*. Nashville: Abingdon, 1996.

Maciocia, Giovanni. *The Foundations of Chinese Medicine: A Comprehensive Text for Acupuncturists and Herbalists*. Edinburgh: Churchill Livingstone, 1993.

Mackintosh, Hugh R. "Does a Historical Study of Religions Yield a Dogmatic Theology?" *The American Journal of Theology* 13/4. (October 1909) 505–19.

Macleod, Donald. *The Person of Christ*. Downers Grove, IL: InterVarsity, 1998.

Mahathera, Narada. *The Buddha and His Teachings*. 2nd ed. Singapore: Singapore Buddhist Meditation Centre, 1988.

Mansukhani, G. S. *Introduction to Sikhism*. New Delhi, India: Hemkunt, 1993.

Masaaki, Tsuchiya. "Confession of Sins and Awareness of Self in the Taiping-Jin." In *Daoist Identity: History, Lineage, and Ritual*, edited by Livia Kohn and Harold D. Roth, 39–57. Honolulu: University of Hawaii Press, 2002.

Maududi, Abul A'la. *Towards Understanding Islam*. Translated and edited by Khi Rshid Ahmad. Tripoli, Libya: Islamic Call Society, 1977.

McDermott, Gerald. *God's Rivals: Why has God Allowed Different Religions?* Downers Grove, IL: InterVarsity, 2007.

Mcleod, W. H. "Essay on Sikhism." In *A Cultural History of India*, edited by A. L. Basham. Clarendon, UK: Oxford University Press, 1975.

———. *Textual Sources of the Study of Sikhism*. Manchester: Manchester University Press, 1984.

———. *Who is a Sikh? The Problem of Sikh Identity*. Oxford: Clarendon, 1989.

"A Message from Buddhists to the Parliament of the World Religions." Chicago, September 1993. In *World Faiths Encounter* 7 (February 1994): 53.

Miller, John, and Aaron Kenedi, eds. *God's Light: The Prophets of the World's Great Religions*. New York: Marlow and Company, 2003.

Milton, John. *Areopagitica*. With Commentary by Sir Richard C. Jebb. Cambridge: Cambridge University Press, 1918.

Mingana, A., ed. and trans. "The Debate on the Christian Faith between Timothy I and Caliph Mahdi in 781 AD." *Bulletin of the John Rylands Library* 12/2 (1928) 11–12. Online: http://tynsemresearch.wordpress.com/.

Mol, Hans. *Identity and the Sacred: A Sketch for a New Social-Scientific Theory of Religion*. New York: Free Press, 1976.

Moore, Charles A., ed. *The Japanese Mind: Essentials of Japanese Philosophy and Culture*. Honolulu: University of Hawaii Press, 1971.

Muktananda, Swami. *Play of Consciousness: Chitshakti Vilas*. San Francisco: Harper and Row, 1978.

Nakamura, Hajime. *Ways of Thinking of Eastern Peoples: India, China, Tibet and Japan*. Edited by Philip P. Wiener. Honolulu: East-West Center, 1965.

Nanamoli, Bhikkhu. *The Life of the Buddha: According to Pali Canon*. Kandy, Sri Lanka: Buddhist Publication Society, 1984.

Naqvi, Ali Muhammad, comp. *A Manual of Islamic Beliefs and Practices: Volume 1*. Edited by John Cooper. London: Muhammadi Trust, 1990.

Nash, Ronald H. *Is Jesus the Only Savior?* Grand Rapids: Zondervan, 1994.

Nasr, Seyyed Hossein. *Islam in the Modern World*. New York: HarperCollins, 2010.

———, ed. *Islamic Spirituality: Foundations*. New York: Crossroad, 1987.

———. "The Quran as the Foundation of Islamic Spirituality." In *Islamic Spirituality: Foundations*, edited by Seyyed Hossein Nasr, 3–10. New York: Crossroad, 1987.

"Native American Prayer." Translated by Chief Yellow Lark, 1887. Native American/First Peoples Inspirational Quotations. Online: http://www.worldprayerfoundation.com/resources/native_american.html.

Neil, Stephen. *Christian Faith and Other Faiths: The Christian Dialogue with Other Religions*. London: Oxford University Press, 1961.

Netland, Harold. *Encountering Religious Pluralism: The Challenge to Christian Faith and Mission.* Downers Grove, IL: InterVarsity, 2001.

Nickerson, Peter. "Opening of the Way: Exorcism, Travel, and Soteriology in Early Daoist Mortuary Practice and its Antecedents." In *Daoist Identity: History, Lineage, and Ritual*, edited by Livia Kohn and Harold D. Roth, 58–77. Honolulu: University of Hawai'i Press, 2002.

Nigosian, S. A. *World Faiths.* 2nd ed. New York: St. Martin's, 1994.

Norris, Frederick W. "Timothy I of Baghdad, Catholicos of the East Syrian Church, 780—823: Still a Valuable Model." *International Bulletin of Missionary Research* 30/3 (July 1, 2006) 133.

O'Mahony, Anthony, et al., eds. *Catholics and Shi'a in Dialogue: Studies in Theology and Spirituality.* London: Melisende, 2004.

Olson, Roger E., and Christopher A. Hall. *The Trinity.* Grand Rapids: Eerdmans, 2002.

Otto, Rudolf. *India's Religion of Grace and Christianity Compared and Contrasted.* Translated by Frank Hugh Foster. New York: MacMillan, 1930.

Oxtoby, Willard G. "The Sikh Tradition." In *World Religions: Eastern Traditions*, edited by Willard G. Oxtoby. Toronto: Oxford University Press, 1996.

———, ed. *World Religions: Eastern Traditions.* Toronto: Oxford University Press, 1996.

———, ed. *World Religions: Western Traditions.* 2nd ed. Toronto: Oxford University Press, 1996.

Padinjarekara, Joseph. *Christ in Ancient Vedas.* Burlington, ON: Welch, 1991.

Pande, G. C. "The Message of Gotama Buddha and Its Earliest Interpretations." In *Buddhist Spirituality: Indian, Southeast Asian, Tibetan, Early Chinese*, edited by Takeuchi Yoshinori, 3–33. World Spirituality Series 8. New York: Crossroad, 1994.

Panikkar, Raimundo. *The Trinity and the Religious Experience of Man.* New York: Orbis, 1973.

———. *The Unknown Christ of Hinduism: Towards an Ecumenical Christophany.* Maryknoll, NY: Orbis, 1981.

Parshall, Phil. *The Cross and the Crescent.* Waynesboro, GA: Authentic, 2002.

Phan, Peter, ed. *The Cambridge Companion to the Trinity.* New York: Cambridge University Press, 2011.

Picken, Stuart D. B. *Shinto: Japan's Spiritual Roots.* Tokyo: Kodansha, 1980.

Pinnock, Clark H., ed. *Grace Unlimited.* Minneapolis: Bethany Fellowship, 1975.

———. *Most Moved Mover: A Theology of God's Openness.* Grand Rapids: Baker, 2001.

———. *A Wideness in God's Mercy: The Finality of Jesus Christ in a World of Religions.* Grand Rapids: Zondervan, 1992.

Pocock, Michael, et al. *The Changing Face of World Missions: Engaging Contemporary Issues and Trends.* Grand Rapids: Baker, 2006.

Pooya, Ayatullah Haji Mirza Mahdi. *The Essence of the Qur'an: The Eternal Light.* Edited by Syed Muhammad Murtaza and Husain P. Taylor. Freehold, NJ: Imam Sahe-bu-Zaman, 1993.

Pope John Paul II. *Crossing the Threshold of Hope.* Toronto: Knopf, 1994.

Prabhupada, A. C. Bhaktivedanta Swami. *Bhagavad-Gita As It Is.* Sidney, Australia: Bhaktivedanta Book Trust, 1986.

———. *The Path of Perfection: Yoga for the Modern Age.* Los Angeles: Bhaktivedanta Book Trust, 1979.

Prebish, Charles S., ed. *Buddhism: A Modern Perspective.* University Park: The Pennsylvania State University, 1978.

Public Broadcasting Service. "New Perspectives on the West: Wovoka." 2001. Online: http://www.pbs.org/weta/thewest/people/s_z/wovoka.htm.

Punnaji, Madewala. *Becoming a Buddhist.* Concord, CA: California Buddhist Vihara Society, 1990.

———. "The Place of Scripture in Buddhism and Its Relation to Doing Good." *Toronto Buddhist* 12/3 (August 1990) 1–14.

Quasten, Johannes. *Patrology: The Beginnings of Patristic Literature: From the Apostles to Iranaeus.* Vol. 1. Westminster, MD: Christian Classics, 1983.

Queen, Sarah A. "The Way of the Unadorned King: The Classical Confucian Spirituality of Dong Zhongshu." In *Confucian Spirituality*, edited by Tu Weiming and Mary Evelyn Tucker, 304–17. New York: Crossroad, 2003.

Quraishy, M. A. *Textbook of Islam.* Nairobi, Kenya: Nairobi Islamic Foundation, 1987.

Radhakrishnan. S. *The Hindu View of Life.* London: Unwin, 1960.

Radhakrishnan, Sarvepalli, and Charles A. Moore, eds. *A Source Book of Indian Philosophy.* Princeton: Princeton University Press, 1957.

Raghavachar, S. S. "The Spiritual Vision of Ramanuja." In *Hindu Spirituality: Vedas Through Vedanta,* vol. 1, edited by Krishna Sivaraman. New York: Crossroad, 1989.

Rahi, M. S. "Unyielding Spirit of the Khalsa." *Abstracts of Sikh Studies* 3/4 (Oct–Dec 2001) 34–40.

Rahman, Fazlur. *Islam.* Chicago: University of Chicago Press, 1996.

Rahula, Walpola. *What the Buddha Taught.* New York: Grove, 1974.

Ramachandra, Vinoth. *The Recovery of Mission: Beyond the Pluralist Paradigm.* Delhi, India: ISPCK, 1996.

Riegel, Jeffrey. "Confucius." In *The Stanford Encyclopedia of Philosophy,* edited by Edward N. Zalta. Spring 2011 edition. Online: http://plato.stanford.edu/archives/spr2011/entries/confucius/.

Rizvi, Sayyid Muhammad. *Hajj: The Pilgrimage to Mecca.* Bloomfield, NJ: Message of Peace, 1996.

———. "Imam Husayn's Mission: Reforming the Ummah." *The Right Path* 1/1 (July–September 1992).

———. *Imam Husayn: The Saviour of Islam.* Vancouver, BC: VIEF, 1984.

———. *The Infallibility of the Prophets in the Qur'an.* Richmond Hill, ON: Al-Ma'arif, 2005.

———. *Peace and Jihad in Islam.* Thornhill, ON: NASIMCO, 2007.

———. *Ritual and Spiritual Purity.* Richmond, BC: Vancouver Islamic Educational Foundation, 1989.

———. *Shi'ism Imamate and Wilayat.* 1st ed. Richmond Hill, ON: Al-Ma'arif, 1999.

Robinson, B. A. "Native American Spirituality: Beliefs of Native Americans from the Arctic to the Southwest." Ontario Consultants on Religious Tolerance, 2008. Online: http://www.religioustolerance.org/nataspir3.htm.

Rommen, Edward, and Harold Netland, eds. *Christianity and the Religions of the World: A Biblical Theology of World Religions.* Evangelical Missiological Society Series 2. Pasadena, CA: William Carey Library, 1995.

Rosemont, Henry, Jr. "Is There a Universal Path of Spiritual Progress in the Texts of Early Confucianism?" In *Confucian Spirituality,* edited by Tu Weiming and Mary Evelyn Tucker, 183–96. New York: Crossroad, 2003.

Russell, Bertrand. "The Essence of Religion." In *The Basic Writings of Bertrand Russell,* edited by Robert E. Egner and Lester E. Denonn. New York: Allen and Unwin, 1961.

Ruvolo, David. "A Summary of Native American Religions." American Religious Experience. Online: http://are.as.wvu.edu/ruvolo.htm.

Sahn, Seung. *The Compass of Zen.* Compiled and edited by Hyon Gak Sunim. Boston: Shambhala, 1997.

Schaefer, Cliff. "A Biblical Look at Native Spiritualism." His Riches. 1997. Online: http://hisriches.com/hisriches/articles/a-biblical-look-at-native-spiritualism/.

Schmidt, Wilhelm. *The Origin and Growth of Religion: Facts and Theories.* London: Methuen, 1931.

Schwartz, Benjamin I. "The Age of Transcendence." *Daedalus* 104/2 (Spring 1975) 1–8.

Schwartz, Stephen. *The Other Islam: Sufism and the Road to Global Harmony.* New York: Doubleday, 2008.

Sherif, Faruq. *A Guide to the Contents of the Quran.* Reading, UK: Garnet, 1995.

Singh, Harbans. *Encyclopaedia of Sikhism.* New Delhi, India: Hemkunt, 2005.

Singh, Nikki-Guninder Kaur. "The Spiritual Experience in Sikhism." In *Hindu Spirituality* vol. 2, edited by K. R. Sundararajan and Bithika Mukerji, 530–61. New York: Crossroad, 1997.

Singh, Sadhu Sundar. *With and Without Christ.* London: Cassell, 1929.

Singh, Santokh. *Fundamentals of Sikhism: Historical and Philosophical Perspective.* 2nd ed. Princeton, ON: Institute of Spiritual Studies, 1994.

Singh, Sardar Harjeet. *Faith and Philosophy of Sikhism.* Delhi, India: Kalpaz, 2009.

Sivaraman, Krishna, ed. *Hindu Spirituality.* Vol. 1, *Vedas through Vedanta.* World Spirituality Series 6. New York: Crossroad, 1989.

Smart, Ninian. *The Religious Experience of Mankind.* 3rd ed. New York: Scribner, 1984.

Smart, Ninian, and Richard D. Hecht, eds. *Sacred Texts of the World: A Universal Anthology.* New York: Crossroad, 1982.

Smith, D. Howard. *Chinese Religions.* New York: Holt, Rinehart and Winston, 1968.

———. *Confucius.* New York: Scribner's, 1973.

Smith, Gordon T. "Religion and the Bible: An Agenda for Evangelicals." In *Christianity and the Religions of the World: A Biblical Theology of World Religions,* edited by Edward Rommen and Harold Netland. Pasadena, CA: William Carey Library, 1995.

Smith, Huston. "The Way of Deliberate Tradition." In *The Ways of Religion*, edited by Roger Eastman, 196–204. New York: Harper and Row, 1975.

Snelling, John. *The Buddhist Handbook: A Complete Guide to Buddhist Schools, Teaching, Practice, and History*. Rochester, VT: Inner Traditions, 1998.

Sommer, Deborah. "Ritual and Sacrifice in Early Confucianism: Contacts with the Spirit World." In *Confucian Spirituality*, edited by Tu Weiming and Mary Evelyn Tucker, 197–219. New York: Crossroad, 2003.

Stark, Rodney. *Discovering God: The Origins of the Great Religions and the Evolution of Belief*. New York: HarperCollins, 2007.

Stark, Rodney, and Roger Finke. *Acts of Faith: Exploring the Human Side of Religion*. Berkeley, CA: University of California Press, 2000.

Stott, John R. *The Cross of Christ*. Downers Grove, IL: InterVarsity, 2006.

Sullivan, Lawrence. *Native Religions and Cultures of North America*. New York: Continuum, 2003.

Sundarajan, K. R., and Bithika Mukerji, eds. *Hindu Spirituality*. Vol. 2, *Post Classical and Modern*, World Spirituality Series 7. New York: Crossroad, 1997.

Tabataba'i, Muhammad Husayn. *Islamic Teachings: An Overview*. Translated by R. Campbell. New York: Mostazafan Foundation, 1989.

———. *Shi'a*. Translated by Sayyid Hisayn Nasr. Qum, Iran: Ansariyan, undated.

Taylor, Rodney I. *The Religious Dimensions of Confucianism*. Albany: State University of New York Press, 1990.

Thera, Nyanatiloka. *The Buddha's Path to Deliverance: A Systematic Exposition in the Words of the Sutta Pitaka*. Kandy, Sri Lanka: Buddhist Publication Society, 2000.

Theon of Smyrna. "Mathematics Useful for Understanding Plato." In *Sacred Geometry: Philosophy and Practice*, translated by Robert Lawlor, 13. London: Thames and Hudson, 1982.

Tsoukalas, Steven. *Krsna and Christ: Body-Divine Relation in the Thought of Sankara, Ramanuja, and Classical Christian Orthodoxy*. Eugene, OR: Wipf and Stock, 2011.

Utter, Jack. *American Indians: Answers to Today's Questions*. Norman: University of Oklahoma Press, 2001.

Venugopal, R. "The Spirituality of Carnatic Music." In *Hindu Spirituality: Post Classical and Modern* 2, edited by K. R. Sundarajan and Bithika Mukerji, 450–8. New York: Crossroad, 1997.

Vivekananda, Swami. *The Complete Works of Swami Vivekananda*. 8 vols. Calcutta: Advaita Ashrama, 1964–1971.

Wachowski, Andy, and Larry Wachowski, directors. *The Matrix*. Warner Brothers, 1999.

Waley, Arthur, trans. *The Analects of Confucius*. London: Allen and Unwin, 1938.

Waterfield Robin. *The First Philosophers: Pre-Socratics and Sophists*. Oxford: Oxford University Press, 2000.

———, trans. *The Theology of Arithmetic*. Grand Rapids: Phanes, 1988.

Webber, F. R., and Ralph Adams Cram. *Church Symbolism*. Whitefish, MT: Kessinger, 2003.

Weiming, Tu. *Confucian Thought: Selfhood as Creative Transformation*. SUNY Series in Philosophy. Albany: State University of New York Press, 1985.

Weiming, Tu, and Mary Evelyn Tucker, eds. *Confucian Spirituality*. 2 vols. World Spirituality. New York: Crossroad, 2003.

Welch, Claude. *In This Name: The Doctrine of Trinity in Contemporary Theology*. New York: Scribner, 1952.

Weller, Robert P. *Unities and Diversities in Chinese Religion*. Seattle: University of Washington Press, 1987.

Wesley, Charles. "Father, Whose Everlasting Love." In *The Canadian Hymnal*, revised and expanded edition, 465. Toronto: William Briggs, 1900.

Whitie, Vibert. *Inside the Nation of Islam: A Historical and Personal Testimony by a Black Muslim*. Orlando: University of Florida Press, 2001.

Wickramasinghe, Chandra. "Maya . . . The Phantasmagoria of Human Existence." Unpublished poem used by permission of the author. Date unknown.

Wilson, Dick. *The Sun at Noon: An Anatomy of Modern Japan*. London: Hamish Hamilton, 1986.

Witherington, Ben, III, and Laura M. Ice. *The Shadow of the Almighty: Father, Son, and Spirit in Biblical Perspective*. Grand Rapids: Eerdmans, 2002.

Bibliography

Woodward, F. L., trans. *The Minor Anthologies of the Pali Canon II*. London: Oxford University Press, 1948.

Yao, Xinzhong. *An Introduction to Confucianism*. Cambridge: Cambridge University Press, 2000.

Yogavacara, Rahula. *The Way to Peace and Happiness*. Taipei, Taiwan: The Corporate Body of the Buddha Foundation, n.d.

Yoshinori, Takeuchi, ed. *Buddhist Spirituality: Indian, Southeast Asian, Tibetan, Early Chinese*. World Spirituality Series 8. New York: Crossroad, 1994.

Yu, David C., trans. *History of Chinese Daoism*. Vol 1. New York: University Press of America, 2000.

Zacharias, Ravi. *Light in the Shadow of Jihad: The Struggle for Truth*. Orlando: Multnomah, 2002.

Made in the USA
Lexington, KY
15 August 2017